BLOOM *Where God* PLANTS YOU

Reflections of a Mission Mom Living in Malawi, Africa

By
Rebecca Wendland

xulon
PRESS

Copyright © 2013 by Rebecca Wendland

Bloom Where God Plants You
by Rebecca Wendland

Printed in the United States of America

ISBN 9781625099112

All rights reserved solely by the author. The author guarantees all contents are original and do not infringe upon the legal rights of any other person or work. No part of this book may be reproduced in any form without the permission of the author. The views expressed in this book are not necessarily those of the publisher.

Unless otherwise indicated, Bible quotations are taken from the *Holy Bible*, New International Version. Copyright © 1973, 1978, 1984 by International Bible Society. Used by permission of Zondervan Bible Publishers; Scripture quotations marked KJV are taken from the *Holy Bible*, King James Version

Edited by Sarah Habben.
Cover photograph - Wendland family walking among Malawi tea fields.
Photography assistance contributed by Melissa Staude.
Several photographs were taken by Reverend James Bartz and used with permission.
Maps prepared by Missionary John Holtz and daughter Rachel Holtz.

Author acknowledges hymn permission to:
Dr. John C. Lawrenz
I Hear the Savior Calling (sts. 1, 3, 5)
Used with permission.

See This Wonder in the Making (sts. 1-4), text by Jaroslav J. Vajda
© 1984 Concordia Publishing House.
Used with permission. All rights reserved. www.cph.org.

We All Are One in Mission (sts. 1-3), words by Rusty Edwards
© 1986 Hope Publishing Co., Carol Stream, IL 60188.
All rights reserved. Used by permission.

All hymns, unless otherwise indicated, are taken from Christian Worship: A Lutheran Hymnal. Copyright © 1993 by Northwestern Publishing House.

www.xulonpress.com

This book is dedicated to the amazing family
God has blessed me with—

My dear husband Robert Ernst

And our four precious children:
Hannah, Nathanael, Caleb and Bethany

It is every one of your lives that help write this adventure
in Malawi, Africa.

TABLE OF CONTENTS

Acknowledgements vii
Foreword ix
Introduction xi
    Map of Africa and country of Malawi xii
    Rob's LCCA congregations in southern Malawi xiii
    WELS missions link xiv
    Why Africa? xiv
    Visiting Africa vs. *Living* in Africa xv

Chapters
1. **September 2003: The Far Side of the Sea** 17
    Setting Off 17
    Settling In 21
2. **Month One: Adjusting** 26
    Neighbors Behind Bars 26
    Matters of Life and Death 27
    Food in Due Season 33
    Sights and Seasons 34
    Health Struggles 37
3. **Month Two: Home, Sick; Homesick** 44
4. **Making Disciples of All Nations** 55
    Job Description for Rob 55
    Job Description for Rebecca 57
    Traveling to Places of Mission Work 58
    Village Church 60
    Language—an Invaluable Tool 61
    You Say "To-may-to" I Say "To-mah-to" 63
5. **Dreaming of a White Christmas** 65
6. **2004: A New Year Toast to Continued Blessings** 81
7. **First Easter; a Fond Farewell; an African Itinerary** 98

8. **A Visit from My Family** 113
    Staude Family First Impressions 114
    Staude Family on the Town 115
    Staude Family on Safari 116
    Staude Family in the Bush 117
9. **Bloom Where God Plants You** 121
10. **Year Two Begins: God Gives and God Takes Away** 149
11. **2005: A Birthing Decision; a Budget Decision** 173
12. **A Baby; a Baptism; a Busy First Furlough** 191
13. **Year Three: Loads of Cares; Loads of Prayers** 205
14. **2006: A Season for Everything** 228
    A Time for Mold 229
    A Time to Mourn 232
    A Time for Grasshoppers 234
    A Time to Weep and a Time to Laugh 236
    A Time to Uproot 237
    A Time to Mend 240
    A Time to Shine Our Lights 242
    A Time to Plant (the Gospel) 248
    A Time to be Tested 250
    A Time to be Sick and a Time to Heal 255
    A Time to Search…and a Time to Give Up 257
    A Time to Give Thanks 258
    A Time for Water Surplus and a Time for Water Shortage 261
    A Time for Tarantulas 265
    A Time to Tear Down and a Time to Build 267
15. **2007: Locked Out, Arrested, Poisoned—Time for Furlough #2!** ... 272
16. **2008: A Visit; a Call; a Fever; a Death** 305
17. **2009: Heaven Sent—Heaven Bound (Furlough #3, Baby #4)** 336
18. **2010: Ministering in Malawi While it is Day** 356

ACKNOWLEDGMENTS

To my husband Rob: Your heartfelt dedication to sharing God's Word with our brothers and sisters in Africa is an inspiration. Your support on the home front is foundational, and it allowed me to write this book. Thank you for your encouragement, editing time and assistance, answering questions, and for your daily help every step of the way. Thank you for giving your heart to Jesus and also to me.

To Hannah, Nathanael, Caleb and Bethany: What joy you bring to my life. Thank you for your smiles, hugs, antics, and zest for life. You each bring extra adventure to my day in Africa. I always have material to "write home about." You are each a wonderful gift, heaven-sent from the Giver. Thank you for sharing Jesus with those around you and living each day for Him.

To my parents: Thank you for your unending support for us and our ministry across the sea. Dad, your zeal to share our ministry highlights with others and hours of manuscript help are sincerely appreciated. Mom, your continuous prayers, holiday packages, phone calls and update letters are very dear and make our life extra special as we stay close to your heart though oceans apart.

To Rob's parents: What a testimony you both are to God's blessings throughout your 40+ years of ministry in Africa. What a privilege for us to live in the country next door. Mom, I appreciate your continued medical help and cherish each opportunity I have to study Scripture with you at the annual retreats. Dad, thank you for your encouragement to write this book. You are a wealth of information and I value your input, experience and example as you continually use your talents to His glory.

To WELS mission-minded readers—especially LWMS members: Thank you for your special interest in missions. How great it is that we work together in our varied mission fields to tell the world about Jesus. May this book help illustrate how your mission gifts and support are used and how God is working through your prayers to guide us, uphold us and keep us safe in His hands on the far side of the sea.

To Sarah, my friend, fellow Malawian sister in Christ, and editor: A million thanks for your countless hours of manuscript editing and help. Your skills and background were the perfect blend for this project. Your complete dedication is sincerely appreciated as you helped prepare my emails and text for publication. Thank you also to your husband Dan and your girls for allowing you to share your time each day with Africa and our story.

To God be all glory!

FOREWORD

I first met Rebecca in 1990 at Northwestern Preparatory School in Watertown, WI. I had transferred there after spending a decade in Malawi as a missionary's daughter. Rebecca was hard *not* to notice. For starters, she was a redhead. Beneath that hair was a friendly, vibrant, upbeat ball of energy—a Christ-centered young lady with high personal standards and a strong sense of morality. Even then she had a particular fondness for puns (which we politely overlooked) and for the phrase, "Bloom where you are planted!"

When her husband Rob accepted his call to Malawi in 2003, I wondered how Rebecca would adjust. She is a person of extreme efficiency, with a work-ethic that would shame a team of oxen. Malawi, on the other hand, is a land of extreme inefficiency, contradiction, and multiple moral shades of grey. Not to mention bugs and dirt. Malawi is a heaven-on-earth for a missionary kid such as I had been: one who figured that it was a normal chore to pick ticks off the dogs or catch flies for the praying mantis living in our porch. For me, a furlough to the States was akin to a trip to Disney World: an entertaining sensory smorgasbord, but who would want to live there? However, for Rebecca to move in the opposite direction, to enter that third world country as a North-American-bred adult, would not be an easy thing. Love for such a world has to grow over time.

That is one path Rebecca's book follows—the leaving behind of family, friends and a well-greased society for the third world. Rebecca tells the tale of laying down roots in a foreign mission field from a wife and mother's perspective. Readers will appreciate how Rebecca tackles the daily challenges with her signature sense of humor and with a Christ-centered knack of blooming where she is planted. You will reflect with Rebecca on the evidence in both Scripture and circumstance of God's wise providence. You will come away from this book with a sharper sense of your own blessings and a deeper appreciation for the sacrifices made by missionary families in Africa and around the world.

The other path this book treads is that of the sure and steady Gospel growth in Malawi since the church began in 1963. You will cheer on God's Word as it is borne on foot, bicycle and the bouncy suspension of a four-wheel drive truck; as it is delivered in the language of the people by faithful missionaries and national pastors. WELS readers in particular will enjoy this up-close look at how their prayers and mission offerings support the work in Malawi and the spiritual growth of the missionary families.

And if you are a reader who happens to be a former Malawi missionary or missionary child, Rebecca's book will draw you into that world you once knew, into the arms of Aunty Africa who takes in orphans and exiles and teaches them to love her despite her idiosyncrasies—or because of them.

Sarah M. Habben (Alberta, Canada 2013)

INTRODUCTION

"If I rise on the wings of the dawn,
if I settle on the far side of the sea,
even there your hand will guide me,
your right hand will hold me fast."
Psalm 139:9-10

Over the years, these verses have held special meaning for me. My high school graduating class selected this passage. I remember looking at my classmates and wondering who might settle on the far side of the sea. Who might live out this mysterious part of God's plan? If someone had told me that someday *I* would be the one settling on the far side of the sea, I would have doubted it to be true! If someone had suggested that I, after traversing the sea, would eat bugs, poison myself, hold over a dozen scorpions in my hand, stand barefoot next to a tarantula and allow a large spider to spend the night a few feet above my pillow, I surely would have laughed. Not me! Arachnophobia runs in my family. I could never eat bugs. How would I, could I, ever poison myself? Those antics are for people who compete for prize money on television! No amount of money could entice *me* to do such things!

No, it was not the almighty dollar that led me into such eyebrow-raising experiences. Rather, it was the knowledge of a people in need of the greatest message in the world. That message is of Christ crucified and the salvation he gives to those who believe in his name. There are people who need to hear that precious message living on a continent far away—the people in the country of Malawi, Africa.

In 2003, our family moved to Africa to do mission work. As of 2013, we are still in Malawi. Throughout the years I have faithfully corresponded with my Stateside family; those emails and letters form the basis of this book. As I reread my correspondence, highlights emerge: heartwarming ministry stories, health struggles, third world frustrations, the beauty and drawbacks of tropical living and unusual happenings on the home front. My emails describe our family's daily routines, how the kids were growing and coping with life in Africa, how we dealt with adverse situations and how God gave us the needed strength and patience to persevere. These letters are a springboard for devotional thoughts and insights that I have gained as a missionary wife in the ebb and flow of life in Malawi, Africa.

I was partly motivated to write this book by the very real possibility that further budget cuts to the Africa mission field may be necessary in the future. I consider this book to be a PR project gone large, to help mission-minded readers better realize who and what their mission offerings support as we each carry out God's Great Commission.

There have been many missionaries before us and, Lord willing, more will follow. Each has their own story to tell. This is my family's unique experience.

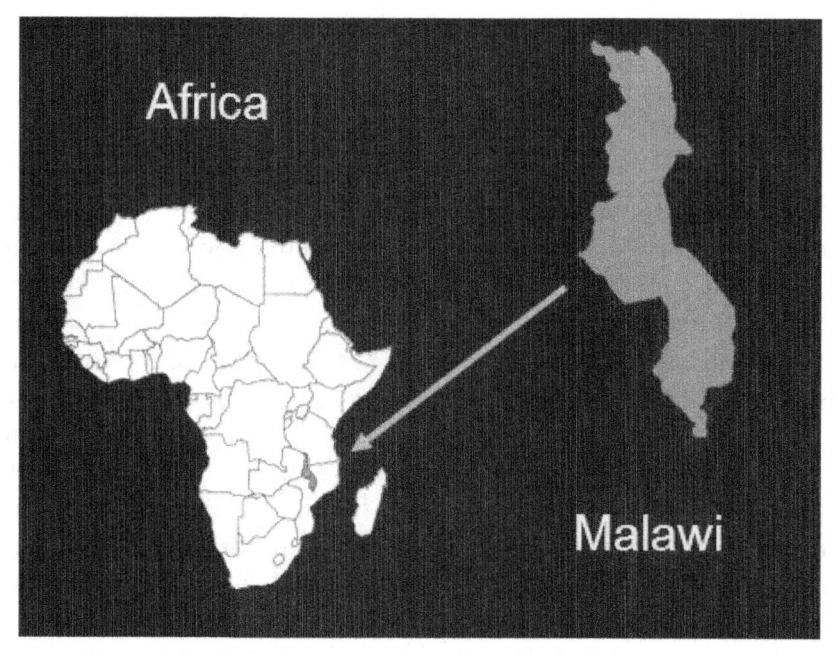

Map of Africa and country of Malawi

Introduction

Rob's LCCA congregations in southern Malawi

WELS Missions Link

The current link to world mission blogs and information is: *http://www.wels.net/missions/malawi*

Why Africa?

Rob was in the thick of his Stateside pastoral ministry when he received a call through the Wisconsin Evangelical Lutheran Synod (WELS) to be a rural missionary to Malawi, Africa in March of 2003. For the previous five years he had served the congregation of Redemption Lutheran Church in Milwaukee, WI. We lived near family. We had good friends close by. We had a wonderful congregation. While there were some who thought we would be crazy to go, others predicted that Rob's childhood in Lusaka, Zambia would entice him back to the "Dark Continent."

It was true that Rob had several generations of "roots" in Africa: his grandparents, Ernst H. and Betty Wendland, had served in Zambia between 1962 and 1978. Rob's father, Ernst R. Wendland, had graduated from Northwestern College in 1968 and returned to Zambia that same year. There he began to teach at the Lutheran Bible Institute and Seminary in Lusaka. A few years later he married Margaret Westendorf, who had just completed a tour of duty as a registered nurse with the Central Africa Medical Mission (CAMM) in Mwembezhi, Zambia. Missionary Ernst R. and Margaret raised Rob and their other three children in Zambia. More than 40 years later, Rob's Dad is still serving at the seminary in Lusaka, as well as doing Bible translation work. Several of Rob's uncles also served as missionaries in Africa. Certainly Rob's many connections to central Africa had taught him firsthand that there are Africans who need to hear about the Word of God and who need someone to minister to them—someone willing to go where the fields are ripe.

Rob was willing. He accepted that call to serve as a rural missionary for the Lutheran Church of Central Africa in Malawi. I was willing too, though I knew that *my* talents, training and calling in life were not the reason we would be on the front lines of mission work in Africa. I had been teaching afternoon classes at Redemption for 6-8th Grade. Now I was caring for our two children: three-year-old Hannah and baby Nathanael, only six months old. I would have been content with the status quo. No need to create extra work. No need to move away from city comforts. No need to break up our close family and church network. No need to spend every waking moment of the next several months thinking about moving, finding boxes and sorting our entire household into piles to give away, sell, send or toss. I wrote in a later diary entry,

"In my heart I know it is right for us to travel ten thousand miles away. But my head says, 'You are crazy!' I sincerely question upsetting my comfort zone

and that of the family. Why should we give up the wonders of America? Why should I have to stress over this daunting task of moving to Malawi? Our family is young and vulnerable. Our son is still not sleeping through the night. I'm nursing. Our three-year-old daughter adores visiting the close relatives. I cannot think straight anymore. I have too many crucial decisions to make by myself since Rob is still working endlessly at church as I pack our household and sell our belongings. It is too much in too little time. I have never been pushed so far to the edge mentally. The only way to keep everything in perspective is to trust in the Lord for REAL!"

In the midst of these stressful preparations, I realized that God equips those he calls with gifts like energy and external support...and even frozen food. A few weeks before Rob received the call to Africa, I had taken advantage of our local grocery store's frozen food sales and stocked up our freezer. During the next month of packing, my well-stocked freezer became a great blessing as a source of easy meals.

Our nearby family members were a wonderful support system during that difficult transition. Though farther away, my parents did everything in their power to lend a helping hand. My mom loyally took on any task, which allowed Rob to complete his full time ministry demands. I know it was not easy for them to prepare to say goodbye to me, Rob and their first two grandchildren. They spent a lot of time on the roads between La Crosse and Milwaukee in order to make the most of our final time together.

At first not many visible tears were shed, since we viewed the separation in light of the *greater good:* this move to Africa would put Rob and our family exactly where the Lord wanted us to serve. But there were many tears shed on the inside. This move meant that our kids would hardly know their grandparents, aunts, uncles or cousins living ten thousand miles away. Our holidays wouldn't include family gatherings as we had come to know them. More than one person had said they would be willing to go anywhere in the world but Africa. Were they right? Were we crazy to go?

Visiting **Africa vs.** *Living* **in Africa**

"The heavens declare the glory of God;
the skies proclaim the work of his hands...
There is no speech or language where their voice is not heard.
Their voice goes... to the ends of the world." Psalm 19

Yes, Africa seemed like the "end of the world." But there is life in Africa. Africa's diversity and beauty is amazing to behold—its starry heavens are just a sampling. What a marvel that God allows us flawed humans to join the celestial wonders in proclaiming His glory!

I realistically anticipated that living and proclaiming God's glory there would be slightly less than *heavenly*. After all, I wasn't a complete stranger to the continent. In 2001 Rob and I, with our 18-month-old daughter, had visited his parents in Zambia—my first exposure to life in Africa. I knew we wouldn't be living in a mud hut. I knew we would have running water, toilets, electrical appliances and even a 4WD vehicle. But in reality, that 2001 trip only meant that I knew Africa as a *visitor*. Visitors don't shop for food, cook from scratch or deal with water shortages. Visitors don't need a back-up meal plan if the electricity goes out. Visitors don't problem solve for flat tires or concern themselves with the all-consuming details of simply living.

I would soon find out that *living* in Africa was a different experience altogether. Like many North Americans, I was used to taking the basics for granted. Turn on a faucet and water comes out. Flip a switch and lights come on. Gas stations always have fuel. Stores send out fliers and stock the shelves predictably. One of my first revelations as a resident of Malawi was that I simply didn't know how to buy things in Africa. In fact, shopping and daily life were so new and strange after we arrived that I began to keep a diary to record all the differences I noticed. I also began to email my family regularly with the latest news. The information contained in those emails and diary entries, along with Rob's correspondence, is what I will share with you in this book.

Fresh vegetable market

CHAPTER 1

SEPTEMBER 2003: THE FAR SIDE OF THE SEA

*Millennia ago God called Abram in Genesis 12,
"Leave your country, your people
and your father's household
and go to the land I will show you."*

It is no small feat to move to Africa: to traverse half the earth via car and airplane with two small kids and suitcases in tow. Yet the Lord had equipped us for this enormous move. Both Rob and I have a childhood history of long-distance traveling and relocation. My dad is a WELS pastor; each divine call that he accepted moved us to a different location. While I was growing up my family moved over a dozen times, calling home places like Wisconsin, Illinois, Florida and Minnesota. I later graduated from Northwestern Preparatory School in Watertown, Wisconsin and earned a teaching degree at Martin Luther College in New Ulm, Minnesota.

After his childhood years in Zambia, Rob went to high school at Michigan Lutheran Seminary in Saginaw, Michigan and then attended Northwestern College in Watertown, Wisconsin. He flew home to Zambia for Christmas and summer vacations. Although relocation was not foreign to either of us, this was a major move for our family. What a comfort to remember Abram, who listened to God's calling to leave all that was familiar and move to a new land. We too followed the calling God had for our family.

Setting Off

On September 12, 2003 our trip began. My family graciously caravanned with us and ferried our luggage to O'Hare International Airport in Chicago, Illinois. It was hard to enjoy our final hours together, knowing they would be the last for a long time. As the clock ticked, the inevitable good-byes drew nearer. I wrote in my diary just how hard it was to leave:

"The good-byes are deep. In the end there are no words to say. Being so choked up leaves one literally speechless. Hannah was truly heartbroken to see everyone so sad. That was hard to watch too. We didn't want to be sad, but you cannot stop true feelings at the last moment. A look into anyone's eyes told the story. Our only consolation is knowing that our family is leaving to do the greatest work God has for us to do: to spread His Word to all nations as God directs in Matthew chapter 28."

The good-byes hurt. They tore at the fibers of my heart. I longed for the two years to pass quickly so that we might say hello again. The truth that we are merely strangers on earth and that heaven is our home had never been more apparent. Even if we would never again see our family on this side of eternity, I knew that I could trust in God's promises that I would see them again in heaven. It still brings tears of joy to my eyes to think that there will be no more good-byes in Paradise!

We collected ourselves and headed down the terminal. This was it.

Sent: September 13, 2003
Subject: Praise God—We made it!
Rob writes: We made it. On September 12 we left Chicago and flew to London. After a 10 hour layover, we boarded our plane to Malawi at 9pm. We spent an hour on the ground in Nairobi, Kenya and finally landed in Lilongwe, the capital city of Malawi, at 11am the next morning. Malawi is one hour ahead of London. We were on that plane for 11 hours. The kids did great.

The Malawi runway sure is short! Everything is very brown and dry compared to the green Midwest. It is quite a novelty to exit the plane directly onto the airport tarmac rather than following a ramp into the concourse.

Several mission families were there to greet us and bring us to the mission property in Lilongwe. That is where the pre-seminary school called the Lutheran Bible Institute (LBI) is set up. The missionaries had a nice get-together in our honor. We fought to stay up as long as we could, but Nathanael "broke" at about 6:30pm. We stayed in an empty house on the LBI campus. We all slept a full 12 hours. The next day Missionary Mark Wendland (Rob's uncle) and Kingdom Worker Stefan Felgenhauer chauffeured us four hours south to Blantyre. Blessings in Jesus, Rob

When God called Abram, the patriarch responded with prompt obedience and complete trust. After Abram arrived east of Bethel, *"He built an altar to the LORD and called on the name of the LORD"* (Genesis 12:8b). We too offered up many a prayer of thanksgiving to the Lord for safe travels around the world. For the first time I pictured how tired Abram and Sarai must have been when they finally reached

Bethel...they were decades older than Rob and I, and they had traveled by foot! The eight hour time change and compounding travel fatigue certainly drained us. Not long after we had met the Lilongwe missionaries and enjoyed a nice dinner together, we were ready to call it a day, or a night, or a nap—or maybe a coma! Equally daunting was the fact that we had traveled with a one-way ticket. We were on our way to a house we had never seen, to make a home in a place we had never been.

The next day we began the four hour journey south to the city of Blantyre and our new home. I felt silly when I hopped into the passenger's seat and found a steering wheel in front of me. I quickly switched seats and buckled in. I would need to. The road trip was hectic! I cringed much of the way as I tried to adjust to traveling on the "wrong" side of the road. I said endless prayers for a safe journey, even as I noted several accidents on the way.

Challenging road conditions

Sent: September 14, 2003
Subject: Home to Blantyre
Rob writes: We witnessed three accidents on our trip south from Lilongwe to Blantyre. First we watched a speeding car try to get around a stalled truck in the road, only to meet a bus head on. Instead of crashing into the bus, the car veered into the ditch at the side of the road. The wheels were still spinning. No one was moving in the crushed cab of the car. In seconds a mob of people came streaming from all around. We saw the second accident as we entered Blantyre. There are people all over the roads. Both people and cars seem to expect the right of way, which is a bad situation when no one gives. A man ran right in front of a car. The car wasn't about to slow down; it just clipped his ankle as he ran. He was spun around but was alert enough to stand up and shout at

the driver. The third accident we saw was when a truck tried to dodge a minibus that was trying to go around another truck. The roads are narrow here and the ditches are deep. There was no room for three vehicles across and the road crumbled under the passing truck. It flipped onto its side but everyone seemed to be okay. Love, Rob

It was apparent on the first road trip that the driving here is seriously dangerous. Many unfit vehicles share the road. They often lack turn signals or working lights at night. They are driven with smashed windshields. Some putter along not much faster than a riding lawnmower. Other vehicles may be roadworthy but are driven at hazardously high speeds. Cyclists weave past, carrying massive and surprising loads: goats, pigs, chickens, mattresses, enormous bags of charcoal, soda crates, metal roofing sheets or piles of firewood stacked higher than their own heads. The side of the road is also shared by running children and women who balance impossible loads on their heads: buckets of maize, massive piles of firewood and tree stumps, or baskets full of market produce like bananas, groundnuts and avocados. Like the cyclists, these women sometimes carry surprises on their heads: an axe sticking straight up, a suitcase, car battery, a cow head or a purse. Add to the road ox-carts, potholes and free-roaming animals and it is no wonder there are frequent casualties. How many of them have *"a knowledge of the truth"* (1 Timothy 2:4)? There is work to do here!

Hauling an amazing load of wood

On the outskirts of Blantyre, in a small area called Nyambadwe, was the house we would call home. The mission house adequately fit our family of four with space for Rob to have a separate office. Indeed, it was great to finally reach "home."

Settling In

Sent: September 15, 2003
Subject: Our home
Rob writes: We arrived at our Nyambadwe home safely. All our luggage made it except our stroller, which is in some airport in Africa. The home is nice, and workmen were finishing up with repairs as we pulled in. We have no electricity and no working phone (welcome to Africa!), so I'm writing this from a fellow missionary's computer. They are rationing electricity. Ours has been out for 24 hours. A neighbor was cutting down trees and a branch fell on one of our phone lines. We will have to contact the phone company to fix it. Hopefully we'll have power and a phone connection soon, but who knows here?

We thank you for all of your help, thoughts and prayers throughout our journey. Most of all we praise Jesus, who brought us here safely, and in whose name we have the greatest of all joy, hope and peace. What a privilege that we now get to share those blessings with our brothers and sisters in Malawi—amazing! The Malawi Wendlands

It was quite inconvenient to have the power off the first night that we arrived. I knew right where I had packed a flashlight in my suitcase, but I had no idea where my suitcase was! Yet somehow it was hard to feel sorry for ourselves over our lack of power and phone when a mile away there were people struggling over the REAL basics, like food, water, clothing and shoes. I felt blessed. Blessed to have a roof over our heads. Blessed to know that our good Lord would help us tackle any trial that might come our way. By the time I wrote my next letter home, we had already faced a few challenges as we worked to get our lives up and running.

Our first mission house at Nyambadwe

Sent: September 24, 2003
Subject: A message from the other side
Rebecca writes: We have been here about a week now. I am amazed at how many people are shoeless or wearing tattered clothes. Many houses don't have doors or windows. The advertising billboards and lines on the road are hand-painted. Scaffolding looks like rickety toothpicks roped together. There are numerous unfinished buildings. I was told they remain that way because the owner most likely ran out of money.

With a little pocket change you can purchase mice on a stick for food! On our drive to Blantyre, people jumped out of the bush to push their black, roasted sticks of mice at the cars to make a sale. The roadside markets that we passed had tomatoes, onions, carrots, beans of all sorts, sweet and Irish potatoes, cucumbers, pumpkins, bananas and eggplant. I was relieved to see those familiar ingredients.

One of the first noticeable differences in our house is how dusty and dirty things get. Within hours, Hannah's white sandals were brown and everyone's feet were filthy. That is why most "wealthy" people have a housemaid. I have been dragging my dirty feet on that option since house workers can also present big problems. We do have a highly recommended gardener/yard worker, Mr. Lackson Chinyama, who takes care of the outside items. He doesn't wear shoes. After seeing our yard and our house I am thankful to have him do the outside work.

We are thinking of waxing/polishing our indoor hardwood floors. It is a parquet floor ('Parkay' only meant margarine to me before this house). Since it is not sealed, it harbors dust and dirt. I mop it and it is still dirty. There are many household tasks to keep me busy for now.

We seem to have a thousand keys, which I hope to sort through and color-code. I will be amazed if we don't lock ourselves out one of these days. After a previous break-in at this mission house, the security was updated. Our entrances have security grates and multiple locks. Most of our windows have double burglar bars. The hallway leading to our bedrooms is closed off by a security grate. We have a cement slab wall around the perimeter with razor wire strung on the top of it. We have two night guards also. I feel pretty safe as long as it is all locked up. The other neighbors have some security, but not as extensive as ours. I guess the surrounding houses had break-ins mere days before we came. We don't have too much in the way of possessions yet. By the time our shipment comes, I hope we won't be a novelty anymore. My red hair is sort of an attention-getter as it is.

I long for my kitchen items that are coming in our shipment. After trying to use a local vegetable peeler, I thought it would have been faster with my fingernails. I

September 2003: The Far Side Of The Sea

did successfully make a banana bread, shepherd's pie and pea soup from all the local ingredients. It all tasted decent. Some of the tastes here are very different. Cornflakes are harder, chewy and expensive. Some of the brand-name boxes are over $10 a box; I've even seen a South African sugar-coated kind for $20 a box.

I don't like the full cream milk that is available. We went to the dairy plant and ordered five liters of skim milk, but it tastes unusual. For now I'll use it in cooking and hopefully get used to something else. I would rather not exclusively drink soda and juice, so our precious boiled and filtered water will have to do for now. Each morning I boil two pots of water, let them cool for several hours, and then run them through a filter. We try to use that for everything that we consume. We have been told to soak raw vegetables in a purple solution of 1% potassium permanganate to make them safe.

We've been shopping a few times in the last week to find the different stores that carry imported items and household staples. Incidentally, I have absolutely no regrets for packing what I did. We were told that you could get just about anything here, but that isn't the whole story. It seems you can get select items on a VERY hit-or-miss basis. You can also get many things for a gouging price. For instance, one can of Campbell's soup is about $5. Only once has the store carried canned orange juice. Oatmeal comes and goes. This time it came...but with weevils. We picked many out. I was also hoping to make my own pizza here. The price of cheese is very high—$10 for a small chunk of mozzarella—if they even have it. There is no pepperoni. It is definitely not like Kansas, Toto.

I have found that our trip to Africa two years ago has helped me to mentally adjust to the challenges here. What challenges you ask? First, Rob did the wash and had to carry about twenty buckets of hot water to the washer for the first cycle and again for the rinse cycle. After the third batch he decided to unhook the hoses and just pour water in the washer from its hose. This is a dangerous solution if you don't watch it carefully—overflow, you know.

Secondly, I was ready to unpack Hannah's suitcase. No sooner did I enter her room when, to my absolute shock, I saw about one hundred tiny wall spiders hatching out of the light fixture. They were slowly spreading across her bedroom. One of the items in the house was bug spray. I did roughly count them as I swept up their corpses.

Thirdly, Rob has killed a large roach every day in his office. It reminds me of when I lived in Florida when I was younger. The bugs will keep coming until they are under control.

Lastly, my biggest hurdle will be gaining my autonomy. The driving here is terrible. There are many bad accidents. There are too many people, too many animals, too many crazy drivers, too many narrow roads, deep drainage ditches about a yard off the road shoulder and unusual roundabout sections instead of stoplights. Learning how to drive on the "wrong" side of the road will be a challenge, to say the least. On top of that, I need to conquer driving a stick-shift Pajero. I will be missing my trusty automatic transmission Oldsmobile for a long time.

Yesterday Hannah wanted to fly back to say hello to Grandpa and Grandma Staude one more time. We miss you all. Thanks for keeping us in your prayers! Rebecca

Roadside fast food—mice on a stick

The mission families in Blantyre graciously showed us around, introduced us to different church members, took Rob to get his driver's license and connected us with helpful people and shopping places. To my astonishment, Rob drove the day after we arrived. Our house and intersection onto the main road were both on steep inclines, so I was reluctant to try my hand at driving a stick shift. In the end it was three months before I attempted to get my license and drive autonomously. For the time being, I was happy to learn about the city and travel around as a passenger.

Something I quickly realized was that in Malawi there are no one-stop shopping centers. Purchasing necessities is a complicated procedure that involves shopping at different stores and even traveling to different cities. There is no internet ordering and no home delivery. If I needed a light bulb or a fuse, I learned to go downtown to Minimax. If I needed a bed net I went to Lambats. Material could be found at Toppers or the Pound shop in Limbe. The Dairibord carried milk and cheese. Empty soda bottles were returned at Metro. Bread items were best fresh at Ellie's Market, but not on weekends. Most stores did not open until 8 or 9am, and they closed for lunch. They opened again around 1:30pm and closed for the day at 5pm. On Fridays the Muslim-operated shops closed early for worship. Most stores did not open at all on weekends. Upon reaching a store there was no guarantee that they would have what I needed in stock. Parking spots were usually difficult to find, especially downtown. I dreaded leaving the car because a dozen vendors would swarm around me as soon as I stepped out. They all seemed to share the same sales tactic: thrust their wares as close as possible to my eyes so I would look at it, like it, and buy it. Shopping was physically exhausting!

To complicate things, the highest bill denomination in Malawi Kwacha (MK) was the 500 note. It was worth less than five US dollars. I'm sure it was a sign that I was blessed, but I often had a wad of MK500s and not much other little change. It was not unusual to get to the check-out counter and find that neither I nor the check-out clerk had the change needed to complete a transaction. I discovered that the only reasonable solution was to buy enough little items to add up to the nearest hundred. Learning to problem solve on the spot was surely better than getting upset and frustrated.

Disarray in logic was apparent in the laws of the land (to my thinking). Laws in Malawi can change, depending on who enforces them. Such was the case when a police officer pulled over a friend to tell her that child car seats were illegal. He insisted that she remove her children from the car seats before he would let her go on her way. In spite of being flustered, my friend cooperated. Then she drove down the street, reinstalled the seats and buckled up her kids again.

In those first weeks in Malawi, some days were more difficult than others. On those days it was particularly challenging to find a silver lining beneath all the frustrations and petty hassles. It was at those times that I was reminded that *in Christ I can do all things as he promises to give me strength*. And not only *do* them but do them with a happy and grateful heart. Hard as it was to overcome the difficulties themselves, it was even more challenging to find the positive in each frustration and to give glory to God for it. So when my faucet handle fell with a clank into a sink full of dirty dishes one day, I thought, "How many other people here even have a kitchen sink, let alone running water?" Contentment in any circumstance was a lesson that God would find many ways to teach me!

> *"I have learned to be content whatever the circumstances…*
> *whether well fed or hungry,*
> *whether living in plenty or in want.*
> *I can do everything*
> *through him who gives me strength." Philippians 4:13*

CHAPTER 2

MONTH ONE: ADJUSTING

Ruth replied, "Don't urge me to leave you...
Where you go I will go, and where you stay I will stay.
Your people will be my people
and your God my God." Ruth 1:16

Ruth the Moabite was committed to her mother-in-law, Naomi. She was devoted to Naomi's God. It is easy to take the details of this familiar story for granted. Yet surely when Ruth left her homeland of Moab and followed Naomi to Bethlehem in Judah, she also left behind friends, family and a sense of routine and security. I wonder if she had second thoughts. What if the move was a mistake? What if her sister-in-law, Orpah, made the better decision to remain in Moab? What if making a new life in a foreign land was too difficult?

Moving to the foreign land of Malawi reminds me of Ruth's story. "Where you go I will go," was also my promise to Rob. In my case, that promise meant following Rob to Malawi. It was not easy to leave friends and family, but if this was where God wanted us, then I trusted God to be with us. Everything was new and most things were difficult. Nonetheless, each day progress was made. We were slowly getting to know the missionaries and figuring out where they lived (without the help of maps or a GPS). We were becoming familiar with the city roads and the routes to the village congregations that Rob would serve. We were learning new terms, unusual names and finding supplies. We were adapting to new foods and different tastes. We were learning how to make this land our home.

Neighbors Behind Bars

Speaking from his many experiences with relocation, my dad has suggested that it is a good idea to meet your neighbors. Shortly after we arrived, we were determined to explore our neighborhood and do just that. As we stepped beyond the threshold of our yard gate and walls, one look down the road told me that meeting people was not going to be easy. Everyone lived behind tall walls topped with multiple layers of razor wire. Dogs barked as we neared any property. When we knocked on a gate it was not the owners who appeared. Instead we were greeted by a yard worker or a guard and had to talk through them. We did not meet any neighbors that day. Who would guess that it would be April, seven months after our arrival, before we met a neighbor face to face! Undaunted, we continued our stroll. It took us down several dirt walking paths that wound around to nearby railroad tracks and back again through the neighborhood. When we later told others about our walk, they were amazed that we had made it safely. They warned us to avoid unnecessary excursions outside of our gate, and said that even the Malawians would not walk on the dangerous railroad tracks. Thieves and witches evidently operated along the tracks and looked for opportunities to prey on others.

The vulnerability of our location dawned on us in time. Our Nyambadwe yard was rectangular. Our east wall bordered a neighbor's property, but the other three walls were exposed to public traffic. Each day hundreds of people traveled past our property. We soon realized that the mango trees around our perimeter were frequently climbed, not only for their fruit but also as a handy way to ogle over our walls. In time we would cut them down. We also learned that a violent break-in had previously occurred in our mission house. The thieves had gained access to the property by digging under the walls. After that incident, the security was beefed up with double burglar bars in most entrances and in the windows. (Even that precaution does not always stop determined thieves...some will pry open burglar bars with car jacks!)

Although we lived those early days with caution, we didn't live in fear. It was a joy to watch three-year-old Hannah and 11-month-old Nathanael adapt to the new culture and absorb the many sights and sounds and smells. They balanced baskets on their heads and played with papyrus "wands" and fallen mangoes. They collected seed pods and searched for the perfect bamboo stick. They watched, wide-eyed, the scurrying geckos and giant millipedes called *chongololos*. I could only imagine what little Hannah and Nathanael would learn, growing up in Africa.

Matters of Life and Death

Sent: September 23, 2003
Subject: Funeral
Rob writes: In Lilongwe an 18-month-old child of a Lutheran Bible Institute student died. Principal Mabedi called off school. He and Missionary Paul Nitz traveled south with a bunch of students and their wives for a funeral in a village east of Blantyre. I went along. We drove through several hilly tea plantations. That congregation is currently served by Pastor Chikwatu. Sadly, I forgot to bring along my audio recorder for his sermon on Mark 5—Jairus' daughter.

We walked in the funeral procession to the house. Ladies from the church

cleaned the home. There were about 150 people gathered. That's today's news.
Love, Rob

Nearness of death gives urgency to mission work

This little one's death was a somber initiation into life and work in Malawi. Deaths like these are very common, particularly among infants and children. It is said that if a child can live past the age of five, they have withstood many of the crucial childhood diseases and troubles and have a chance to see adulthood. Praise the Lord that this little boy belonged to a family of believers and now enjoys the wonders of heaven with God!

Rob mentioned Principal Daison Mabedi in his email. In 1997, this pastor became the first national principal of the Lutheran Bible Institute (LBI) in Lilongwe. The LBI is a three year pre-seminary school for men from Malawi and Zambia who are interested in entering the ministry. When one of his students lost a child, Principal Mabedi showed support by calling off school to attend the funeral several hundred kilometers away. This kind of Christian support is crucial when so many LBI students are surrounded by the belief system of their culture: ancestor-worship, belief in a spirit world and the practice of witchcraft. Though none of us could have known at the time, a year later Principal Mabedi would lose a child too and need his own share of Christian comfort in the face of death.

Even though death is a grim reality of living in a third world country, giving life and having a large family is important to Malawians. A large family means many helping hands and a sense of being blessed. This way of thinking was evident when a Malawian lady at a local shop asked me how many children I had. I told her I had two. She replied, "Oh, you are better than me; I only have one." How contrary to North American culture, which measures success by the number of *things* you have, not the number of children!

Mothers care for the next generation

Many families in Malawi have between six and a dozen children. Our gardener, Mr. Chinyama, had eight. He, like many Malawians, made certain sacrifices to support his large family. For example, he only visited his village home on weekends. On Saturdays he would bike an hour to the nearby city of Limbe. Then he would leave his bike and take an hour-long bus ride. This was followed by a two-hour walk before he finally reached his home.

Several weeks after we settled in Nyambadwe, Mr. Chinyama told us that his daughter's home had burned down. Malawians cook over an open fire on the floor of their village huts, so the possibility of a house fire is high. Mr. Chinyama asked to leave work early so that he could buy her a roll of plastic sheeting. That way she could rebuild the hut with plastic under the thatched grass roof. Malawians have to be innovative with the tools at their disposal.

It soon became clear to me that missionaries need their own share of innovation as certain projects found us tapping into previously hidden talents.

Sent: September 29, 2003
Subject: Garden of Eden...?
Rebecca writes: Rob installed his own florescent light fixture in his office. I was quite amazed. I didn't realize he could tackle electrical items. As we sat down

to eat dinner yesterday, our power went off for an hour. Thankfully the food was cooked. Hannah likes the candles. I've decided that candles are a novelty in the States because they CAN be!

Nathanael is eager to keep pace with everyone and is walking now. Next time you see him he won't be a baby anymore.

This Sunday we went to church at Beautiful *Saviour* (British spelling here), where a small but established group of English speaking members worship in a "Reading Room" located in downtown Blantyre. Missionary Ron Uhlhorn (who previously lived in the Nyambadwe house) was instrumental in gathering the core group of members here. Currently the services are being led by mature lay-leaders, nearby national pastors, or missionaries from Lilongwe. I will play keyboard this Sunday and ask if there is a Sunday School in the works.

Missionary Paul Wegner and family stopped by. They live in Zomba, about 60 km away from us. They have been in Malawi for almost 5 years. They brought some rhubarb from the Zomba plateau. Evidently the conditions on the plateau are conducive for growing it. I would have never guessed there would be rhubarb in Africa! You'll have to tell Great Grandma Staude that we are enjoying rhubarb and have several mango trees on our property. Since she thinks Eve was tempted with a delicious mango, we might possibly be living in the original Garden of Eden! (Okay, maybe not.)

News on our shipment...it hasn't left Chicago yet! It has been waiting Stateside for four months already; what is another few? God bless, Rebecca

One transition that I mentioned in the email was the milestone of Nathanael walking. Our families were too far away to be a part of that exciting time as he started to walk, talk, grow and learn. He was so young when we came that I was afraid that he would not even remember our extended family members when we saw them again. For the time being I pointed to pictures, said their names and talked about them frequently.

In spite of missing our overseas family, we were grateful to be surrounded by an immediate family of believers in Malawi, both missionaries and church members. It was a blessing to worship with such a variety of people and join together in proclaiming the good news and praising our awesome God. I also felt extremely blessed to be able to worship in English. That is something I will not take for granted. It is hard to grow spiritually when God's Word is shared in a language you can't yet understand.

When we arrived in 2003, the small congregation of Beautiful Saviour had a growing core of members. The members were mostly Malawian, with some expatriate families mixed in. They were meeting in the Lutheran Reading Room, which had opened in Blantyre in 1999. The Reading Room was set up with Christian books, periodicals and various media. Throughout the week various classes were offered, such as English lessons and a Children's Hour. The goal was to attract people to use free Christian resources, learn English and perhaps find a church home in the process. Outreach had been successful enough to lead to the formation of Beautiful Saviour. Now the members had plans to build a proper church building downtown. We looked forward to being part of that exciting transition.

Rob's call was to village congregations. He would spend the bulk of his first year in language immersion so that he could serve as a shepherd to village churches. Some of my most cherished early experiences included worshipping in a few of those rural churches. There I could see firsthand the mission work that was being done and the kind of work my husband would be doing. After all, that is why we moved to Malawi in the first place. Rob was similarly inspired by the joyful faith of the members in the village congregations. He wrote home about a particularly stirring church service in a village called Mboola. He had attended a special service to celebrate the opening of their new church building.

Sent: October 1, 2003
Subject: Mboola!
Rob writes: Wow—yesterday was a great day! I was invited along to one of the village congregations that is served by a local man, Mr. Mission (that is his real name). He has been serving the Lutheran Church of Central Africa (LCCA) for almost 30 years. He is now 76 years old and continues to serve 4 congregations, the farthest about 10 miles apart. Even now he bicycles from one to the next on a Sunday morning on the dusty bush roads. Those congregations are also in the most densely populated area of the LCCA. I have been told that we have more members down that Thyolo road than all of the rest of Malawi and Zambia combined. As a result, Mr. Mission serves more than 1000 members.

Yesterday I attended the dedication of a new church building at the village of Mboola. Mr. Mission was one of the first to greet me. When he heard that I was Robert Ernst, oh, he was so happy. He told me that he held me in his arms when I was 3 days old; at least I think that's what he said—he was speaking Chichewa and I'm still learning the language. He invited all the pastors to his house for a meal before the service. It was a fine meal of rice, beef and cabbage. One of the pastors gave Mr. Mission a hard time, calling it only "breakfast" since there was no *nsima* (a cornmeal porridge). All "proper" meals include *nsima*. After breakfast, the pastors gathered to discuss the finer points of the service.

At 12 noon, we marched from Mr. Mission's house to the new church, two by two. As we walked, we were joined by choirs and members of the congregation. There were over 400 people in attendance. It was awesome to hear the different hymns and singing as we approached. In front of the church doors, Pastor Meja silenced the crowd and conducted a small liturgy asking God to bless His house and its members before we went inside. Then all the people joined behind us. They walked two by two as we entered the new church. I had expected to be sitting in the back, as a mere observer, and had brought along my video camera and audio recorder. Mr. Mission would not allow me to peel off. He invited me to one of the chairs reserved for the pastors, set up in front of the altar facing the congregation. I didn't want to be a distraction waving my video camera around, so I didn't get much recorded.

After everybody was in the church who could fit, a choir marched to the front. They were the only choir to use instruments the whole day. If you or I were to look at these things we might wonder if they were simply toys. There were homemade drums, two homemade guitars (made from sticks and wire), and a bass (which was a box on the ground with one wire fastened to a wooden arm). It took two to play the bass. One person pressed down on the wire string and the other hit the box in rhythm—not much—but *miyo ine* (oh, my) the music! It is something one has to see and hear with one's own eyes and ears. The sound, the rhythm, the singing, the clapping and the response from the congregation was fantastic and a wonderful taste of things to come.

We used the liturgy from our Lutheran Hymnbook—*Nyimbo Za Mpingo wa Lutheran*. I was glad I could record the liturgy as it was spoken. Now I can hear how it is supposed to be done when I practice at home. Wow! I have a lot of work to do.

After the body of the service, different congregation elders and tribal leaders were given the time to say something. When they were done, the choir sang two more songs and was joined by the congregation in singing, dancing, clapping and rejoicing. It truly was a blessing to be there and rejoice with them. It finished at 3pm. Wonderful! 400 people joining together for a special worship on a Tuesday for three hours was amazing. I truly cherish this zeal for worship and am blessed to be a part of it.

After the pastors disrobed, we went back to Mr. Mission's house, this time for a "proper" meal—with *nsima,* chicken and cabbage. We finally got home at about 5:30pm. After taking several national pastors home, Uncle Mark joined me for a wonderful dinner that Rebecca had waiting for us. All in all it was a great day.

Tomorrow we head to Lake Malawi for an overnight trip with the Felgenhauers. Stefan and Kathy Felgenhauer have lived here in Blantyre for about a year. Stefan is the mission business manager with WELS Kingdom Workers. Love, Rob

P.S. Mr. Mission sends his greetings to all those with whom he has worked. He said to me, "Ha, how blessed I am to serve with all these Wendlands over the years!"

A traditional *nsima* meal

Food in Due Season

Traditional food is fairly simple in Malawi. Their staple carbohydrate is called *nsima*. *Nsima* begins as maize or field corn. The women take a large mortar and pestle and pound the maize into a fine white powder called *ufa woyera*. Over an open fire, which can be outside or even on the floor of their hut, the women add the *ufa* to a pot of boiling water and cook it to the desired thickness. The finished product resembles grainy mashed potatoes…but only in looks. The taste is bland and starchy. *Nsima* is prepared to be eaten "now-now" (soon), not as leftovers. It is scooped into patties and served with *ndiwo*. *Ndiwo* is a relish that usually consists of cooked tomatoes, onions, greens such as pumpkin leaves, kale or spinach, and beans of many sorts, all prepared in a generous amount of oil. This simple vegetarian meal becomes a feast with the periodic addition of a boiled egg, *kapenta* (tiny dried fish), goat, beef or chicken. Not all meals have meat since it is only affordable on occasion.

The words of Psalm 145 in the King James Version were becoming more tangible to me*: "The eyes of all wait upon thee; And thou givest them their meat in due season. Thou openest thine hand, And satisfiest the desire of every living thing." (KJV)* Food "in due season" doesn't register in quite the same way in North America where many shoppers pile imported fruit and vegetables in the cart and swipe their credit card at the checkout counter. Shoppers hardly pause to wonder where the strawberries come from in the middle of winter. Here in Malawi, seedtime, rain and harvest means that the diet of the local people consists of exactly what can be grown, harvested and eaten NOW! The subsistence lifestyle puts Malawians in a position to realize just how much of their food and life depends on the Lord.

Over our years in Malawi, Rob has been a guest at many such local meals, served to him by the congregation to demonstrate their support for the spiritual food he provides for them. Incongruously, this traditional meal is often accompanied by a bottle of Coca-Cola for honored guests. Coke—*in Africa*? I still find it humorous to see that red and white symbol in such a rural setting. A soft drink in the middle of the bush may seem a bit extravagant, but when the water supply is contaminated and possibly full of gastrointestinal bugs, a soda is a safe drink. On occasion there is nothing to drink at meals. The local water supply, such as a river or stream, is not only used for drinking but also used for washing clothes, cooking and bathing. Water from villages with bore holes, or wells, is more available as the people are able to use a hand-pump to pump fresh water from the ground. But since we *azungu* (white people) didn't grow up with the local water, or any bugs that are in it, we often get sick if we drink it. A soft drink is about the only safe option when you are far away from a western-style town.

Washing day down at the river

Sights and Seasons

With our travel plans to Lake Malawi announced, we received caution from Rob's mom:

INCOMING EMAIL: October 2, 2003
Subject: RE: Mboola!
Mom Wendland writes: Hi Rob, What a wonderful, uplifting message! Thanks!

Month One: Adjusting

You had great observations. Be sure to keep all these emails in a file to read (or print) at a later time. I hope you don't swim in Lake Malawi. Remember that you have only one good kidney. I love you all—you are constantly in our prayers! Much love, Mom

Rob's mom proved to a blessing that I could never have fully appreciated had we stayed in the States. Not only did she have 40-some years of experience of living in Africa, but she was also working as a nurse for the US Embassy in Lusaka, Zambia. Her medical expertise in times of dilemma has been invaluable. In this email she added a motherly reminder to Rob, since she knows that Lake Malawi is contaminated with bilharzia. Bilharzia, or snail fever, is caused by a parasite that is harbored by snails and can infect humans who come in contact with infested waters. The disease can wreak havoc on certain internal organs, a risk that Rob can't afford since one of his kidneys is already impaired. We have not spent our years in Africa in paranoia about such illnesses, but we do take precautions…and we do not go in the water of Lake Malawi, inviting though it looks.

Lake Malawi is one of the great African Rift Valley lakes. It is the third largest lake in all of Africa and the eighth largest lake in the world. It runs north to south for two-thirds the length of Malawi; it is about 560 km (348 miles) long, and its widest point is about 75 km (47 miles) across. That's some significant water for a country that is a little smaller than Pennsylvania! One phenomenon periodically seen over the lake is dense clouds of lake flies (*kungu*). When these "clouds" pass through villages, the locals take baskets and swing them around in order to gather the flies to eat as fly cakes.

Beautiful Lake Malawi

Sent: October 6, 2003
Subject: trip to the lake
Rebecca writes: Sorry to hear about Grandma Staude's broken bone, as well as Grandpa Wendland's stroke. God knows the plans He has for them yet.

We came back from our neat trip to Lake Malawi on Saturday; we almost felt like we were in Aruba or Maui instead of Malawi since palm trees lined the sandy beach. We got a cabin by the lakeshore. We had a cookout right on the beach and went to sleep to the rhythmic washing of the waves.

Each day we walked by the public beach to get to the dining area. As Kathy put it, "It is sort of like walking through a page of National Geographic." No swim pants for the kids and bathing in the buff for many. There were lots of ladies doing wash and kids playing in the water. A group of Malawians was leaving the beach and was almost out of sight as we approached. I thought, "Good, maybe they won't notice us." Wrong. They backtracked and stood there gawking at our passing. We stayed out of the water. It is such a shame that the beautiful lake is so contaminated. I wonder how many of the local people live with bilharzia.

One night we heard a bush baby in the tree and it did sound like a baby crying. We got a fleeting glimpse of it by flashlight as it climbed through the trees above us.

Matt and Dad—I couldn't help but think of you both on the travels to the lake and back. Craftsmen were cutting down big eucalyptus trees. Without an electric saw or planer they were cutting the boards with something like a huge bread slicer to keep their saw blades straight. It was amazing they do that all by hand. There are also many coffin workshops along the roadside.

On our travels we almost hit a kid—as in a child, not a goat (though there are lots of those too)—who darted into the road. Then we almost got sideswiped by a huge truck. My blood pressure must have doubled. AGHH! I think our angels are in the hospital with broken wings.

After we returned from our trip I played the keyboard on Sunday at Beautiful Saviour. Then we all went to a bush congregation for a second service that afternoon. Even though it made the day a bit long, I enjoyed the experience of worshipping in the village. When we arrived at the village church, the ladies of the congregation all surrounded the vehicle and sang a welcome song thanking God that we had come. It was a highlight to sit elbow-to-elbow on a cement bench with members of a different tribe and praise God together. I recognized every fiftieth word or so. I smiled as the members looked on. I am glad they have an English service in town.

Hannah threw up after supper. Our health is in a state of flux. Love, Rebecca

This email included an update on two of our grandparents. When we learned of their health struggles we were forced to face the possibility that we might never see them again on this side of eternity. It was a difficulty that we had known we would one day face. We did what we could from our great distance: we prayed. As it turned out, the Lord allowed us to see my grandmother once more on our first furlough and to see Grandpa E. H. Wendland several more times before he died in 2009.

We were also hoping Hannah's sickness was short-lived. Prayers for good health are right up there with the traveling prayers. I am certain my *prayer* life was healthier than ever here in Malawi.

Sent: October 7, 2003
Subject: Question Answered
Rob writes: In answer to your question about our weather, our temperatures during a typical day are around 80°F and about 70°F after the sun goes down. In the lower-lying bush areas the temperatures hover in the mid-90°F. In the Shire Valley, which is where my future congregations are, the temperatures can be close to 120°F. The humidity is very low and you have to remember to keep drinking water. Love, Rob

That first October in Malawi I enjoyed walking around with comfortably warm hands and toes. It was a delightful difference from the cold, tingly appendages I had in the Midwest from October through April.

There are roughly three seasons in Malawi. There is the **warm and wet** season from December to April. The first rains often begin in December and last several hours each day. Often this provides several inches of rain in a short amount of time. Humidity is high. The months of May to August are the **cool and dry** winter months. In Blantyre, the conditions in winter occasionally allow for *chiperoni*, a Malawian term for the drizzle or heavy mist experienced in the Shire Highlands. *Chiperoni* makes the temperature feel even cooler, but the vegetation appreciates the moisture and soaks up the late rain. During a Malawian winter the nights get cold (50°F), but the days are often warm and pleasant. Conditions are dry and very dusty during these months. Usually a pungent smoke fills the air as people burn leaves and grass to clear their land and burn charcoal and wood to cook and keep warm. During September through November the conditions are **dry and hot**. October is usually the hottest month with hot days and very warm nights.

Health Struggles

So far, our family had coped decently as we became accustomed to life in Malawi. However, we didn't just need to adjust mentally. Our bodies were also *physically* adjusting to life in a foreign country. Soon we faced inevitable health complications. We had been eating different kinds of food in various places and our systems were not pleased. Hannah's tummy problems spread to Rob and me. Little Nathanael, who was just shy of his first birthday, had a different symptom: he developed a high fever. Was he just teething? Or could it be something worse? We looked for advice from the most experienced person we knew: Rob's mom. It was the first of many times we have relied on her vast African medical expertise.

Sent: October 10, 2003
Subject: Nathanael's fever
Rob writes: Nathanael has had a fever of 103°F since yesterday. Another note: a couple of days ago the rest of us were down with something. Hannah and I were throwing up. Rebecca had a bad case of diarrhea. Nathanael hasn't had either symptom. The rest of us are recovering. I tried to call you in Zambia but couldn't make an international call without "making arrangements with customer service on Tuesday." I wanted to see what you thought. Thanks! Love, Rob

We figured that Nathanael's fever was not food related. It was impossible not to consider malaria as a cause. Our trip to Lake Malawi would have exposed him to anopheles mosquitoes. However, his fever did not fit the malarial pattern (in which it becomes increasingly elevated every other night and drops during the day). Also, malarial symptoms don't arrive for about two weeks after the initial bite. Time would tell. In addition to health struggles we had other issues that neither one of us had ever dealt with. One was a "killer"!

Sent: October 12, 2003
Subject: under the "nice" weather
Rebecca writes: Bill and Cathy Meier drove the kids and me to church today since Rob was in the bush. There was no power for half the service, so I didn't play most of the hymns. Our reading from the book of James caught my attention like never before. The reading talked about treating the man with fine clothes really well, but giving a beggar who comes along a poor seat. At that exact moment in the reading, a lame man tentatively entered the room. He sort of crawled in, wearing flip flops on his hands. He was wearing a tattered suit coat and did his best to sit unnoticed in the corner of the room. The whole reading stood still as I saw firsthand a real-life Biblical application come to life.

Earlier in the day I discovered a huge swarm of "killer" bees by our house and sprayed them with bug spray. They aren't giving up. I swept up at least a hundred dead ones today. They make me a bit nervous, since it seems they are living in our roof.

As per the title... the temp is nice and warm outside, but we are all a bit under the weather yet. Last week Hannah wasn't well. This week Rob and I woke up not feeling great. I have the runs and am extremely weak. I'm trying to drink to

Month One: Adjusting

avoid dehydration. Nathanael has had a fever for four days. He was tested for malaria and it was negative.

This week the Administrative Committee for Africa (ACA) is visiting Malawi. This committee makes routine visits to the field to evaluate the work being done, as well as to encourage, advise and ensure good communication between the missionaries and the WELS World Mission Board. They will be here for the 40th Anniversary celebration of the LCCA-Malawi Synod on Friday. Two of the ACA men are staying with us.

Yesterday afternoon Rob returned from Ntcheu (halfway between Blantyre and Lilongwe), where he had meetings with the Lilongwe missionaries in order to get their ministry plans and goals ready to present to the ACA. He returned just in time to join the welcoming party organized for us in Blantyre. All the missionaries from Zomba and Blantyre came: the Wegners and Meiers from Zomba along with the Janoseks, Felgenhauers, and Uncle Mark Wendland from Blantyre. We had a good night of fellowship. It is officially Mother's Day in Malawi tomorrow. God bless, Rebecca

Nathanael's fever would have caused me only mild concern in the States. In a tropical third world country, however, a fever could be much more dire. I realized how little I was in control and how much I needed to rely on God's promise in Romans 8:28, *"And we know that in all things God works for the good of those who love him, who have been called according to his purpose."* It was a great feeling to leave our health troubles in such capable hands. We were not sure how to proceed but patiently waited and prayed that Nathanael's fever would break soon.

Our missionary gathering was enjoyable. What a mix of fresh enthusiasm and far-reaching experience there was among these missionaries, their wives and kids. Missionary Paul and Kristy Wegner had been in Malawi for almost five years. Two years before Bill Meier had been called as a permanent business manager/lay missionary for the mission in Zomba after his Kingdom Worker term was completed. Stefan and Kathy Felgenhauer had arrived a year before us. Rob's Uncle Mark and Louise Wendland were in their twelfth year of mission work in Malawi, having served in both Zambia and Malawi. Missionary John Janosek and his wife Yvonne had an astounding 40 years of experience in Africa, most of it in Malawi.

As we approached the 40th anniversary of the LCCA in Malawi, we realized how privileged we were to serve with someone who had been instrumental in its inception. Since the beginning of the Malawi mission in 1963, the Lutheran church had grown to over 30,000 members in 135 congregations served by 18 national pastors and aided by 9 missionaries. The gospel was being proclaimed in rural and urban communities from one end of Malawi to the other. Future national pastors were being trained. A plan was in place to develop the LCCA-Malawi Synod into an independent sister body of the WELS. God's hand had surely worked wonders during the last 40 years in Malawi.

In less than a year, Missionary Janosek would be retiring. Rob was his replacement on the field. We were certainly thankful in the meanwhile for the experience and guidance they could share with us. Months later I would interview the Janoseks before they left the land that had been their home throughout their adult years. I asked them what advice they had for newcomers to the field, and their response still resonates with me. Yvonne, who raised five daughters in Malawi, noted, "Don't look for America in Malawi. Instead look for what you can do and use here." John advised future world missionaries to "first find a *wife* who wants to be a world missionary."

Sent: October 12, 2003
Subject: Amai amasamba
Rebecca writes: This week *amai amasamba* (vegetable ladies) came to our gate. I bought $5 worth of lemons, carrots, onions, broccoli, cauliflower, zucchini and strawberries. I even got a watermelon for 50 cents.

I recently learned that the Africans eat chicken with the bones and all. Malawians are very resourceful and nothing goes to waste. God bless, Rebecca

P.S. The watermelon had worms. Rob was eating the first piece as we made the wiggly discovery. I wonder how many worms we eat and never see. Any wonder we're getting sick!

It was one of those neat things about living in Malawi: fresh produce delivered to our gate. The previous missionaries, the Uhlhorns, had been regular customers of the *amai amasamba*. By word of mouth the ladies knew the house was occupied again, so they came selling their locally-grown goods. They arrived with huge baskets on their heads and spread their wares on our lawn in the hopes of making a sale. If I bought a whole grouping, such as a whole basket of strawberries, they would give me a "good price" and often threw in a "prizey" of an extra veggie. The *amai amasamba* saved me many hassles of the market, street vendors and gawking crowds.

We were told that as time progressed, buggy food would be easier to deal with. Not because it would have fewer bugs, but because one's outlook changed. Newcomers who find ants, weevils, worms or bugs in their meal tend to throw the food out. Those who have lived here a little longer might pick out the bugs and then eat the food. A seasoned resident of Malawi regards the bugs as extra protein and is satisfied to eat the food, bugs and all. I realized I was clearly at the newcomer stage.

Month One: Adjusting

Vegetable ladies

Sent: October 13, 2003
Subject: "Happy" Birthday?
Rob writes: Thanks for all Nathanael's birthday wishes. He has not been himself. Late last night his fever rose to 104.6°F. I went to the new Mwaiwathu hospital by our house. They did a malaria and blood test. The malaria test came back negative again, but the doctor could see that his platelets were a bit low—164. He treated for malaria and prescribed Halfan (halofantrine) since the parasites can eat platelets. We returned home at 1am. Today his fever has lessened slightly. For his birthday he had a brownie "#1" cake topped with colorful imported Nerds candy—the only remotely cake-decorating item in the pantry.

Last week was busy. On Wednesday we were all sick. Some were throwing up, others had diarrhea...not pretty. We spent most of the day resting.

The next morning I went out to the district of Chiradzulu to visit two congregations with Missionary Janosek. These 2 congregations are pretty new, so they worshipped in buildings with grass walls and thatched roofs. The first congregation, Chongwa, didn't even have benches built. Chongwa was recently allotted a church building by the Synod if they can meet their *chikole*, which is a small payment of MK1200 or $12. It is the first step in ownership of the building. If they can't pay their *chikole,* they will lose the money for their church and they would have to petition again. If they fail, that might be the end of the congregation, which is 40 members strong. The other congregation is newer, about 2 years old.

They worship in a nice thatched church that looks better than many of the brick churches. They have about 90 members and recently submitted their request for a WELS-subsidized building. We were back in Blantyre at 4pm, having traveled 160 km (100 mi) round trip.

On Sunday I went back out with John to two Chiradzulu congregations. These are the most established ones, with 150 communicants apiece. We arrived at Khanyepa, and I found out that's where our garden worker, Mr. Chinyama, is a member. They have a good choir with a really neat instrument I hadn't seen before—a bicycle bell. It functioned like a triangle. John shared that he had to limit the choir's singing because otherwise they would "take over the service."

This week won't slow down much either, since I'm off to Lilongwe for meetings with the ACA, then home on Friday to regroup for the 40th Anniversary service in Chonde.

Thanks for your emails. Grandpa Wendland, we especially keep you in our thoughts and prayers after your stroke. We rejoice that the love of Jesus gives us the courage to face all things and the supreme comfort that He is with us. May He continue to keep your heart soaring in the freedom of His love and care for you. Love, Rob

Nathanael's fever was worrisome at such a vulnerable age. But I was also struggling in the health arena. I could not seem to shake off my gastrointestinal issues. Just when I thought I had recovered, I would have another troublesome bout of diarrhea. I would spend much time and effort in the coming weeks, months, and years trying to pinpoint the cause of these recurring symptoms and trying to function despite them. I experimented by cutting out particular foods for months at a time. I tried to drink only *our* boiled and filtered water. I tried to eat only foods that *I* had prepared. I even avoided raw vegetables and tried cooking everything I consumed. But those attempts could only last so long. My health struggles were yet another reason to kneel before the Lord in prayer. That was not hard—my symptoms often brought me to my knees anyway.

> *"Be joyful always; pray continually;*
> *give thanks in all circumstances,*
> *for this is God's will for you in Christ Jesus."*
> *I Thessalonians 5:16-18*

Sent: October 14, 2003
Subject: RE: Happy Birthday!
Rob writes: Nathanael is doing much better today. His fever is gone and he has been acting more like his normal, joyful self. Thanks for your thoughts and prayers. Love, Rob

Month One: Adjusting

We, along with our families from afar, were so happy and thankful when Nathanael's health crisis seemed to have turned a corner. Perhaps the malaria medicine had wiped out a parasite; although in a few days I would develop another theory about the cause of his illness. Either way, we prayed he would remain healthy.

We had also reached the **ONE MONTH** mark of living in Africa! So much had happened in our first month that it seemed to defy reality. On one hand, it seemed like yesterday that we had stood on US soil. On the other hand, it seemed like a few *years* had passed in the space of one action-packed month. Malawi didn't exactly feel like home yet, but it felt like there was work to be done and we were in the right place to do it. Rob had experienced a positive start to his bush ministry, and it seemed that his gifts were well-matched to his calling. I was glad to see that. My role as a mission mom in Malawi may not have looked like much on most days, but my gifts were being used too as I encouraged and supported Rob in his ministry and worked to keep my family clean, fed and healthy.

> *"Therefore encourage one another*
> *and build each other up,*
> *just as in fact you are doing."*
> *1 Thessalonians 5:11*

CHAPTER 3

MONTH TWO: HOME, SICK; HOMESICK

*"My grace is sufficient for you,
for my strength is made perfect in weakness."*
2 Corinthians 12:9a

Our first month on field had been a rollercoaster in many respects. We had experienced uplifting and wonderful mission high-points even as we began an ongoing struggle to remain healthy and productive. For the foreseeable future we would have to live with the frustration of precarious health. But the Lord knew our situation and would help us cope one day at a time, whether we were sick at home... or just plain homesick. Meanwhile, Nathanael developed new symptoms in the wake of his weeklong fever that seemed to point to the cause.

> *Sent: October 16, 2003*
> *Subject: Just rosey*
> **Rebecca writes:** This morning Nathanael had a light rash all over his torso. I had heard roseola was going around. I did a bit of reading and, sure enough, the symptoms matched. I thought, "Why couldn't the silly spots come first for us to know how to react to such a high fever?" Praise the Lord for a non-malarial ending—we are thankful!
>
> I went to a local moms' group. There were expatriate ladies from the United Kingdom, Belgium, South Africa, Germany, Hungary, Norway, Australia, New Zealand and the USA. It was neat to listen to their stories and meet new people. They spoke great English. It reminded me of this fitting story:
>
>> A mother mouse and her three children crept out of their hole into the kitchen and began eating some food. Suddenly, Mother Mouse saw a cat slinking between the mice and their hole. The mother mouse puffed up her lungs and shouted, "Woof! Woof!" The cat turned tail and ran. With that, the mother quickly led her children back to safety in their hole. Mother Mouse

asked her children, "Now, what's the lesson from that experience?"

"We don't know," the baby mice squeaked.

"It is this," said Mom Mouse. "It is always good to know a second language."

We press on to communicate in another language as well; Rob more so than I. I am trying to learn a few Chichewa phrases for vendor communication, such as, "How much does that cost?" Then I'll proceed to subject agreement, noun classes, etc. Rob is in Lilongwe for the ACA meetings. He comes back tomorrow. The last few nights we have had power cuts. The other night I had invited guests for dinner and it was hard to heat up supper. This evening we ate and took baths early. Hannah had just pulled the plug in the tub when the lights shut off. I have flashlights strategically placed for such emergencies. Hopefully the batteries will last. It is not so quaint sitting next to a warm lamp or candle when it is already 90°F. Love, Rebecca

As distressing as Nathanael's symptoms had been, we realized that there are Malawians who face the same struggles daily. We knew that as a white, relatively wealthy, educated family, we had access to information and medicine that most Malawians do not have. The gloomy stats tell the story. Infant mortality rate is high in this part of the world: one in ten kids die before their fifth birthday. Every six seconds a child dies because of hunger and related causes. Deaths from malaria are not far behind. One in every 100 childbirths claims the life of the mother. The life expectancy in general for a Malawian is under age 50.

Health care in North America is so good that the tendency is to give credit to doctors and medicine. Here it is more clearly by the grace of God that we live and move and have our being. Here it is obvious that life and death are truly in His hands. Knowing health can be so volatile here added urgency to our call to spread the saving message of Jesus' salvation.

Sent: October 18, 2003
Subject: Busy Week!
Rob writes: At the end of last week I carpooled to Lilongwe with the other missionaries for meetings with the ACA and WELS President Karl Gurgel. A passing truck kicked up a stone that cracked our truck's windshield. That same day the Zomba missionaries had their windshield smashed by a brick that bounced off a truck. Thankfully, in spite of the excitement, we all arrived safely. Our meetings (8am-5pm) were held at a place outside of Lilongwe—the Dairy. It is a functioning dairy and made the Wisconsin people feel right at home with the sights and smells. The Malawi mission field is in a state of flux and will be for a while.

Please keep a space in your prayers for both the national church and our mission during these tough times.

The next day we left Lilongwe at about 7am and had an uneventful trip back to Blantyre. I regrouped with the family and we immediately headed to Chonde, where the "40th Anniversary of the LCCA in Malawi" service was to be held. It was a great service. Some of the choir members sat on the floor so we could have the front bench. The sermon was on "Amazing Grace." It was preached once in English by President Gurgel and then translated by LCCA President Chinyama. Two choirs sang. Their homemade guitars, drums and instruments were all right in front of us. The service, the fellowship, the music and a church full of rejoicing were all very special. It was an enjoyable week. God's great blessings to you on Son-day! Rob

Celebrating at Chonde

Hannah and Nathanael had especially enjoyed the multiple gatherings of the past weeks. The fellowship temporarily filled the void of get-togethers with our family and church family back in Wisconsin. As the excitement and sensory overload of our move to Malawi began to give way to the reality of day-to-day living, loneliness was also waiting in the wings. We were grateful that we could at least *receive* phone calls from far-off family, though our phone connection was not able to handle outgoing international calling. Rob's mom gave us a special call to see how we were doing in the health arena.

Sent: October 20, 2003
Subject: phone call—thanks
Rebecca writes: Thanks much for your phone call, Mom Wendland, and medical info concerning my gut troubles. After we hung up I forced myself to drink, but I'm not sure it did any good. Almost on cue the liquid would simply come out the other end. Rob went to the pharmacy to get the Cipro you recommended. I forced myself to eat some lunch, though it turned my stomach. Today I am slightly better. God Bless, Rebecca

Month Two: Home, Sick; Homesick

> *"He who did not spare his one and only Son,*
> *but gave him up for us all—*
> *how will he not also, along with him,*
> *graciously give us all things?" Romans 8:32*

Maybe it is a testament to my healthy life before Africa, but I never thought that the *"all things"* in this passage could refer to my health. Now it had become a prayer for God's gracious gift of health...a topic that entered my prayers more frequently than ever before.

Sent: October 21, 2003
Subject: Not out of the woods yet
Rob writes: A truck carrying a full load of dry cement crashed Saturday night near the ESCOM (our electricity company) major generators. All that powdery cement blew into the generators. ESCOM has been cleaning and repairing ever since. Our power was out about 16 hours on Sunday (5am-9pm) and another 20 hours today (midnight to 8pm). Thankfully we have a generator at home to run our stove and cool our fridge.

Rebecca and Nathanael are sick again. Rebecca has had serious diarrhea and lil' Nathanael has a fever again—102°F.

My Temporary Employment Permit (TEP) is still not done after waiting four months and counting. My driver's license is still not done either, after one month and counting.

We hired a man today to make me a bookshelf/storage unit (6x6 ft.). Materials cost about $90 and his labor is $60. He has done work for other missionaries and built a few of our rural churches. All he uses is a meter stick, cross-cut saw, wood glue, sandpaper, a level and nails. We love and miss you all! Rob

For the next few days the man building our bookshelf parked himself in our front yard. He sawed and glued, pounded and sanded hour after hour. As the days went on, more and more sand and dirt were becoming a part of the bookshelf as they fused into the glued joints. By the end of the week the bookshelf was finished. I had to pick a few pieces of grass out of the cabinets and dust it before it was transferred into the office. It was so heavy we could hardly lift it. Maybe he should have built it on location in the office instead of on our front lawn!

Sent: October 24, 2003
Subject: lil better
Rebecca writes: Today Hannah observed, "Mom, you are walking around standing straight up again!" Not only was I not well recently, but Nathanael had

a fever again and our power was mostly off. I laid low and wrote some snail mail correspondence by candlelight. Thankfully, as of this writing, the electricity and our health are all much better. I didn't even realize today was Friday.

Sunday afternoon Rob drove us out to Chilimoni and I drove home. At one point he told me to beep so the people would get out of the way. I hung on to the wheel, kept my feet in position and told him that beeping was not possible right then. On the way home I did manage one little beep in between the shifting and I didn't stall the vehicle. The new drivers here hang a plate with a red "L" on their cars for "Learner." I refuse to buy one—it reminds me of the Scarlet Letter. They are mainly used by driving schools. Rob says, "They still teach driving as if they were living in the 1930's." Each new driver learns hand-signals. The new driver must extend their arm out of the window and, depending on whether they want to turn left or right, flap their arm up and down like a flying bird. It is amusing, considering automatic turn signals have replaced arm motions for almost a century now.

Thanks for your faithful email updates. It is special that you take the time to keep us posted, and it makes the distance easier to bear. God bless, Rebecca

It was good I was feeling a bit better since Rob was gone often and every task here took so much longer to complete. Simply leaving the house took a ridiculous amount of time. I had to make sure I had the necessities in the diaper bag (including water and hand sanitizer). If we would be gone until dusk I needed to put the mosquito nets down around all the beds and shut the drapes and windows before we left. Then I had to make sure I had the correct fistful of keys so I could lock three sets of house doors on the way out. Often by this time Hannah had to use the toilet again, or we forgot something…and I had to open the doors and repeat the process!

My driving progress was slow. Driving would have been difficult enough on a typical Malawian road without also having to negotiate a stick shift for the first time. One reason for the perilous driving here is a lack of road-safety education. Because the majority of Malawians don't drive, they don't know common road rules. They have not been trained to look both ways before crossing a street or how to use a crosswalk properly. Particularly in rural settings, pedestrians and cyclists seem to assume that after one vehicle has passed by, the road must be clear. Without looking, they veer into the middle of the road. Any driver following another car's lead has to be extra careful of this phenomenon. Another common problem is the many cyclists who share the road. They often weave all over the place, especially when they are startled by a vehicle behind them. Defensive driving here is essential in order to avoid tragic accidents. I have learned never to take safe travels for granted.

Soon Rob planned to head south to a congregation near Mt. Mulanje with Missionary John Janosek. I had already heard much about the beauty of that area. The

Month Two: Home, Sick; Homesick

Janoseks personally listed Mt. Mulanje as one of the top three attractions in Malawi and I was anxious to hear Rob's impression of the area. He was not disappointed!

Majestic Mount Mulanje

Sent: October 26, 2003
Subject: **Zirombo!** *(Actually, "Akafumbwefumbwe"!)*
Rob writes: Friday was a neat day at Muhapokwa. It is located in the shadow of Mt. Mulanje, an impressive mountain. Mulanje is 10,000 feet tall (half the height of Kilimanjaro and one third the height of Everest) and rises out of a flat plain. It's not the typical upside-down "V" mountain but a "massif." It rises steeply with peaks and valleys that spread over a large area.

Before we saw the mountain we saw *zirombo!* When I got to the Janoseks' house to pick up John for our trip, his pickup was loaded with twenty-one bags of maize—a grain offering from some of his bush congregations. Some of the congregational members are really poor. They don't earn money but live a subsistence life by planting their crops and living on that throughout the year. These places give their offerings to the LCCA in the form of maize, chickens, squash, sweet potatoes and seasonal produce. Every year after harvest the congregations take all of the maize and put it into sacks. John then sells the grain to different buyers. The money translates into the congregational offering that he sends to the LCCA synod treasurer. This year there has been a glut of maize on the market, so John had been storing some maize in his shed for months. Finally, he got someone to do him a favor and buy it. The plan was for us to drop off the bags at a processing factory on our way to the congregation in Muhapokwa.

Well, every one of the 21 bags of maize was totally infested with crawling *akafumbwefumbwe*: weevils. John called them *zirombo*, a term for any group of destructive creatures. The weevils were crawling all over these bags: millions, seriously! Looking at those bags I got an idea of how some of the plagues in Egypt must have looked back in Joseph's day. There were so many you could hear them scratching through the bags, walking on the bags, walking on the truck. Many were mature enough to fly. My job was to brush at least some of the creatures off before we sold the bags, but it was like rowing up a waterfall. With the hot sun beating on the maize bags, those critters wanted to get out.

The factory people graciously weighed the bags anyway, all the while making jokes with John: "Maybe we should weigh the *zirombo* to see what you (John) owe us!" And, "Hurry up and weigh otherwise we'll get zero kg!" Most bags weighed 70 kg (154 lbs) and earned about MK1000 ($10) per bag. Afterward it was a 2 hour trip to Muhapokwa, the whole while flicking off weevils that were still crawling all over us.

Muhapokwa congregation is new. The church building had grass thatch for walls and ceiling. They are nice people who greeted me warmly. We had 31 for worship, 14 for Lord's Supper and 2 baptisms. It was a good day. We got back at about 6pm. Today is in the 90°s, sunny and dry as a bone. Rich blessings in Jesus!
Rob

Rob's weevil story had me crawling for a long time. I could hardly wait for our deep freezer to arrive in our shipment, so I could freeze my dry goods rather than holding my breath to see if something had hatched in my flour.

Sent: October 27, 2003
Subject: Nyala Park
Rob writes: Today the Janoseks took us to Nyala Park. It is a small park (maybe 600 acres) an hour south of Blantyre, in the Shire Valley, and located where Illovo is based. Illovo is a giant South African sugar company that owns huge swathes of sugar cane fields in the area. It was neat to see the sugar fields and the humongous harvesting trucks transporting the sugar cane. Each truck had ten axles. To keep the dust down, the company paves the roads with molasses, which is a byproduct of sugar. In the middle of it all, the company keeps an area wild with indigenous trees and plants. They have brought in various animals, including the fairly rare Nyala antelope. There are no big predators, so the animals live in peace.

In the park we reached a high temp of 53°C (127.4°F)! Thankfully, we had air conditioning in the car. When we rolled down windows for a better look we would immediately start to sweat. Nathanael had rivers of sweat running down his pink cheeks. It was like a preheating oven that kept getting hotter. We saw impala, giraffe, bushbuck, wildebeest, zebra, red hartebeest, a long-crowned eagle, several nyala and the white-faced blesbok. We got out of the car when we came upon five giraffe near the road. We had a great time. Blessings in Jesus, Rob

The nyala antelope is an impressive animal with spiraling horns and unique markings that include stripes and long white "socks." Southern Malawi is one of the few places in the world where this particular nyala is found naturally. This park had such a healthy population of nyala that they were able to trade them to other parks in exchange for a variety of animals. It continues to be extraordinary to enjoy such flora and fauna in "real life" rather than in a zoo or a greenhouse. It is a blessing I hope never to tire of.

The tremendous heat we experienced in the park was because of its location in the Shire Valley, a wide floodplain with conditions that are perfect for growing sugar cane (and propagating mosquitoes). The Shire Valley is an extension of the Great Rift Valley that has its origins in Israel: a neat geographical connection to consider. The great Shire River, whose outlet is Lake Malawi, descends to the lower valley through a series of rapids and waterfalls before it broadens out and meanders through the bottom flats of the valley. Eventually the Shire flows into the Zambezi River in Mozambique. Haze-obscured mountains frame the edge of the valley, and thin plumes of smoke from many little bush fires rise from the valley floor. Traveling to the depths of this hot valley was now all in a day's work for Rob, who had begun serving congregations in the Lower Shire. At this time of year Rob might set out in 90°F heat. By the time he reached the bottom of the escarpment, the temperature could become an astounding 40°F hotter! He would come home with salt marks just below the knees of his pants, literally sweating through his clothes in the intense heat.

Sent: October 28, 2003
Subject: cool trip
Rebecca writes: We are all feeling well, which is wonderful! The kids and I went to a Baby Bible Group. It meets weekly on Tuesdays. We spent time with our kids learning Bible stories, singing Christian songs, doing related crafts and talking about Jesus. Our church currently has no Sunday School, so it is a highlight during the week for the kids to hear God's Word at their level. Both Kathy Felgenhauer and I are trained WELS teachers and teach for the group. It is amazing to meet other Christian ladies from all over the globe. I know that our pathways will inevitably part here on earth after the short time we share in Malawi. However, we anticipate meeting again for all eternity.

I made sweet rolls the other day since I was feeling better. I shared some with the night guards. The next day they made it a point to come around and say "Hallo, Madam" instead of only greeting Rob. My guess is they never had a sweet roll before. They were smoking by our window yesterday…so we'll see how "sweet" things remain.

This Friday is the annual Malawi Ladies' Bible Retreat. Each October the Malawi missionary women host a retreat, and each February the Zambia missionary ladies host one. The Bible study topics are chosen in advance and are prepared and presented by the missionary ladies. I hope Rob enjoys his time with the kids. I am thoroughly looking forward to the fellowship and spiritual renewal with the mission women. Rebecca

Sometimes it seemed that for every beautiful experience in Malawi there was a frustrating or negative one just waiting to balance the scales. We were quickly realizing that dealing with our hired night guards would be an ongoing frustration. In response to a previous breach in security, two night guards had been hired. I began to wonder if the guards, whom I often found sleeping, were part of the problem rather than the solution. After reading the company's operation manual, I decided to talk to the guards about their multiple conduct violations. To my horror they laughed and thanked me for my "advice." I told them that I wasn't giving them *advice*; I was reminding them of the company rules. Rob later explained that Malawians tend to laugh when they are nervous or attempting to diffuse a situation. That was a "custom" I did not think I would ever get accustomed to. It seemed better for Rob to deal with the guards, since ladies simply do not have the same prestige, presence or respect that men have in Malawi.

I often thought of the Biblical account where God led the children of Israel in a cloud by day and a pillar of fire by night. I wished that we could forgo the guards and have a pillar of fire by our gate, or angels with flaming swords around our perimeter. But I knew that even if I could not see God's protection, He had promised that it was there.

> *"For he will command his angels concerning you*
> *to guard you in all your ways;*
> *they will lift you up in their hands,*
> *so that you will not strike your foot against a stone." Psalm 91:11*

(As an added bonus, I was certain that our celestial guardians would never pound on the bedroom window at 6am to announce that it was check-out time.)

INCOMING EMAIL: October 29, 2003
Subject: Update on Dad/Ernie/EH/Professor/Grandpa/Uncle
Grandma Kathie writes: Dear Friends and Family, many of you know of Ernie's recent stroke. Your visits and cards have meant a great deal to us. Being reminded of what we know is true in a stressful circumstance is one of the blessings of being in a Christian community and family. My mom was the one who, early on,

Month Two: Home, Sick; Homesick

encouraged us both by reminding us that this stroke too is a blessing from God. It's already proven to be so. We've come closer to the LORD and to many of you during this time. Thank you and praise Him. Love, Kathie & Dad

If Grandpa Wendland's stroke had happened a few months earlier while we were still in Milwaukee, we could have driven up to see him in Two Rivers, WI. Now that was impossible. Experiencing a family crisis from such a vast distance is very difficult, no matter which side of the sea you happen to be on. There was no opportunity for a face-to-face conversation or for the simple consolation of being in the same room as a loved one. We were thankful for email. Since our phone line was not working well, email was a quick and easy way to communicate across the miles. It was hard to imagine the old days when the only options were telegrams and snail mail. But there was no need to explain communication difficulties to Grandpa Wendland. Not because he wouldn't understand—just the opposite. In the "old days" he was a missionary in Zambia. In his book, *The Diary of a Missionary*, he wrote about sending important telegrams in the 1960's that never arrived. Even if we could not visit Grandpa, at least we could send up-to-date wishes electronically. More importantly we could keep him in our prayers—prayers that were never dependent on technology.

Sent: October 30, 2003
Subject: Veggie tales
Rebecca writes: I'll type a note while the kids play nicely. It should be quick, ha ha. I let Hannah play with some veggies while I worked in the kitchen. When I took them away to chop them up she was heartbroken. They were her people. She lamented, "Mom—you can't take them away, they will be so *lonely*." It seemed like a veggie tale come to life. Being separated from family is often on Hannah's mind. She wants to tell you, "I will come back from Africa, write letters, play play-dough and dip chocolate strawberries. And you should come over to Africa and sleep in my bedroom under a mosquito net." We think of you all often! Love, Rebecca and family

Loneliness. When she thought of her far-away loved ones, three-year-old Hannah felt deeply touched by loneliness. A part of each of us was empty from being so far away. Making new friends, fitting in and starting over would take some time. I also felt the pangs of loneliness. Leaving behind dear family and cherished friendships created a big hole. However, I was so busy coping with daily life that I truly did not have much time to sit around and reminisce. In that sense, the many tasks I faced each day were a blessing. They kept my mind focused, rather than allowing me to wallow in thoughts of what I had left behind.

Jeremiah 17 reminds me that whatever comes my way—whether issues with health, security or separation—can be weathered if my roots are planted in the life-giving stream of God's Word.

*"But blessed is the man who trusts in the L*ORD*,*
whose confidence is in him.
He will be like a tree planted by the water
that sends out its roots by the stream.
It does not fear when heat comes; its leaves are always green.
It has no worries in a year of drought and never fails to bear fruit."
Jeremiah 17:7-8

My goal wasn't to be the most productive and beautiful tree around, but it was obvious that life on a mission field would either wither me or toughen me up pretty quickly. One thing was certain: I had to keep myself rooted in God's promises.

CHAPTER 4

MAKING DISCIPLES OF ALL NATIONS

*"Therefore go and make disciples of all nations,
Baptizing them in the name of the Father and of the Son and of the Holy Spirit,
And teaching them to obey everything I have commanded you.
And surely I am with you always, to the very end of the age."*
Matthew 28:19-20

Job Description for Rob

Rob's divine call opened with this passage. They proved to be the words that would outline his job description and begin our journey. That journey would take our feet off the ground of Milwaukee, Wisconsin and plant them in the city of Blantyre, Malawi. There was a weight of responsibility in those words of Matthew 28, but we were reassured by verse 20: the special promise that God would be with us in the days ahead. Since God was calling Rob, then He would also make good on his assurance to equip him as needed. I knew that Rob's talents and his mission-centered heart were a good fit for ministry work in Africa. He had grown up surrounded by African people and culture. He understood the ways and workings of the African mission field, and he was ready for the journey.

In our first year in Malawi, Rob served over a dozen churches in two main areas of southern Malawi: Chiradzulu and the Shire Valley. Chiradzulu is the closest area of the two, about an hour and a half away from Blantyre. This area was home to some of the oldest churches of the LCCA in Southern Malawi; some had been established for 40 years. It was Rob's goal to phase out of this area as the individual churches or parish unions called their own national pastors. In the meantime, he provided these churches with stability and parish experience as he preached and ministered the sacraments to the members. Because Rob managed over a dozen churches, he could only visit each church once a month on a rotation basis. Although these congregations had the spoken goal of calling and providing for a national pastor and his family, they were hesitant to lose the involvement of a missionary and still appreciated even a monthly visit from Rob.

However, a monthly visit doesn't allow in-depth nurturing and spiritual care. Growth toward independence was slow.

The second area Rob served was the Lower Shire Valley. Traveling to this deep, hot valley also "meant business" for Rob. Blantyre sits at about 2,700 feet above sea level. Rob's congregations in the Shire were at the bottom of the escarpment, between 140-350 feet above sea level. It was a three hour trip, one way, from Blantyre to the farthest congregation in this area.

The people who live in this region depend on the Shire River. It is their lifeline. When—if—the river flows as it should, life is good. When it floods, the crops are destroyed. When it is too dry, crops can't grow. For the people of the Lower Shire, food shortages are a recurring theme. The conditions are perfect for growing sugar cane but not as ideal for growing maize, a staple in the Malawian diet. When crops aren't bountiful the people turn to the river for provisions, even though crocodiles are a real risk. The sweltering heat makes this region a breeding ground for mosquitoes, and every year malaria claims many lives.

In spite of the heat, people come to worship. Rob has said that preaching in such hot conditions is like conducting church in an oven. Some churches have metal roofing. When the sun beats down, it begins to bake anything underneath. On beastly hot days, the congregations will hold church outdoors in the shade of a tree where the air moves more freely. (Interestingly, the members of the Lower Shire do not seem fazed by the heat, the intense smells or the sweat of such gatherings. They dress in their best for worship. Men appear in suit coats and dress pants. Ladies wear dresses or skirts and then wrap a second layer around their waists: a two meter long piece of material called a *chitenje*. Babies often wear knitted bonnets even in the hot season and are secured to their mothers' backs in a second *chitenje*.) Life in the Lower Shire is difficult and precarious. Pray for these believers. And pray for the willing messengers who deliver to these Malawians the sure and certain message of Christ crucified, sins forgiven and a heavenly home where all their former troubles will pass away.

Rob dedicated his days to language learning and visits to his bush churches. This type of ministry has a steep learning curve before one becomes productive. It also requires a Christ-like heart to reach out, understand and minister to people of another land, language and culture. A good sense of direction is helpful too: Rob gradually learned the many routes to his churches in Chiradzulu and the Shire Valley by following landmarks. Once you leave the main road, there are neither maps nor any decent road signs to help locate these bush churches. Rob learned the names of his congregations and their corresponding villages slowly but surely. This wasn't as simple as it might sound. His congregations were named Bangwe, Balala, Khanyepa, Khobili, Katunga, Chikunumbwi, Diwa, N'singano, Tcheleni, Muyere, Muhapokwa, Chongwa, and Mpira. Rob also worked to learn the names of the many members of these congregations: names such as Chimwemwe Banda, Sizi Kashort, Casebell Phiri, Tadala Tafatatha, Giant Danger and Sautian Cabbage. Even without a language barrier, this was not a simple task. Some tribes in the village use the last name of the father as one of the first names of each of his children. Many Malawians have multiple names: their given name, a baptized name, an English name and even names suggested by relatives. Rob found that the members of these churches were equally eager to learn *his* name and to welcome him with open arms in true Malawi fashion.

Typical worship at Tcheleni

Job Description for Rebecca

"We have different gifts, according to the grace given us.
If a man's gift is...serving, let him serve; if it is teaching, let him teach;
if it is encouraging, let him encourage; if it is contributing to the needs of others,
let him give generously; if it is leadership, let him govern diligently;
if it is showing mercy, let him do it cheerfully." Romans 12:6-8

My gifts, on the other hand, were geared for *za chizungu* (white people's) church and culture. My childhood years were molded by the parsonages I grew up in throughout the United States. I knew how to run off bulletins, organize a church potluck, serve for coffee hour, play the pipe organ and direct four-part-harmony chorale pieces. My MLC training had prepared me to share Christ in a grade school classroom. As helpful as these gifts and talents were to a church in North America, they hardly seemed to equip or qualify me for life on a Malawian mission field. Questions crept into my mind about my vocation and my ability to rise to the inevitable challenges. God's promise in Isaiah 41:9-10 reassured me: *"'You are my servant'; I have chosen you...So do not fear, for I am with you; do not be dismayed, for I am your God. I will strengthen you and help you; I will uphold you with my righteous right hand."*

Though I felt inadequate, I could trust the Lord to be with me. He had chosen me for this new role of missionary wife and would strengthen me through Christ. The strength

God promised me would not arrive in a big warehouse box; it would come in increments that allowed me to endure one challenge at a time. Any progress I made would be to His glory, not mine. Any achievements would be a testimony to God working directly through me to fulfill a purpose in His eternal plan.

Knowing God was with me gave me comfort and a bit of courage to embrace my new vocation as a mission mom in Malawi. It was a role that was at once daunting and humbling. My personal harvest field had shrunk in scope, though not in importance. My vocation was now on the home front. The souls I would nurture were those of my own children. My time and efforts would be spent on "behind the scenes" jobs, which were necessary though often menial in nature: haggling with vendors and beggars, learning how to cook from scratch and without electricity, locating repair people in town, discovering the ins and outs of cloth diapers, keeping dead bugs out of the baby's mouth, keeping the mold at bay during the rains and dealing with leaky roofs. My role as mission mom would include painting over seasonal water stains on the ceiling, extracting bugs from shoes, eliminating spiders of all sizes from the house, shopping with a foreign currency, fumbling through language barriers, coping with security and all the other issues of an average day in Malawi.

1 Corinthians 10:31 reads, *"So whether you eat or drink or whatever you do, do it all for the glory of God."* As a mission mom in Malawi, I don't have awe-inspiring agendas each day; I don't frequently accomplish anything grand and glorious by dusk. Daily life in Malawi is often daunting. Progress is slow and projects are frustrating, but it is my calling to stick with it and do whatever needs to be done. It is not in my job description to proclaim the Word of God to hundreds of people in the villages throughout the week. But it *is* my calling to support my husband who does. With that in mind, I can see all I do with a higher purpose. I can glorify the Lord and know I'm furthering His kingdom…even if I do not step out of our yard but step on a roach instead. It is truly by the grace of God that I live each day, accomplish anything and make a difference in my small space in an unimportant town in a very poor country on the vast continent of Africa. Some days it seems that it hardly matters what I do, how well I do it, or how much I did or did not finish. But that is exactly the secret. If I do anything, whether great or small, **to God's glory**—then I am doing **what God asks of me.** To that calling I daily try to be faithful.

Traveling to Places of Mission Work

I rejoiced with those who said to me,
"Let us go to the house of the Lord." Psalm 122:1

Travel is a very real and volatile part of mission work. So much depends on the vehicle, fuel availability and the road conditions. If any of these become an issue, there is trouble. Rob's bush work takes him to some very remote places. He and his trusty 4WD Land Cruiser go through many tanks of diesel and navigate over pot holes, streams and rugged terrain to reach the established southern congregations within the LCCA of Malawi. On several occasions Rob has tackled roads so thick with mud that his Land Cruiser has been buried up to its axles, leaving its 4WD utterly powerless. Rob can sometimes remedy those sticky situations by wedging branches and stones under the tires to gain traction. Other times it has taken sheer manpower—and possibly the assistance of angels—to boost the truck from the muck. This note home from Rob describes one such heart-pounding incident.

Sent: November 2, 2003
Subject: washed out
Rob writes: On Sunday I had a service out at Chizilo, which is reached by driving into the Lower Shire Valley and then back up into the Thyolo Hills. I have to cross a washed-out bridge to get to this place by driving down the embankments of a creek and driving up the other side of it. During our service it rained and rained. On my way home, the banks of the creek were muddy and slippery as ice. I was able to get down into the creek fine. It was getting out that was the problem. Even in 4WD low gear I would slip back into the creek. My skidding wheels did nothing to help our situation for further attempts. The evangelist I was traveling with went to the nearest village for support. Fifteen men came and could not push my truck out. The best we could do was to get about halfway up the embankment. Then I would slide back down. I was quite concerned that I might slip backwards over one of my helpers. I was wondering if the truck was going to be my home for a few days until the embankments dried up. Then the men decided to cut down some elephant grass to throw on the embankment for traction. They cut arm-loads of grass, even a small tree, and piled it all the way up the embankment. They told me to go "full blast." I gunned it…and shot over the rim of the embankment. Needless to say, I was very thankful to be out. After consulting them, the men felt that MK100 (about $1) would be good for their help. That's not $1 each, it's $1 for all of them—for two hours of pushing, getting splattered by spinning tires, cutting grass, laying it down and standing in a creek with a steady rainfall the whole time. I certainly feel blessed to be home after a long day in the bush. Love, Rob

Many rivers and bridges must be crossed as you travel in Malawi. Often the bridges look less than reassuring: a cobbling together of mismatched logs and planks. I have closed my eyes—not that it helps any—as I have ridden across many-a rickety bridge, simply because I cannot bear to watch as the vehicle and our lives are entrusted to the substandard construction. Though, like it or not, when *I'm* driving my eyes must stay open.

Village Church

"Consequently, you are no longer foreigners and aliens,
but...members of God's household,
built on the foundation of the apostles and prophets,
with Christ Jesus himself as the chief cornerstone.
In him the whole building is joined together...
And in him you too are being built together
to become a dwelling in which God lives by his Spirit." Ephesians 2:19-22

The typical church building in Malawi is a rectangular space a little larger than the size of a modern three-car garage, often with a mud floor. It is enclosed by mud bricks and has a thatched or metal roof, cement benches or grass mats to sit on, an altar and a lectern. There are a handful of open cinder blocks to let in air and anything else, like creepy crawlies or flying insects. The men generally sit on the right side of the church, while the ladies and children sit on the left side. The choir often waits in the back of the church until it is their turn, at which point they will sing and walk—or dance—their way to the front. Many churches have a ladies' choir, a youth choir and a senior choir. Sometimes the choir members will continue to sing until they are told their time is up. The music reflects both their passion for Jesus and their love of singing. It is a beautiful part of worship life in Africa.

The choirs keep tempo and beat with clapping hands and stomping feet. Sometimes homemade instruments augment the rhythm. The first time I heard a village church choir I was sitting in the front of the church. The choir began their singing and playing in the back. From the sound behind me, I assumed that the musicians were playing quite a variety of decent percussion and stringed instruments. As the choir and musicians moved up the aisle I was shocked to see the tools they used: a large homemade bass guitar, a homemade acoustic guitar, metal cymbals, a bicycle bell and a drum made from an old paint can. My favorite was a string of metal bottle caps. The string was struck with precision for just the right metallic sound. From those basic tools came a very deep and rich sound to accompany the harmonious singing. It is truly a joy to see such natural talent and heartfelt praise be lifted up in spite of meager conditions, to the utmost glory of God.

Sunday morning worship in the village

Language—an Invaluable Tool

To best serve the national church and care for the national flock in Malawi, Rob began diligently learning the local language of Chichewa. It is a Bantu language and is similar to Chinyanja, the language spoken in the area where he grew up in Zambia. Perhaps having heard the language as a small child explains the speed, efficiency and accuracy with which he progressed. I shouldn't overlook the fact that Rob's Dad is also gifted in languages—working as a professor of languages at the LCCA Seminary in Lusaka and as a Bible translator with the United Bible Societies. Rob decided that his study of Chichewa would improve with the help of a language teacher. Missionary Paul Nitz in Lilongwe suggested that Rob hire a gifted student from a local high school, perhaps one who had graduated but was waiting to be accepted into a university.

Sent: November 4, 2003
Subject: Language information
Rob writes: I went to Nyambadwe Secondary School to see if I could find a language helper for my Chichewa learning. The students must not see very many white people in their school because there was a great cry of, *"Mzungu!"* (White person!) from all the students. (I guess African high school students aren't that different from their American counterparts.) I cleared the gauntlet and made it to the headmaster, who directed me to their Chichewa teacher, a young man named Mphatso Dzoole. I came looking to use one of his better students, but he informed me that he would teach me instead. I left a little concerned. He has training in Chichewa, but I don't think he has taught an English speaker how to become a Chichewa speaker. We will meet on weekday afternoons for about two hours. Love, Rob

It may seem like a huge expense of time and money to learn a national language. Some church denominations skip this process and simply use a translator. The advantage of a translator is that a missionary can begin preaching and teaching almost immediately. The disadvantage is the lack of control over the accuracy of the message being proclaimed. In contrast, taking the time to learn the vernacular allows a missionary to better understand the culture of the national people, since so much of a culture is revealed in its language. It also shows them respect: in a post-colonial land where many white people don't make the effort, a missionary who speaks Chichewa demonstrates a spirit of good will and solidarity toward the people with whom he is sharing the Gospel. Since the early days of WELS mission work in Africa, it has been strongly felt that language acquisition is worth all the effort.

Sent: November 6, 2003
Subject: Meet Mphatso
Rob writes: One of the village congregations, Khanyepa, organized a welcome for me. Their choir sang songs and the people marched up one by one to present their gifts to me. There were several big bags of tomatoes, okra, maize on the cob, and an unidentified leaf. I am grateful that these people would give us so much—*zikomo kwambiri!* (thank you!) That bounty has kept Rebecca busy for the past few days. There were so many tomatoes that she has been boiling and pureeing them for three days. She is making tomato sauce with our own home-grown oregano.

Lolemba, mphunzitsi wanga, abambo Dzoole, anabwera kunyumba yanga (On Monday, my teacher, Mr. Dzoole, came to my house). He started with nouns and their meanings, but it wasn't as simple as that. He put them into sentences. He asked me to repeat and then to fashion my own simple sentences based on what he had taught in Chichewa. This forced me to break each word down. He knows that I am a pastor and so some of his exercises fittingly revolved around God's Word. I'm very glad for the teacher the Lord has blessed me with. His plan is to come here four days a week, and on Fridays we will go to the school to speak with his students...Chichewa *basi* (that is all)! So my days are now spent reviewing and repeating what we went through in our lesson and then my two hours with Mr. Dzoole. Rebecca also helps me in the evening by quizzing me on what I've written from the lesson...and thereby getting a lesson herself. This phase of my language learning has just begun, but I'm excited and pray that I can drum all this in my head and use it. Love, Rob

I was able to practice small Chichewa sentences on the vegetable ladies during their weekly visits to the house. However, I lacked the time for the intense lessons that Rob was taking for 10 hours every week. My spare moments were absorbed in a learning curve of my own: managing the household, cooking from absolute scratch and being a mom.

At least gift-giving is a custom that transcends any language barrier. The members of the congregation at Khanyepa were eager to show their appreciation for a new missionary by presenting gifts of produce. It reminded me of yesteryear in the States. A few generations ago, a pastor's pay would be augmented with chickens, beef, vegetables, eggs or grain. In Malawi that is still a common practice. A national pastor receives a base salary—a meager one at that—and this is padded with gifts of produce from the members, the vast majority of whom are subsistence farmers. The bags of produce that Rob wrote about in his email kept me busy for days, chopping, boiling and cooking in 90°F weather. I even made coleslaw, starting from scratch with homemade mayonnaise!

Rob and I understood the importance of learning the language of the people. However, committing a foreign vocabulary to memory is tedious no matter how you slice it. The job of learning the words well enough to let them roll off your tongue takes practice. The skill of listening to a native speaker, understanding what was said and responding in a coherent manner can take a lifetime. I was prepared to take one day at a time and trust the Lord for the strength and wisdom necessary to deal with language learning, culinary challenges, health and security.

> *"Because of the Lord's great love we are not consumed,*
> *for his compassions never fail.*
> *They are new every morning; great is your faithfulness.*
> *I say to myself, "The Lord is my portion;*
> *therefore I will wait for him." Lamentations 3:22-24*

You Say "To-may-to" I Say "To-mah-to"

Chichewa wasn't the only barrier to clear communication. Sometimes I couldn't even understand the Malawians who spoke *English* to me! I would hear, "There is the basko," or "Can I have a bob?" The accent and intonation of their words had me completely puzzled. It turns out that they were NOT referring to hot sauce or a haircut. "Basko" was "bicycle"; "bob" was a light "bulb." Living here, the story of the Tower of Babel comes to mind daily!

I made a list of common language differences we encounter here in Malawi. Malawian pronunciations (or mispronunciations) of English are only part of the communication difficulties. Added to this, Malawians have adopted many British English terms from the 73 years they spent under colonial rule until their independence in 1964. Throw in a few Afrikaans terms, and things can get very confusing!

American English Term	**Malawi English Term**
Porch	*Khonde*
Flashlight	Torch
Napkin	Serviette
Feminine item	Napkin
Underwear	Pants
Pants	Trousers
Printed: month/ day/ year (4-21-03)	Printed: day/ month/ year (21-4-03)

Food items

Barbecue/ grill out	*Braai*
Tangerines	*Naartjies*

Eggplant	Aubergine
French fries	Chips
Chips	Crisps
Cookies	Biscuits

English	**Chichewa**
Hello, how are you?	*Muli Bwanji?*
I am fine and you?	*Ndili bwino, kaya inu?*
Thank you very much.	*Zikomo kwambiri.*
I'm sorry.	*Pepani.*
Yes.	*Inde.*
No.	*Ai.* (ee aye)

Language barriers are daunting and can be the source of many frustrations in overseas mission work and life. Thankfully, we can find unity and strength in Christ. Without that bond the frustrations would divide. *With* that bond the difficulties are seen as a transitory obstacle. United by Christ, fellow believers—regardless of color and mother tongue—can continue working toward the same goal: to share Jesus with those around us.

"For he himself is our peace, who has made the two groups one...
His purpose was to create in himself one new humanity out of the two,
thus making peace, and in one body to reconcile both of them
to God through the cross...
He came and preached peace to you who were far away
and peace to those who were near."
Ephesians 2:14-17

CHAPTER 5

DREAMING OF A WHITE CHRISTMAS

Give thanks to the Lord, call on his name;
make known among the nations what he has done.
Look to the Lord and his strength;
seek his face always. 1 Chronicles 16:8, 11

We had officially passed our two month mark in Malawi and it was surreal to think Thanksgiving was right around the corner. Here Thanksgiving Day is not a public holiday. There are no festive autumn decorations and rarely a frozen turkey in our local store. The shelves aren't lined with canned pumpkin, Cool Whip is unheard of and no candy corn is to be had. Despite the lack of commercial hype, we were looking forward to a celebration with the mission families nearby. After all, every day is an opportunity to say "thanks" to God for the blessings we have been showered with…whether or not those blessings include turkey, stuffing or pumpkin pie!

November in Malawi is not fall. The cool winter months are past, and November is more like a hot, dry "spring" before the rainy season of December-April. On this particular November the rainy season made an early appearance. The heavens seemed to open up and pour down water. I guess from Noah's perspective a spring rain in Malawi is small potatoes, but for me it was strikingly different than a typical Midwestern shower. The great volumes of rain filled the air with a rich, earthy humidity, replacing the distinct smell of powdery dust that was part of the dry season. The fine particles of dust that settled on every surface each day in the dry season were soon replaced by a new invasion: rapidly growing mold. As Christmas drew nearer, we knew (despite the incongruous "Let It Snow" message we saw on a Malawian man's T-shirt) that a white Christmas would not be an option this close to the equator. The memories, sights and sounds that had accompanied a lifetime of Thanksgivings and Christmases in the USA would have to be replaced by an entirely new set of traditions.

As I adjusted my cleaning battles from dust to mold, Rob continued to enjoy and practice his Chichewa. He began to add Chichewa proverbs to our email signature, which you will see in the next group of emails. One such proverb that struck home at this time of year was, "*Walira mvula walira matope.*" It means, "Crying for rain means crying for mud"—in other words, accept the consequences of what you wish for.

Sent: November 16, 2003
Subject: Veggie Lady
Rebecca writes: We are in the middle of a huge storm with heavy rain. Now I know why there are BIG drainage ditches everywhere.

Our devotion today (based on Numbers 11) was about the Israelites and how they complained about manna and whined for meat. I shook my head about the whole scenario—especially when some finally got their meat and then ate too much. Maybe it was McManna and that will happen to us when we return to the land of fast food.

Hannah is immersing herself in Malawian culture and says, *"Dzina langa ndine Hannah."* (My name is Hannah.) After the vegetable ladies came on Monday, she found the basket of produce I had bought, sat on the floor, spread out the vegetables and played her own version of vegetable lady. She also walks around with baskets on her head and wonders why I don't carry Nathanael on my back in a *chitenje* like other ladies. Recently Hannah used Rob's old clear deodorant cap on her Barbie's head as a scuba helmet. It is fun to see the imagination that develops with ordinary items.

Nathanael's latest thing is locating ants and following them around. This morning he woke up with his mosquito net over himself so he looked like a little ghost.

I threw out our old monitor Styrofoam, and some of the local kids walking by our trash can went crazy for it. I would guess an average weekly garbage collection from a typical North American neighborhood could supply a village for a month.

Last week Rob set up the outdoor *braai* (grill) and grilled the maize given as a church gift. It was sort of like eating unpopped popcorn. It had good flavor but could do some serious tooth damage. It took so long to cook that after using a flashlight for about an hour we called it quits. Fortunately, I had thrown on some other things to eat.

Our shipment has reached Durban, South Africa, but I don't know more than that.

Does anyone know if we could do a chat room to "talk" together without the expensive international fees? God Bless, Rebecca

---

"*Kuthyola ndiwo ndi kuwerama.*" = "To pluck vegetables one has to bend down." (If you want something good you have to work for it.)

Dreaming Of A White Christmas

It certainly had been a blessing for us to keep in touch by email, but the possibility of a chat room—where our whole, scattered family could communicate in real time—seemed extraordinary! Eventually we did set up a chat room. We managed to write a few lines back and forth before our internet connection was broken, leaving our conversation hanging. Since the appearance of Skype, we have made Skype phone our communication vehicle of choice…if and when the internet and electricity cooperate simultaneously.

As the holidays approached I was eager to hear what events were taking place back "home" in the States. Even though we could not participate, it helped to stay connected and hear about all the activities. Rob was missing his annual deer hunting excursion. Hannah wondered when she would be able to go to McDonalds with her grandparents. Many of our thoughts drifted to those familiar gatherings taking place across the incredible distance.

I wrote in my email about the local kids capitalizing on the Styrofoam I tossed out. Resourcefulness is a way of life in Malawi. Objects (like the deodorant cap) and ordinary items are used to their full potential—and then some. Shoes are worn until the soles simply fall off; even then they may be repaired on the side of the road using an old car tire as a new sole. Clothes are worn until threadbare and then cut up and used as "wasters" (rags). Old plastic bottles, packaging (such as rice or sugar bags) and container caps are often fashioned into toys, used as wheels and played with over and over again. I am not sure a local Malawian would fill up a typical garbage can's worth of waste in several months.

Sent: November 20, 2003
Subject: update of late
Rebecca writes: Yesterday I climbed up a ladder to clean our clogged eaves. I also cleaned away a rotting rat and accidentally disconnected our phone line. The wires are completely out in the open (or in this case, draped under rotting leaves) and exposed to the rain, with no protective tape around the twisted wire. Who knows when someone will come to fix it? This morning I got back on the ladder to look at the phone wires. I lined up the length of the wires to see where the disconnection happened and twisted them back together. Wonder of wonders…I fixed it. A big help living here is doing things yourself to save time, money, hassle and headaches. Maybe I'll have to take some classes from my brother Matt on electrical wiring. Now at least I can send this letter!

I drove the Pajero around town with Yvonne on Sunday. It is quite a task to leave our road, since it connects steeply uphill to the main road. I succeeded after several tries. I guess I could manage to go somewhere if I had to now.

God bless your Thanksgiving week. We truly rejoice that our family is spiritually close and has God as our focus. For that I am very thankful! Rebecca

---

"*Mfulumira anadya gaga.*" = "Mr. 'Let-me-do-it-fast' ate husks."

Living in a different country, town and neighborhood, far from familiar people, was challenging. Rob was gone often, which meant all household tasks fell on me. In general, I coped fine. But being home alone without a working phone made it seem like the last lifeboat had left while I was still aboard a drifting ship. Okay, maybe that's an overstatement…but the idea that I couldn't call for help if trouble arose did make me feel vulnerable. Our previous walks around the neighborhood did not give me any confidence that I would even be able to contact a neighbor for help. I could hardly believe that I had accidentally disconnected the phone wires by cleaning the eaves. With determination and frustration backing me up, I astonishingly repaired the phone line myself. To hear a dial tone again was like reeling in that lifeboat and putting it back on its docking station.

Sent: November 21, 2003
Subject: Africanizing **pang'ono ndi pang'ono** *(little by little)*
Rob writes: In our family devotion we had a little Q&A with Hannah. The point was to show all the blessings Jesus gives to us and to remember to say thank you. It went like this (Hannah's answers in parentheses): "Every day the sun rises and…(sets). Every day you have food to…(eat) and water to…(boil!)" It seems the little girl is catching on!

With that little story I reintroduce myself to all of you. It has been a month since I last wrote. The big item on my agenda has been Chichewa training. My teacher, Mphatso Dzoole, comes over every weekday afternoon and we are progressing well. I want to know Chichewa grammar because I like to know the "why" of things. Just when I fear that it's getting too academic we have a day where we only attempt to converse in Chichewa. My big bane is noun class/ personal pronoun-demonstrative pronoun-verb agreement. Chichewa seems much more of a poetic language than English. Chichewa likes words to sound like they fit together. Some examples:
1) *Tanthwe limeneli munaliona kuti?*
    Where did you see this rock?
2) *Magazi amenewa munawaona kuti?*
    Where did you see this blood?
3) *Chakudya chimenechi munachiphika liti?*
    When did you cook this food?
4) *Zipatso zimenezi munaziphika liti?*
    When did you cook this fruit?

As you can see, the sentences are saying pretty much the same thing in the same tense, but the demonstratives change depending upon noun class. I spend much of my day reviewing…and then it's time for the next lesson.

Yesterday I went with John to Tcheleni, a congregation at the southern tip of Malawi. It was an hour down the escarpment and then two hours following the eastern bank of the Shire River. On the way we passed the sites of at least three other congregations that I'll be serving. We also passed some land we hope to build on (though I'm finding that that can be a real hassle—one day the village headman says you can have this land, the next he wants to give you a different piece, usually not so nice and accessible as the original). I got a good look at the Shire Valley. The bottom of the valley is very flat once you are past the escarpment. I can see why many places become submerged when the Shire River floods. Being so low, it is also a place filled with palm trees and baobabs side by side.

Tcheleni congregation is a neat one. It was wonderful to experience the singing, the choirs, the smiles and the enthusiasm all the way out in the Lower Shire, in a "building" nothing more than grass and sticks. I know the people are planning to build a new church, but to me it seemed the perfect building as I listened to the Word, straining mightily to discern what I could out of the Chichewa. I watched the low rain clouds swooping over the palms and the baobabs. I watched people in the nearby village who could hear our singing. Every once in a while they'd look up to see what was going on over at that Lutheran *tchalichi* (church).

The congregation president, James Tembo, has built a small hut used specifically as a place to serve the missionary lunch before he returns home on his long journey. He served us a great meal—and I mean it—of *nsima*, chicken and Coke. Somehow these people afford such a meal every month when pastor comes. It makes me wish to learn Chichewa all the faster.

We did have one setback at the service. Because the thatched building was so small, John served communion outside the building. When re-entering, he didn't duck low enough and hit his head on a low, protruding beam. Later he said he felt as if someone had speared him. The beam tore a flap in his scalp and the service was suspended a moment as he tried to stop the flow of blood. Then John got the service going by pointing out the difference to the people—"*magazi a Christu, magazi a Janosek*" (the blood of Jesus, the blood of Janosek)!

The ride home was as pleasant as the day. As dusk descended on the African bush, my heart said that there is no place in the world that I would rather be than the central African bush in the evening: escarpment rising to the right, the bush of the valley sprawling to the left, believers behind, home ahead.

Have a happy Thanksgiving wherever you may be. Here a live turkey has been secured, a large pumpkin has been found, even imported cranberry spotted...though our temperatures will likely be in the upper 80°s, and we'll be at the mission house in Kabula Hill that sits on a hillside and looks over Africa to the north. God's richest blessings! Rob

P.S. Yiiihaaa! I was about to send this email when I caught a fast movement across my office floor! Running around was the biggest insect I've ever seen in a house. It has legs that are about 4 inches long, huge jaws and resembles a gigantic ant. What IS it? It looks like some type of scorpion/big spider. It has 8 legs and 2 smaller appendages. I was going to send some cute pictures of the kids with this email (some of you no doubt wish I had). I'll send those later. For now (Mom?), what is this thing?

P.P.S. Rebecca is hiring someone to spray our house—*soon!*

"*Ndinatha ngombo ndi akamundi, kuli achanga ndisanafike.*" = "I ran out of hunting sticks at the lemurs, before I arrived at the bush-babies." (I wasted time and strength on trifles when the real issue was around the corner.)

Solifugae—a real creepy crawly

I had never seen Rob so unnerved by a creepy crawly. We did not know if the bug was poisonous, or if it was looking to make a home or a nest. All we knew was that it needed to go… and we hoped no more would return.

Sent: November 26, 2003
Subject: discover a bug
Rebecca writes: Nathanael is now asking, "Whazz-zzaatt?" One child is asking what things are, and the other is asking why they are that way. What an opportunity I have to share God's Word with them and to tell them so many things, especially living in Africa.

We had rice and chicken for dinner. That in itself is not important—but I found over a dozen weevils burrowing in our locally-purchased rice. Painstakingly,

Hannah and I began sorting each granule to make sure there were no more weevils. We found a few tiny stones that had also made the cut. Maybe I should always sort the rice! I put the rest in the freezer for a few days, hoping to kill anything we may have missed.

You wouldn't believe—another one of those huge spider-bugs just darted full speed across the office floor. Its quickness reminds me of a fast centipede. I called loudly for Rob. The fear in my voice also made the night guards come and look. I did not need the attention, since I am sitting here in my pajamas. By the time Rob came, the bug was finished checking things out and was ready to go back out the door. It was a smaller one than yesterday and not a novelty anymore. YUCK! These critters will have to answer to the professional exterminator next week. God bless, Rebecca

---

"*Nkhwangwa yatema bondo.*" = "The axe has cut your own knee." (If your own axe cuts you, you don't throw it away. Likewise, learn to forgive—especially those who are close to you.)

We have learned since then that the spider bug is called a solifugae. This is what Wikipedia has to say:

*"**Solifugae** is an order of Arachnida. The name derives from Latin, and means those that flee from the sun. Their common names include camel spider, wind scorpion, sun scorpion and sun spider. In southern Africa they are also known as beard-clippers, relating to the belief they use their formidable jaws to clip hair from humans and animals to line their subterranean nests."*

Our gardener told us that in the village they call it *"yochotsa mfumu,"* which is translated as, "It removes the chief." Usually the chief is the one sitting down while everyone else in his presence is standing in respect. If this creature comes along, even the chief gets up! I was relieved to find out that the shockingly ugly creature with its huge jaws was neither poisonous nor very interested in humans. Still, I'm glad Rob took care of it. I do not think I could have slept well at night if I knew one of those was running around the house.

It is no coincidence that when times are rather unnerving or difficult, amazing words of encouragement find their way to strengthen me. Sometimes that encouragement is in the form of a fitting Scripture verse from my morning devotion. Sometimes it is an encouraging card or email. A few months after our move, my father-in-law sent me a supportive email from his home in Zambia. I include it to show an example of how God has worked through people, even in distant countries, to encourage me.

INCOMING EMAIL: November 27, 2003
Subject: mission work
Dad Wendland writes: Dear Rebecca, we're so thankful to the Lord for you and the great support that you've been to Rob in his ministry. You have a wonderful attitude toward your situation, Rob's ministry and the opportunities that also lie before you in Africa. May He bless your family as He has ours over the years—it has been truly amazing to see how the Lord strengthens and helps those who commit themselves to his service; more than you could ever imagine! Much love from Mom and me, Dad-W

The frequent communication allowed by email has been the most beneficial part of modern technology for me in Africa. Phones are too unreliable. Conversations often have a time lapse after each statement, pauses, bleeps, robotic sounds and frequent cut-offs. It is also a challenge to connect at decent hours due to substantial time zone differences and busy schedules. In 2003 I may have had trouble sending email with our dial-up internet connection, but at least the message was in one piece and could be read at the recipient's leisure. Our families and friends were not only interested in the latest happenings, but they also kept every situation in prayer as we shared the highlights, struggles or patiently waited for a resolution to different trials. One response to an update was, *"Your letters let us know what the Lord's servant's daily routines consist of, how adverse situations are dealt with and the strength God has given you to persevere. We also rejoice with you that the Lord is guiding you to many souls to help them learn that Jesus is the Lamb of God who takes away the sin of the world."* That was indeed my goal, and I was privileged to be able to share our news with others so easily, at the touch of a button.

Sent: November 28, 2003
Subject: Happy Thanksgiving –God bless!
Rebecca writes: We had a wonderful Thanksgiving here with the missionaries. The day before, the kids and I went to the Felgenhauer's place to roast squash, prepare pies and make some window decorations. I returned again at 8am on Thanksgiving Day to help with the turkey. Rob had a nice devotion after lunch and we sang hymns. It was great to celebrate our American holiday by gathering to thank our Lord for all we have been given. All the cooking was done from scratch for the meal. I was glad we started a few hours (and literally days) earlier than necessary, since we faced several power outages trying to get the food cooked. All the hours I stood by Dad as he carved the turkey were finally put to good use.

Today we went to Limbe and found AntiPest. They are scheduled to come this week and spray for mosquitoes, house pests, roaches, spiders and ants.

Hannah has been asking people if they soak their produce in potassium permanganate before she will eat anything. I see she pays more attention in the kitchen than I thought—a lil' survivor. We gave her hugs from all of you and updated her on the family news of the birth of her cousin Leah. We certainly thank the Lord for you all! God bless, Rebecca

---

"Kulasa mtengo ndi chamuna chomwe." = "To hit a tree is also manliness." (A person targeted a buffalo but shot a tree instead. i.e., an honest mistake is no dishonor. Keep giving your best effort and success will come at last.)

Our first Malawian Thanksgiving was special because everyone put in so much effort to make it an "American" celebration. In the end, some tastes were just different since we couldn't get the same brands or items. We decided it was best not to consider the costs of such a meal, since it could easily spoil the enjoyment. Many of the import shops purposely mark up the prices of special holiday items: one can of cranberries can be over five dollars; the imported frozen turkey alone can set the pocket book back about seventy dollars. Consequently, we thought it was not out of the question to celebrate with chicken in years to come.

Of course we missed our US family celebrations and traditions. Nevertheless, we knew it was still essential to give glory to the Giver of all gifts. Tradition and family are beautiful extras that the Lord allows us to enjoy and anticipate. Soon after Thanksgiving we found ourselves giving thanks for a new reason…our shipment had arrived!

*"Every good and perfect gift is from above,
coming down from the Father of the heavenly lights." James 1:17*

Sent: November 30, 2003
Subject: **kaTUNdu!**
Rob writes: The big news today is *kaTUNdu wambiri* (lots of stuff)! Our shipment has arrived! We had been warned about the slowness of customs, so we weren't getting our hopes up. We arranged to meet the crew after church at the main shopping center and lead them to our place. All went according to plan.

Now we wade through boxes once again. Every box is accounted for. Many thanks, Mom Staude, who helped every step of the way as they were packed. One thing we cannot wait to set up is our wonderful bed. Rebecca's been anticipating its arrival for months. The Malawi foam mattresses and locally-made bed frames leave a lot to be desired—including less back pain. We are blessed! Love, Rob

---

"Mlomo wakumwamba ndi wakunsi, pho!" = "The upper and lower lip, snap." (Proverb used when one has been asked too many questions and now is stranded—he doesn't even know how to begin to answer!)

Our shipment was an amazing blessing. We certainly did not NEED the extra comforts. We had been able to survive since June living mainly out of suitcases and without the majority of our belongings. However, our tool box, linens, proper kitchen utensils and kids' toys, along with their clothes and shoes for the next several sizes, were all a welcome sight. It was pure joy to put them in their places and then put them to use! For me, the most valuable shipment item was our box spring and mattress. Years later, I am still fond of our lovely, extremely comfortable imported bed!

Sent: December 1, 2003
Subject: RE: kaTUNdu!
Rebecca writes: Hello. Rob updated you yesterday on our shipment. Nathanael is grateful to finally sleep in a crib. The Pack N' Play served us well for the past six months, but I will be happy to finally put it away and use it only for traveling.

    I melted right into the bed last evening. The night guards came by the window to "check-out" at 6am. I mumbled a *"pitani bwino"* (go well). Either they sneak out at 4am or check out at our window at 6am.

    A note for my brother Matt: I think of you often when I see the local men selling things in their make-shift booths by the side of the road. They often fry up potato chunks that they call "chips" (fries) or sell cell phone top-up cards. The fort you built out of sticks in grade school was sturdier than some lean-to shelters here. Love, Rebecca

---

"*Chikondi ndi kutherana zakukhosi.*" = "Love means saying all that is in one's heart."

The days became busier as we unpacked our shipment. It was a blessing that we did not take for granted. Now it was a matter of keeping off the dust and bugs. I certainly didn't want roaches making nests in anything or spiders making their webs all over. I was thankful that AntiPest was on their way—hooray!

Sent: December 4, 2003
Subject: Bug free for now
Rebecca writes: Our house is hopefully bug-free for a while now. It is odd to see no movement in the kitchen. Usually there is a determined group of ants around or the resident geckos are on the move. Not anymore! That is because the AntiPest sprayers came yesterday. We had to leave so we would not inhale the fumes.

    Mom and Dad Staude, thank you very much for the Christmas envelope with the piano music and cards. Rob wanted to let you know that there is a better guarantee that a package will arrive without pilfering if you make all descriptions quite vague, such as "periodicals," "confectionary" or "personal effects" and estimate fairly low for the declared value. Otherwise it might be "Merry Christmas" for the mail room. God bless, Rebecca

---

"Wopusa adayimba ng'oma, ochenjera anabvina." = "The foolish one beat the drum while the clever ones danced." (Even "clever" people can benefit from those they look down on; something can always be appreciated in others.)

It was such a boost to get mail from "home" and have a few Christmas presents to open later that month. But it can be risky to send things to Malawi since the mail system here does not have many checks and balances. If dishonest postal workers see something declared on a package that they would like, there is not much to stop them. The cost of shipping is expensive enough without losing part of the treasures enclosed.

Sent: December 17, 2003
Subject: Hello again
Rebecca writes: Our power has been out because an electric line was chopped in half. That meant no computer and no electricity. It is crazy how much I rely on electricity, whether for cooking, using the computer, hot water or listening to music.

We are considering buying a cell phone. With all of Rob's traveling it should be a worthwhile investment.

I finally have conquered driving stick shift and have driven a few times here and there. As a passenger I have mentally turned onto the wrong side of the road, but I have not had trouble when I am actually driving. I am using the parking brake to manage getting uphill from a dead stop. Now I'm not so worried about rolling into the car behind me. Being an independent driver is a wonderful feeling, especially with Rob's frequent absences.

Our neighbor's house across the street was broken into. The neighbor suspects that the plumber, who had come to do work, had scouted out more than the plumbing necessities. On Monday night, the thieves grabbed the huge ladders that were stored on the property, removed the roofing tiles (there was nothing underneath) and let themselves down. Since the house has electronic sensors on the doorways, the alarm immediately went off. The thieves escaped empty-handed. We asked our night guards (who work for the same company) why the neighbor's guards allowed the thieves to get that far. "Oh, the thieves are so quiet," they told me. Two days later I heard our night guard snoring.

Our unpacking is glorious. I am jumping for joy at the things we brought. Mom,

I'm finding all the treasures that you and I snugly fit into each crevice. We did a great job packing. I am floored that next week is Christmas. God bless, Rebecca

---

"Patsepatse nkulanda; mwana wa mfulu apatsa yekha." = "Give me, give me is to steal; the free child gives on his own."

Wow, our first Christmas in Malawi was ONE WEEK away! That crept up on us. It simply did not feel like Christmas. The weather was so warm and there were no decorations, no advertisements and no Christmas music playing. We also had no midweek church services, so the Advent season simply passed me by. I hoped I had packed an Advent calendar in our shipment. Next year it would help us to better prepare our hearts for the coming of our tiny King. We were especially excited for Christmas since Rob's parents planned to visit us from Zambia. We had never celebrated a major holiday with Rob's parents before, except maybe the Fourth of July on one of their furloughs. We were thankful for the chance to celebrate Christ's birth with family and minimal distractions.

Unpacking our shipment really felt like unwrapping early Christmas gifts. However, after I heard of our neighbor's break-in, I knew we had to be extra careful about locking up and not drawing attention to the piles of household items that we had been unloading. Hannah and I counted the layers of security we had at Nyambadwe. We had a wall topped by double razor wire rolls, a locked gate, two night guards, burglar bars on each window inside and out, hallway grates, and an alarm that notifies a team of security men to come and secure the premises. Not to mention God, who provides us with the best security and sense of peace, bar none!

This time of year, which is the end of the dry season before the rains come, is called "the hungry time." The crops from the previous harvest are gone, stored food has been used up and people are hungry and looking for a way to feed themselves and their families. In Malawi, people who have MORE are culturally obligated to share with those who have LESS. This is particularly true of relatives or employers who have a surplus. This could mean sharing food, school fees, seeds, household supplies or clothing. Of course this cultural expectation also affected us. Even if we only lived with the "basics" we would be wealthier than most in Malawi. As it was, we not only had a decent house to live in, but we also had electricity, indoor plumbing, appliances, a vehicle and more possessions than many Malawians would deem necessary. In time we would find ourselves helping those in our employment to pay for funerals, transport, school fees and myriad supplies. It is sometimes difficult to walk the fine line between generosity to those in need and avoiding an unhealthy handout-mentality. Thanks be to our God who has the most amazing ***giving attitude*** this world has ever seen—and whose gift of a Son and Savior we were preparing to celebrate in a few days.

Sent: December 22, 2003
Subject: Merry Christmas from Malawi
Rob writes: Thanks for the notes and the Christmas wishes. There is no fancy letter from us this year, no pop-out cards, no poetry; just a sincere, from-the-bottom-of-our-hearts wish that you have a wonderful and richly blessed celebration of the birth of Immanuel. Imagine! "God with us!" The concept is so fantastic; the mercy behind the event is too deep for us to truly comprehend it. How can it be that the Creator, the Ruler of all things and the One before whom the angels fall in worship, is this tiny baby in a stable, forgotten as the rest of the world bustles by? And that He should be here and do this because of me, for me…words fail. Indeed, what great things our Lord has done for us! Because of Immanuel, this baby, this Messiah, what even greater things are guaranteed to come! Have a wonderful celebration of the Christ's birth! Love, Rob

---

"Wadzoladzola kumatope, koma kumunda kulibe ndime." = "He is completely full of mud, but in the garden there is not one row hoed."

With Rob's parents coming soon, I was valiantly trying to unpack supplies and get things set up for them. The task of packing all our possessions into boxes before we moved had not been exactly fun. But now the task of unpacking all our treasures was a bigger blessing than I ever would have imagined—at least, as far as earthly blessings are concerned. Even if the boxes had no fancy wrapping, ribbon or bows, they were a joy to open!

Only a few more days to go and Christmas would be here. I was rapidly filing new images of Christmas in my memory bank: warm fingers and toes, the smell of rain in the air, candles lit less for mood than for power outages, and an airport trip planned to pick up Grandpa and Grandma Wendland. Even as these new images flooded in, a part of my mind was registering what was absent: no major music selections for organ or choir, no recitations to polish, no last minute shopping, no snow-clad pines and no large family get-togethers.

Sent: December 23, 2003
Subject: Christmas wishes
Rebecca writes: I have been going non-stop and have not gotten on the computer. I also have not felt the greatest since Friday. We had no power that evening and now I seem to be losing *my* power. Nathanael is off again too. He fits into the same clothes that he wore before we left. I think that is a bonus, since I feel I missed out on enjoying his baby stage this past summer when the days were consumed with packing and moving.

Hannah is thrilled over the two small Christmas stockings I unpacked. I have had to rubber band anything big to the outside of her tiny stocking—but it works. It seems odd to sing about the snow and cold winter's night when that isn't the case here. I don't miss the snow…but I miss what the snow meant = Wisconsin = Milwaukee = bundling up for the church services = practicing organ = choirs = family gatherings.

Thanks for parting with Grandma Dobberfuhl's large cooking pot, Mom. I only need to boil one pot of water daily. I use it every day and think of her.

We finally bought a queen-size bed net for $50. This morning a gecko dropped a cricket on Hannah's bed net while she was in bed. She stayed still and very matter-o-factly called out, "MOM, there's a big bug on my bed net."

We praise the One who was born to make it possible for us to be together for eternity. Merry Christmas, Rebecca

---

"Wopempha salira tololo." = "The one asking does not cry for the bundle." (i.e., when you are dependent on the goodness of the giver, you don't dictate how much they give you.)

Picking up Grandma and Grandpa Wendland from the airport was so exciting. They were our first family members to visit our new home. Having departed from the relatively modern Lusaka International Airport, Mom Wendland found our Blantyre airport, Chileka, to be pretty quaint. She thought its old-fashioned verandah overlooking the runway looks like it came straight out of a Hemingway novel. The runway is very short and the plane rolls to a stop directly in front of the baggage claim. The open-air balcony above the runway allows everyone to watch and wave as the passengers disembark on the outdoor stairway. In fact, Chileka Airport is too "old world" for major airlines. British Airways will not fly into Chileka anymore, since the security is not tight enough. To be fair, the airport has *a few* security measures in place: there is a conveyor belt at the entrance to screen baggage, and only checked-in passengers can proceed to the departure lounge. Before passengers board their plane they have to walk up to their baggage and point to it. A porter then carries the identified baggage to a cart to load it onto the plane. Third World ways have their charm. Though it is not so charming when none of the baggage carts have working wheels, and you find dirt and grass stuck to your bags.

Sent: January 2, 2004
Subject: Holiday Review
Rob writes: Greetings everybody! It was wonderful to be able to spend Christmas with Mom and Dad Wendland—in Africa. The last time I celebrated the Christmas holiday with them was in high school back in 1990! Here are a few highlights:

December 24 – Meet Mom and Dad at Chileka Airport. Whirlwind tour of

Blantyre. Christmas Eve worship at Epiphany in Ndirande.
December 25 – Christmas day in the low 90°F. Worship with Mom and Dad at Beautiful Saviour in downtown Blantyre.
December 26 – Boxing Day—the Malawi missionaries gather for fellowship and fun. This event also served as the farewell for Uncle Mark and Louise Wendland, who are returning to the States after 12 years in Malawi.
December 28 – We travel to the Zomba Plateau. We take the "old road" up and finally make it to the summit, buy rhubarb since it is the only place you can get it here, haggle with vendors, enjoy spectacular sights of the vistas of Malawi and take the "proper" road down.
December 29 – Dad sits in on a portion of my language class.
December 30 – Quiet day to enjoy each other and the weather. We play Spades that evening. The girls cream the guys.
December 31 – We visit Mua Mission, about 200 km north, near Salima. It has top-notch wood carvers, a picturesque church, an ornately decorated museum with frescos of Chichewa culture, an animal orphanage and old buildings all around. The priest in charge, Father Chisale, recognized Dad W. from his book, _Preaching that Grabs the Heart_. We got home and I attempt to make caramel corn with Rebecca—it was a disaster…twice. Maybe the different brown sugar or higher altitude wreaked havoc on our good intentions. No popcorn that night. We resume our Spades feud. The guys eke out a last-hand victory.
January 2 – All good things (well, except for grace and glory and life in Jesus…ach, you know what I mean!) must come to an end. Mom and Dad sojourn home and we get back to the business of everyday life here. Hannah sheds big tears. _Tiyamike Ambuye wathu_ (Let us praise our Lord) for all His great blessings! Rob

---

"*Ichi chakoma, ichi chakoma, pusi adagwa chagada.*" = "I want this one, I want that one, the monkey fell in between." (A warning against greed: a monkey grabbed for two fruits at once and instead fell down with nothing.)

One of our Christmas highlights was our day trip to Zomba, a city about 64 km (40 mi) northeast of Blantyre where the LCCA also has a presence. Zomba Plateau looms over the city, rising over a thousand meters above the plain below. The top of the plateau is crisscrossed by streams and dotted with waterfalls and lakes. The air on the plateau is filled with the smell of African juniper. Once again we found ourselves marveling at the variety in landscape and scenery that makes up the country of Malawi.

We thoroughly enjoyed sharing some day-to-day experiences with Grandma and Grandpa Wendland. But best of all was the special blessing of being able to celebrate

Christmas together, African-style. Taking Rob's parents back to the airport after their visit was unexpectedly hard. Airports did not seem fun and exciting anymore, especially if you are left behind. We were very sad to see Grandpa and Grandma Wendland's airplane disappear into the clouds. But with upcoming mission meetings to be held in Zambia, Rob would soon be traveling to Lusaka. The meetings were being held at the LCCA Seminary, where his dad was currently a professor. It was hard to believe that Rob could go to a mission meeting, see his parents and even sleep in his old bed. It is a small world after all!

"Glory to God in the highest, and on earth peace to men on whom his favor rests." Luke 2:14

CHAPTER 6

2004: A NEW YEAR TOAST TO CONTINUED BLESSINGS

*"Therefore encourage one another
and build each other up,
just as in fact you are doing."
1 Thessalonians 5:11*

*H*appy New Year! When I looked back on all that had transpired in 2003, it made my head spin. Shortly into the New Year my head started spinning once again because of some uplifting news: *My family was coming to visit!* The WHOLE Staude clan was planning a trip from Wisconsin to Malawi. All of them! My mom and dad. My brother Matt with his wife Melissa and their one-year old son, Luke. My sister Sarah and her husband, Aaron Mueller. And my youngest sister Stephanie! My parents and siblings planned to visit us in Malawi in June, about five months away. They had been such an encouragement to me across the miles. Now they were taking an elaborate and expensive step to see exactly where we were, what their prayers were for and how the Lord was working in our mission field in Malawi. Suddenly I couldn't wait to finish unpacking and start planning for their arrival.

There are so many details and questions to iron out for any trip overseas. Rob and I were well aware of the preparations and hassles this trip would create for my family, since we had just gone through the process ourselves. Current passports, transit visas and vaccinations were the beginning of their travel arrangements. We also knew that overseas travel was worthwhile, exhilarating, enlightening and eye opening…but *not cheap*. Oddly enough, a round-trip ticket costs less than a one-way ticket. As certain as I was that my family would enjoy their holiday with us, I also knew they would be happy to have their return ticket home!

Sent: January 6, 2004
Subject: Happy Epiphany
Rebecca writes: The New Year has brought us electricity outages again. I was glad that the electricity cooperated while Mom and Dad were here, because since then it has been hard to get anything done. Since they left, no water has been boiled, and it was tricky to get meals cooked all weekend long. It also has been difficult to get online.

On Sunday we were thrilled to have the power click on during Mom Staude's final attempt to call us from La Crosse. I finished blowing out the candles right about the time they told us more about their exciting plans to visit Malawi. The time will fly by.

Happy Epiphany. God bless your week as you daily live for HIM. Rebecca

---

Knowing I was going to see my family again before our furlough in two years was exhilarating. Our first few months of separation had not seemed that unusual; there had often been a space of several months between family visits even in the States. Yet, as the calendar pages kept turning, the distance widened. The memories of family gatherings seemed to get glossed over. The thought of being together again, of refreshing old memories and making new ones, of talking to people who knew us — without needing a preamble of explanation — was super special. I could not wait. I pointed to our family pictures and quizzed the kids every so often to make sure they could remember who was who.

Some might think that the fact we could leave our family to go live on a mission field means that our family bonds weren't particularly strong. I suppose it *would* be easier to leave a place if you did not have much reason to look back. But in my situation that certainly was not the case. My family structure was close and our ties were strong. Those family ties made the separation difficult; those same family ties supported us wholeheartedly while we were apart.

Even though on one level it seemed like a huge sacrifice to leave our family, we realized the truth that all earthly family is a gift. In our case, following the will of the Giver meant we had to temporarily let go of the gift of family. Jesus' words in Matthew 10:37 gave us a proper focus: *"Anyone who loves his father or mother more than me is not worthy of me; anyone who loves his son or daughter more than me is not worthy of me; and anyone who does not take his cross and follow me is not worthy of me. Whoever finds his life will lose it, and whoever loses his life for my sake will find it."* Our separation from family was merely a transitory earthly trial connected with doing the Lord's work in a distant place. And God would not fail to provide for us in their absence, just as he promised in Mark 10:29, 30: *"I tell you the truth," Jesus replied, "no one who has left home or brothers or sisters or mother or father or children or fields for me and the gospel will fail to receive a hundred times as much in this present age…and in the age to come, eternal life."*

Sent: January 9, 2004
Subject: More visions of Africa
Rob writes: My language lessons now go from Monday—Saturday for a total of ten hours a week. The bulk of my time each week is spent preparing for class. The goal is for me to go to the village congregations on my own by April. Time is ticking. Spare time has been spent:
- Building a small bookshelf out of the leftover wood from our shipment crates. I'm glad we brought power tools, even if they need to be run with a step-down transformer. The shelf turned out well considering the condition of the wood. Our gardener helped hold a board and said that was the first power tool he had ever seen.
- Saying farewell to the Mark Wendland family who left the field yesterday.
- Getting our crippled Pajero fixed up.
- Going to a missionary meeting in Zomba. We will try to plan the Malawi Mission Field's future and determine what calls should be extended to replace two positions.

We have had three days of solid rain. Now all the frogs (and every other chirpy creature) are going full blast. *Mulungu akudalitseni nonse chaka chatsopanochi*—God's richest blessing this New Year! Rob

The rains in Malawi seemed to bring everything to life—green and growing things as well as creatures. The vegetation in our garden—fruit trees, roses, gardenias, lady of the night—gave off multiple layers of scent. But the layers of sound were almost more overwhelming: the birdcalls of louries, sunbirds, weavers and crows were accompanied by the zing of grasshoppers and cicadas and the click of geckos. Even after years in Malawi, this cacophony of chirping, calling, singing and cawing can still surprise and amaze us: recently Hannah called me to the window and said, "Mom listen, it sounds just like a jungle!"

We were settling into a post-Christmas routine…but I kept one eye on the calendar. The days seemed to be passing like sands through an hourglass that would turn over with the arrival of my family in June.

Sent: January 10, 2004
Subject: Hannah cannot wait!
Hannah writes: Dear Grandma and Grandpa, I can't wait until you come. I am going to play games with you, read books, and do playdough. I am excited to see you in June.

(Hannah is anxious. She frequently says, "When they come I am going to show them…" Each day she likes to walk down and see how our new bunch of bananas is growing.) Love, Hannah (and Mom)

Hannah truly missed her grandparents and could not stop talking about their upcoming visit. In turn, there was not a day that went by when my parents did not think of Africa. They continued to pay our US bills that trickled in long after we left the country. They assisted us in necessary, ongoing Stateside paperwork and phone calls. But their efforts continued well beyond obligatory maintenance. Over our years in Malawi my mom has remembered every special day and holiday with cards, phone calls and even packages. She has been completely committed to finding a way to provide anything we might lack. My dad wouldn't let us leave the country before he was sure we were supplied with the proper tools and fix-it items. He also took on the enormous task of tackling our yearly Stateside taxes. They both field questions and inquiries about us and constantly and positively promote the Malawi mission work that we are a part of. <u>We have their total support.</u> Those few words do not scratch the surface of what they continue to do for us, though we are worlds apart.

The Lord has provided both Rob and me with out-of-this-world parents. I know their support is no coincidence; it is founded on their faith in Christ. That is apparent in the way our parents brought us up, the way they serve and trust in the Lord each day and the way they still passionately study and hear God's Word.

Sent: January 11, 2004
Subject: eat your veggies first…
Rebecca writes: Hannah's latest quote while she played was: "And God told Adam and Eve: 'You eat vegetables before you eat apples!'"

We have had days of heavy rains! This is great for the crops. Our pink hibiscus plant is taller than our roof. We have to watch out for falling mangoes lately. Really—they hurt! We have been sharing our mango abundance with beggars.

I saw some vendors on the streets selling what I thought were brown shiny peanuts. No; they were large fried *inswa* (termites) about two inches in length. I'm told they are a great source of protein and free for the taking after the rains—if you wish.

Today in church I saw a parade of ants. I wasn't sure what they were after. Rob informed me he knew after he drank his wine for communion.

Hope all is well on your end. It is simply great to hear from so many of you. It shrinks the miles—creating smiles! God bless, Love, Rebecca

When the first big rains of the season soften the earth, it is a signal to a large variety of underground termites to send out their flying explorers. These termites, also called *"inswa"* or "flying ants," can be over an inch long. They have four large wings, come out by the thousands and attempt to fly around to find a mate. After a time, they drop their wings and crawl around. If they are successful kings and queens, they will unite and establish a new colony.

At this time of year, the wings of these termites seem as abundant as snowflakes; they gather in drifting piles against every surface. Each morning when we open our front door, we disturb a fresh pile of *inswa* wings. The discarded wings flutter up and redistribute everywhere, even inside our house. The sound of *inswa* pelting our door, scratching against our screens or dropping to the floor with an audible "toc" becomes mundane background noise. But what is a nuisance to us is a welcome and healthy source of protein to Malawians. It is not uncommon to see barefoot children leaping to catch the first swarm of flying *inswa* as they emerge from the ground… and popping them into their mouths, raw. Many Malawians carry empty shopping bags as they go about their daily business, so they can collect *inswa* for a later meal. The *inswa* are most commonly fried in oil. Their plump, greasy bodies turn crisp and crunchy…and are rumored to taste like peanuts.

Fried *inswa* wasn't the next thing on our menu list—birthday cake was. Hannah turned four on January 16th. Being the first grandchild on either side of the family, Hannah was accustomed to plenty of attention on her birthday. This time there were no familiar cars pulling up the driveway and no chorus of relatives to sing birthday wishes. Our erratic dial-up internet access prevented even a birthday phone call. We did our best to make it special anyway and were thankful for the blessings of beautiful January sunshine and our lovely four-year-old daughter.

Sent: January 17, 2004
Subject: Thanks for all the wishes
Rebecca writes: Thanks for Hannah's 4th birthday wishes. I asked Hannah how she felt to be four. She announced, "Oh, I turn four after I eat my birthday cake." Good thing I had baked a cake so she could be officially four by dinner time.

Here is a list of what Hannah will do (so she told me) when she turns five next year: ride a rollercoaster (which Dad promised her back in America—and she hasn't forgotten), lift up her brother, stand and cook at the stove, turn on lights, work a drill, turn on flashlights, turn on the generator, light a candle…I stopped her there to get my pencil and grab the video camera. She was spouting these off like she had pondered them for years. (Can you tell our sporadic electricity affects her?)

Sorry we never got to connect, Mom and Dad Staude, for your phone call. Rob had a huge file from the synod that he tried to download most of the day. That tied up our phone line as his computer struggled to receive it. Our power was fine until yesterday. God Bless, Rebecca

When emails arrived with big attachments, files, or video clips, our system simply could not manage. We rarely went on the internet for information, since the glut of information would often freeze up our computer. It seemed we were standing still on dial-up internet access while the rest of the world zoomed ahead on broadband and wireless.

Sent: January 22, 2004
Subject: my temp
Rebecca writes: I'm happy to report that the title has nothing to do with thermometers; after many hours I received my Malawi driver's license—a temporary copy. Yvonne Janosek spent the morning with me at the driver's place going back and forth from rooms 1-6, while being smooshed between sweaty, smelly individuals. It was the most unpleasant experience I have had so far in Malawi. Each line took hours to get to the front. I accidently stood in a wrong line once since there are no helpful signs. It is poorly organized and the people behind the counter must have no incentive to work efficiently. I'm glad it is over with. I didn't even take a driving test, only paid. Maybe a Wisconsin driver's license holds enough clout.

Here are a few things on my list from this week:
- Rob made homemade vanilla ice cream. It was terrific; best I've had in a long time.
- We have had several days of heavy rains.
- Yesterday morning we woke up to two ceiling leaks. One was right over the pot of water I had boiled and was letting cool on the stove. I used it to water plants instead.
- I attended a Blantyre Music Society choir practice on Monday evening. It was comprised of various musically-inclined individuals from all over the world who live and work in Blantyre; a nice, talented group. The director wondered if I could accompany some of the pieces on the piano. I have been trying to practice the pieces. I surely miss my piano!
- It is pineapple season and each week we buy several fresh ones. They sure are sweet.
- The night guards have been getting a dinner bonus at our place. Not only are the mango trees loaded, but the guards take shopping bags and collect the *inswa* (flying ants) that swarm by the security lights.
- The guards also asked for an onion last week. I was a bit puzzled—fried *inswa* and onion? No; they had seen what they thought was a meter (3') long cobra slither across the pavement and into the grass. They tried to hit it with rocks and mangos but missed. They thought if they scattered onion, the snake would surely come out. Nothing happened. I hope it left

the property for good. We've seen nothing since.
- Rob got a new battery for the Pajero. It was dead when we planned to drive to church this past Sunday. It also has a nail in the tire, which we hope to get fixed before Rob takes it to Zambia on Monday. Never a dull moment. God's blessings. Love, Rebecca

After several months of stick shift practice I had conquered our steep driveway, acclimated to driving on the other side of the road, discovered that I actually LIKE roundabouts, and become accustomed to all the obstacles along the roads. Little did I know that the hardest part was yet to come…applying for a temporary license. The formality of getting the license wasn't formal at all: it was chaotic and seriously frustrating. I stood in line (or rather *six* lines) hour after hour for the better part of a day, battling with the crowds to keep my place. I hoped I would not have to repeat the scenario anytime soon. But if it meant that I had a Malawi driver's license on the way, it was worth the trauma—I hoped.

Sent: January 25, 2004
Subject: Tropical!
Rob writes: Our rains are in full swing and we are thankful. It doesn't always seem overly humid, but books and papers left near an open window usually have curled pages after a couple of hours. Rebecca was shocked to find that her passport cover was completely curled over the other day. With all the wet and warmth one can easily understand how a rainforest could form if this kept up much of the year. Rich, green, slippery moss is covering the bricks in our yard, frogs are croaking at night and mushrooms are popping up all over our lawn. Hannah has been stamping them down, aside from the enormous one that measured 12" long and 8" wide.

Bits of news: the ACA called two men to fill the Malawi vacancies. One would be an additional rural missionary; the other would be the next urban pastor at Beautiful Saviour. This congregation is currently a small group of English speaking members who meet at the Reading Room in downtown Blantyre. The plan is to build a new church and Reading Room facility. It would also have a conference room, a small kitchen and be a type of headquarters for the LCCA in Blantyre. Please keep those men in your prayers.

John Janosek is undergoing surgery in February. He called to tell me that he wants me to take some of his services during that time. I will be going from observing a service to conducting one…nothing like "sink or swim."

This week I head to Zambia as a representative of our Malawi mission. Tomorrow I'll pick up Missionary Ib Meyer in Lilongwe, cross the Malawi border and drive to Chipata, the Zambia border town. Tuesday we journey to Lusaka…

and I sleep in my boyhood bed. Wednesday it is meetings, Bible Study and fellowship. Friday it's back to Chipata, and Saturday back to Blantyre. Then the following week...the aforementioned "baptism by fire" begins.

Here are a few interesting points about Malawi currency learned from language class this week: "*Kwacha*" (the paper bill) is translated "dawn" (as in, after the night of colonial rule); "*Tambala*" (the coin) is translated "rooster" (crowing as it dawns). Love, Rob

When we arrived in Malawi, the mission field was preparing to say goodbye to two missionaries and their families: Mark Wendland and John Janosek. About a year after our family's arrival, two new missionary families would join the field. The men who accepted the calls were Pastor Jim Bartz in Michigan, who would serve as a southern rural missionary, and Pastor Mark Johnston in Wisconsin, who would serve Beautiful Saviour, the Blantyre urban church.

Sent: January 26, 2004
Subject: Lil' update
Rebecca writes: WOW, the roads here are bad with all the rains. The potholes keep growing and are filled with mud. It has been damp and rainy each day and feels like a rainforest. Other missionaries told us to watch out for moldy shoes. The milk has been spoiling fast too. A lot of old trees are tipping over with their roots pulling right out of the saturated ground. God bless, Rebecca

P.S. I saw a mongoose in the yard. It ran away as soon as I tried to take a picture.

In grade school I studied different climates around the world. I remember being amazed when I learned that some areas have growing seasons all year long. Now I had an opportunity to experiment and explore the vegetation in Malawi's temperate climate. I really enjoyed visiting plant nurseries and browsing through the stunning flowers, various plants and flowering shrubs. So far this was the only shopping I had managed to enjoy in Malawi.

Sent: February 11, 2004
Subject: Lil' contact
Rob writes: Greetings from Lilongwe! Our phone line at Nyambadwe has a loud hum. We've tried calling Malawi Telecom. They've promised every day for a week now that they will come.

I am sending this email from Missionary Paul Nitz's computer. We all left Blantyre at 5am this morning and came to Lilongwe for mission meetings. At that time the scenery was quite spectacular, especially the 40-some miles through the

Dedza Plateau. We ascended the winding northbound road through hills and cliffs. The early morning sky was full of intense reds and blues that shone on the rocky outcroppings. In a few spots the road rises so high that we could see entire villages from a bird's eye view: smoke ascending from their early morning fires and people and animals walking around, seemingly unaware of their roadway visibility. On the hills and plains there was a patchwork of gardens and maize and a variety of indigenous trees—baobab, acacia and banana—and tropical vegetation. At one point in the clear morning air we could see Lake Malawi on the horizon to our right. Later, we passed near the Mozambique border to our left and saw their flags blowing in the breeze.

We got to Lilongwe in time for my morning meeting. (I'm on the LCCA Mission Board as secretary.) After the meeting I dropped off Rebecca at the Zambia border. She is on her way to the annual Zambia missionary Ladies' Bible Retreat. The Chipata missionary wives graciously offered to pick her up from the border and take her to the retreat.

On Wednesday, I went to three congregations in the Lower Shire and enjoyed it. I led the liturgy in Chichewa and distributed communion for the first time. The evangelist did the readings, prayers and sermon. It's coming along. Blessings in Jesus! Rob

Our trip to Lilongwe was multi-purpose. Rob had meetings and I tagged along since the four-hour journey north took me that much closer to the Malawi-Zambia border. I was on my way to the annual Ladies' Bible Retreat in Lusaka, the Zambian counterpart to the Malawi retreat I had attended in October. It was a bonus to be close enough to attend this one too—only one country and 1000 km (600 miles) away! The missionary Holtz family, who lived in the Zambian border town of Chipata, graciously collected me from the border and transported me to and from Lusaka. I was grateful for the experience and opportunity to travel "next door" to study God's Word with fellow believers.

Sent: February 17, 2004
Subject: Back online... at last!
Rob writes: My inbox says I last downloaded emails three weeks ago. We have had a terrible humming noise, which we think is from the rain hitting the poorly-connected, non-insulated phone lines. You should see the major junction boxes! It is a wonder that any phone calls are made. Every few days we contacted the phone company and every few days we received assurances that they would fix the problem asap. Well, asap must mean February 17: *tikuthokozani* (thank you) Malawi Telecom—at last! I sent them home with a packet of cookies for their assistance.

So many things have happened since I was last able to send a message to you all: congratulations, Uncle Paul, on accepting the Lord's call to serve as president of Wisconsin Lutheran Seminary. I cannot fathom the length and breadth of the task you have, though we have the wonderful confidence that whatever the Lord asks of us He also gives the power to do.

I'm still "bacheloring" it with the kids. After we took Rebecca to the Malawi/Zambia border, the kids and I returned to Blantyre. Police on the way doubted my ability to handle the kids. At police check points I heard comments like "Surely the little one should have gone with Mummy" and "Will they survive?" We hope Rebecca has had a wonderful Ladies' Bible Retreat in Zambia and that the Lord grants her a safe journey back to Blantyre. Love, Rob

The North American work ethic that insists on a job done in a timely, efficient, predictable manner is hard to find here. Comparing a Malawian work ethic to a North American one is futile and frustrating. More than once I have approached a business counter and found the receptionist snoring in a chair. Work often seems to be treated like something to be endured. I shook my head one day when I saw a wheel-barrow-shaped pile of hardened cement next to a building. Maybe lunch time had arrived and the call of wet cement was not as compelling as the call of a hungry stomach. Perhaps it is Malawi's proximity to the equator that causes so many to follow a tropical pace. Perhaps we didn't yet know the right people or we lacked the right connections—like being a relative of someone's sister's cousin and of the same tribe and therefore friends. Instead of steaming over such issues, we have taken to keeping packets of cookies or nuts on hand. They can be a "sweet" thank you to workers who are perhaps poorly rewarded for completing their work in a timely manner.

Sent: February 21, 2004
Subject: safe at home
Rebecca writes: The retreat topic of "creation versus evolution" was very worthwhile and enjoyable. The trip to Zambia is long to be sure. It ends up being about 28 hours round-trip. In the States that might be 2 days' worth of travel—here it meant almost 5 days spent exclusively in the car. The pace of travel is so slow because of the very rough road conditions and slow speed limits (50 kph/30 mph) through every village, not to mention dodging cattle and stalled vehicles, and the lack of nighttime lighting. For safety reasons, people avoid traveling in the dark if at all possible. That limits the length of daily car trips. However, there are not that many opportunities to study, worship and have fellowship with other Lutheran, English-speaking women—so it was well worth the long haul.

I got to know the Holtz family better as they graciously hosted me on my transient way through the Chipata border to and from Malawi. There was no diesel on our way back to Chipata. In Petauke we needed to fill up. A group of Zambian men swarmed the car to sell us diesel. Soon a bunch of men were lifting up a 10 liter container and siphoning it with a black rubber hose into our vehicle. That was quite an experience.

I feel so refreshed from the retreat. It was encouraging on many levels. God bless, Rebecca

Rob is quite capable of holding down the fort during my brief absences, and it was a terrific bonding time for Rob and the kids. For me, the days away were a great chance to dig deeper into the Word with ladies of the same faith. Studying, sharing and applying Scripture is always time well spent. Despite the arduous travelling, I returned home with renewed zeal to deal with the frustrations of daily life and to complete the tasks that the Lord had placed before me here in Africa.

Sent: February 24, 2004
Subject: Cloth Diapers
Rebecca writes: We got a garden planted yesterday. Rob is out in the bush again today.

Our phone line is still bad and our power is crummy again. Blantyre city is on a power rotation. Evidently a major transformer blew. The chief in charge of the area where the transformer is located won't allow anyone to fix it, because his maize crop, which is planted around the transformer, might be ruined.

I've been giving cloth diapers a try (for Nathanael). I miss the free diaper testing that I used to do in Brookfield, WI. I can scarcely believe they paid me for it. It is difficult to save money here, because if you need a special product (such as disposable diapers) you either pay the seriously inflated prices—often quadruple—or you remain empty-handed. God bless, Rebecca

A village chief wields a significant amount of power—enough to delay maintenance on a local transformer for the sake of his crops. On the one hand, the chief was protecting his interests at the expense of a city's electricity. But from the perspective of the average Malawian, to whom electricity is a rare luxury and a maize harvest is a necessity, the chief had a legitimate concern.

Unlike the average Malawian, I am dependent on electricity. When the power is out I still find myself automatically flipping light switches throughout the house, even though I know they can't turn on. I wonder why the music isn't playing, or I put things in the microwave only to take them out again, shaking my head at my lapse in concentration and realizing just HOW MANY things I use each day that require power. When the power is off for long periods of time, I have learned to use a cooler and a few cold packs to keep a day's-worth of items readily available without having to open the refrigerator a dozen times.

Sent: February 28, 2004
Subject: Back online
Rob writes: We're back online! For how long is unknown. Our phone had been out for weeks. Last Sunday we got a telephone call—it was Mom and Dad Staude. It seemed to be a miracle, since the phone worked just for them. I think the Lord intervened yesterday, because I don't think Malawi Telecom did!

We've had some big storms in Blantyre, with lightning and thunder right on top of each other. I think a strike must have fused a few loose lines, because our phone was working fine after that storm. I would have sent this email last night…but the same strikes also blew a couple of electricity transformers, leaving us with no power. I've included a picture of our phone line junction box here in Nyambadwe. Maybe some of you technicians can tell us what the problem is. Yes, that is a bird nest in the middle of all the wires—poor Frankenstein phone box!

I have been frequently traveling with John Janosek to his/my congregations—16 of them. Last week was busy. On Tuesday I presented an exegesis on Galatians 3:10-14 for the area called workers (Dad Wendland—they really enjoyed the Chichewa included in the exegesis: Greek to English and Chichewa. Afterwards one national pastor commented, "I think all of us who went to Seminary have seen something—an orange tree cannot produce mangoes." It was an African way of saying that an apple does not fall far from the tree—kindly comparing the son to his father.)

The next four days we went to village churches. It is neat going out to serve those places, even though it can make for some long twelve-hour days. I come home tired—but I tell you, it is wonderful traveling through the African bush in the evening: a day of rejoicing with believers behind you, dusk falling on the baobabs (with leaves even!), the smell of rain heavy in the air, the bush birds singing away when home and family are ahead.

A couple days ago John and I were coming home from Chizilo. There had been quite a rainstorm in the Thyolo Escarpment, causing water to wash down to the Shire River—and cross our road in a number of places. We made it through all of the flooded streams, but one was a close call. After we crossed the stream I asked John why he had driven crooked, since our vehicle had edged uncomfortably close to a small waterfall. He told me that he'd had the wheels cranked in the opposite direction. We made it a across with a few inches to spare. If the river had been a bit higher (it was to the top of the wheels and flowing fast), or if we'd had to go a bit farther, we might have had a swim.

While we were at Khobili congregation on Sunday, a big rainstorm passed right over us. They don't have a roof other than a few strands of grass. Sadly, I didn't bring the camera. It would have been quite the picture: the service continued as umbrellas were opened inside the church, the people were standing ('cause the mud floors and benches were...well...mud), and rain was just pouring in. Needless to say, we left quite wet that day—with another service to attend at Bangwe. Currently I conduct the liturgy, consecration of elements, distribution of communion and also baptisms.

Missionary Paul Nitz asked Rebecca to be the update coordinator for the Malawi mission field, with the goal of boosting its Stateside visibility. She agreed that she would be willing, but it will depend on our telephone dial-up internet service. The kids are well, Hannah is 102 cm tall and Nathanael is 76 cm (we've gone metric). Love, Rob

Bird's nest in neighborhood phone box

I was ready to make my own static about our crummy telephone lines. It was an unending frustration that our most convenient connection to other mission families and to people both local and overseas was so unreliable. I was eager to contribute to the Malawi mission's public relations back in the States, but even that ministry was dependent on our erratic phone line.

The bird's nest snuggled into the twisted wires of our phone line junction box was a rather revealing comment on the mystery of Malawi maintenance. At times it seemed to me that the Malawi work motto was: "The squeaky wheel gets the oil (don't bother to oil the other wheels) but the oil is finished, so now we cannot continue to work... and you need to buy us more!" I realized that, in contrast, my own mind works in a proactive and preventative manner. It took some mental adjustment to wait patiently for progress when matters seemed to be out of control. This was yet another valuable lesson in tolerance for me.

Sent: March 5, 2004
Subject: water log...
Rebecca writes: While Rob was recently away at meetings in Zambia, I went with Yvonne Janosek to a wildlife meeting on Liwonde Park and Mvuu (hippo) Camp. Yvonne picked up the kids and me shortly after 7pm, and we didn't get home until almost 10pm. Upon our return, the night guards announced that the shower had been running. I was puzzled. The guards explained that they had heard running water near the office shortly after we left. I whisked the kids to bed and opened the door to the office. It looked like a wading pool. The nearby toilet had blown its hose when a metal part broke. It seems the cheap fixture combined with irregular water pressure caused the calamity. The remaining part of the pipe was spurting (thankfully clean) water all over. Everything in the bathroom and Rob's office was soaked in two inches of water. I found and turned off the crucial knob to stop most of the water. Then I wrapped rubber strips around the pipe (saved from Stateside blood draws for such an occasion), and that stopped the flow completely. After that, I opened an outside door and water gushed out. I spent the next four hours mopping the area dry, rotating a fan in different areas and unloading all the tables and bookshelves to tip them over and dry the wet bottoms. What a mess. **At least the electricity stayed on!** At about 2am that night the neighbor's house alarm went off. Who knows, maybe the commotion staved off a potential break-in here. Thankfully, the Lord also provided three sunny days following that incident to dry things out. It felt like He was smiling on my clean-up efforts.

Rob is now safely home and has almost finished restocking his bookshelves.

The rains have subsided since our flood. I'm told recent rains are the result of a cyclone over Madagascar. If the rain stays away we may have improved phone lines soon. Love, Rebecca

> *"Be joyful always; pray continually;*
> *give thanks in all circumstances,*
> *for this is God's will for you in Christ Jesus."*
> *Thessalonians 5:16-18*

A water-logged bathroom and office in Rob's absence meant an exhausting all-nighter for me. Thankfully, the kids were asleep and the power cooperated, so I had an uninterrupted block of time to manage the clean-up. The Lord gave me the needed strength and endurance to finish the task by early morning. It was good exercise in spite of my new constellations of bruises!

2004: A New Year Toast To Continued Blessings

Sent: March 23, 2004
Subject: climbing Mt. Kachisi
Rebecca writes: What an amazing scenario: my computer is on, I've downloaded all the mail, read the letters, stayed connected and may be able to send another note all in one sitting (provided the kids also cooperate). There are a lot of variables to this whole operation.

One happy item to report is that the sea shipment (with US mail and packages) from five months ago has arrived in Blantyre and has been distributed. Mom and Dad, your package from September—with the hand sanitizer wipes and goodies—has arrived! We certainly appreciate all the practical things and are putting it all to use. Mom, you taped the box amazingly well and packaged things great with shrink wrap and zip-lock bags. Something to keep in mind is to declare packages at a worth of between ten and twenty dollars. It may seem quite low, but devotional booklets, church magazines, trinkets, hand sanitizer and snacks do not have much market value here.

Since I mentioned water filters…that was one thing we should have taken on our recent excursion to Lake Chilwa and Mount Kachisi. This past Saturday, Missionary Paul and Kristy Wegner babysat our kids while we met up with the Wildlife Society in Zomba. A group of about 40 people had gathered to carpool to Lake Chilwa. We rode in the back of an ambulance with 8 others. We arrived at the edge of the lake where six wooden fishing boats waited to ferry us to a large island. Everyone chose a boat and paid $1 to embark. As soon as I stepped in our boat, I saw water seeping in from several places. The bottom was covered with green moss and slippery algae. One lady couldn't swim and kept asking questions about the integrity of the boat. The owner of the boat used a huge bamboo pole to propel us across the lake like a gondola. It probably would have taken ten minutes to cross the lake by motor boat. Instead it was a relaxing 45 minute ride by "pole power." After four of the other boats passed us, I wondered what was wrong with our boat. A local man sat in the corner of our boat and was bailing water almost the entire time…giving me quite the "sinking feeling."

The men must know the limits of their boats, because we crossed the lake in one piece. We were all introduced to the chief of the island. I had worn a jean dress and tennis shoes for the occasion. I figured it was a practical hiking outfit but still looked respectful enough to meet a chief. After a picnic lunch, our carpool driver announced her plan to hike to the summit of Kachisi, an extinct volcano on the island. We hired a guide to find the trail that would take us to the top. It turns out that this so-called guide could not find any path up. We trekked through village cornfields, hiked through thorn bushes and briar patches and gradually ascended areas of steep, slippery rocks.

I was snagged by countless thorn bushes, had half-a-dozen thorns imbedded in my hands from grabbing for dear life any tree that could give me support, and had two very scratched, bloody and dirty legs by the time we reached the summit. I had no idea we would be in for mountain climbing like that, or I wouldn't have worn a dress. It really felt similar to a climbing wall at times. By the time we reached the top, everyone was beat, out of water and not looking forward to climbing down. It had taken us three hours to get to the top. Rob had predicted there would be no view at the top since the summit gets the most sunshine and trees like sunshine. Sure enough, it was solid trees.

Some ladies in the group had heard that there used to be a motorcross (motorized dirt bike) trail somewhere. We headed for the area that they wanted to check out and sure enough—we stumbled on the "real" trail. It was free of thorn bushes and only took us one hour to descend. People hesitated to pay the guide since the consensus was that he should pay *us* for showing him the trail! He did get a few tips. Then we were back on the boats for the 45 minute trip back to the mainland.

A few people in the hiking group decided to drink the local water since they were completely parched. Rob and I refused to take that risk since the temporary refreshment would likely result in troublesome, persistent health issues. When we returned to Zomba we were parched and it was almost dark. The kids had enjoyed their time with the Wegners. We drove home to Blantyre in the dark and thankfully made it safely.

The other day as I was driving in town, the passenger door of an oncoming minivan (packed with people) flew open as it drove toward me. It is a blessing that it wasn't the driver's door or it would have crashed right into me.

We tried a new vegetable called shu-shu, or *chokos*. Hannah loved it. It was different than anything else we have tried. It seems like a cross between a potato and squash. I'll try planting some. Sending—happily via email—our love, hugs and prayers, Rebecca

Lake Chilwa is the second biggest lake in Malawi after Lake Malawi. The lake is about 40 km (25 mi) long and 30 km (18 mi) wide. It is surrounded by wetlands that are home to water birds like pelicans, flamingos, herons, egrets and ducks. The islands in Lake Chilwa are said to be some of the most isolated communities in Malawi, having little contact with travellers. We thought they looked similar to many other villages in Malawi, including their centrally-located hand pump for water. Some of Rob's remote congregations are more off the beaten track than the Kachisi island community. Kachisi has tour groups that visit occasionally, allowing some interaction between the villagers and white people. Rob says that his Lower Shire congregations would likely never see 40 white people in their whole lives, let alone in one sitting!

Our exhilarating, exhausting and memorable experience climbing Mt. Kachisi gave me a few things to ponder. One of the tourists on the hike had a GPS along. What was interesting about the device was how ultimately useless it was! The man kept holding it out and declaring that we were going the right way. But his GPS could not direct us around the briars, the thorn bushes or the steep rocky inclines. In fact, it didn't register the proper hiking path at all. To me, the whole scenario seemed to parallel life in this sin-filled world. We could have a busload of advanced equipment to gain information, but if that equipment fails to inform us of the true path to heaven, it is useless. Only in God's Word do we find a valuable GPS: **G**od's **P**romised **S**avior. Only through Christ our Savior can we be assured of the correct way to eternal life in heaven.

Your word is a lamp to my feet
and a light for my path. Psalm 119:105

CHAPTER 7

FIRST EASTER; A FOND FAREWELL; AN AFRICAN ITINERARY

So the women hurried away from the tomb, afraid yet filled with joy, and ran to tell his disciples. Suddenly Jesus met them. "Greetings," he said. They came to him, clasped his feet and worshiped him. Then Jesus said to them, "<u>Do not be afraid</u>. <u>Go and tell</u> my brothers to go to Galilee; there they will see me." Matthew 28:8-10 (underlined emphasis mine)

"*Do not be afraid. Go and tell…*" Jesus' words to the fearful, joyful women make me nod in understanding. I too have great joy sharing the amazing gospel with my children, friends and neighbors here in Malawi. Yet I too am sometimes filled with unsettling fear. That's when I remember that Jesus' words to the women are for me too: "Don't be afraid. Go and tell." Whatever comes my way each day, I am reminded not to be afraid. I know that God has work here for me to do, and that He guides my daily walk. This was true as we approached our first Easter in Malawi—another special celebration far from our family and familiar traditions. This was true as we bid farewell to the Janoseks and realized the role we now had to fill without them. This was true as we watched little Nathanael struggle with his health again. It was also true as Malawi anticipated a presidential election that brought with it the possibility of riots. How encouraging to have Jesus himself telling me not to be afraid!

In the midst of all this it was a real blessing to prepare for the arrival of my family. As we planned an itinerary for them, I couldn't wait to add "show and tell" to my "go and tell!"

Sent: April 2, 2004
Subject: "powerful" birthday
Rebecca writes: Thanks for all your wonderful phone calls and birthday messages. It made my 30th birthday—and my first Malawian one—extra special.

Today one of our neighbors was digging a ditch and dug a deep trench right next to the two main poles of the electricity transformer for our area. The poles fell over and landed in a tree. We heard an ominous bang, smelled smoke and lost our power. On our way into town later we saw the transformer and tree in flames. We changed course and drove to report this to the ESCOM-power managers. They knew nothing about it and claimed that they would fix it that day. To my sheer amazement, it was indeed fixed later that evening. A real "powerful" birthday for me!

I went to a farewell party for Yvonne Janosek. Our phone has been out, so I didn't know what to bring for the potluck. I made a rhubarb dessert, since Rob brought back another bunch from Zomba. When I brought the dessert, it was put next to the chicken. Later, they carefully placed it at the end of the table all by itself. Many ladies asked me about it. After the main meal it was a big deal for everyone to go to the end of the table and taste a piece. I had been the only one to bring a dessert. It wasn't one of the things to sign up for—but I didn't know that. I took home a very empty pan.

I went to look up a phone number the other day but I couldn't find it. I paged around until I found a whole section of "late entries" at the end of the phone book. It includes people and businesses that submitted their numbers late. Who looks up a number twice or realizes that this late section exists? Today we went to the milk factory. They had no milk. How can a milk factory have no milk?

We had a Peace Corps couple, Stephanie and Joaquin Ramsey, over for lunch. They have bats that live in their *chimbudzi* (toilet), which sometimes fly out unexpectedly. Thankfully we don't have that problem, since we have flush toilets at our house. They told us that a friend of theirs had a break-in. The thief stole toothpaste but left his camera. When their friend developed his film, he discovered that the thief had accidently taken his own picture. They figure the flash went off and he got scared, dropped the camera and ran. Crazy!

Today the kids emptied the cupboard that had my metal pie plates and cupcake pans. They pretended to be drumming for the church choir. Love, Rebecca

As we were beginning to settle in to our new home in Malawi, the Janoseks, whom we were replacing, were preparing to depart. The women at church gave Yvonne a nice send off. The multi-cultural nature of the church made the meal unlike any potluck I had ever been to. This potluck had assorted chicken dishes, rice, *nsima*, boiled cassava, a plate of Indian *samosas*, Chinese spring rolls and—apart from my rhubarb dish— no desserts. Malawians generally don't eat desserts, although this is not necessarily because they don't like them. Desserts are quite impractical for the vast majority of Malawians. In a village there are no conventional ovens for baking. Nor is there access to ingredients like sweetened condensed milk, cream or chocolate. Apparently some Malawian children do not care for chocolate because they so rarely have it.

A Malawian's sweet tooth is most often satisfied by chewing on stalks of sugar cane (which I find similar to chewing on mildly sweet toothpicks). Malawians peel back the tough outer bark and tear off strips of the inner cane with their teeth. This they chew to a pulp, sucking out the sweet juice. Then they spit out the dry pulp, remnants of which are found scattered on every major thoroughfare. Chewing on sugar cane is actually healthier than it sounds. The juice is a source of hydration. The potassium in sugar cane aids digestion. Sugar cane also contains calcium, magnesium and Vitamin B. Some say that chewing the woody pulp strengthens a person's gums, but it doesn't do much for their pearly whites. Sugar cane is harvested in Malawi by burning the fields. When locals eat sugarcane, they bite through the burned outer layer (often containing ash), and their teeth become brown or even take on a blackish tint or streaks.

I was interested to learn that potlucks can be a sensitive issue here in Malawi. Food that is prepared in private is regarded with suspicion by some Malawians, because someone may have done *juju* "*w*itchcraft" to it. A potluck requires them to trust that no one did any funny business to the food. My mother-in-law told me that this is a big issue at their urban church in Lusaka, Zambia. The ladies there will often prepare food together for gatherings. Thankfully, at Beautiful Saviour the topic has been discussed and we have not had issues. As our church demographic becomes more integrated with different nationalities, these issues continually diminish.

I am not one to have a potty mouth, but I did mention in my email a *chimbudzi* that our Peace Corp friends have for a toilet. A *chimbudzi* is an African outhouse that consists of a hole in the ground around which four brick walls are built for a little privacy. A gap between the walls becomes the entrance. Sometimes there is a roof, sometimes not. The hole itself is often ringed by inlaid bricks. A fancy *chimbudzi* might have an old toilet seat strategically positioned on a ring of bricks built up around the hole. Rob recently saw one village *chimbudzi* that had no hole in the ground; just a pile of bricks. This puzzling arrangement must be on the low end of *chim* designs but easier to make. Fancy or not, they are usually an unsanitary, stinky place to visit. But when nature calls, they serve their purpose.

Sent: April 7, 2004
Subject: "Cell"ebrate
Rebecca writes: We are "cell"ebrating today because we got a cell phone! The phone will be a wonderful addition, since we rarely have a working phone at home.

On Tuesday Rob wanted to record his two radio sermons downtown. That didn't work and he'll have to go another time. Today he is out all day at two village churches. He is observing while John conducts the services and confirms some members.

Despite Rob being busy with church items, I had him set some rat traps and put rat poison in our attic area. We'd heard some mighty loud scratching and footsteps up there. It was high time to get the critters before they multiplied. Yesterday as I walked outside to greet a visiting friend, I stepped near a good-sized rat that was still squirming. Our gardener stabbed it with a stick.

This morning the church women and I made plans for when the Lutheran Women's Missionary Society (LWMS) ladies visit from the States. We will host them in Blantyre from May 6-9. That is the same weekend of our Music Society's choir concert. Since I'm performing some piano music in the concert, I'll see if I can be involved in both events.

I hope to take some baked goods and an Easter card over to our neighbors. We have only briefly met them. I think it would be good to be able to recognize our neighbors if they ever showed up at our gate. I'd like to let them know about our church and why we are here. One of our neighbors' security alarms went off again last night. Maybe we'll get an update on their security situation as well.

Before Hannah went to sleep, she looked at her pillow and announced, "My pillow is very big. I only use a little bit of it. I think there is room for Aunt Stephanie on this side and Grandma on that side. I'll sleep in the middle and there will be room for all three of us." She is very willing to accommodate everyone! She must have overheard us talking about sleeping arrangements recently. She listens carefully to what we say and is like a living tape recorder, ready and waiting to play back our conversations.

I hope you are having a meaningful Holy Week. (I do miss the special services here. I don't think you ever really appreciate things completely until they are gone.) God's blessings as we humbly follow our Savior to the cross and triumphantly to the empty tomb! Rebecca

I had missed the Advent preparation for our first Christmas in Malawi since we did not have midweek services. Now I found myself caught off guard again at Lent. Without any midweek Lenten services, I hardly knew Easter was around the corner. During our Stateside ministry, the midweek readings, choir songs and Easter preparations gave me ample time to prepare my heart and to contemplate the necessity and purpose of the first Easter. I realized I had hardly thought about the Passion history this year, until I saw Malawians carrying palm branches to church on Palm Sunday. I would have to augment my home devotions with more seasonal readings in the years to come.

Our new cell phone allowed me to be in contact with people despite our horrible land line. I took it in our room at night and felt safer knowing that I had a lifeline to the outside world if the need arose. It also helped ease the stress of Rob's frequent absences.

Sent: April 10, 2004
Subject: sharing Easter
Rebecca writes: Yesterday we saw two vervet monkeys playing in the trees. It was bizarre to think we weren't at the zoo and the monkeys were free to go anywhere!

I made two pounds of soft pretzel dough and formed them into crosses for Good Friday coffee hour. I also kept some for the beggars. I baked four mini cakes, put them in a tray with some crosses and an Easter card and took them to the neighbors. The west neighbor lady's name is Barel Tubb. She sent her cook home because of malaria, so she appreciated the plate of goodies. I think all our neighbors have cooks, house cleaners, gardeners and watchmen.

Last night the Wegners from Zomba asked if we wanted to join them for an Easter meal and games. They had already bought a ham and invited all the Blantyre gang. Rob and John will try to wrap up their services and confirmations quickly and join us if possible. It will be great to spend the day celebrating with the other families.

May you have a very joy-filled Easter celebrating Christ's resurrection. It is such a highlight in the church year and especially in our daily lives. Ultimately it is our reason for being here and sharing this Good News with others. He is risen—INDEED! Rebecca

We finally met our neighbors after being in Malawi for half a year! It took all afternoon to make it past the guards, gates, dogs and schedules to meet them. I was glad we now knew each other by name. As they enjoyed the home-baked treats, I hoped they would read the Easter message in the card. If they were looking for a place to worship, I had also included the details of our church, Beautiful Saviour.

Sent: April 11, 2004
Subject: Blessed Easter blessings to you all!
Rebecca writes: Happy Easter to you all! We had a nice service this morning downtown. We served dyed, hard-boiled eggs for coffee hour. At first the members were a bit skeptical to take a funny colored egg. But as we left church, the ground looked similar to Palm Sunday—except substitute colored egg shells in place of palm branches. We were literally walking on egg shells!

We are off to Zomba soon for the Easter dinner at Wegners. I am bringing a few dishes to pass. Thankfully I had done my baking yesterday morning—the power went off from 2pm until 9pm. We will also be gone for a few days at the mission Easter Retreat. Love, Rebecca

Each year, if funding allows, the missionaries from Zambia and Malawi gather after Easter for an Easter Retreat. The retreat is a time for the mission families to gather around God's Word in devotions, Bible studies and Sunday School. It is also a time for fellowship, games and family activities. The retreat closes with a communion service. This is a very special way to connect as fellow Lutheran Christians before heading our separate ways to continue spreading the Word in Africa. Over the years, our African mission families have been grateful for these refreshing spiritual retreats and for special offerings that make them possible.

Zambia and Malawi missionary families 2004

Sent: April 25, 2004
Subject: Blantyre update
Rebecca writes: We are in the dark again. Our phone has been out ever since we returned from the Easter Retreat. I'll send a message from someone else's computer this afternoon.

No news isn't exactly equal to good news. Nathanael has been quite sick. He wouldn't eat the day we left for the retreat. That night he had a fever and threw up repeatedly. We used a malaria test kit to test him for malaria. Throwing up is often a tell-tale sign of the disease. It registered negative. In addition to throwing up, he started terrible diarrhea. We were at our wits' end since he was very sick.

Rob preached for the Easter Retreat. One lady told him it was the best sermon she had ever heard. To God be the glory! We did enjoy being there, but our participation was scaled way back when Nathanael got sick. I thought it was a fine scenario in which to take care of a sick kid: I could hold him while I sat in my chair listening to devotions, and know that I had nothing more pressing to attend to. I even saw a monitor lizard dig around some bushes and then climb a tree as Nathanael slept.

After several days of Nathanael's sickness, we took him to a doctor who prescribed Flagyl (metronidazole)—a powerful antibiotic for bacterial infections. Nathanael has finally stopped the terrible diarrhea and is getting back to normal.

Hannah had a 104°F fever after church on Sunday. We had a quiet afternoon and read books together. I am using hand sanitizer wipes like they are going out of style to keep any more germs from spreading.

We thank you for your prayers—and I **really** mean that. While we were gone, our three neighbors—the ones I gave Easter cards and coffee cakes—all had thieves on their properties. Our neighbors to the east had their dogs poisoned and killed. Amazingly our house was left alone. One missionary said if we don't feel safe we could relocate. Just what we want to think about—moving—AGAIN! If our house is locked up, it is very safe. I lock it when Rob is gone and now early in the evenings too. The days when my family lived in Florida prepared me for safety and security awareness. We dealt with burglars and prowlers there too. As always, we leave the rest in the Lord's capable hands. Love, Rebecca

"For the eyes of the Lord range throughout the earth
to strengthen those whose hearts
are fully committed to him." 2 Chronicles 16:9

This passage from Chronicles did not make much of an impression on me until we moved to Malawi. I felt like only the Lord could possibly know our neighborhood security situation and help. I did not feel like we were just waiting in line to be sabotaged, but the recent break-ins at our neighbors' houses certainly made us aware of the potential danger.

A few verses later in Chronicles (16:12) there is another obscure verse. It reads, *"In the thirty-ninth year of his reign [king] Asa was afflicted with a disease in his feet. Though his disease was severe, even in his illness he did not seek help from the Lord, but only from the physicians."* King Asa was afflicted and sought earthly help but did not seek the Lord. Two years after this affliction he died. Our family had already encountered afflictions of health. Now our sense of security and safety was afflicted too. We had earthly measures of deliverance in place: a property wall, razor wire, guards, a siren that signals a rapid response team, grates, gates, burglar bars and locks. However, I felt if we solely relied on these earthly measures then we were no better off than King Asa. He left out the Lord. He was not delivered. We are encouraged in 1 Peter 5:7, *"Cast all your anxiety on him because he cares for you."* With the almighty God of the universe on our side to protect, guide and deliver us, I knew I did not have to be anxious. Instead I could be thankful for God's ranging eyes and His deliverance. In fact, I should give thanks for that daily—without ceasing!

Sent: April 30, 2004
Subject: wonder of wonders
Rebecca writes: (Sing to Fiddler on the Roof*'s "Miracle of Miracles" song)*
"Wonder of wonders, miracle of miracles,
God took a problem once again

Used a Malawi phone repair man.
We are hooked up for now, you see;
You never know when you'll hear from me!"

Currently the power is on and we have a dial tone, so I'll type an update.

We are still getting rain and I keep discovering moldy things. We are keeping closet doors open and fans blowing to reduce the moisture.

I am happy to report that Nathanael is finally doing MUCH better. The Flagyl helped him but altered his appetite for a week. Nathanael walked over to me at the computer just now with something in his hand. I opened up mine to catch his treasure. It was a dead beetle—thanks.

Hannah has been doing well. Today she was playing with plastic people. Her play mom was saying that her son was very sick with bilharzia and hoped he wouldn't die. She also told me (after a sermon on Revelation), "In my room I saw seven lampstands and upon them was Jesus holding seven stars. In one of these seven churches we go to church." Be assured her bedroom has one lamp, and no one stands on it.

We cut and hung the first bunch of our bananas in our garage. There are about eight dozen on the bunch. I think a bunch of bananas is called a hand. Let me tell you, I must "hand" it to the women who carry these bunches on their heads. They are seriously heavy! We'll surely "go bananas" when they all ripen at once.

We recently found a sisal cactus plant that dropped hundreds of little sisals on the ground. Rob got a big bucket and collected a few dozen for our gardener to plant all along the outside of our wall. That will make a good protective barrier in a few years.

Those with upcoming Malawi travel plans might want to know our weather has turned much cooler. Wearing layers is helpful so that you can add or remove as the temperatures fluctuate. I know some of you have asked about bringing dresses and skirts. It was a law about 10 years ago that women must wear skirts/dresses. The hem had to touch the floor if you knelt on the ground. Women don't have a dress code anymore, but I still prefer to wear a dress or skirt to town so I don't get more stares. You will stick out no matter what you wear. God bless, Rebecca

Packing, getting shots and applying for passports and visas are just some of the hurdles of a trip to a third world country. But my family was jumping over those hurdles—and jumping for joy—that we would see each other again soon.

INCOMING EMAIL: April 30, 2004
Subject: Tickets purchased
Mom and Dad Staude write: How wonderful it is to hear from you! It's been so

long. We purposely have been trying NOT to write much because we suspected that your phone lines were down. Then we figured that after you were reconnected, you'd be so back-logged with emails that it might crash your computer and you'd have to start over.

It is five weeks and five days to our departure. So much of our daily lives now focus around "the Staude Safari." We started taking our typhoid pills. We have our passports and tickets and are getting excited. Now we are working on our Zambia Visa Applications. The itinerary you sent was the highlight of the week!

Rob, we can't wait to see firsthand the African mission work that you are doing. You are in our daily prayers that God will keep you safe and bless your ministry in Africa. Wishing you God's continued blessing as you serve Him. Lots of love, Mom and Dad

One drawback of traveling halfway around the world is that there are no direct flights and many legs to the trip. A Wisconsin traveler en route to Malawi, Africa passes through eight different time zones on multiple airlines, with layovers at each exchange.

My family would not require a visa to enter Malawi, but we would all need visas to travel across the border into Zambia to visit the South Luangwa Game Park. This outstanding park would prove to be well worth the extra effort and additional fees.

Sent: May 2, 2004
Subject: in the dark
Rebecca writes: Rob is at Khanyepa congregation today. Next month when Rob is scheduled to visit that church, we'll all go along!

Yesterday we spent the entire morning in the dark. I had planned to put my power juicer (birthday gift) to work on a bag of lemons. First, I had the kids play with them on the floor to soften them. Secondly, I tried getting the juicer to work. I plugged it in twice, checked that I had the correct adapter for the plug and flipped the switch a few times. Finally it dawned on me that our power was still off. Ha ha. After the power returned the juicer worked slick.

I interviewed the Janoseks for a website write-up on his ministry, since I am the official Malawi Public Relations person. One of John's striking comments was that he'll miss the life-and-death driving here. On any given trip, a crash or accident is a distinct possibility. John concluded that it is too easy to fall asleep while driving in the USA, because the roads are smooth and clear. After they move, we will be the solo Blantyre missionary family for a time.

At church I talked to a couple from Norway who had visited South Luangwa National Park in Zambia. That is the one we are planning to visit in June. The couple raved about it. They saw elephant, hippo, lion and leopard. They even had armed guards walk them to dinner at night because there were elephant close to their camp. How about that to whet your appetite?

Our power is off, so the generator is running to make this possible. I should shut it off since it is blowing a heavy exhaust into the house. God bless, Rebecca

Hearing about South Luangwa was thrilling. It has been called one of the greatest wildlife sanctuaries in the world. The 9050 km^2 (5620 mi^2) park is situated in the Luangwa valley. Its prolific animal and bird species concentrate around the Luangwa River and the surrounding wetlands. There are 60 different animal species and over 400 different bird species that roam freely through the park. As my family would soon find out, the hippopotamus is one animal that a visitor cannot miss—according to estimates, there are at least 50 hippos per kilometer of the Luangwa River!

Sent: May 7, 2004
Subject: gathering staples
Rebecca writes: We were notified that our power will be on for about 15 more minutes this morning and then will be cut all day until 5pm.

The LWMS ladies came and went. Marilyn Ewart, Sally Valleskey and Lois Meyer were the ladies who came to Blantyre. They had a lovely presentation. We had them for dinner on Friday and enjoyed visiting.

Recently we were warned that there may be some minor rioting in town, since there are presidential elections next week. We were told: get all your staples and fuel up your car just in case you need to stay put for a while. Rob wondered why staples are so important, ha ha! Hey, I've got lots of food in the freezer (bought and prepared ahead for your coming), so if need be I could use that for such an emergency! Love Rebecca

Between 1891 and 1964 Malawi was controlled by the British Central Africa Protectorate. Independence was gained in 1964 when Malawi became a one-party state with Hastings Kamuzu Banda as its first president. Banda was regarded as a hero and soon declared "president for life" of Malawi. He ran a mostly peaceful dictatorship for 30 years, enforcing loyalty with the help of a paramilitary wing of his government. President Banda enacted many laws. Women couldn't wear pants, or skirts that revealed their knees. Men couldn't grow their hair below their collars; those who arrived from overseas with long locks were treated to a haircut before they left the airport. Every public building had to hang a picture of President Banda on its wall; nothing could be placed higher than his portrait, not even a clock. Censorship was rampant. Churches had to be government-sanctioned. (When the LCCA asked President Banda for permission to expand our mission arm into Malawi from Zambia in the early 1960's, he wouldn't allow it unless the LCCA also provided medical care to the Malawian people. What seemed to be a barrier soon became a blessing—a door to sharing the gospel—since the Malawi Medical Mission was born.) When President Banda was finally deposed in 1994, he and several associates were put on trial for the 1983 alleged murder of four politicians. Later they were acquitted of all charges.

Increasing domestic unrest led the Malawian people to vote for a multi-party democracy. The first free and fair national elections were held in May, 1994. Bakili Muluzi was elected President. He was re-elected after serving his first five-year term, although this re-election brought Malawi to the brink of civil strife. Christian tribes dominant in the north did not approve of Muluzi, a Muslim from the south. As a result, Muslim property and mosques were destroyed.

By the time our family had arrived in Malawi, President Muluzi had served his two allowable five-year terms and Malawi was poised for its first transition between democratically elected presidents. Democracy was still in its infancy in Malawi, as in many African countries. With elections came the possibility of a breakdown of peace in the form of riots, strikes and random violence. White foreigners could be particular targets in such incidents; we were told to be prepared to hunker down.

Sent: May 15, 2004
Subject: farewell
Rebecca writes: Today was the Janoseks' farewell worship service at Epiphany congregation. Many national pastors and congregation members came. Many church choirs sang and danced. The majority of the service was in Chichewa. It was a fitting send-off to worship and celebrate with missionaries and nationals alike; after all, that was the essence of John's ministry.

After we were fed with God's Word there was a feast (Malawian style) for those in attendance. Hannah loved the rice and chicken lunch that she ate with her bare hands. She wore the African dress from Grandma Wendland and fit right in. I did not eat any of the food since I seem to be too sensitive to the different cooking; though the smells of the good food did make me hungry. Others happily ate whatever portion I didn't.

Here is the poem I wrote for the Janoseks:

God Bless Your Retirement 2004
Jesus motivates your African day
A family you raised in Malawi
New life to Christians in the bush
One day at a time; 40 years it took
Seeing growth; enjoying God's creation
Educating, baptizing, many-a-confirmation
Keep the great commission in daily prayer
Special blessings, John and Yvonne, as you retire!

Yesterday the Music Society outdoor concert went well. Several choir members are leaving Malawi permanently. Official good-byes were said after the concert. I am learning that constant turn-over is a part of life here. I invited a lady from the orchestra to Bible Group. The choir is a great avenue to meet other expatriates and let them know about the LCCA and our work here. I also met a doctor whom I'll keep in mind for future medical needs.

Our phone has been remarkable. We have used email for several days in a row. I wonder if our phone service has recently improved to make a good impression for the upcoming elections, which have now been moved to Thursday. May that be peaceful. Great to hear from you all—it shrinks those daunting miles. Love, Rebecca

I was finding out that an unavoidable part of living here is the sadness of saying goodbye to people heading back to their home countries. It is neat to befriend so many different people from around the world, but the friendships are all too temporary. As their contracts expire, they leave. Goodbyes are common enough even in our LCCA circle as missionaries retire or receive a call back to the States. That part of living here continues to be wearisome.

Saying goodbye to the Janoseks was difficult, but their departure from the field came with one small consolation: I bought their piano before they left. Now I could have music at my fingertips again!

Sent: May 22, 2004
Subject: go bananas
Rebecca writes: Amazingly, our phone line has remained in good order for almost **one week** now. The rains have pretty much subsided, so maybe that is the difference. At this time of year our daylight hours start shrinking. The sun falls so quickly below the horizon it's as if someone cut its string. Of course this means our upcoming traveling will be affected, since safe traveling is bookended by dawn and dusk.

The election results should be calculated today—no word yet. I liked Election Day: it was so quiet around here AND we had no power cuts! That is great because I have been cooking like crazy. One whole shelf in the freezer is now dedicated to pizzas. (125 imported pepperonis in all—nothing like killing the fattened calf to celebrate when you come!) I also made several banana breads out of our very own bananas. The next bunch is ripening in our garage.

We have a spotted eagle owl on our property. The other night it was in the tree right by our kitchen window. We had a terrific view! (Some Africans don't like owls. They believe if an owl is hanging around it implies there will be a death.) God bless, Rebecca

Thankfully, Election Day went by peacefully and was a good example of how elections should be conducted. Bingu wa Mutharika won the election, a man with a long career as a civil servant and a doctorate in economics. Our gardener went to town to vote. To no one's surprise, he spent the entire day waiting in a line.

Sent: May 25, 2004
Subject: sew what?
Rebecca writes: Our phone has been bad again, probably from the late heavy rains. Rob could see an email with a picture attachment awaiting us. However, with the bad phone line, fickle online service, and computer crashing, it has taken us several days to try and download it.

I spent all of yesterday making the guestroom bed nets. I bought two rectangular twin-size nets and sewed them together. I felt like I was sewing a wedding dress with all that netting. I managed to keep it all straight, and it turned out exactly how I wanted it. Hooray! Love, Rebecca

My mom gave me a heavy-duty sewing machine for Christmas shortly before we moved to Africa—and what a blessing that has been. Even though I've never had a formal sewing class, I have frequently tackled mending and alterations. After our shipment came and I got my sewing machine hooked up to a step-down transformer, I decided to make drapes along with my bed net project. In time I would also repair rugs, sew play clothes and pillow coverings, install zippers and even make zebra-striped aprons for the kids. All this practice and experimentation means I have broken my fair share of needles…but I can rethread the machine in seconds!

Sent: May 27, 2004
Subject: u.t.w.
Rebecca writes: Thanks for all your updates. It is great to enjoy the festivities—graduations, confirmations, showers and wedding events—vicariously.

Rob was under the weather (u.t.w.) last week, and it seems the rest of us caught up. My other projects will have to wait now.

I couldn't believe our phone yesterday. Rob was planning to send some emails. He checked the phone line and it was dead. Then he checked again and told me it was playing a tune. I put my ear to the receiver and heard "FÜR ELISE." I listened in astonishment. Since when does Malawi Telecom play filler music while they take our phone off the hook? Could this be the latest improvement? God bless, Rebecca

Sent: June 4, 2004
Subject: mefloquine
Rob writes: Hi! You asked what the most common side effects of mefloquine

(a malaria prophylaxis) are. They are upset stomach and more vivid dreams than usual. When our family has taken it (for traveling outside of Blantyre), we have had no problems. The side effects pale in comparison to one potential side effect of malaria: death. Mefloquine needs to be worked through your system two weeks prior to provide maximum protection against malaria.

Rebecca is planning and preparing meals for when everybody's here. That way she can spend more time with you and less time cooking for 12. I am squeezing in extra trips to my congregations now. They are long days, but it is worth it! If we're not able to communicate again before you leave, may you have a wonderful time through Europe! May you see lots, wonder lots, expand your minds and horizons lots, find many more things to praise our Savior Creator about and have a safe and blessed journey! We eagerly look forward to seeing you next week! Love, Rob

Sent: June 5, 2004
Subject: counting down
Rebecca writes: We returned from Lilongwe meetings yesterday. It was VERY DRY there and my lips chapped the whole time. I'm told that is very good for game viewing (the dryness, not necessarily the chapped lips).

Some bad news: our yard worker has malaria. Apparently the Chichewa word for malaria, *malungo,* is also equivalent to "fever." It can be quite a challenge to know if someone who says they have malaria simply has a fever or is sick with the dreaded illness from the anopheles mosquito. Either way, I pray he recovers soon.

With the election over, we are back to untimely power outages. Hopefully we'll have power when you come so we can **heat** and eat our food!

Earlier today we went with Rob to his bush congregation, Nalipa. During church Hannah was excited to give the offering, since members walk up to the front of church to put it in the basket. One lady gave us MK50 (about 45 cents) to buy sodas for the kids on the way home. That was a generous gift from their extremely meager incomes.

This morning as I drank the fake orange-flavored Sobo juice we buy here, I thought I'd remind you to savor the American foods and familiar tastes before you leave. Food here won't taste the same. Not always in a bad way—just different. God bless, Rebecca

I wanted my family to be prepared for the different tastes that they would experience in Malawi. However, that would probably be the least of their cultural adjustments. I also planned to explain our mosquito precautions, mention our different voltage (220 voltage in Malawi, rather than 110 voltage as in the States), point out the outlet converters and transformers and remind them not to drink the tap water. I would inform them of the current exchange rate and give them some local currency. I wanted them to know the whereabouts of the flashlights, matches and candles. I knew it would be a helpless feeling to be in the dark in an unfamiliar place if the lights unexpectedly went out. And of course they needed to be aware of our security matters. They would have to note the locations of the quick-response panic buttons and the keys to unlock all the doors and door grates. They would even have to be shown how to lock the front doors of many vehicles here, which require that the outside handle is held up while the door is being shut. It's all too easy to unknowingly leave a door unlocked; I'm sure more than a few free lunches have been "harvested" from such vehicles parked downtown.

Sent: June 10, 2004
Subject: almost here
Rebecca writes: Thanks, Mom, for your nice email letter. We won't expect to hear from you again until we hear your voices at Chileka Airport in Blantyre. They may search your things. Stand and watch carefully. We'll be waiting for you. One more warning for tourists has popped into my head: if you see a group of kids who are trying to entertain you…watch out! Sometimes it is a scam that involves another kid in the background, scouting out valuables to grab.

Enjoy the magnificent sites and sights enroute. You have family history in the making! Lord willing, we'll see you soon! God bless, Rebecca

The grains of the proverbial hourglass had almost drained; my family was almost here! It had been the better part of a year since we had left America to start a new life in Malawi. Before our departure, my sister Stephanie had hoped out loud that I would not change too much. I had thought of her comment often in the intervening year, because I *had* to change in order to survive and function in my new environment. I had to change to fit in. I had to change to deal with the tasks at hand. Those changes were hopefully all for the better. It was going to be interesting to see if my family had changed much themselves. I would find out soon enough. Meanwhile I prayed that their long trip would be problem-free. I kept this passage from Philippians foremost in my mind:

> *"Do not be anxious about anything, but in everything,*
> *by prayer and petition, with thanksgiving,*
> *present your requests to God.*
> *And the peace of God, which transcends all understanding,*
> *will guard your hearts and your minds in Christ Jesus."*
> *Philippians 4:6-7*

CHAPTER 8

A VISIT FROM MY FAMILY

*"Seek first his kingdom and his righteousness,
and all these things
will be given to you as well."*
Matthew 6:33

This passage from Matthew was an encouragement to me after our move to Malawi. Rob's call had required us to put God's kingdom in priority position: in front of family and familiarity with first world comforts and convenience. When Rob accepted this call, we had trusted that God would take care of us in every way. And He had. Nine months later we were not lacking any necessity, and we enjoyed abundant blessings in Malawi despite our difficult separation from family. When I stepped onto the airplane in Chicago in September 2003, I had fully expected that two years would pass before I would see my family again. Now the Lord was heaping an extra and unexpected blessing onto our plate: the opportunity to spend the next few weeks, from June 15-29, with my family. The fact that they were coming around the world to visit our home meant worlds to me!

Rob's parents had traveled from Zambia to visit us in December. Their Christmas visit has become an annual tradition that we eagerly anticipate and cherish. It is a blessing to share time with them: two people who understand firsthand our adjustments and struggles. When we visit with Rob's parents, *I am the one* learning from their 40 years of valuable cultural experiences. I knew that the visit of my family was going to be an entirely different kind of visit. My family had never set foot on the continent of Africa. Everything would be new to them. I had spent many email hours trying to communicate effectively what we were experiencing here. That had been a difficult task without a shared cultural context. For that very reason, Stateside mission committee members often visit the African fields. If someone wants to truly *see*, *understand* and *empathize* with the struggles, challenges and blessings of those who live in a foreign mission field, that person must walk the same paths and in the same shoes. The fact that my family wanted to share a piece of our African lifestyle despite the distance and expense brought me immense joy.

And now they were on their way! All the bedrooms were ready with extra beds, linens and nets. Food was prepared, little personalized clay huts awaited each person's place at the dining table and we had even scattered bougainvillea flower petals down the path to the front door for a tropical feel. We wanted this to be a very special African welcome. When the day came, we waited patiently for the South African Airways 10pm flight, which this evening carried extra-precious passengers and cargo. Finally it arrived—landing abruptly, as is usual, on the very short runway at Chileka. Attendants wheeled the outdoor staircases to the plane's exit doors, and people began streaming out. I saw my sister first and we wildly waved our flashlights from the outdoor balcony to catch her attention. Tears came to my eyes. We had been preparing and waiting so long; I wondered what they would think of Blantyre, of Malawi, of Africa as they stepped foot for the first time in this unfamiliar part of God's creation!

Staude Family First Impressions

To "shock" vegetables means to pull them from boiling water and plunge them directly into an ice bath. Culture "shock" is a transition that can be just as extreme and jolting. It had been several years since my first visit to Africa in 2001, but I could easily remember the feeling of stepping onto foreign turf for the first time. I had been bombarded by unusual sights, sounds and smells, none of which bore much resemblance to any of my other experiences. My family's sensory shock began the moment they disembarked their plane. In the following sub-chapters I have recorded my family's impressions, to give you a taste of visiting Malawi for the first time.

As soon as we got off the jet, we were met with immediate differences that put us way outside our comfort zone. It felt like true culture shock. The runway seemed too short; the airport, which consisted of a single building, looked primitive and makeshift. There were neither terminals nor concourses nor an exit-tunnel to guide us to the building; we just walked straight off the plane and onto the runway. We picked up our luggage right off the pavement. The runway lights turned off immediately after our arrival—before we were even in the building! Inside the airport, everything was dusty and dirty, and there was no toilet paper in any of the airport bathroom stalls. We noted that flights between Blantyre and South Africa, a major destination, only come and go twice a week. We felt overwhelmed at the customs desk, especially since we could not understand the questions that the lady was asking us...IN ENGLISH! We were immediately swarmed by porters who wanted to make tips. We all remember very clearly how Rebecca took charge, got us through customs and chased away the throng of porters. We could not imagine what it was like for people to arrive without such help.

Merely getting to Africa can be an overwhelming experience. But all eight family members (and their luggage) had arrived safely. Their familiar voices were music in the house. Hannah and Nathanael were in their element with the extra family attention. It had been almost a year since we had seen each other, but it felt like hardly any time had passed once we were together again. Email had kept us up to speed on many big issues, but now we were eager to share the small day-to-day aspects of African life with them. We also found ourselves reconnecting with USA culture and events as we chatted with my family about recent Stateside news and sports trivia.

Staude Family on the Town

In the days to follow, we showed my family our tropical property and ventured into town for a tour of Blantyre.

The sights, sounds and smells of Africa were very different. All our senses were aroused. The smells, in particular, were strong: we could smell the pungent burning leaves and trash, diesel exhaust, different pollens and strong body odor. Bugs swarmed around us and grasshoppers abounded. As a large group of white Americans we stood out like a sore thumb. The constant gawking we attracted made us feel like movie stars at times...or easy targets. The language barrier was evident, and often it was English that we could not understand. Burglar bars, razor wire and security were everywhere. It was quite a job to keep things locked up and secure. At dusk, taking mosquito precautions and putting down all the bed nets was quite time consuming.

Providing food was a major undertaking. Grocery stores were scantily stocked compared to stores in the States, and none of them carried convenience foods. We had to plan ahead for milk and bread items. All meals were made completely from scratch. The meats, cheeses, milk and even desserts had unusual tastes. Rob treated us to a batch of outstanding homemade ice cream—that thankfully tasted familiar! Water had to be boiled and filtered, even for brushing teeth. Having safe tap water in the States is something we had taken for granted. Raw foods were soaked in chemicals. On the side of the road we could buy sugar cane, grilled maize—which tasted like eating "old maid" popcorn kernels—and the infamous mice-on-a-stick. Those sure caught our attention when we first saw them! Malawians skewer about a dozen mice on a stick, roast them until they are almost black and crispy and wave them at passing cars in hopes of winning a customer. We did stop to take some pictures. None of us was brave enough to try eating them.

Driving on the left side of the road took adjusting. People and animals were walking everywhere—even on the road! The contrast between shantytown inhabitants and the better-dressed business class people was very noticeable. Minibuses—crammed with an unsafe number of people—weaved in and out of traffic and were a real menace. Many vehicles, including large trucks, were broken down right in the road. Branches were cut down and placed near the truck as a warning. The road conditions were poor by USA standards. Gasoline/diesel fuel was expensive and at times hard to get.

Staude Family on Safari

We packed in the sights so my family could enjoy the breadth and depth of the beauty of God's creation on this side of the world. Within Malawi, we journeyed east to the Zomba plateau, north to Lake Malawi and then south to Nyala Game Park in the Lower Shire Valley. We took them across the border into Zambia for our much anticipated trip to South Luangwa, the world-class game park nestled in the Luangwa escarpment. That trip required extra visas and extremely rough traveling, but it was a highlight of a lifetime for my family. Rob and I had tried to describe Africa's beautiful scenery, stunning night skies and amazing wildlife, but somehow none of these things could mean as much until my family had experienced them firsthand.

The diverse beauty of Malawi is amazing! We traveled from mountains to plateaus to rain forests to the dry dusty African plains. We saw palm trees, banana trees, acacia trees, baobabs, poinsettia bushes and blooming flowers of all kinds.

We stopped a few times to look at curios (souvenirs). The vendors swarmed around us and kept reminding us that, "It costs nothing to look." Malawian children often ran after our vehicles as we pulled away. They would shout some of the few English words they knew: "Give me money!"

We ran over a dog that darted in front of us as we started out for Zambia. But that was just the beginning of the animals we would see. South Luangwa Game Park was outstanding. It reminded us of the Garden of Eden. Once, as we gazed from left to right across a wide plain, we could see in that single glance zebra, wildebeest, impala, waterbuck and warthogs. We were also treated to sightings of kudu, giraffe, Cape buffalo, elephant and throngs of beautiful birds. We never tired of seeing in the wild what we could only see in a zoo back in the States. The kids loved seeing the monkeys, though the creatures became a nuisance. They took food right off our outdoor dining table and ate it in the treetops above us. At night we had the rare treat of seeing lions, a lioness with twin cubs, and hyenas. Crocodiles and hippos were ever-present near the water's edge. We were escorted by armed guards at night if we ventured out of our chalet. We realized why this was necessary when we awoke one morning to find large hippo tracks right outside our front door. It is not every day that we get to wake up next to a hippo!

We were all amazed at the beautiful night sky and the multitude of stars in the southern hemisphere, undiluted by city lights.

Staude family safari

Staude Family in the Bush

We all are one in mission; We all are one in call,
Our varied gifts united By Christ the Lord of all.
A single great commission Compels us from above
To plan and work together That all may know Christ's love. (CW 566:1)

This hymn had often come to mind in the last nine months as I thought of my family working *together* for Christ, even though we were separated by thousands of miles. Each of us, on our separate continents with our varied gifts, was supporting the work of the Lord. Now they were right here with us and we had a golden chance to share some aspects of the Malawian ministry with them. During their whirlwind two-week stay, we managed to visit some of the African villages where Rob conducts his mission work. This was the most special opportunity of all, since that was why we were here: not merely to revel in the adventure and beauty of a foreign country, but to share Christ's love with the people of Malawi.

If anyone thinks that a missionary just grabs his Bible, hops on a plane to Africa and goes hut-to-hut evangelizing people in the bush—they should know it is not that simple. We saw that there is a LOT more involved than one would imagine to travel to Malawi, to live there, and to share God's Word in the villages. It was a privilege to experience.

The roads off the beaten path were really rough and full of potholes and ruts. We were amazed at how much the native women carried on their heads. Malawian women obviously do a great deal of the work to manage their families. As we drove, we saw them working in fields, gathering large quantities of firewood, washing their clothes at the river and gathering water in large pots to take home. Even the young children carried buckets of water on their heads. Sometimes we saw a brother or sister strapped in a chitenje *on their older sibling's back.*

We were met with great enthusiasm when we reached a village church. The joy these Christians have is awesome, especially considering their physical poverty. We all enjoyed their beautiful musical ability and were eager to listen to the choirs in church, even though we could not understand the Chichewa words. We were presented with gifts of food from the members in honor of our coming. That was truly humbling, since we have so much already and they have so little. Ultimately, no matter what our physical circumstances, when we have Christ, we have everything! That treasure is something we share in common with these Malawian believers, both in this life and in the next.

We all are called to service, To witness in God's name.
Our ministries are different; Our purpose is the same:
To touch the lives of others With God's surprising grace,
So every folk and nation May feel God's warm embrace. (CW 566:2)

Rob and I had experienced God's guiding hand as we settled on this far side of the sea. My family had been able to see that as they spent some time with us. Then, all too soon, they were packing to return to the States. As the hymn verse says, though our purpose was the same, we had different ministries on different continents. It was difficult to say goodbye. While my family was visiting, I felt like the beaming kid at the top of a teeter-totter: on top of the world. After they left, it felt as if the kid at the bottom of the teeter-totter had jumped off when I wasn't looking. I came jolting to the ground, hard. It hurt. But with their visit behind us, we needed to pick up the pieces and continue the work that we were called to do.

Sent: June 30, 2004
Subject: homeward bound
Rebecca writes: We certainly treasured the time that you were here with us. I

A Visit From My Family

wish I had brought my camera to the airport when your plane took off at 6am. The sun rays were just beginning to radiate from the horizon as your plane ascended. It was a spectacular shot! I will keep that picture in my mind as an "uplifting" ending to our time together. Your departure reminds me all the more that heaven is our home. The good times on earth seem too short and can never last as long as we would like. Thankfully we will share time together for all eternity.

I'm pleased that you all can picture our place now. Many thanks again for all the gifts. We really appreciate you remembering (and finding space in your luggage) to bring all the little things that make our life easier here and remind us of America—thank you! We are blessed here and have all that we need. The extras are a great bonus. Thanks a million. We love you all, Rebecca

With their departure came a simultaneous yearning to see my family again. I found myself turning the proverbial hourglass over and beginning the countdown to our furlough, still about a year away. In the meantime, I needed something to focus on. The Malawi Ladies' Retreat was the next big event in October, and Rob's parents were planning to visit again at Christmas. Those few rays of sunshine broke up the chunks of time that seemed lengthy, lonely and tiring.

Tearful farewells are a part of mission life

Sent: July 1, 2004
Subject: airport special notice
Rebecca writes: Today we received this letter concerning the Chileka (Blantyre) airport. I'm glad your travels here weren't affected by anything like this!
SPECIAL NOTICE: *Air Traffic Control Malawi has advised all flights must be airborne from Chileka Airport by 17:15hrs. This is due to nonfunctioning runway lights.*

I wasn't too far off the mark when I was marveling that the Chileka airport even <u>had</u> night lights. I don't think the Staude family's 10pm flight would have worked out with these present conditions. We were certainly blessed with smooth travels during your stay. We pray that God is keeping you safe on your long return journey.

Rob has had two rigorous days out to the valley congregations. We are still adjusting to the lull after your departure. God bless, Rebecca

Rob has figured that with all the intercontinental travel he has done in his life, he currently has enough mileage to take him to the moon and most of the way back. It felt like I had prayed more about traveling in this past year than in all my other years combined. And pray I did. In my mind ran the constant thought, "May God be with you 'til we meet again." We prayed that God would keep us all in His care as we carried out our different lives and different ministries around the world.

Now let us be united, And let our song be heard;
Now let us be a vessel For God's redeeming Word.
We all are one in mission; We all are one in call,
Our varied gifts united By Christ, the Lord of all. (CW 566:3)

Words by Rusty Edwards
© 1986 Hope Publishing Co., Carol Stream, IL 60188.
All rights reserved. Used by permission.

CHAPTER 9

BLOOM WHERE GOD PLANTS YOU

*I walk with Jesus all the way; His guidance never fails me.
He takes my ev'ry fear away When Satan's pow'r assails me,
And, by his footsteps led, My path I safely tread.
In spite of ills that threaten may, I walk with Jesus all the way. (CW 431:5)*

At this time one year ago, in the summer of 2003, we were in the midst of packing, moving and transitioning from Wisconsin to life in Malawi. One way the mission helped us to prepare for the upcoming transition was through an orientation class for new missionaries. The week-long orientation class spent time on world mission policies and procedures, as well as on interpersonal relationships such as language learning, stress, conflict management, spiritual renewal, culture shock and cultural adaptation. After we had lived in Malawi several months, I was asked by the orientation committee to write a list of "Do's and Don'ts" that might be helpful to other new missionaries on their way to Africa. I don't know if it was helpful to anyone else, but it was a good exercise for me!

DO:
- Use a battery-powered alarm clock daily.
- Freeze your flour to eliminate crawling creatures.
- Meet your neighbors in spite of difficulties.
- Try to learn about the new animals, spiders, snakes and vegetation in your area. This knowledge will help you marvel at God's creation and could also be a lifesaving skill.
- Have a flashlight or headlamp handy, especially at dinner and bath time.
- "Bloom where God plants you!" He alone gives us the strength to face each day no matter where we are in the world.

DON'T:
- Expect local food to taste like USA food; you'll be disappointed.

- Store things under your bed in the rainy season.
- Be embarrassed to ask AGAIN to clarify a conversation.
- Get frustrated by in-your-face vendors. Their livelihood depends on their skill at being a living commercial. They usually "turn off" when you politely walk away.
- Ever take your phone, power or security for granted.
- Get so caught up in the differences of your new environment that you miss the good things it has to offer. Doing without a certain item or living under different conditions can be a new way to serve the Lord and show thankfulness for his blessings.

When my dad accepted a call to a church in Florida years ago, one of my mom's friends gave her a cross-stitched hanging with the words, *"Bloom where God plants you."* Her friend realized that being in the ministry meant moving around periodically—sometimes far away from friends and family. It was a special reminder to my mom that adjusting to her new home was one way she could support Dad in the ministry. We children learned to adjust too. Each ministry-relocation meant making a different house our home, switching schools and making new friends.

Here in Malawi I also have a *"Bloom where God plants you"* reminder sign by our front door. Every time I see it I am reminded that I am able to bloom here because God has promised to be with me. Of course, blooming means first putting down roots. My family's visit had reminded me that I had one network of roots deeply planted with them in the States and another, newer, network of roots here in Africa. The life of a missionary must include both sets of roots. I had to maintain my family connections and USA ties for my own sake as well as for my children, who would one day go to school in the States and perhaps settle there. But I also had to bloom where I was now planted, in Malawi. That meant shifting my focus from the wonderful visit of my family to the work at hand.

Sent: July 2, 2004
Subject: back to work
Rob writes: We are so happy that you all returned safely and are thankful to you for coming and sharing such a wonderful time with us. And now, wow, things have picked right up! We spent Tuesday cleaning up and getting used to the shock of an "empty" house once again. We also have to shift mental gears, because what we had looked forward to for so long and enjoyed so thoroughly is now only being seen in the rearview mirror of memory. How wonderful that in heaven we'll enjoy a perfection that will never come to an end.

On Thursday I spent eight grueling hours trying to get all the road licenses done for my truck. Even so, I accomplished only half of the task. Today I had to go back again. I also recorded my radio sermon and got instant-messaging set up on the computer. Tomorrow I travel out to two more congregations for worship. Blessings, Rob

We praised the Lord for the safe return travels of my family. Now life moved on, Malawi-style.

Sent: July 3, 2004
Subject: done being pampered
Rebecca writes: A few kidbits: Hannah poured sand around our palm trees to resemble the beach at Lake Malawi! I'm back to using cloth diapers for Nathanael. I sure prefer disposable. We're done being "pampered" in more ways than one. My new theme song is: "Back to life…back to reality…back to the here and now!" It is back to reality now that we have turned the calendars to July, and one more year exists between our next reunion. It seems trite to say again how much we enjoyed the time together, but it's the truth. I miss showing you all the neat things here.

Have a great 4th of July weekend. I'm going to make a fresh strawberry pie for the occasion. May God continue to "Bless America…home sweet home!" Love, Rebecca

Of course there is no Fourth of July celebration here. Malawi Independence Day is July 6. We paused to remember the independence of America and explained the meaning to the kids.

Soon after the departure of my family, Hannah thought she heard additional "visitors"…in the roof!

Sent: July 4, 2004
Subject: oh rats
Rebecca writes: Our weather is quite warm and lovely these days, especially considering it is winter. Throughout Blantyre, city workers are digging underground trenches to bury the phone lines. Some existing city wires were accidently cut while the phone company was installing underground cable casings. More phone problems.

Today in church it was announced that Rev. Mark Johnston is gearing up to move to Malawi. We're excited for their family to come.

Hannah informed us that she heard a rat in the roof. Rob went in the attic crawl-space and found one caught in the big steel rat trap. That rat was 14" long from head to tail. We had eaten, so we weren't tempted to skewer and roast it… too big for you, Dad? Ha ha. God bless, Rebecca

It seemed we needed to get the unnerving rat population under control again. We were on the lookout for some watchdogs, hoping they would help deter both thieves and rats.

Meanwhile, we were very excited to have a new missionary on his way! Since 1999, urban outreach in Blantyre had been conducted through the LCCA's Lutheran Reading Room. That had led directly to the formation of Beautiful Saviour. Missionary Uhlhorn, our predecessor, had been instrumental in forming that core group of members. After he left, they had no formal shepherd. Lay members, nearby national pastors and missionaries took turns preaching sermons for the group. Now land had been purchased and a new church was being built downtown. The new facility would be across from the marketplace and have prime visibility. The plan was to move the Reading Room, which was surrounded by shops in its current location, into the new church building. Regular programs could be held in the new facility, such as Bible classes, English lessons and children's groups.

Sent: July 5, 2004
Subject: little moths
Rebecca writes: Our power has been very iffy, but I've managed to cook between the outages. I've been using the great headlamp from my sister Stephanie (thanks!). The kids stared at me as I was "mining" my own business. I did feel like a miner...and Rob thought the kids looked like moths flocking to the light.

We have a National Independence holiday tomorrow. We *azungu* (white people) were warned to make sure our licenses and insurance disks are up-to-date. We are also supposed to have a set of red reflective triangles ready to show the police.

I should start planning supper. It is best to have things ready long before we actually want to eat, in case our power fails again. God bless, Rebecca

Back in the States before we moved, I remember browsing through the camping section of a sports store. I ran across a selection of headlamps, snickered to myself and wondered who in the WORLD would buy one of those. Hardly a year later, I knew firsthand why someone would buy that specialized equipment! My headlamp proved to be such a handy item. It made washing up kids and dishes during a nightly power outage *much* easier and more efficient...and we had much cleaner results.

Independence Day in Malawi doesn't bring out the parades, but it does bring out the police. Even on a normal day there are random police stops throughout the city. A policeman will step into the middle of the road and raise their hand at whomever they want to stop. On Independence Day I was stopped at a police check and asked to show my driver's license, my set of reflective triangles and my insurance and license disks (which are posted on each vehicle's windshield). Being required to show two reflective triangles at any given time and place on the roadways of Malawi may seem rather strange. In theory, each vehicle is required to have them so that in the event of a breakdown the driver could place one triangle on the road in front of the stalled vehicle and one behind it, for better roadside safety. In reality, the vehicles that have the triangles are rarely the ones breaking down. Instead it is the cars or trucks that avoid these police checkpoints that end up breaking down. Instead of the triangles, a few tree branches are typically placed on the road to warn of a stalled or abandoned vehicle. The more severe the breakdown or accident is, the more branches that are stacked on the road. At night this system is both hard to see and dangerous; yet it is a very common roadway occurrence.

Sent: July 10, 2004
Subject: plugging away
Rebecca writes: I have been asked to write for and update the Malawi website information. I plan to get current missionary family pictures displayed soon. I'm not so savvy at the extra computer stuff. I have email down, though!

Recently, the import store had one rare, tiny jar of applesauce—with a broken safety seal—for $5. It made me hungry for apple turnovers. Surprisingly, I also found cottage cheese. I splurged and bought one container, so I could make a pan of lasagna. After calculating the price of imported noodles and cheese and other ingredients, it ended up costing about $25. (Back in Wisconsin, I could make several pans for that price!) Not to mention the hours I spent buying and preparing those ingredients. The first bite was such a letdown and sadly didn't taste the same.

The weather is cooler, and the kids wore mittens today for the occasion.

Rob is in the bush again today. Hopefully it isn't raining there…N'singano's new worship facility is still in the building process. God bless, Rebecca

July is winter here and the temperatures are quite cool considering there is no indoor heat or insulation. The temperatures in the mornings and evenings hover in the low 50° Fahrenheit range. That feels cold, especially when the wind is whipping around during the *chiperoni* rains. When the sun shines and there is no wind, the winter days are quite lovely. I enjoyed each one of these warmer winter days, since memories of snow, ice and below-zero wind chills were still fresh in my memory.

Cool weather in Malawi seems to bring out far more unusual attire than my children's mittens: once I saw a baby wrapped in a hooded towel for warmth. A little farther down the road was a man zipped into a snow suit. I had to laugh. It wasn't quite THAT cold. Another time I saw a man draped in bubble wrap for protection from the rain.

Perhaps Rob would have been glad for some bubble wrap during his church service in N'singano. It turns out that it *did* rain, heavily, and the bush church did not yet have a roof. Rob was curious how the members would react to the downpour in their unprotected facility. It seemed this was nothing out of the ordinary, because most of them simply popped open their umbrellas and continued as usual—all set to praise the Lord, rain or shine.

Sent: July 11, 2004
Subject: humdinger
Rebecca writes: I went to the import store today to buy one more cottage cheese to make apple turnovers. I was VERY disheartened; all they had left was feta cheese. I looked on my substitution cooking page for ideas. I saw that you can substitute sour cream for cottage cheese—and you can substitute plain yoghurt for sour cream—so would Pythagoras agree that I could substitute plain yoghurt for cottage cheese? Mom Wendland, do you have any tips on whether I could make my own cottage cheese? I hate to waste a lot of time and precious ingredients for funny-tasting mush.

Today I noticed a very large, colorful spider (a Golden Orb Web spider) spinning a golden web outside the back *khonde*. As I was walking back into the house, two sunbirds (like hummingbirds) were singing, chattering and flying all around me. They like the blooming hibiscus plants. I stood still and they flitted in the air all around me. The male had beautiful iridescent markings. I'll take a colorful bird over a spider any day.

I got out the preschool activity box for Hannah. I'll start her on a schedule of Bible stories, letters, numbers, weather, songs, and arts and crafts. She seems eager for "school work," so I'll channel that as best as possible. God bless. Rebecca

Splurging on that first container of cottage cheese and remembering the jar of applesauce at the store made me think about my mom's apple turnovers, which called for both of those ingredients. Finally, I decided that it would be worth paying the high price for a second container of cottage cheese. Much to my chagrin, when I returned to the store the shelf was completely empty. It seemed others were willing to look past the inflated prices and were happy to get the rarely-available products. I was disappointed and would learn. Now I was on a mission: I was determined to make the turnovers whether I could buy cottage cheese and applesauce or not. It was time to start getting creative!

Even though spiders aren't my favorite creatures in Africa, it is true that they can be amazing in their own right. Apparently, a Golden Orb Web spider spins its web with a water-based silk that is almost as strong as Kevlar, the strongest man-made material. Bullet-proof webs aside, I still prefer birds: having those beautiful sunbirds flying around me and chattering as if I were a part of their conversation was truly awesome. Malawi has an incredible variety of birds. It is as close to living in an aviary as one can get without being a zookeeper. I usually share any neat discoveries with the kids, but for once I was glad they weren't with me. The few seconds I enjoyed with the chattering birds would not have happened around my chattering kids!

Sent: July 12, 2004
Subject: A is for Africa
Rebecca writes: Today we began with the letter "**A**" for Hannah's home-schooling. We covered several workbook pages, played some games, did singing, exercised our **A**rms and put together a Noah's **A**rk puzzle. She is also "keyed" to use the preschool computer program. Wednesday will be computer day, if and when we have electricity.

The vegetable women came with lots of good-looking broccoli today, so I'd better start chopping for supper. Curried chicken divan recipe is in the works, with warm thoughts of my Mom attached. Love, Rebecca

P.S. I just listened to the phone line and it is playing "*Für Elise*" again! Hannah currently has her ear to the phone and is making up words to go with the music. She is singing away. When you get lemons, make lemonade...right, Dad?

I had decided to try home-schooling Hannah for her Reception year, which is roughly equivalent to Preschool in the States. My biggest motivation was to give her a solid base in a Christ-centered curriculum. I had seen how invaluable such a base was as a parochial school teacher. Rob and I agreed that if we remained in Africa long enough, we'd like the kids to return to the States for high school; another reason to prepare Hannah both spiritually and academically. As time went on, my trial period became a permanent choice. Hannah proved to be a delightful little student and we both enjoyed the structured time together.

Sent: July 14, 2004
Subject: notes
Rob writes: Dear Dad Staude, you had asked about my bush congregation helper, Spider Chinyanga. He works with me at our congregations at Katunga (way down by Nsanje) and Muhapokwa (over in the shadow of Mt. Mulanje). He visits each place twice a month—once when he comes with me, and another time by himself. When he goes by himself he visits members, teaches classes and conducts worship. These congregations have no other called worker (and not very strong lay people), so it is nice to have his help. If it weren't for him, they wouldn't be getting much in the way of spiritual food except my monthly visit. Spider also helps to keep the books on my congregations and any current building projects.

On a sad note, last week I took Spider's wife to the hospital. Tests revealed that she has advanced ovarian cancer. There is nothing the hospital can do. They gave her pain medication and sent her home to her village, where her family and friends will take care of her until she is called to glory.

Please give our greetings and congratulations to Rev. Mark Johnston. We are their pre-field orienters (as long as our phone line holds). Blessings in Jesus,
Rob

Our phone-line problems weren't merely inconvenient to us; our best efforts to share information with the incoming missionaries were often foiled by our unreliable connection. International calling was also very expensive. We tried to sign up with a company called Global Phone. However, we ran into the same problem that always pursued our attempts to set up anything internationally: our mailing address was in Malawi, but our billing address was in Wisconsin. Also, most standard computerized forms would not allow us to skip the zip code section; yet we have no zip code here in Malawi. The more computerized things became, the more this happened.

It was a classic Catch-22 that if we ever got the international phone system working, we could call someone and explain our plight. Then again, we would probably be connected to a voicemail network and be put on hold so long that our phone connection would fail, or our power would go out, or both.

Sent: July 15, 2004
Subject: alphabet train
Rebecca writes: This morning was Hannah's computer morning. WOW, did she enjoy that. An alphabet train chugged into view, whispering "Alphabet Express" and she giggled away. It was good for her to practice maneuvering a mouse.

Thanks for the cottage cheese recipes, Kathie and Mom; I'll try the Africa version. We can usually get fresh milk…so I'll be patient and wait for the cheese product to "cure" so I can fill my craving for apple turnovers!

This morning I thought I had plenty of time to get lunch going and also start a pea soup for supper. Mid-morning I started boiling water for the peas. I opened two local bags of split peas. I put one bag in the colander to rinse and to my dismay found many, many weevils. I began picking them out. Half an hour later, Rob came to help. By noon we had finished picking out the live adult bugs but realized that there were too many peas remaining with larvae burrowed inside to use after all. What a waste. Then, right when I was ready to start lunch…the power went out.

Such is life in the Malawi lane these days. We still have music playing on our phone line. Paul Nitz tried calling and wondered what was happening. After his failed attempts to phone us, he questioned whether or not we should continue to be the field orienters for the Johnston family. In the end we all decided that the phone lines in our area were just too unpredictable. God bless, Rebecca

I decided that I would give the homemade cottage cheese recipe a try. First I would have to cure some milk on our kitchen counter. Next I would have to drain the cured milk through a dish cloth to separate the cheesy product from the whey. That cheesy product would become my substitute for cottage cheese. THEN I would finally be able to attempt my apple turnover recipe. I hoped that by that time they wouldn't have run out of apples to make into sauce for the filling. I felt like I was in a living rendition of "There's a hole in my bucket!"

Not long after my email, I received one back from Rob's mom in Zambia. She wrote,

"Rebecca, your problem with weevily split peas is VERY familiar. I get so tired of planning a meal, only to have to throw out the whole thing and make something else.

Your family's visit sounded like it was fun and happy and too short! It is always hard to get back into the routine of everything after a nice break like that.

Thanks again for all your faithful and interesting emails, Rebecca. I really appreciate them. I pray that Jesus continues to watch over and guide you all. I love and miss each of you! Perhaps we can visit again at Christmas. I have to have the next family visit to look forward to and plan to keep me going! Much love, Mom."

I would never have guessed that someday I would relate to my "African" mother-in-law on so many levels. Rob and I had dated almost two years before I even met his parents during their furlough in 1993. Before we moved to Malawi, I had only seen them a handful of times. The past Christmas had been a very special celebration since we could share it with both of Rob's parents. In spite of our infrequent visits, we are able to relate well because of our shared faith, family ties and African experiences. What a blessing!

Sent: July 16, 2004
Subject: odds and ends
Rebecca writes: Rob is out again today. Last week things did not go so smoothly in the bush: He and aDzoole, his language teacher, drove three hours to Katunga, Rob's most distant congregation. (Rob learned that putting an 'a' in front of a name is a polite gesture. Now Dzoole is aDzoole.) ADzoole had agreed to ride along and assess Rob's language progress in action during the church service. However, when they arrived only the chairman of the church was there. He said

no one else would show up because of a village funeral...and he wasn't staying either. So Rob and aDzoole drove the three hours back to Blantyre. They had an informal language class on the trip. Otherwise...what a complete waste!

    I had a dream last night that there was a McDonald's that I didn't know about. I saw someone eating a bacon-egg-cheese biscuit in town. They gave me directions. I found the McDonald's...but all I had in my wallet was 100 Kwacha. I got a brownie. One more year before I can make that dream a reality (food from home is on my mind again)! God bless, Rebecca

Canceling church without notice is culturally acceptable here, even though the fuel costs of this particular trip and the inconvenience to Rob's language teacher made the situation expensive and rather embarrassing. A church service—even one led by a missionary who can only come once a month—does not take precedence over a funeral. In Malawi, attending a funeral means far more than being physically present. Attending a funeral has deeper roots that include showing respect to the community and the deceased and representing your family. If a family member or even a village member *fails* to participate in a funeral, that person could be accused of having killed the deceased through witchcraft. At the least, they could themselves become a target of malevolent witchcraft. There is also a fear that the soul of the deceased might try to gain revenge on the family member who didn't participate in their funeral rites. The "spirit" might haunt the individual or make his life difficult: perhaps by not allowing crops to grow, or causing sickness, loss of friends or the collapse of business deals.

Sent: July 18, 2004
Subject: time to get cookin'
Rebecca writes: Rob left for Lilongwe for a week of summer school on the LBI campus.

    Today I got an American Women's Association cookbook. The book is published by American women writing American recipes adapted for Malawi. It uses available ingredients and lists different names for items. It also contains a handy metric equivalent page. Much of the book contains recipes to make things from scratch. One of the first listings I saw was a cottage cheese recipe! It also has recipes for English muffins, granola, homemade noodles, marshmallows, Fritos (I'm trying that one soon), saltines, Wheat Thins, tomato soup and curry. I am thrilled to add it to my kitchen shelf.

    Our power is crummy today. I have my headlamp on already since I don't like being left in the dark when I am in the middle of something. Once the lights went out as I was about to pour our huge pot of water into the filter. I didn't even trust if I knew where the counter was, so I put the pot on the floor and went for the flashlight. Such fun you get to live without! Love, Rebecca

The recipes in my new cookbook have been fun to try, although they've had varying results. The English muffins turned out fine but were rather time consuming to make. The homemade Fritos sadly did *not* taste as I expected. I had to remind myself of the Do's and Don'ts list that I had written: "Don't expect local (or homemade) food to taste like USA food; you'll be disappointed."

Sent: July 19, 2004
Subject: Beautiful B
Rebecca writes: Today Hannah and I began the letter "B." The learning treasure chest was full of items beginning with "B." There was a Bible, ball, baby, battery, etc... At the end of the "B" things I looked at Nathanael, and he responded, "Bub-Bye!"

A learning activity in one of Hannah's American-published preschool books was to name any of the seasons. Hannah replied, "Rainy." I guess that would fit the weather pattern here: we do refer to the "rainy" and "dry" seasons. Of course the book was teaching the four seasons north of the equator, so we talked more about each of those. I did not even realize how "American" much of our literature is until I started using it in this very different context. Of course seedtime and harvest will continue no matter how we label it!

The Dairibord was out of milk again yesterday. The man at the sales counter joked that the cows were on strike. I did not think it was particularly funny, since they supply the city with milk. If they don't have it, no one will. Love from "B"lantyre, Rebecca

Our local Dairibord spells their brand name kind of like they carry milk—*unusually*. Rumor has it that they make all their milk from powder. One of these days when I am standing in line I'll ask the guy at the desk if they actually have cows or not.

My mom grew up on a farm in Wisconsin—with real cows—and her mom, my Grandma Lydia Dobberfuhl, had a small treasure chest in her attic on the farm. That chest, which I inherited, was now the same treasure chest that I was using with Hannah each day for our alphabet "treasures." That old chest had great memories attached, and we were making many more memories as we used it here in Africa.

It struck me how very American a lot of our literature is. Even the devotionals I read have many pointed references to American items, sports, phrases or products. I realized this more clearly one day when I began looking for a devotion to share with the ladies at Beautiful Saviour. Our women's group at the urban church is primarily made up of Malawians, with a smattering of other cultures represented. It was more difficult than I thought to find a relevant devotion. I hadn't realized how different an audience could be 10,000 miles across the ocean. I needed to become a translator of sorts, trying to bridge the gap between cultures. In the end, I prayed that though the words or application might be lacking, the true message would shine through.

Sent: July 21, 2004
Subject: Pumpkin plan
Rebecca writes: Today the kids and I drove the 60-plus km to Zomba for the monthly missionary wives' Bible Study. One of the side roads to the mission house is very bad. WOW. Deep gullies from the rains. Our Bible study was on Christian discipline. On the way home we were stuck behind MANY slow-moving trucks. I stopped to buy six pumpkins. I will bake, puree and freeze some for Thanksgiving to make sure we have a pumpkin pie for the occasion. Pumpkins will not be in season then.

We have had so many power outages lately that I've been living with my headlamp on. It makes for a weird hairdo afterward—function versus form.

I'm doing a few Malawi website write-ups. The website is beginning to take shape with statistics, pictures and a few articles. We are eagerly waiting for the new mission families to come; soon their profiles will be added. God bless.
Rebecca

At this point in time, the mission wives from Zomba and Blantyre were getting together once a month for a Bible Study. In 2007, when mission cuts meant our numbers had dwindled in the Blantyre area, we shifted to family Bible studies instead. We are so often bombarded with difficulties and trials here that it is a priority to stay connected to Christ. However, that continues to take a real effort here in Malawi. Resources and opportunities for spiritual growth are not as plentiful as in the States. Personal study is crucial, or we could so easily stagnate. Just like real muscles, our spiritual muscles are either strengthened with use or begin to weaken from disuse. Studying and applying God's messages to our lives is a workout with colossal eternal importance, allowing us to build muscles of faith and trust that go beyond skin-deep.

Sent: July 25, 2004
Subject: Lilongwe meeting update
Rob writes: I had a wonderful week of summer school in Lilongwe with "the guys." Every year a Seminary professor teaches a class in either Malawi or Zambia, on a rotating schedule. This year Prof. Mark Zarling came and had some great classes on Genesis (Names of God) and Christian Leadership. Jason Paltzer had a wonderful and straight-to-the-point HIV/sex education class. (Jason was originally connected with the Medical Mission and was very effective in health education. He has since been hired by the mission.) Missionary Paul Nitz also had a great class on breaking down a text and teaching it.

> In Lilongwe, Jason saw an ad for bullmastiff puppies. The puppies are purebred from South Africa for $400. I couldn't convince Rebecca that we need a $400 dog. The search continues.
>
> Mom and Dad Wendland, have you given thought to your furlough schedule next year? It would be great if we can both be Stateside during the same year to share furlough time together. Blessings in Jesus, Rob

In the hope of extra security, we were keeping our eyes open for a dog. I saw no need to break the bank, considering that our neighbor's dogs had recently been killed by thieves.

As we began to plan and try to coordinate our furlough—still more than a year away—I was reminded yet again how much preparation and foresight it takes to travel around the world. Little did I know at the time what an extraordinary amount of planning and coordinating, sacrifice and prayers that first furlough in 2005 would involve. This would be due to the schedule of someone *other* than Rob's parents... but that would become apparent soon enough.

> *Sent: July 26, 2004*
> *Subject: shoe surprise*
> **Rebecca writes:** I put on my tennis shoes this morning and felt something like a pebble inside one of them. After I walked into the kitchen I took it off. Inside was a large roach. It was still alive. I won't do that again without looking first. YUCK!
>
> Yesterday I boiled and baked two quarts of raw peanuts to make into roasted sugar peanuts. They are great. I also tried dehydrating some banana chips in the oven. Those weren't so good. God bless, Rebecca

Roaches. They were right up there with the rats that we were attempting to get under control. Soon after we moved in we had found roach egg pouches—dark brown, shiny capsules about one inch long—in several corners of our house. After the exterminators came we saw a big improvement in the amount of wildlife around the house. However, some rogues were still making unwanted appearances. The one in my shoe was utterly disgusting. I am not sure how it survived with me walking on it, but it did. Cockroaches are expert survivors: supposedly they can live for almost a month without food and a week *without a head*; they can climb walls, swim, hold their breath for up to 40 minutes and run at a respectable clip of 3 miles an hour. Some female cockroaches mate once and are pregnant for life. Rob's mom once bit into a locally-made sandwich and found that a cockroach was part of the "fixings." I have to put things like that out of my mind. The more I dwell on them the more creeped out I become.

On a sweeter note, I tried a recipe from another missionary lady and made my own sugared peanuts. Although they were time-consuming to make, they turned out great and exceeded my expectations in flavor—a pleasant surprise after other disappointing recipes. I was finding that it is sometimes more rewarding to embrace and enjoy Malawi's unique flavors, rather than risk the disappointment of trying to recreate a USA flavor. It might be a short list, but Malawi does have some flavors and foodstuffs that are truly appealing—like the lovely, flaky texture and mild flavor of fresh *chambo* (a lake fish) and the intensely sweet flavor of fresh pineapple and other seasonal fruits. Malawi also features other foods that are just plain unique, like "crisps" (potato chips) that come in flavors such as chutney, biltong, tomato and mutton.

Sent: July 28, 2004
Subject: GSE
Rebecca writes: Today is another Grapefruit Seed Extract (GSE) day. I woke up really feeling crummy. After a good dose of GSE I've only had to run to the bathroom once. I don't know what brings on the stomach junk.
　My cottage cheese is nearly ready. Enjoy your day. Rebecca

GSE is a concentrate from the seeds and pulp of grapefruit. It is supposed to be very effective for gastrointestinal upsets. The Nitz family had found it to be helpful and gave us some to try. I was eager to put the natural cleansing capabilities to the test.

I pass through trials all the way, With sin and ills contending;
In patience I must bear each day The cross of God's own sending.
Oft in adversity I know not where to flee
When storms of woe my soul dismay; I pass through trials all the way.
(CW 431:2) [underlined emphasis mine]

When my homemade cottage cheese was finally ready, I made a batch of homemade applesauce. And THEN I was able to make and bake the apple turnovers that I'd had my heart set on. The familiar, special smell in the house was terrific…but the lengthy process meant I would not make them again anytime soon. For the time being they satisfied my craving for a taste of home.

Sent: July 30, 2004
Subject: "C" is for cookie
Rebecca writes: The kids are watching a "C" Is for Cookie video since it is "C" week. Nathanael is completely in awe since he's seen about as many videos as he is old.

I read a chapter of <u>Charlie and the Chocolate Factory</u> to the kids while they bathed. Much of that humor is lost on kids. Now I'm picking up the little extras, such as, you need to use a whip on cream to make "whipped" cream; and a "poached" egg needs to be stolen in the middle of the night! That one is quite fitting for Africa.

Speaking of whipped cream, I heard an interesting story. A fellow missionary family recently took a trip to South Luangwa Game Park. At the start of the trip they had given their kid a sippy cup filled with our local, high fat milk. When they arrived at the Game Park their kid wouldn't drink the milk. They took off the lid and looked inside…evidently all the bumps, along with the warm temperature, had turned it into butter! (I should try that method in bulk since butter is expensive and hard to find.)

The rhubarb-starts that I bought from the Zomba plateau are doing well. I planted them in various spots. The black raspberries I transplanted are taking off too.

I'd better check on the little "C"hildren. Love, Rebecca and "C"lan

The kids sure admired our television a lot—the outside of it, that is! It had been a living room decoration ever since our shipment arrived. The local TV station was not very informative. DSTV service via satellite was expensive. For the time being we used the TV occasionally to view DVD's. I rather enjoyed the quiet evenings and uninterrupted family time. Besides, we were more likely to share a favorite childhood chapter book without the TV as competition.

Years ago I thought <u>Charlie and the Chocolate Factory</u> was written on a kid's level. Reading it again showed me that many details go beyond a child's comprehension. I have found the same to be true as I read Scripture. Bible passages and hymns that I read and memorized as a child now have so much more depth, meaning and possibility for personal application as I mature and as my realm of experience grows. God has truly authored a Book that can both nourish a child and feed an adult, leaving those who read it satisfied…yet yearning for more!

Sent: August 1, 2004
Subject: time for a spin
Rebecca writes: Dear Mom and Dad, thanks so much for the phone call. I used to wonder how Rob could talk so long to his parents when he would call home to Africa during our dating years. Now I understand.

We noticed many potholes on our road were filled in with gravel. I think it was a private resident willing to dish out money to avoid vehicle damages. The trip down our road was amazing. We crossed over the (filled) potholes without our seatbelts immediately tightening. The kids didn't bounce around in their car seats either.

I stopped at the Dairibord after church but they didn't have milk. They claimed it was coming "soon." I was behind a dozen others. We all stood there waiting.

Nobody was speaking English, so I wasn't completely sure if milk was really coming or not. We were out of milk at home. To give you an idea of how long we waited, I watched a spider spin a web on the man in front of me. It crawled out of his tattered handbag and was trying to make its web from the handbag to his pants. I knew if I didn't "snuggle up" to people I'd probably lose my place in line...but I felt I needed to keep a bit of distance in case other critters would emerge. The man who works there (and knows me by name) came on the milk truck shortly after the spider web was spun. He delivered the milk and I was on my way. God bless your week. Rebecca

I was doubtful whether our recent road improvements were due to a city crew, although in this particular case the potholes were at least filled with gravel. More often, fix-ups are very temporary efforts by local people, or kids who fill the potholes with old bricks and dirt. They stand nearby with an empty bowl to collect tips from grateful drivers. I guess it is a step up from outright begging, since they actually expend some effort. However, the rains make short work of this type of "solution" and leave the potholes as big as ever.

Sent: August 6, 2004
Subject: enjoyed the ride
Rebecca writes: Our family enjoyed two bike rides recently. Our equipment is officially initiated with layers of dust and dirt. We got tons of stares and were stopped at five police stops, probably for a closer look at our bike gear. We had a great day of exercise, fresh air and togetherness. As we neared our gate, we saw a car had smashed through our neighbor's wall...a few meters from **our** wall. I did have a sense of relief when I realized it was not our wall, but we are praying for the protection of our vulnerable neighbors. Love, Rebecca

If thieves were waiting for a target it seemed they needed to look no further. The hole in the wall was like posting a "Now Open" sign on the property. I also realized that easy access to our neighbor's yard was a stepping stone into our yard. It was tempting to worry about the breach in security. Satan the Deceiver certainly loves to use situations like this to shake our faith and replace it instead with a cycle of anxiety. That danger is worse than the first.

"I walk in danger all the way; The thought shall never leave me
That Satan, who has marked his prey, Is plotting to deceive me.
This foe with hidden snares May seize me unawares
If e'er I fail to watch and pray; I walk in danger all the way. (CW 431:1)

Our family said extra prayers for safety and followed our usual security measures. Amazingly, nothing happened during the night. No house alarms went off and no thieves seemed to be enticed by the smashed wall. Within a week the neighbors had bricked up the hole and our sense of security was restored.

Sent: August 8, 2004
Subject: 2 bee or not 2 bee
Rebecca writes: A few days ago we stopped in Limbe at an import shop. This shop carries hard-to-find imported items such as specialty foods, toiletries and cloth diaper inserts. Things there are quite expensive...but if you are looking for a familiar brand or product, it is worth a stop. I walked past the bakery section and was delighted to find whole-wheat rolls, small ones and big ones. With such a selection I decided to take a few bags of each. That evening I served the small rolls with dinner. They tasted funny. I cut one roll open. Baked into the roll were about five black bugs with their legs sticking out! The bakers must have used very old and bug-infested flour. Now I'm completely paranoid and beginning to see little black specks in all my food.

Rob stopped at the store yesterday to show the manager the bug problem. The shop owner gave him a replacement batch of rolls. In the car Rob cut one roll open and found more baked-in bug parts. The man refunded Rob's money. I won't buy rolls from there again for a long time.

Rob conducted 22 confirmations and a dozen baptisms yesterday. The congregation members were very happy and presented him with lots of produce gifts. He returned home with three cabbages, a half dozen yams, onions, a bucket full of peanuts, peas and enough tomatoes to make three jars of pizza sauce.

I just heard LOTS of bees outside the house, so I got up to look. I'm telling you, it is like the killer bees that you see on TV. There must be tens of thousands, if not **millions** of bees, right outside. I was going to try to take a video or picture, but I got spooked. This is surreal and scary. I'll lock the grate so the kids don't accidentally go out. I am not sure what they are doing so close to the house. 2 bee or not 2 bee...maybe 2 million bees...bee-yond bee-lief! What a blessing to keep in touch despite the thousands of miles. God bless, Rebecca

P.S. I'm amazed. Mere hours ago I wrote about the bees. Now they are gone. Half-a-dozen stragglers got trapped in the house, but they have all conveniently died.

Shopping here continued to "bug" me. I could not help but compare it to the great shopping in the States. After buying many whole wheat rolls, I was disgusted to find them filled with beetles. I am not a gourmet cook nor do I have a highly selective palette...but I do draw the line at paying for and eating unwelcome bugs.

The Lord was blessing Rob's village church work. There continued to be an encouraging number of baptisms and confirmations and strong church attendance. The high numbers here in Malawi attest to God's grace at work in spiritual fields that are ripe and ready for harvest. Since Rob is only able to visit each church on a monthly basis, the procedure followed in the village churches is to have the church elders teach confirmation classes. The missionary then tests the confirmands on all parts of the catechism and Bible. In this way the Malawians receive a well-rounded, Bible-based education comparable to confirmands and members in the States.

The bee encounter was something I will not forget. I have since learned that their behavior is called "swarming," and it is a phenomenon that happens in spring, or whenever food is scarce. Often they are close to starving when they swarm. It was truly spooky to be so suddenly surrounded by multitudes of bees and their all-encompassing, deafening buzz. I wanted to document the encounter, but I quickly abandoned the idea for fear of injury. I knew the African bee could be volatile. If one bee is killed, the dying bee lets off a pheromone that signals other bees to attack. The thought of being attacked by bees in Rob's absence, with no reliable phone and two helpless kids in tow was not a happy one. I played it safe, stayed inside and in a short time they were gone…or so I thought.

"Be still and know that I am God." Psalm 46:10

Sent: August 11, 2004
Subject: "kraft"y
Rebecca writes: Today I used the Kitchen Aid shredder attachment (thanks, Mom!) for cheese. That worked slick. I shredded 2 kg of mozzarella and 1 kg of cheddar. I froze portions in bags, so making pizzas and adding cheese will be much easier now.

Rob successfully fastened on the washer attachment that you sent, Dad. For the first time in almost a year we have a washer that works all by itself! No need to manually fill it with water, have minor flooding or wait hours until we remember to add water for the rinse cycle. Rob thinks our overly-hot water and frequent power surges wear that part out prematurely. For now, we're squeaky clean with ease! Dad, please thank the repairman that helped you order that.

We're so thankful for the tools we brought in our shipment. Rob talked with someone who bought a pipe wrench here. That very day it broke. He replaced it with an imported one for $100! To finish the job, the man needed another one. So for $200 he has 2 pipe wrenches. Quality hardware stores are a "pipe dream" here!

Unfortunately, the bees did not go away and are nesting in our roof. When they swarmed a few days ago they must have been scouting things out. We'll try Dad Wendland's advice to paint diesel in the area. Although, I **could** use the honey and have wax for candles!

Our power and phone have been really crummy again. The city is still trying to string new underground phone cables. It is a nice effort; however, they are digging up the pavement and merely filling in the holes with dirt. I hope they fill in the holes with pavement before the rains.

The kids played with sidewalk chalk. Hannah drew a cross and a cell phone. The necessities!

We have our monthly ladies' group at church on Saturday. I am planning a card-making craft to do together. God bless, Rebecca

Our urban church, Beautiful Saviour, has an active group of about a dozen women. The group, like the church, is a cultural melting-pot but is primarily made up of Malawian ladies. We get together for monthly Bible studies and periodically for crafts. In Blantyre we have a local papermaking store called PAMET. They make paper and envelopes from banana bark, baobab bark, papyrus and cleaned elephant dung (which is very fibrous and useful if you get past the idea of it), as well as many other varieties of recycled paper. I bought an armful of supplies from them and went home to design a card for the ladies to make. I wanted a craft made out of local material so it could be sustained without many imported supplies.

I came up with a few Christmas card designs that incorporated Christian stamps to make sure each card carried the important message of Christ. The ladies seemed eager to do the craft. I set up an assembly line. They did well in spite of difficulties with gluing, stamping and cutting. I had not fully appreciated what a skill it is to position a stamper and produce a clean image on paper until our session was over. The women had never seen a pinking shears and thought each zigzag would have to be cut by hand. When the ladies looked at their completed cards, they were happy to have been part of the process. The plan was to sell the cards and use the money to buy communion supplies and cleaning items for the church. I was glad I could use my skills to teach some crafts, so the ladies could play a part in supporting our church.

Sent: August 15, 2004
Subject: we bee getting there
Rebecca writes: The builders are saying Beautiful Saviour's new church building will be done in four weeks. That would be nice!

We sprayed the bees and hopefully much of their nest. I cleaned yesterday and swept up a few hundred dead ones. I was looking through my recipes last night and realized I may have missed an opportunity. I saw a recipe for *"Ana a Njuchi"* (Bee larvae). It says, "Remove the nests and boil. Then take out the larvae from the comb and dry. Fry with a little salt, and dry again if desired. Serve as a relish or as an appetizer." So, as I struggle to come up with meal ideas, I'll think of the potential that lies in our roof—though now tainted by poison.

Necessity is the mother of invention for sure. I discovered that if you pour about ¼ cup of popcorn kernels into a Pyrex bowl (with a little oil at the bottom), cover it with a glass cover, and microwave it for about three minutes you get nice results. Since bags of popcorn are about $4 each here, this is the way to go. (I had chemistry class flashbacks when I was painfully reminded that hot glass looks like cold glass. Now I lay out the pot holders before I start!)

I cleaned **again** today. With the dry weather comes endless dust. It is relentless. I moved a bookshelf and a plastic tote. They required dusting…but underneath them the wooden floor was covered with mold.

Hannah wants a purple lollipop when we return to America. I'll start a furlough list so I don't forget to fulfill these wishes. If I forget, she'll have to wait four years! God bless. Rebecca

Sent: August 17, 2004
Subject: bush work update
Rob writes: Last week I went out to Tcheleni with my language teacher, aDzoole, as a make-up day for Katunga. I picked up Evangelist Matengula and a choir from Mpemba-Beni congregation. When Matengula found out that my language teacher was along, no more English was spoken that day—3 hours there and 3 back in Chichewa. He gave me tests and grades. It was a fun ride and we laughed a lot. By the end of the day my brain was so fried that I said "*ine*" (me), then "*ndithu*" (certainly), before I could spit out "*inde*" (yes) to answer a question.

At Tcheleni the congregation was waiting and singing as we pulled in. We had a great service—3 hours with the choirs all taking turns. The congregation fed us all *nsima* and chicken. On the way back we had a flat tire, but we had 20 hands to help. I got home after 9pm, wonderfully tired.

The last two days have been unexpectedly busy. Before church yesterday, Spider told me that his wife, who was diagnosed with ovarian cancer last month, had died. As Spider's employer I was responsible for paying for the funeral. I paid MK3,000 for food and bought a MK3,000 coffin. The grand total for the funeral was about $60; I didn't think that was too bad.

Next it was out to Tsobola village (about 1.5 hours from Blantyre) for the funeral. We got there, waited several hours, ate (the meal I paid for—which was goat and *nsima*), put Mrs. Chinyanga in her coffin and had the service. After the service it was out to the graveyard where, in 20 minutes, the coffin was in the ground and covered with dirt. Then Pastor Chinyama led the committal and introduced me as I put a bouquet of flowers on the new grave. We sang hymns and returned home at 7pm, having left at 9am.

Tomorrow I travel to Katunga again. On the way back I will pick up Evangelist Master and head over to Chikwawa, where a group says they want to "join our church with 500 new members." Evangelist Master has had to work overtime down there. The LCCA has three nice new churches going up. Since no other church body has built churches like that there, we have people coming out of the woodwork to "join us." Evangelist Master has done the screening.

I'll close...as I praise the Lord for the 32 years of grace he has given me.
Love, Rob

Spider's wife died and was mourned. In her death she had become another statistic, another funeral to attend and another sad result of sin. But for the grace of God, death would be nothing but a horrible end. Through Christ, her statistics were behind her and her glory was realized.

In Malawi, death seems close. Maybe it is because the life expectancy—around 40 years of age—is so low. Maybe it is because each funeral is a community event. Or maybe it is because there are no funeral parlors to act as buffers between the dead and the living. Ordinarily a person is buried within 24 hours of dying. Relatives are contacted immediately and try to arrive at the home of the deceased by evening, so they can spend the night mourning with the family. A Christian family will sing hymns all night long. By early the next day a coffin is purchased, and someone is hired to dig a deep hole. Two sets of branches, one for each lane of traffic, are placed on the main roadway near the house as a public signal that a funeral is taking place. Before preparing the dead, relatives and important guests gather at the house and eat a meal. After dining, the relatives wash the dead body and place it in the casket. The portion of the dirt floor that the person had died upon is dug up with a hoe. That dirt is put into the casket, along with the deceased's clothes and grass mat. Usually children are buried in the morning or early afternoon, and adults are buried in the late afternoon.

In a Christian funeral like the one Rob attended for Spider's wife, the casket is then placed in front of the house. Ladies surround it and sing hymns. Then the official funeral service takes place. Afterwards, different speakers and preachers take turns saying something. Next, the ladies lay flowers on the casket as they sing. Family members then lift the casket to their shoulders, and the whole group walks to the graveyard. Traditional superstition often asserts itself at this point, as pregnant or nursing women do not enter the graveyard. Many believe that an evil spirit could harm their babies. Thankfully, with Christ such fears can be put aside. At the graveyard, the mourners sit on the ground. After the casket is lowered, everyone grabs a hoe and covers it with dirt. If the family can afford it, the burial site is also covered with thick layers of cement. This is to prevent living things from getting in and, as many Africans still believe, to prevent anything dead from coming out. It looks like an ending. But for a Christian, death—so close, so seemingly final—is not a termination but a transition. What joy it will be to join together on the other side of eternity, sing praises to our Savior and have no more reason for fears or tears!

Village graveyard

My walk is heav'nward all the way; Await, my soul, the morrow,
When you farewell can gladly say To all your sin and sorrow.
All worldly pomp, be gone! To heav'n I now press on.
For all the world I would not stay; My walk is heav'nward all the way. (CW 431:6)

Sent: August 18, 2004
Subject: odds and ends
Rebecca writes: Our gardener killed a harmless Cape wolf snake this morning in our flower bed. It had a skink (a type of lizard) in its belly when it was killed.

I'll share some comments from 4 ½ year old Hannah that I thought you'd enjoy:
- "When I'm 65 then I'll drive a car." (That means Rob will be 90…AGH!)
- "Why can't we touch the touch-lamp?"
- In keeping with "F" week, I made French Fries, chicken nuggets and onion rings for Rob's birthday supper. Hannah asked me, "Are the chicken nuggets for dessert?"
- At Bible Group I mentioned that the devil is the father of lies. I also gave two other names for the devil: Beelzebub and Satan. At supper Hannah stated, "Mom, at Bible Group you forgot to mention 'Lucifer' as another name for the devil." Next time!

We have had a lot of sweet potatoes (from church offerings) lately. I decided to slice them thinly and fry them like potato chips. That worked great. They are extremely crispy and quite good. I'll take a batch of the chips to the Bartz missionary family's welcome party on Saturday. Pastor Jim Bartz, his wife Jayne, and their four children will be living in Blantyre. Pastor Bartz will serve as a village missionary in the outlying Blantyre areas. Like Rob, he'll be submerged in Chichewa lessons to help him minister to the national congregations. We pray they travel safely and adjust smoothly once they are here.

Nathanael just handed me a dead bee and ran away with Rob's stapler... better go catch him! Love, Rebecca

Rob's congregations in the Southern Shire Valley often bring sweet potatoes as their harvest offerings. They are a hearty crop and are more drought-resistant than maize. Rob bought the potatoes with our money. That payment then became the congregation's offering to the LCCA synod. It was a kind gesture to help the members out…but now we had sweet potatoes coming out of our ears! When I looked at the enormous pile of potatoes in our garage, I wondered what I could possibly do with all of them. It didn't seem practical to try to sell them. We gave many away. But when we discovered they make fantastic sweet potato chips, I felt like I had just spun straw into gold. They quickly turned into a family favorite and a "sweet" way to utilize the offering.

Sent: August 18, 2004
Subject: all in a few days' work
Rob writes: Dear All; during the past three days I traveled almost 1,000 km. There was one funeral, lots of transporting, one communion service, one investigative meeting with those who want to join the LCCA, one evening village service conducted solely by my Land Cruiser headlights, four meals of *nsima* and one building project begun and $2,000 spent to do it. I'm ready for a "day in" tomorrow. There's no rest yet…tomorrow Rebecca goes to clean and prepare the mission house before the Bartz family arrives, while I play Mr. Mom here at home.

Maybe I'll open some of my birthday gifts after supper tonight. Thanks again for the great support across the miles! Rich blessings in Jesus, Rob

Rob had been traveling so much. As the sun would start to sink below the horizon, I would watch for his truck. If he wasn't back I said extra prayers, since driving in the dark is extra dangerous. I had full confidence that Rob was in the Lord's safe keeping.

Sent: August 25, 2004
Subject: **sadzapezekanso**
Rob writes: Ever since Rebecca's family witnessed this *mbusa* (pastor) leading the Chichewa service, especially for the singing of "*Ulemelero*" (Glory to God),

they have been requesting a video clip. Yesterday I went to Chizilo congregation. They had been asking me to take their picture, so I thought the timing was perfect. I got a clip of one of my favorite Chewa hymns, "There is no one like Jesus." During the clip the people are singing, "*Sadzapezekanso. Palibe wofanana naye.*" (Rough translation: "Another like Him will never be found. There is no one like Him.") In the rest of the song the people sing, "I've walked all over the place (*Ndayendayenda ponseponse*), I've gone around all over the place (*Ndazungulira ponseponse*), I've searched all over the place (*Ndafunafuna ponseponse*), and another like Jesus will never be found." The people act out the "walking," the "all arounding," and the "asking" parts of the song. I was so glad I had the camera along. It was a church full of happy, pumped up people, and I had the Word to share and hear as we worshiped in the amazing beauty of the Thyolo Hills. Absolutely marvelous! (I didn't even have a flat tire or get stuck on the way home this time.) I hope the video clip was worth the wait. Love, Rob

Worship here in Malawi does not always fit neatly into a weekly one-hour increment. And it shouldn't! Worship of our Almighty Creator should preempt anything else crowding our agendas. As Rob's mom has commented, "Everything else is a colossal waste of time." When it is necessary for me to prioritize my daily tasks, I ask myself, "If Judgment Day were next week, would the items on my schedule today make an eternal difference to me or anyone else? Does my schedule strengthen my relationship with God or detract from it? And as I follow that schedule, do my actions and words and attitude glorify God? Nothing I have been given, including my time, is too great to sacrifice for God—the Giver of every gift. As the Chichewa song declares, "I've looked all over and there will never be another one like Him!" Praise our most loving God that *He* has found *us*!

> *"This is love: not that we loved God,*
> *but that he loved us and sent his Son*
> *as an atoning sacrifice for our sins." I John 4:10*

Sent: September 3, 2004
Subject: latest here
Rebecca writes: I am completely convinced that I will not ride my bike in our neighborhood. After our anniversary bike ride I had been itching to ride around like I used to in Milwaukee. Here is why I **won't**:

Two days ago our gardener, Mr. Chinyama, went out after 5pm to the nearest village to buy groceries. On his return trip he was mugged by 20 people (we were gone at the time). They held a gun to his head, took his shoes and stole all his remaining money and groceries. It happened around the railroad track area beyond our back yard... the same area that our family had been warned to avoid a year ago when we first arrived and took a neighborhood walk. Rob asked Mr. Chinyama if he had been roughed-up and he replied, "Oh, they'll never fail to do that." Please keep him in your prayers.

If that wasn't enough to get us thinking again about security—our neighbor three doors down had a robbery the same night. The thieves evidently got away with a lot of items. We heard their alarm in the night. Just when I felt like throwing my hands up and asking, "Why Lord?" I realized it was more important and much more effective to throw them together in prayer and ask all the more for HIS protection. After doing a recent visual enactment of the parting of the Red Sea for Bible Group, using a candle for the pillar of fire and cotton balls for the cloud, I picture the Lord as a pillar of fire right by our gate. It helps me to better visualize HIS presence and help. (Unfortunately, the thieves probably **don't** envision that.) We certainly appreciate your continued prayers for safety.

It is "H" week for **Hannah**. She is pretty excited that it is the same letter as her name! Hannah...Heaven...Helper...Hooray! Nathanael's latest word is "gecko!" Just in time for letter "G" last week! I would not have imagined that someday I would be writing in his baby book that one of his first words was "gecko." It's hard to believe he's almost two.

Hope all you teachers and students enjoyed your summer break and that the coming school year isn't too stressful. That is one huge change I have noticed here. Malawi has no run–around-until-you–drop syndrome. Things are busy but with notably less stress. Then again, standards here are much lower all the way around, so I'm not sure where the happy-medium lies. I guess only in heaven! God bless, Rebecca

It was becoming clearer that our Nyambadwe property was not in the safest area. The price was right when the mission had purchased it years ago, and the security had been upgraded to a very tight level...but that was of no benefit once off the premises. We were quite safe if we were locked inside the house by the evening. Even though it was tempting to enjoy the outdoors a little longer while the weather was agreeable, I decided that once the sun began to set we would call it a day. Then everything got locked up, especially when Rob was gone.

Our gardener had a small room on our property and lived there by himself during the week. He did his own shopping at the market and had a small garden to help supply his needs. On weekends he returned to his home village and his family of nine. Mr. Chinyama wanted each of his kids to attend school, a goal that could not be achieved through a subsistence life in the village. Earning a city living helped Mr. Chinyama support his family...but what an irreplaceable loss it would be to them if he was injured or killed in a mugging! This particular market trip left him shaken. We happily replaced all his tangible losses, but can you ever replace someone's sense of security? Mr. Chinyama no longer left the premises after dark but instead completed his shopping during daylight.

We were all sadly reminded of the dangers that lurked beyond our property walls—not only physical dangers but spiritual ones also. I thought of the passage in 1 Peter 5:8, *"Be self-controlled and alert. Your enemy the devil prowls around like a roaring lion looking for someone to devour."* With our high walls we could not see what might be stalking us. We could only see the things above our wall: the trees, the nearby mountains, the sky, clouds, sunshine and rainbows. The rainbows reminded us that God still keeps His promises. God promised to be with us, knowing full well we needed His help while the enemy prowled. Looking over our walls kept my eyes heavenward, where the source of my strength and help dwells.

Sent: September 10, 2004
Subject: light work
Rebecca writes: Rob's latest project was replacing two outdoor security lights. The kids and I went outside to admire his handiwork. As we were walking back inside, Rob said "*zikomo*" ("thank you") to the night guard who was helping carry the ladder. Hearing this, Nathanael piped in, "Gelcome!" ("You're welcome!") He must be processing it all. His vocabulary is exploding.

A night guard was snoring under our window last night at 8:45pm! Every time I describe our sleepy guards I feel like I am anthropomorphizing: ascribing human qualities to inanimate objects. Given the latest neighborhood security issues, it is very frustrating.

I am preparing a Ladies' Bible Study on angels. I made some angel wings that I'll wear for my introduction. God bless, Rebecca

I repeatedly have to remind myself that we have two lines of defense against intruders: our earthly guard and our heavenly guard. Obviously one is vastly superior to the other…what a comfort to know that when our earthly sentry is snoring, our angels are still standing at attention!

> *I walk with angels all the way; They shield me and befriend me.*
> *All Satan's pow'r is held at bay When heav'nly hosts attend me.*
> *They are my sure defense; All fear and sorrow, hence!*
> *Unharmed by foes, do what they may, I walk with angels all the way. (CW 431:4)*

Sent: September 12, 2004
Subject: 24-hour service the Malawi way
Rebecca writes: We had a packed church today at the Reading Room. Every seat was taken. Even the preacher willingly gave up his chair. Thankfully, we will

be worshiping in our new church building soon! We also eagerly await the arrival of Beautiful Saviour's new pastor, Mark Johnston. He, his wife Jane and their daughter Rebekah will be in Blantyre in November. They are leaving four grown children behind in the States, as well as their first grandson.

My email title isn't referring to the church service. Instead it refers to a comment that we heard from the Ramseys, whom we had over on Friday (the couple who had bats in their *chimbudzi* a while back). They were talking about a gas station in Southern Malawi that had a sign claiming they were open 24 hours. Their friends decided to go around 3am to get some munchies. Lo and behold, it wasn't open. They returned the next day to ask why the station hadn't been open, despite their 24-hour advertising. The employees replied with all seriousness, "Yes, we are open 24 hours...just not in a row!"

The Bartz family arrived. Jayne Bartz said she is really struck by the poverty. She is also tense and worried about hitting someone while driving. That could be a chronic problem, since I **still** feel the same way! There by the grace of God go...the missionaries on the roads of Malawi! God bless, Rebecca

---

On September 13 it was official...we had been in Malawi for ONE YEAR. We had survived our first year in spite of some bumps in the path of Malawi life. There was no email announcing the benchmark day. That was because our phone was out again—as it had been when we arrived a year ago! Rob was away at meetings and it was just another ordinary day in the life of this mission mom holding down the fort in Nyambadwe, Malawi, Africa.

As we welcomed a new mission family, I was reminded of a harsh comment that I had recently heard. An expat teacher at a local international school had ranted, "I think highly of missionaries who set up hospitals and aid organizations; it takes a special person to do that. But missionaries who just come and preach should not be in Malawi. *Anyone* can do that...and what good does it do? Religion confuses the local people and takes away their culture. It's more important to help and educate people than it is to teach them about the Bible and Jesus." When I heard that comment my jaw dropped. I thought of Rob's efforts to respect the Malawian culture by eagerly studying their language, sharing their food, attending their funerals, sincerely mourning their losses and rejoicing over their gains. This wasn't an attitude of railroading over a culture. To claim that Malawians, or people *anywhere* in the world, do not need to hear about their Savior from sin was to buy into Satan's lie that the welfare of the body is more important than the welfare of the soul. The only part of African culture—of *any* culture—that Christianity strives to erase is SIN and the lust for it.

It is no coincidence that Christians around the world are found organizing worthy community projects that provide medical assistance (such as our Central Africa

Medical Mission), digging bore-holes for drinking water, building schools, assisting orphans and donating seeds, food, clothing and personal time. Those projects all reflect a Christ-like love and concern. They can also create opportunities to share the message of Christ. Society rightly applauds such projects because they have a visible impact on outward problems. However, the smile on the face of society often fades to a frown when the primary goal of a project or mission is to share the gospel. Sometimes people like that expat teacher do not understand that all the physical aid the world can offer is of no eternal value if it is not accompanied by spiritual aid. When did Jesus ever heal a broken body or feed a hungry stomach without also healing a broken spirit and a hungry soul? Food, water, schools and clothes are necessary gifts that God wants us to provide for those in need; but if we are only preparing people for life in *this* world, then we are truly not helping them with what matters most.

The truth is, missionaries like us are essentially preparing people for death—or more specifically, for their life after death. Romans 6:23 says clearly, *"The wages of sin is death, but the gift of God is eternal life in Christ Jesus our Lord."* Once our final breath fades, there are no second chances. Our destination is set. We will either enter eternal life through Christ or eternal torment in hell. Neither earthly poverty nor riches will change the outcome of our souls; only whether we have believed in Christ or rejected him. It is not a politically correct message. It is not one that the world wants to hear. But it is a message that compels every Christian, on the mission field or in their own backyard, to proclaim Jesus as the Savior from sin.

CHAPTER 10

YEAR TWO BEGINS: GOD GIVES AND GOD TAKES AWAY

Take my life and let it be Consecrated, Lord, to thee.
Take my moments and my days;
Let them flow in ceaseless praise. (CW 469:1)

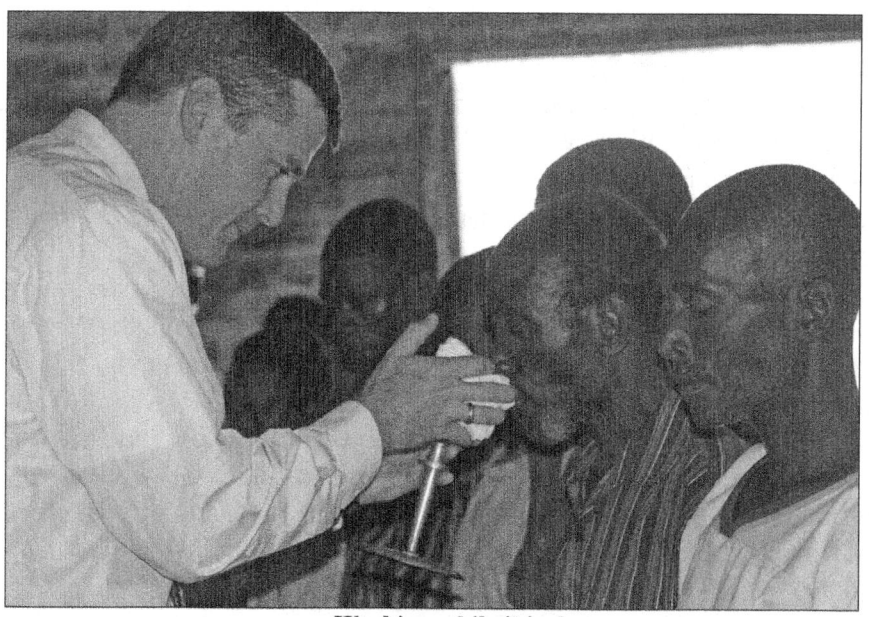

Working while it is day

It is said that a missionary needs to be on field for a few years before he can become productive. It certainly did take time for us to learn to live in a foreign culture and land. The day-to-day details from the emails I wrote that first year (including the oft-repeated refrain about our lousy phone and power!) make it clear what a slow process it was to adjust to the newness of African life and mission work. Those details also show how God used circumstances to train us in patience and trust. I had recited Luther's explanation of the First Commandment for decades: *"We should fear, love and trust in God above all things."* Implementing that command is taking me a lifetime...certainly our first year in Africa accelerated my practical application of it in ways I never anticipated.

Our productivity on field followed with baby steps. I was finally beginning to feel settled, more confident of my surroundings and more capable of managing the tasks at hand. My focus changed from merely coping and surviving to meaningful living and growth. Looking back, I can see that it was often the challenges we weathered that promoted growth! Before 2004 ended we would find ourselves confessing with Job that, *"The LORD gave and the LORD has taken away; may the name of the LORD be praised"* (Job 1:21). In our gains and in our losses, we strove to place our trust in our loving God. As we began our second year in Malawi we became aware of a God-given gain: a very significant *new arrival* that we were eager to announce in person to our families—if only our crummy phone would allow it! Some aspects of life in Malawi, it seemed, would never change.

Sent: October 7, 2004
Subject: Re: is your phone ok?
Rebecca writes: Hello from a drought of email correspondence. Our phone is extremely frustrating! We have learned that the new underground cables that the phone company has been installing in the ditches are merely for show. The city spent all the money on the piping and now can't afford to buy the fiber optic phone lines to fill them.

Our poor phone is particularly frustrating because we have been trying to call all of you and talk to you in person throughout the last month. **We found out that I am expecting baby number three!** I wanted to tell you this great news in a more personal way.

We recently had a lightning strike come out of the clear blue sky—literally—and it fried our modem that was plugged in. Also, for two weeks ALL of our outdoor security lights have been out! That is trouble. It is pitch black outside at night. An electrician was here today and thankfully located the problem.

We worshipped in our new Blantyre church this past Sunday. No more downtown cramped worship services! The church is very lovely and spacious with lots of potential for our congregation to expand and reach out to the urban crowd with the WORD.

I started a beginners' Chichewa language class a few weeks ago with Jayne Bartz. We're first learning how to buy things from vendors using Chichewa terms.

Hannah informed me that she does not want to eat chicken pox. She also asked, "Did Adam and Eve get dusty and dirty and get slivers since they didn't wear any clothes?" Love, Rebecca

It was good that I was feeling more settled, especially with the exciting news of baby #3 on the way. Our new arrival would likely come in April and would mean big changes for me and our family. I felt excited but also very sick and tired. I wanted to talk to both of our families in person. After an entire month of trying—with many failed attempts—we finally managed to reach a few family members. Much to my chagrin, I did end up having to send an email to inform the rest.

One major decision we needed to make was where exactly baby #3 would be born. Nearly every previous Malawi missionary family and Kingdom Worker that I knew of had delivered their babies at local private hospitals. Our own local hospital, Mwaiwathu, had a decent facility, relatively advanced equipment, and it offered some of the best medical care in Malawi. The pressing question was whether or not they would have the proper staff to operate the equipment at any hour of the day or night. A friend of mine who had delivered her baby at Mwaiwathu Hospital had imported her own injectable pain killer for the impending birth. The hospital kept it in a locked cabinet until she needed it for her delivery. When she finally went into delivery in the middle of the night, the cabinet was locked and the person with the key was not available.

The unpredictability of our local medical care made me apprehensive because Rob and I have an Rh blood incompatibility. This condition occurs during pregnancy if a woman has Rh-negative blood and her baby inherits the father's Rh-positive blood. The mother's body then creates Rh antibodies that can attack the baby's red blood cells, leading to potentially fatal oxygen-deprivation in the baby. The problem is, once these antibodies develop in a mother, they remain in her body and pose a greater risk to each subsequent pregnancy. What I required in my third pregnancy was prompt prenatal care and screening. If I were in the States I would receive an injection of RhoGAM to prevent the problems of Rh incompatibility. However, a little personal research revealed that our Blantyre hospital would *not* be proactive in dealing with my negative blood type or providing RhoGAM. I was advised to find other people with my blood type and build up my own blood bank in case I needed it. I found one blood-type match: a person who lived in the capital city of Lilongwe, over 300 km away.

Another difficulty was Rob's schedule. He spent the majority of his time traveling and conducting church services in the bush. The million-dollar question was whether our phone would work if I needed to contact friends or neighbors for help in his absence. Our land phone was exceedingly unreliable, as I am sure you are beginning to understand now. Even my cell phone coverage was iffy; one family told me that every time they called me on my cell they got a busy signal—even if I was not on the phone. I learned that our carrier blocked certain cell areas when their call levels reached maximum. Nyambadwe must have been in that target area.

If we had not been living overseas on a mission field almost all of these struggles would have been non-issues. Instead, we found ourselves weighing our options with a lot of thought, research and prayer.

Sent: October 18, 2004
Subject: powerless weekend
Rob writes: Our weekend was...powerless for the most part. The "technicians" flooded one of our electricity turbine stations at the hydro plant. A feeding duct malfunctioned, and water filled half the station (it is mostly below river level). Last year the same problem happened and the *whole* station flooded—this is progress. Now they have to take apart their soaked computers and dry their circuits in the sun. It worked last year! This means we have had electricity about 50% of the time since Friday. No phone, no electricity; water next? The beat goes on; unpredictability is rather predictable here.

In other news, we had rain all weekend. That was our first big rain. I tell you—there is nothing like the smell of that first rain after the long dry season. The dust is put to rest and the air is filled with the fragrance of all the plants and trees, including the sweet jacaranda. Combine this with the comfortable warmth of mid 80°s and the greening all around and it stirs old memories—it's beginning to look (and smell and feel) a lot like Christmas!

This week we head to Chipata, Zambia to see how our fellow LCCA missionaries conduct their ministries. Currently, we Malawi missionaries don't have decades of experience serving in the bush; so it's over to Zambia to watch those who have been working at it longer than we have. Rich blessings in Jesus, Rob

Sent: October 19, 2004
Subject: October update
Rebecca writes: Rob is currently taking a load of cement to finish up the Kobili building project. Nathanael's second birthday came and went. I attempted to cut a cake into the numeral "2" for his dessert. No Grandma Staude to bring cake masterpieces for these special occasions.

The Malawi Ladies' Retreat was held in Nyambadwe this past weekend. I had the opening session on "Brokenness Caused by Sin." It so happened that a mirror fell off our wall a few weeks prior, which provided some great visual aids for my topic. In the end I developed the idea of our "brokenness" by talking about our sharp edges and how we can easily cut each other—yet the Lord has made us into a new creation. Our sharp edges can no longer hurt others when we are working together in Christ. In the same way, broken pieces of glass work side by side in a stained glass window. (I had cut colored tissue paper into pieces that matched the broken sections of my mirror and fashioned them into a stained glass window.) Just as the light shines through the sections of a stained glass window, we are working together to let His light shine through us and our efforts here as we carry out the great commission.

We told Hannah yesterday that she will be a big sister. She had a huge smile on her face. She insisted that she will help with the name and went straight to her Bible to start looking. She understands my constant tiredness now. God bless, Rebecca

The annual Ladies' Bible Retreats have been an incredible spiritual highlight for me as I live on field. A computer analogy comes to mind when I think of the value of these retreats. I used to use a relatively old computer. After performing countless operations in different systems, my computer ran a bit slower, the RAM bogged down and errors crept in. When that happened, it was obvious I needed to shut it down to renew the RAM and reboot the system—before it crashed! Like that old computer, I begin to drag after the countless operations of daily life here. At times I find errors creeping in and realize I could benefit from a break—before I crash! Our annual Bible retreats are a temporary shutdown from the daily grind of household life and from struggles on the home front. At these retreats I can reboot around the Word of God with fellow Christian ladies. The Word unfailingly rejuvenates me and revives my zeal to continue in the supportive role that we missionary wives have. It helps me prioritize and gives my spirit a boost. I feel extremely blessed to be able to gather with fellow missionary wives, empathize with each other's challenges, enjoy our weekend fellowship and, most importantly, grow in faith.

The Lord rejuvenated me at an opportune time; it wasn't long before our next big challenge came along that would find me drawing on my reserves of trust and patience in the face of loss.

Malawi Ladies' Bible Retreat 2004

"Those who hope in the LORD will renew their strength.
They will soar on wings like eagles; they will run and not grow weary,
they will walk and not be faint." Isaiah 40:31

Sent: October 28, 2004
Subject: transformers

Rebecca writes: My title references the plastic toy Transformers that start as a plastic car and then transform into a mechanical man. The theme song was, **"Transformers...more than meets the eye!"** (I know at least my brother Matt can sing it with me.) That tune has been running through my head since last night, when most of the electronics that we own—110v items that were plugged into a (real) transformer, along with assorted 220v items plugged into the wall—were fried and damaged. Malawi's terrible electricity has resulted in us paying quite a price.

Rob woke very early when he heard our step-down transformers in the house begin to hum loudly. The hum was a telltale sign that a power surge was sweeping through and frying anything plugged in. Our whole house was stinking! Our 220v stove was fried, along with our refrigerator, camcorder battery charger, CD player, several entertainment center items, my computer printer and microwave. Thankfully the computer, one kitchen appliance and Rob's printer escaped the blowout. I had unplugged ALL these things when we went to Zambia. But after our return everything had been gradually plugged in again.

Hannah's room was the stinkiest because our security-system box is plugged into the wall next to her bed. It still works but only by battery. Its transformer will have to be replaced too. Her wall around the outlet is black from smoke and smoke had filled her room. I asked her if she had noticed it; she told me that when the smoke got bad, she covered her mouth with her blankie. UGH. I have tried to impress upon the kids exactly what emergencies are and what to do during them. Then during an emergency, instead of getting help, little Hannah covered her mouth and stayed in bed! I told her that SMOKE IN HER ROOM is considered an emergency, and she should tell us immediately. (I can't help but think that if a fire **did** ever break out, even if everyone responded promptly we would be hard pressed to open all the necessary locks and grates to escape in a timely manner. All our windows are encased in double burglar bars, so they are not an escape option. The Lord knows our situation, and I trust Him to take care of us and provide a way out if and when we ever need it.)

On to a happier subject: we had a good trip to and from Chipata, Zambia. Rob enjoyed the bush trips with the missionaries. The Missionary Holtz family graciously hosted us for a few days. On the way home we bought lots of peanuts—more than Nathanael weighs. If we ever get our stove working again, we may actually get to prepare the peanuts...plus any other meals.

Dad, thanks for the neat autumn deer picture. I looked past the deer and marveled at the beautiful scenery: smooth pavement, clean open roadway, and wide gravel shoulders. That was the feature right? Ha ha! God bless, Rebecca

We knew that our possessions were a gift from God. He had given us our material blessings; now He had allowed many of them to be taken away. We were thankful for His grace that kept us all safe. An electrical repairman later estimated that a power surge of 600 volts had swept through our house. As soon as we heard the loud hum we had unplugged everything as quickly as we could. But it was too late. As we assessed the damage, it was quickly apparent that we had lost most of our electronics. Even the surge protectors were absolutely melted. We checked the information on the back of them: they were only effective up to 400 volts. Thankfully, we had a superior surge protector on our refrigerator. Though it burned out, it did save the fridge. That kind of voltage protector costs a hefty $60 each…but if they could save our electronics, it would be a worthwhile investment.

The power surge was so drastic that Rob figured we actually had power rushing in straight from the high power lines. The incoming high voltage simply bypassed our nonfunctioning neighborhood transformer and traveled straight into our outlets. It came with such a blast that it actually blew apart previously-connected wires in our circuit box. It blew out all of our security light switches as well. Later we found out that our neighbors' light bulbs had exploded in their homes. I was thankful to have avoided that kind of mess. We had enough to deal with, cleaning up the black singes on the walls from the burning outlets and the plugs that had melted into the outlets.

We visited the electric company's office and asked them what they would do to prevent a reoccurrence, and how they would compensate our loss. They told us if we listed all our losses on paper they would have their insurance company reimburse us. I estimated that our losses were to the tune of several thousands of dollars. (Of course, that was the only "tune" we would be singing, since we could not play music any more.) The electric company's insurance never did reimburse us, in case you were holding your breath. I was not holding mine.

Take my silver [electronics] and my gold [appliances];
Not a mite [kwacha] would I withhold.
Take my intellect and use
Every power [220v-110v] as thou shalt choose.
(CW 469:4) [brackets my own]

Sent: October 30, 2004
Subject: big debate of late
Rebecca writes: My thoughts are a bit scattered at the moment as to the final plan for the delivery of Wendland baby #3. Thank you, Mom, for the offer to fly to Malawi if I need assistance. It would be a stretch to deliver the baby here in April and get all the paperwork and passport items cleared in time for our furlough in late June. (The last family waited five months before their child's passport was

completed. That wait is too long if we wish to return to Malawi by September for Hannah's transition to school.) However, if we took an early furlough, Rob would completely miss his *parents'* furlough, which is scheduled around his Dad attending the Seminary's summer quarter in July.

An April due date is possibly close enough to our regularly scheduled June furlough that I could consider coming to the USA early. Stateside health care for the baby and me would be light years ahead of Malawi. However, Rob would not be able to accompany us, since he is required to work until the middle of June. That would mean the kids and I would fly back early by ourselves. I am required to fly before 36 weeks, which is mid-March. No housing or car would be provided until Rob's scheduled arrival in June. Where we would stay is up in the air. I don't think this choice is Rob's first preference. On the flip side, having a baby here with questionable health care isn't my first preference.

Rob has mentioned that if I remain here and deliver at Mwaiwathu hospital, I can trust that the Lord will take care of things. That is certainly true. It was true even as we cut our ties to move here. I also see that the Lord has given me my abilities to make an educated judgment. My previous deliveries each had their troubles—though no major problems developed. But I was thankful to have reliable health care at hand. I am praying I do not have to deal with serious swelling as I did with Nathanael's pregnancy. Figuring out what is best for everyone is not easy. God bless, Rebecca

Delivering in Malawi would be the most convenient choice but also the riskiest. Delivering in the States would put us in the hands of first-world health care, but our family would not be together and Rob might not be around for the delivery. I would have to depend on Stateside family for help. I knew the Lord would care for the baby and me in either place. Trouble can happen anywhere in the world, regardless of the quality of health care. The impact of one decision versus another kept me teetering back and forth on where this new baby should be born.

Sent: October 31, 2004
Subject: strike 2
Rebecca writes: Today Rob preached at Beautiful Saviour. It was an edifying service. It was a foggy, rainy morning so the attendees trickled in long after the service started.

We recently went to Shoprite, only to find that they were on strike. Then we tried the Dairibord to get our usual bale of milk (10 liters) and strike two—no milk today. Their homogenizer was broken. So we drove all the way back into town to go to a third store. Thankfully, they were open and had about half the things on my list. I picked up other produce from a street vendor.

Our stove is working, but our oven still is not. We're using our griddle often.

Last evening our power was out for a long time. The kids don't even make a sound any more when the lights go out. They patiently wait for someone to get another light source going and carry on as usual. I could see a splash mark on the kitchen floor where someone dropped a cup when the lights went out. It must have been Nathanael, because a minute later the two-year-old appeared with a cloth and started to wipe it up. That evening our three-wick candle burned to the bottom. The holder wasn't designed to catch that much wax.

Happy Reformation! What a blessing it is to take a moment to appreciate Martin Luther's dedication to true Biblical teachings. God bless. Rebecca

Meager groceries. No milk. No oven. No power. Some days in Malawi require extra patience and multiple attempts to accomplish anything. Days like these also require some creativity, since meals still have to get on the table and tasks still have to be completed.

Sent: November 2, 2004
Subject: Malawi update
Rebecca writes: When I drove home from choir last night it was after dark. As I pulled into our yard, I noticed that the night guard didn't lock the gate behind me. I asked him to lock the gate. He claimed the other guard was bringing the key. I found the other guard and he had no key; in fact, he had completely lost our keys. This is a serious offense. Rob is waiting to see if they can turn something up tonight. I put a whole lot more stock in a metal lock than I do in one of them sitting by the gate all night "watching" (their eyelids).

Hannah asked me the other day how to open a door with a round door knob after seeing a picture of one in a book. I never noticed that there are no round knobs here; we have thin-handled levers. That will be another discovery awaiting her on furlough.

I included the presidential election in our morning prayer with Hannah. We are resting on our preliminary absentee ballots that we sent via the American Embassy in September. Love, Rebecca

Soon after I sent my email about the guards losing our key, Mom Wendland in Zambia dashed off a reply:

INCOMING EMAIL: November 2, 2004
Subject: RE: Malawi update
Mom Wendland writes: Hi; the guard "losing" your keys is VERY serious! It could mean that the guards have given them to people to use when you are gone

or sold them. You should change the locks on whatever the guard had keys for, AND report them to their company. This is how thieves can get onto a property and spend the rest of the night breaking into the house and no one can see them! This is serious, and the guards need to know that—like NO JOB! Jesus keep you all in His care! Much love, Mom

Yet again we faced the frustration of hiring men to protect our property who at best seemed incompetent, and at worst, accessories to crime. Certainly a night-guard's job here involves long hours and poor pay. Their company promises them four hours of overtime-pay per day, but their paycheck does not reflect this. The management barely supplies them with what they need. The guards are constantly running out of pens to fill their operations book, and they are happy if they get good quality uniforms with working zippers and without holes. They have no workers' union to uphold their cause. Many of the guards struggle to communicate in English. Most of them struggle to stay awake! Several have told me that they also work day jobs in order to support their families. We had to ask for one guard to be removed because he simply could not stay awake past 8:30pm. The night guards frequently ask us for money, or help, or for us to hire them privately. We willingly provide them with occasional small gifts throughout the year and a Christmas and Easter gift-assortment of helpful items. However, becoming their private employers would require taking on some undesirable obligations: having to hire relief guards for their sick days, funerals, days-off and holidays, as well as being responsible for their family's health issues. It has crossed my mind that life would be easier and we could save the mission a load of money by simply not hiring guards. But, though it is hard to live with them, the risk of living without them is too high.

After this incident we continued to reinforce with each guard we were sent the importance of following rules and keeping track of keys. We also informed the management of our recent key loss and let them follow through with the appropriate consequences. And we changed our locks!

"So do not fear, for I am with you;
do not be dismayed, for I am your God.
I will strengthen you and help you;
I will uphold you with my righteous right hand." Isaiah 41:10

Sent: November 4, 2004
Subject: odds and ends
Rebecca writes: I'm slowly getting some energy back. It feels nice NOT to be exceedingly wiped out all day long with morning sickness. Thank the Lord; it is none too soon with many activities coming our way. One main item on our

calendar is a visit from the ACA next month. We're hosting, driving and feeding people, so I can't afford to take it easy and rest much longer. Every task here takes so much longer to prepare for.

We heard the election results. May the Lord continue to bless America through President Bush. Love, Rebecca

P.S. (This is so silly—I tried to log on to send this and **MY** phone is busy!)

Each mission family hosts and feeds many visitors throughout the course of a year here in Malawi. The Administrative Committee for Africa (ACA) sends representatives almost every year to the field. Hosting such visitors is another small way that mission wives quietly serve the Lord and support mission work. We obviously don't provide Michelin-starred cuisine or five-star Hilton accommodations, but we gladly share what we have on these special occasions and visits.

Take my hands and let them move At the impulse of thy love.
Take my feet and let them be Swift and beautiful for thee. (CW 469:2)

Sent: November 11, 2004
Subject: Now we're cookin'
Rebecca writes: Our phone is causing us trouble again. Sometimes I feel like a prank caller when we actually make a connection but no one can hear us at the other end.

Our oven, thankfully, is fixed. Yesterday I baked and cooked most of the day. That was a nice change; I haven't been cooking for almost two months of morning sickness.

I had my second prenatal appointment. The doctor had lots for me to chew on. He is not happy that I'm not on a malaria prophylaxis since the rainy season is upon us. He's suggesting a Fansidar dose every trimester. I do have friends taking a combination of paludrine and chloroquine. The combo is supposed to be effective and safe for pregnancy. I don't know. Also, the doctor doesn't think I'll need my RhoGAM shot at 26-28 weeks. I told him I've read a lot about it and would like to have it, especially since this is my third child. I don't know if the hospital here will have it—and if they do, I am not sure my doctor will be willing to administer it.

We went to Limbe for my first ultrasound. In the middle of nowhere, past some abandoned railroad tracks and warehouses, there was this little clinic that had a paved driveway and decent equipment. The kids liked watching the little baby on the screen. I paid $40 in cash. He even printed out a picture for me to take home, though it is very grainy and difficult to make out. Could be my gall bladder for all I know.

We planted a nectarine tree along with our orange trees. Our newly planted citrus grove might soon be enjoyed by someone else. What do I mean? This morning Paul Nitz, the Malawi field coordinator, called. He is concerned about our security and communication issues and asked if they could look around for new housing for us. We wouldn't potentially move until after our baby is born and after our upcoming furlough. No more landscaping. I'll put things on hold and be glad I didn't make more drapes. Love, Rebecca

I suppose if our family lived in the bush, a working phone line or power would be completely luxurious. But we were living in the city. Emails were our lifeline. More and more companies in the West were assuming their clients had access to an internet connection. We were expected to stay up-to-date on WELS news, mission policies and insurance information. We also needed to stay connected to the "outside world." We were often directed to online information and website details, but trying to glean *anything* online from our home in Nyambadwe was nearly out of the question. Not every area in Blantyre was affected with such a poor phone line. Nor was every area in Blantyre subject to our security issues. We finally felt settled and did not relish the thought of moving again, but a change in location within the city could improve both our problematic phone line and our security. It was something more to think about.

My Malawian prenatal care was definitely in a different category than the Stateside care I had experienced with my first two pregnancies. Sometimes the care seemed so minimal I would wonder why I had bothered—I could weigh myself at home! I requested an initial ultrasound; mostly for a confirmation on my due date. If I wanted another I was told to ask for a referral slip.

INCOMING EMAIL: November 12, 2004
Subject: RE: Malawi update
Mom Wendland writes: Hi Rebecca, Your doctor is right about a malaria prophylaxis. Pregnant ladies should take some kind of prevention. Malaria is known to cause late-term miscarriages and is very dangerous for pregnant women and their babies. Taking the Fansidar is common here in Zambia too, especially in government clinics. It is safe and you could use this. The US Government uses mefloquine. The research finds that this is safe in pregnancy too. Your doc probably wouldn't recommend this because it is expensive. The chloroquine/paludrine combo is safe in pregnancy, but there is parasite resistance to these drugs so they aren't very effective protection. Jesus keep you in His care! Love, Mom

I really struggled with the idea of taking a malaria prophylaxis. I wondered what kind of drug research had been done. I knew I should make a decision soon. I was supremely thankful this was not my first pregnancy.

Sent: November 16, 2004
Subject: the latest from here
Rebecca writes: I'm happy to report that the Johnston family safely arrived in Malawi. They were welcomed at church on Sunday. Mark Johnston is eager to "get started." We've had mission get-togethers almost daily since their arrival. We hosted a gathering on Sunday afternoon. There are no bakery buns to be had in all of Blantyre; thankfully I had made some ahead of time (with our newly repaired oven) and had precooked my meat also. I was nicely ahead of schedule with the food when, sure enough, the power went out shortly after I put the dinner in the oven. It sort of slow-cooked in the warm oven for several hours. I organized a scavenger hunt for the kids. They had fun running around and learning the names of local flora and fauna: I'm all for educational. They picked treasure-box prizes at the finish. God bless, Rebecca

"The LORD gives..." We were thrilled to add the Johnston family to our list of blessings. Now our new church building in downtown Blantyre had a new pastor who would lead us in worship of our amazing God...in English even!

Sent: November 23, 2004
Subject: litchi league
Rebecca writes: Hello! No, I haven't joined the nursing mother's league...but (as the title suggests) we have tried some litchis. It is a fruit that looks like a hand grenade on the outside, with a thin, hard, bumpy brown shell that you peel away. The fruit is milky white and tastes like a sweet, juicy grape. In the center of the fruit is an almond-shaped pit. Rob thought the peeled fruit looked like an eyeball. Hannah was intrigued. She was happy to have her Grandpa Wendland (who is briefly with us as he travels through Blantyre) try some. He had eaten litchis before in South Africa. We're still new and learning many things here.

In addition to Grandpa Wendland's visit, we also spent Saturday evening with Great Grandma Kathie Wendland. She was a registered nurse in Central Africa in the 1970's. She now works in the States as a nurse recruiter and advisor for the Central Africa Medical Mission and traveled here with the Lilongwe Medical Mission nurses.

The weather here has been HOT, HOT, HOT! Temperatures have been in the upper 90°s in the shade. It was so hot in our kitchen that a bottle of crystallized honey began to re-liquefy. Last evening there were dust devils everywhere, churning up garbage from the road, plucking mangos and small branches from the trees and pelting debris against the car. Something was brewing. Thankfully it was a storm that left cooler weather behind.

Last week a man was at the gate talking about a salve he needed for a burn. In the end, Rob let him in our yard. The man went immediately to a tree in the corner of our property and cut off some bark. When the sap began to ooze out he wiped some on his burn. I should find out what that tree is. As I mentioned, we're still new and learning many things.

Over the last few weeks, mail from early 2002 has been trickling in. Malawi Post must have found a pouch of "lost" mail. Nathanael wasn't even born then, and we weren't on field yet. Love, Rebecca

I never guessed when we moved to Malawi that we would be blessed to have so many family members visit us in a single year. These delightful visits have erased any previous assumptions that we would be swallowed up by the Dark Continent and only found years later, wrapped in loin cloths, chiseling messages into rocks and starved of human contact. I'm kidding. Of course Rob and I would wear something more than a loin cloth! All our visitors and hosting opportunities, even here in the heart of Africa, made us feel like we were at least accessible, if not exactly a global hub. Still, when we got a pile of mail that should have been delivered two years ago, Malawi did feel a bit like "the land that time forgot."

Sent: November 24, 2004
Subject: good news-bad news
Rebecca writes: Matt and Dad—good news: we received a check from the United States Treasury for our 1999 tax refund! That was a big surprise. I collected it by certified mail from the American Embassy in Lilongwe. Thanks for your work... you obviously cleared something up to our benefit. Since we cannot process any USA checks here, we hope to send it back to the USA to you via an ACA member when they visit in December. Bad news: there is no sign of the Christmas package that you sent a few months ago, Mom. For once, the tax news is the best news.

Rob came home with his truck half full of sweet potatoes from a church offering, so I made sweet potato chips all afternoon. He was supposed to go to a congregation in the Shire Valley today. Due to a bad accident on the road down, no one could get through. Now he's trying to do tomorrow's work in order to have the day free for our Thanksgiving celebration.

I have two more weeks of language classes before I'll call it quits. With the baby on the way I'll be happy with what I was able to learn thus far. We are getting into noun classes and that will be quite labor-intensive to study and put to memory. (Of course **that** kind of "labor-intensive" might be easier than the one I will soon be facing!)

Today Hannah lamented that she can't remember things from America. I asked her to tell me what she couldn't remember—trick question—and then she told me she couldn't remember the color of the Milwaukee garbage trucks. Funny, Rob and I couldn't remember either. I thought they were orange, but Rob thought they were white and green. So it goes with trash talk here.

Pastor Johnston's installation was very nice this Sunday. The installation rite is always a great reminder of what the Lord expects of His called servants. May the Lord continue to bless all of our ministries, big and small, as we thankfully share his Word with those around the world. Rebecca

Just when I had mentally rolled my eyes over mail in Malawi that was two years late, we received a USA tax refund that was five years late. I am reminded so often that no place on earth is perfect. It cannot be. For perfection we keep our eyes heavenward and our hearts with Jesus.

Sent: November 28, 2004
Subject: Camahady & Co
Rebecca writes: I didn't sleep well on the eve of Thanksgiving because after I went to bed Rob came down the hall exclaiming, "Oh…no…I forgot to tell you…" The detail was significant. He had received notice earlier in the day that our electricity would be off from 8am to 7pm on Thursday: Thanksgiving Day! I was glad I wasn't hosting the celebration. I was awake at 6am and was able to get all the pre-cooking and preparations done with existing power (and even took a hot shower) before the kids woke up. I ended up with an overflow pan of zesty corn stuffing and ate part of it as my breakfast! This was the first time I ever made my own croutons. It took several days to bake the bread, dry the bread cubes and finally make the stuffing.

We had an enjoyable Thanksgiving with the mission families. Pastor Johnston prepared a worship program and shared a meaningful Scripture message. All the ladies had prepared a wonderful feast. We had a great time worshipping, feasting and fellowshipping the night away.

Hannah opened a restaurant in her room. It was called "The Malawi Camahady Chicken Restaurant." I ordered Peanut Chicken and she aptly replied, "Oh, sorry we don't have that today—pick something else." Then the scenario would repeat. It was truly a Malawian-style restaurant!

This Sunday the ACA members come for a few days. We're hosting Dr. John Johnson (Missionary Support Services), Pastor Walter Westphal (Board for World Missions) and his wife Diane. The Westphals were missionaries in Lilongwe in the 1980's. Their daughter, Sarah, was my classmate at Northwestern Prep. Sarah (Habben, *née* Westphal) commented once that she thinks heaven will be like Malawi, except without all the dirt and dust. This will be old stomping grounds for the Westphals, since Sarah commuted from Lilongwe to attend Blantyre's international high school, Saint Andrews. It is located mere minutes from our Nyambadwe house. She attended Saint Andrews before she transferred to Northwestern Prep as a junior. It is a small world after all!

I hope to put up Christmas decorations before the visitors come, along with getting the bees exterminated and the floors waxed. At least I'm feeling up to doing more. I'm still obliged to rest more than I wish, but it is progress from those early months of heavy morning-sickness!

I had a little insight into the true resourcefulness of the Malawians today from a local lady. She told me many Malawians reuse old batteries. (I figured that much.) She explained that she cooks a "porridge" and puts the old batteries in it. When the battery acid and the porridge are "just right" she uses the paste as a floor sealer for the inside of her house/hut. I wonder who experiments with these things. Does she use gloves? What you don't all learn!

We pray you had a wonderful Thanksgiving. It is hard to put into words just how incredibly blessed and thankful we are. God bless, Rebecca

The idea that when you work hard for something you appreciate it all the more proved to be true for our Thanksgiving celebration. Preparing a feast with all the delicious fixings and familiar American Thanksgiving flavors required a considerable investment of time from all of us.

Take my voice and let me sing Always, only for my King.
Take my lips and let them be
Filled with messages from thee. (CW 469:3)

Sent: December 1, 2004
Subject: not as planned
Rebecca writes: Rob drove the 300 km north to Lilongwe for meetings to prepare for the upcoming ACA visit—but no business was conducted. In fact, he and the other pastors were soon headed south again for a funeral in this area. This sad message from Lilongwe explains more:

"Yesterday, many pastors and laymen of the LCCA Malawi gathered here in Lilongwe at the Lutheran Bible Institute. The next two days were to be Synod meetings. One of the laymen was Clifford Mabedi, the second-born son of LBI Principal Daison Mabedi. Clifford had arrived in Lilongwe a few days early but soon felt ill. The doctor admitted him into the hospital and later he died. His sudden death was caused by the cerebral form of malaria. Our meetings have been cancelled. Today we will have a service here at Crown of Life. After the service many of us will travel to the Mabedis' home village near Kamoto in the Southern Region for the funeral and burial on Wednesday."

Year Two Begins: God Gives And God Takes Away

While Rob was away, Hannah kept dinner conversation lively. At supper she asked me, "Mom, which bed would you sleep on if you were in jail?" Now what do you say to something like that? Later I wondered if her question had been prompted because I ran a red light that evening. Lest you think that my driving has gone criminal, I have been told—and in fact, encouraged—to drive carefully through a red light at night rather than become a sitting target at an intersection. There is no police presence on the roads at night; once the sun goes down, police are off duty.

Nathanael saw a bug yesterday. He pointed and announced exuberantly, "FLY!" Hannah looked at it and declared with precision, "It is a *chongololo* curled up into the shape of a 6." I thank the Lord for their varied personalities daily.

At choir practice the power went out. I felt like I was part of the Ten Virgins parable. When the lights went out it was a test to see who was prepared, since no one had known "the hour." Only a few of us had flashlights. I'll take my headlamp for the next practice. Our concerts are this weekend. The ACA comes on Sunday, so it will be a very busy weekend.

Yesterday our language instructor never showed up. Our lessons are winding down but not THAT quickly! Instead, I took the other two mission wives shopping downtown. We had fun exploring. We found a garden shop, a Halaal meat place and an office-furniture supply store. It was fun shopping with them, but by myself I have no desire to explore new shops. I'm at a zero for adventure right now.

Hannah is excited to get the Christmas decorations up, so I'll "wrap" this up.
Love, Rebecca

While I was holding down the home front, Rob was in the midst of a plan-change due to the abrupt death of Pastor Mabedi's son, Clifford. You may remember Pastor Mabedi being mentioned earlier in this book. Shortly after we arrived in Malawi, Pastor Mabedi had cancelled school at the LBI to attend the funeral of a student's infant son. Now it was Pastor Mabedi's turn to receive comfort from fellow Christians. He had lost a son of his own, a young man not yet 30 years old. Death has long fingers in Africa; plucking its victims from every age and stage of life. Many in Africa believe such family deaths are caused when an ancestor's spirit is angered. Their grief has no hope. Pastor Mabedi knew the truth: that because of sin, death comes to everyone…but the fingers of Death are broken. They cannot hold on to those who are in Jesus' arms.

Sent: December 1, 2004
Subject: the wages of sin…
Rob writes:…is death. We know this. We believe this. And yet it does not lessen the pain when it happens, especially *mwadzidzidzi* (suddenly). I'll add my side to the story.

Monday morning I drove my truck to Lilongwe with 750 lbs of "starter seed packs" as humanitarian aid for the northern congregations. I stayed in the mission guest house with the Bill Meier Family. Cathy graciously invited me to dine with them. While we ate, we received the shocking news that Pastor Mabedi's son, Clifford—age 29—had died. Clifford worked with me on the Mission Board, so I knew him well. He had been sick a few months ago with cerebral malaria but had recovered. What happened?

It turns out Clifford and his family had come to Lilongwe a day early. On Sunday, Clifford didn't feel well and had a fever. On Monday, Pastor Mabedi visited Clifford, but he was sleeping and his temperature kept rising. At 5:45pm God called his child home. "*Malungo*" (fever/malaria) was the official cause written on the death certificate.

At around 7pm I went over to the Mabedi home. Other pastors were there. The wailing had begun. Pastor Mabedi was outside, and I tried to comfort him with words that can never seem to begin to convey the feeling inside. I reminded him of the hope we have in the return and resurrection of our Savior Jesus *("comfort one another with these words"!)*. Pastor Mabedi responded with an African perspective (for indeed I never heard such a thing in 40 funerals Stateside), "I have comforted many others in the past under similar circumstances, but now I too need to be comforted. It is my turn."

I guess so, isn't it? We each "get" a turn sooner or later. We each lose those who are near and dear, until we too are dragged down into the dust of death. What a comfort there is in the solid hope of redemption and resurrection; a hope that is mine all because He loved me so much that He became a wretched human— He obeyed, He died—*chifukwa cha ine* (in my place / because of me). That was Clifford's hope and also that of his parents.

By 10pm it was decided. The next two days were funeral days. The meetings were postponed. About that time Pastor Wowa invited me back to the Mabedi's. There the pastors sang hymns until midnight. The wailing stopped and many of the mourners sang along. It is etched into my memory. Beautiful Chichewa hymns sung by firelight with the pastors and LBI students, staving off the *midima ya chisoni* (darkness of sadness).

The next day, my truck was emptied of starter seed packs by 7am. With my truck empty, I picked up the LBI choir and Pastors Mabedi and Msowoya and drove to the mortuary. It was about 10 km out of town. Another pickup drove to get the casket. The mortuary was set up with concrete benches in a semi-circle around a concrete table. With the bills taken care of, we sat on one of those benches and waited. The immediate family had also come to wait. It was not long before the wailing began again, because the coffin had arrived—the definitive (apparent) finality of the rough wooden box. We stood while it was carried into the side room

Year Two Begins: God Gives And God Takes Away

where the morticians worked. For almost two more hours we waited, singing hymns as they completed their business.

Then everything was ready. The now-full coffin was placed on the concrete table. The wailing began again. Pastor Msowoya stood, calmed the crowd and shared a devotion based on 1 Thessalonians 4, "We believe that Jesus died and rose again and so we believe that God will bring with Jesus those who have fallen asleep with him." Then we loaded back up again to return to the LBI. We moved at funeral speed: 20 kph. Many, many people from the surrounding community had come to the LBI. The coffin was placed in front of the church; a "flap" was opened to reveal Clifford's face, and people filed by for their final viewing.

The service was in English and Chichewa. The English was led by Pastor Ib Meyer and the Chichewa by Pastor Liwonde. They both preached on Psalm 116:15, "Precious in the sight of the Lord is the death of His saints." What does that mean? How is it possible? What comfort can this give to us even now? And again, the only hope any can have—that of the Savior Jesus—was clearly proclaimed.

After the service it was time to go south. South past Blantyre into Thyolo District to Kamoto village, the Mabedi home. On the way down we passed through regular rain; then the "rain" of greasy *inswa* (flying termites). So many of those things hit my windshield that I ran out of windshield fluid and I had to use my drinking water. The roads were wet, so we slip-slided around as we wound through the darkening Thyolo hills, passing macadamia farms and tea plantations until at last we made it to the Mabedi home at 7pm. We found everything ready. Plastic chairs were set up and food was prepared. I shut off the vehicle and the darkness of Africa enclosed. It was cloudy with no moon and no stars. The only light was cast by the little fires outside and by small kerosene lanterns. It was by the light of one of those lanterns that I ate with the pastors: *nsima*, fish and boiled cabbage. I was told the people would sing all night this time. Pastor Mabedi quietly dismissed the missionaries. Paul Nitz led me out of Thyolo and I was home by 10pm. Faithful Rebecca had soup waiting and I ate again.

Today it was back to Kamoto village with the other Blantyre missionaries. The darkness had been banished by a sparkling clear day, and we were stunned by the beauty of the land and mighty Mt. Mulanje. We arrived by noon and were shown our seats of honor in the shade. Pastor Chikwatu hosted, Pastor Msowoya preached on Psalm 23, and Pastors Kambalame and Kawelama prayed. Two choirs sang. It was neat to be able to translate the vast majority of what went on for the two new missionaries.

After the funeral activities we walked to the grave site. It was probably over a kilometer away, on paths that often forced us into single file. We walked through the hills, past villages, over a river and finally found the grove of trees that marked the *manda* (graveyard). In the African way, most of the men helped put the coffin into the ground. After a committal service, all the men filled in the grave with dirt and women sang while placing flowers around it. Then it was done. We had mourned. We had remembered. But most of all we had called on and leaned on the promises of our wonderful Savior.

As I was leaving, Pastor Mabedi said to me, "My son is dead and I will always carry that burden; but you have done a lot to lift that burden for me, to carry it with me. Thank you." With tears stinging the edges of my eyes I responded, "And together we look forward to the time when we will never have to say good-bye again." Love, Rob

The Lord's gracious timing was evident. He had called Clifford home while surrounding his father and family with supportive Christian friends, who all "just happened to be" gathered in one place for meetings. Through the devotions, sermons, songs and prayers that filled this time of mourning, many were reminded that Clifford's will and life and heart had belonged to the Lord—who had redeemed him and raised him from death to life eternal.

Take my will and make it thine; It shall be no longer mine.
Take my heart—it is thine own;
It shall be thy royal throne. (CW 469:5)

Typical village in Malawi

Sent: December 2, 2004
Subject: postal smile
Rebecca writes: Our phone has worked nicely for a few days in a row. Rob took the kids on errands in town, and on his way home he stopped at the post office. He collected the straggling, West Salem-mailed Christmas package! "We thank you we do," and we have big smiles at the treasures that wait under our artificial

tree. It certainly is looking like Christmas...indoors, anyway! God bless, Rebecca

Our families and fellow Christians were and continue to be a never-ending source of encouragement in the form of words, actions, prayers...and even packages. THANK YOU!

Sent: December 7, 2004
Subject: CD smile
Rebecca writes: This week zoomed by. The ACA arrived here in Blantyre on Sunday. We had a nice evening meal and visit. Pastor Westphal told me about an insurance program currently being explored by the Board for World Missions (BWM) called International SOS. It is a company that provides a variety of health and medical assistance to international travelers and expatriates. Apparently a recent incident has the BWM looking deeper into health care matters...and recommending that any missionary wife in Africa diagnosed with pregnancy concerns should travel to the USA prior to the birth of her child.

The subject title (CD smile) was for this morning. At Bible Group my blown-out CD player was waiting for me. A German friend had worked on it. But without a step-down transformer it couldn't be tested. When I got home I tested it, and it worked! We had our Christmas music playing again after lunch. Hallelujah!

In our attempt to eradicate our bee problem, we encountered yet another typical Malawi run-around. Rob called AntiPest last week and discussed our situation. In the end, AntiPest told Rob that if they came to spray it would be too expensive. They advised Rob to go to the city council for cheaper service. So Rob dutifully tried all the city numbers listed in the phone book and no one answered. (Now that I think of it, we didn't check the late-entry section at the back of the phone book!) So, to bee or not to bee remains the question for yet another day/month/year. I'll still try my best to get rid of them before our next dear visitors come for Christmas: Grandma and Grandpa Wendland!

Another huge hand of our bananas, over 100, ripened almost all at once. I shared lots with the other families and we're "going bananas" with the rest! I made seven banana breads and several dozen muffins. I pushed my limit of running around the kitchen. I had to sit down as I finished putting the batters in the pans. I can't go bananas quite like I used to. Love, Rebecca

I had written off most of our electrical items from the power surge at the end of October. What a gift it was that my friend helped repair my CD player...and it WORKED. When I see the Lord work through people unexpectedly, it makes me stand back in awe that He cares that much. I started enjoying music again that very day!

Sent: December 8, 2004
Subject: Barbie dream house
Rebecca writes: Today Hannah and I played Barbie Dream House Colorforms together. It is amazing what you learn from a child's dialogue. She was Barbie and I was Ken. It was soon their bedtimes. Then Barbie wanted to get up. So she got up and walked to the kitchen. Hannah said that Barbie could do that because they had no grates on their doors. There were no thieves—therefore she could walk around wherever she wanted. I thought, "That is the truth! I can't think of anyone who is 'locked' into their bedroom area in the States for security reasons." Grates certainly would not be in a Barbie dream house! I'm banking that my heavenly mansion won't have them either! God bless, Rebecca and a "grate-full" family.

I have come to realize that no place on earth is ideal. Each place has its advantages and beauty; each place has its drawbacks and aggravations. I think that God allows this so that we keep our eyes heavenward and don't get too comfortable on this side of eternity!

Sent: December 10, 2004
Subject: RhoGAM run-around
Rebecca writes: We bought a German Shepherd puppy: Shadow. She is destroying flower beds, potted plants and has shattered two bird baths. Puppy love—not really!
My doctor appointment was cancelled. They tried to contact me but couldn't, since our phone was out of order yet again. They rescheduled the appointment for today. I called to reconfirm. The clinic told me that my appointment had been cancelled again, since my doctor was "not available." Instead, they suggested that I show up tomorrow after 9am and I'll be put on a waiting list. I replied, "No thanks, I'd rather be rescheduled for a proper appointment next week." I was told that wasn't possible since my doctor would be moving to South Africa. Surprise! Maybe that's why he was insisting I didn't need my RhoGAM shot…he wouldn't be there to administer it anyway. I will have to find another doctor to manage my health care here.
I'm happy to report that Mom Wendland will be able to bring my RhoGAM shot when she visits at Christmas. My other RN connection, Jane Johnston, will administer the shot. How is that for fast circumvention of the irregular service here? Love, Rebecca

In typical Malawi fashion, my prenatal checkups and even my doctor were "subject to change." I counted my blessings that I had two registered nurses in my African circle of family and friends: Mom Wendland, who could bring the necessary RhoGAM shot, and missionary wife Jane Johnston, who could administer it. Thank you, Lord, for letting things fall into place so nicely!

Sent: December 22, 2004
Subject: wonders
Rebecca writes: Greetings! It's been a while since we had contact; the phone company shut us down. It seems people are somehow calling long-distance to India using our number and running up a handsome total. Rob went to the phone company and talked over our situation with the powers-that-be. It turns out we had to set up an "A" account (a second account that is used while disputing an outstanding bill). The lady advised him to pay our October bill and she would hook us up that evening. We were doubtful. Lo and behold, we had a dial tone. She even called later to make sure that it was working. Must be the Christmas spirit!

The garbage men—a whole truck-full for the occasion—all wanted Christmas presents today when they came. I could hear the truck coming. It rumbled down our street as the whole chorus of men was shouting, "MERRY CHRISTMASEE!" Those words really mean, "You need to give us our Christmas gift now!" I looked outside and saw the whole group of garbage men had climbed on top of their garbage truck to see over our wall. Many of them were wearing some very dirty and tattered Santa hats and big smiles on their faces. Last year mangoes were the gift, but I didn't have any picked. This time I gave them rice. Chicken and rice is a traditional Christmas meal here. Love, Rebecca

P.S. Hannah told me that if Dad isn't back for supper tonight (and he probably won't be) I should **practice** opening her soda bottle, since it is her one night to have a soda.

That evening I "managed" (even without practice) to open a bottle of grape Fanta for dinner. It smelled strangely like turpentine. We decided not to drink it until we had shown it to Dad. When he got home, he took a sniff and a sip. It not only smelled like turpentine, it tasted like it! Rob figured that someone, probably in a village, had used the bottle as a handy vessel in which to store turpentine. When the turpentine was used up, the bottle was returned to the bottle depot, "cleaned" and refilled with Fanta. It was not quite clean enough for our standards, though.

Sent: December 23, 2004
Subject: bee careful
Rebecca writes: It is pouring as I type. This morning Nathanael found a lethargic bee on the ground and picked it up. One millisecond later, the stinger was in his thumb and he was screaming. I was truly hoping to have those bees taken care of BEFORE this happened.

Five-year-old Hannah stumped us with a theological question. She asked what a martyr is. We told her that the Greek word *"maturos"* means "witness." We explained that martyrs are people who died because they witnessed, spoke about and lived their faith in Jesus. She asked, "Does that mean that Jesus was a martyr when He died?" I told her to ask our family seminary grad, Uncle Aaron Mueller. God bless your worship of the newborn King. Love, Rebecca

The approach of our second Christmas in Malawi still took some getting used to. Green lawns, heavy rains, different church activities and celebrating with Grandpa and Grandma Wendland were our memories from 2003. We looked forward to forming similar ones in 2004. I was thankful for the Advent items and devotions we had packed in our shipment and could use this time around. Our family devotions helped focus our hearts in a most fitting way for our Savior's birth. And being an expectant mother sure made the Christmas story come to life in an extra-special way!

Sent: December 27, 2004
Subject: Merry Christmas
Rob writes: Dear all, Mom and Dad arrived on Friday, safe and sound. Church went well. Hannah did a great job on her recitation. We returned home to enjoy Rebecca's excellent homemade pizzas and open presents. Thank you to all of you who planned months in advance and sent packages. "We thank you, we do!" Your thoughts, prayers and gifts that were flown and floated across the earth are very precious to us.

Saturday we enjoyed a joint English/Chichewa service at Epiphany in Ndirande. The Johnston family joined us after church for a Christmas meal, games and fellowship. On Sunday, Dad W. was going to accompany me to one of my bush congregations, but my truck wouldn't start. Even after 30 minutes of trying to jump it, the battery was still dead. Plans changed; we all went to Beautiful Saviour instead. It was the first time Mom and Dad had been to the new building, and they agreed it's a beautiful church.

We wish we could all celebrate together. Someday in glory, at least. Tomorrow we plan to head into the shadow of Mt. Mulanje to visit Lujeri tea plantation. When we met there with the ACA we were struck by its spectacular beauty: a place where waterfalls plummet into the clouds that ring the middle of the mountain, where you can hike one of the three Malawi rainforests, and where you can swim in pristine mountain streams. Merry Christmas, Rob

Take my love, my Lord, I pour At thy feet its treasure store.
Take myself, and I will be
Ever, only, all for thee. (CW 469:6)

CHAPTER 11

2005: A BIRTHING DECISION; A BUDGET DECISION

The King of love my shepherd is,
Whose goodness fails me never;
I nothing lack if I am his,
and he is mine forever. (CW 375:1)

The new year dawned with some difficult decisions brewing. Rob and I had to decide where our third baby would be born: in Malawi or in the States. Meanwhile, the Malawi mission board had its own "tough call" as it faced the beginnings of a synodical budget crunch—a crunch that would become a crisis by 2009, forcing difficult decisions throughout the WELS.

For now we basked in the great memories of a Christmas celebration with the Wendland Grandparents. An email from Grandpa/Dad Wendland recaps our special family time:

INCOMING EMAIL: January 2, 2005
Subject: Back from Blantyre!
Dad Wendland writes: Mom and I returned from our Christmas excursion to Blantyre. We had a wonderful stay with Rebecca and Rob, being served hand and foot by their attendants, Hannah and Nathanael!

I write as if they, R&R, can read this message, which is 70% un-likely due to their POOR phone service. The Zambia phone company, even in the worst years, was never as bad as they have it—rarely a dial tone, and even then so much on-line "noise" that the connection to their ISP can barely be made. I connected at 2.4 KBps last night, for about 5 minutes.

We went down south to the Lujeri Tea Plantation at the foot of Mt. Mulanje, about 90 km from their home. We stayed on a high bluff overlooking the tea-bush-filled hills and valley—a beautiful site and sight! We hiked up a mountain trail to a dam one morning and toured a local tea-processing factory the next.

On the way back to Blantyre we picked up our Christmas present: a carved box made from Mulanje cedar wood. On our return trip the customs lady wondered where Margie had found such a nice Malawian carving. Love to all, M&E

The area by Mt. Mulanje is stunning. The mountain massif rises into the air out of the surrounding plain and is ringed by lush green tea fields, each with thousands of tea plants. Lujeri is nestled among those tea fields. During our stay, we saw many people in the fields picking the leaves by hand. Tea leaf picking takes skill since only select inner leaves, new and green, are picked from each established plant. We also toured the tea factory and saw how those green leaves are dried and processed into shredded, dark-brown tea leaves.

A section of tropical rainforest is also located on the side of the massif. We took in some of the gorgeous scenery on a hike through the forest and admired the fascinating birds, plants and trees. We had an unpleasant encounter with biting ants after we unknowingly crossed their trail and carried away some painful passengers. Only Nathanael escaped their biting jaws, since he was riding on Grandpa's shoulders.

Harvesting tea

Sent: January 3, 2005
Subject: so suddenly
Rob writes: Again a wonderful holiday time comes to an end since Mom and Dad left.

We got word that Principal Mabedi's daughter (in her mid-20s) died. She was ill suddenly, went to the hospital and was dead the next day. Love, Rob

It was difficult to hear of Principal Mabedi losing yet another child so suddenly. What a comfort it is for a Christian to be able to confess, *"For to me, to live is Christ and to die is gain"* (Philippians 1:21). We continued to count our daily blessings, aware that at any day or hour our own earthly walk could come to an end.

In death's dark vale I fear no ill
With you, dear Lord, beside me;
Your rod and staff my comfort still,
Your cross before to guide me. (CW 375:4)

Sent: January 6, 2005
Subject: New Year greeting
Rebecca writes: Happy Epiphany! As the saying goes, "Wise men still seek him!"

Yesterday evening I heard rain…**in our attic**. The hot-water heater was getting so hot and condensing so heavily that there were droplets lining the underside of our roof. When the droplets got heavy enough they rained into the attic, leaving very ugly water marks on our ceiling. The thermostat had blown completely apart with so many power fluctuations. Thankfully, it was a quick fix for the electrician, who installed a new element and thermostat. We are slowly compiling a list of "fix-it" people to contact.

On Christmas Day the power went out as our special ham dinner was baking. We ate about an hour later than planned. Splurging on an $80 ham sure lightened our pocketbook, but we looked past the price tag and truly enjoyed the wonderful treat with family and friends.

We returned from our Mulanje trip and found a dead bird, a black and white wagtail, in our kitchen. It possibly came in through the chimney. It had a snare on its foot; it was probably going to be someone's New Year's meal. (We do have some noisy frogs by our bedroom window. Maybe someone could eat those things instead—they taste like chicken, right?!) Love, Rebecca

Sent: January 9, 2005
Subject: PBG
Rebecca writes: I have a doctor appointment this week. I'll see what her input is on my delivery location. The little one does kick in the evenings, while I sit at church, or when I'm eating. Quite a wonder when they remind you that they are there. Quite a miracle that they are entrusted to our imperfect care.

Yesterday Hannah announced that from now on I should call her "Princess Barbie Girl" (PBG). We talked about why her name is Hannah and how Princess Barbie Girl wouldn't send a good message to other kids who can't even afford a

Barbie. Reluctantly, she agreed that "Hannah" was fine. I agreed to call her Princess Barbie Girl until supper time, and she settled for the compromise.

I'm typing this off-line. We unplug the modem EVERY time we log off now. God bless, Rebecca

My new Malawian doctor was fine, but she did not volunteer much information on what she was doing or why unless I asked. So I kept asking! We talked over the options of where the baby could be born. The doctor told me that if *she* had the means to deliver in America, she most certainly would go. (Maybe the thought of me badgering her made that option seem preferable!)

Sent: January 21, 2005
Subject: gotta bee
Rebecca writes: Every afternoon this month has brought storms and rain. Things are incredibly green and lush but also damp and starting to mold.

I'm struggling again with gut issues. I am taking GSE which seems to be keeping it at bay. I'll stay close to toilet range. I'm concocting my Kool-aid packets into homemade Gatorade.

We finally had our bees taken care of by the city. I wasn't keen on the chemicals being sprayed all over (nor the stains they left on the walls), but the bees are now officially exterminated. We had a garbage can full of beehive remnants to show for it.

Hannah turned five. She requested homemade donuts and chicken nuggets for dinner. Nathanael's key word is NOW! Pray NOW. Amen NOW. Want it NOW. Open it NOW. He followed Shadow (the dog) into the compost heap—dirty NOW! During his bath we found a live ant crawling around in his belly button. God bless, Rebecca

It was time to take two-year-old Nathanael's new word, "NOW," and apply it as I finished deliberating on the location for the birth of baby #3: "Pray NOW!"

Sent: January 25, 2005
Subject: back to the dark ages
Rebecca writes: I'm typing this by generator power. The electricity is out and our phone is terrible. Not only is our land line trouble, but the cell phone network headquarters has burned down! Now we have no cell phone coverage—back to the Dark Ages.

I recently made a double-batch of homemade cheese, since the hot weather made our fresh milk begin to sour earlier than expected.

I'm still not over my stomach trouble. It got better and then worse. Love, Rebecca

2005: A Birthing Decision; A Budget Decision

In the midst of my teetering back and forth on a decision for the birth of baby #3, the major cell phone company's building burned down. Now I had no phone coverage, period! The thought of potentially going into labor without a reliable phone finally helped to tip the balance. Rob and I made a decision: the kids and I would fly back to the States in March, three months prior to our scheduled furlough, for the birth of baby #3. Lord willing, Rob would join us for our regularly scheduled furlough in June, but also for a brief few weeks around the expected birthdate of the child. We knew the separation would be difficult, but it was on my conscience to make every effort to ensure a healthy birth. With a decision made, we could now move forward with our preparations. We prayed our efforts would be blessed and left the details in the capable hands of our Almighty God.

> *"Trust in the LORD with all your heart*
> *and lean not on your own understanding;*
> *in all your ways acknowledge him,*
> *and he will make your paths straight." Proverbs 3:5-6*

Sent: January 26, 2005
Subject: March ideas
Rebecca writes: Thanks, Matt and Melissa, for the kind offer to stay at your Germantown house as needed. I will take you up on borrowing a car seat. Is Hannah required to use one at 40+ lbs? I'd better familiarize myself with the current Wisconsin laws again.

My plan will be to resume medical care in Milwaukee. I'd like to keep things as familiar as possible, since my sense of adventure is at its limit lately.

Mom, you asked about the sick child at church that we had talked about. He is able to walk again. They found a living parasite in his system. There is also a missionary who has an amoeba permanently living in his liver. They simply cannot eradicate it with medication; there is a real danger of damaging or killing the missionary in the process. God bless, Rebecca

Family is a beautiful blessing in life. My parents and siblings were very supportive of our decision to fly Stateside. My brother Matt and sister-in-law Melissa generously offered to share their home with ALL of us. That was a big prayer answered in many ways. Their Germantown location would allow me to resume the medical care I'd had when we lived in Milwaukee. We could spend treasured time together, and the cousins could finally be playmates on the same soil.

The parasitic amoeba that had taken up residence in the missionary's liver reminds me of life with sin. Christians live in serious competition with the unwelcome and dangerous parasite of our sinful nature. While an unchecked tropical parasite *may* cause death, the parasite of sin *will* eventually kill us. The Bible makes a clear and chilling diagnosis: *"The wages of sin is death"* (Romans 6:23). Not only will we die because of sin, but our death is impending from the very start. *"Surely I was sinful at birth, sinful from the time my mother conceived me"* (Psalm 51:5). What patient wouldn't be horrified by this diagnosis? Yet even as we sink into despair, Christ reveals his unconventional cure: he offered his own body as a host to our parasite of sin. Our sin consumed him on the cross. He died our death. He rose again to guarantee us eternal life through faith. His power inoculates us against temptation. There is no need for us to live in fear. Praise God for his love, protection and deliverance!

Sent: February 2, 2005
Subject: phony
Rebecca writes: We will finalize our furlough tickets soon. The missionary discount prices are good until Friday. The June dates we wanted are fully booked already.

Our phone is terrible. Today the repair man came at 11am to fix the line. He hooked up his beeping gizmo from our line to locate the fault. It is now 3pm. His gizmo is still here, he hasn't returned, and our line is still dead. I'm typing this hoping he'll fix it soon. I don't like the "phony business," but what can you do?

The other day I went to town. While I was gone, our power spiked to ridiculous volts again. We had more blowouts. The power company had no idea it was happening until Rob reported it. It is a real pain to unplug everything after each use, but it is also costly to forget. We are still in the process of buying needed voltage guards. So it goes...or blows! God bless, Rebecca

Because the kids and I were flying to the States during low season, in March, we had no trouble scheduling our departure dates. Rob's tickets during peak season were another story. Although June was still four months away, travel dates during that month were almost booked solid. We were none too soon in securing him a seat.

Sent: February 3, 2005
Subject: few updates
Rebecca writes: Rob is running more building-project errands. Buying building supplies is not an easy task here. He pulled in from Lilongwe this morning bearing good news: the "committee in charge" supports the plan for me to fly Stateside for the upcoming delivery, as well as Rob's extra trip for the birth and baptism.

The kids and I have March tickets. Rob will join us from April 21-May 5. Then he'll return for his official furlough in June. We cannot forget to order a separate ticket for the baby after the birth. They won't issue one until you give the child a name. Love, Rebecca

With tickets purchased, our rapidly approaching furlough began to feel real. At first it had seemed that the two years in Malawi were going to feel like twenty. Now our trip was one calendar page-turn away. Full steam ahead!

Sent: February 5, 2005
Subject: how quaint
Rebecca writes: Today I awoke to loud thuds in the rafters. Rob found a rat in the steel trap.

Rob picked up our blown-out microwave. It works, but we cannot read the numbers on the display. It was fixed for $60. That is the price of a good outlet voltage guard—live and learn.

We went to an Italian restaurant last evening for pizza. It was a nice break, since yeast items are difficult to manage with unpredictable power outages. The restaurant had a pleasant atmosphere. When they lit candles at our table, Hannah commented how thoughtful it was in case of a power outage. Rob thinks her third-world exposure is showing through. Nathanael's chin was hardly over the table ledge. No high chairs or anything much in the way of kid safety, but we enjoyed an evening out. Love, Rebecca

Dining out was such a treat for our family. Aside from church and school-related gatherings, we did not get out very much. I was trying to stay off my feet a little more...so *not* cooking in the kitchen was "healthy!"

Sent: February 9, 2005
Subject: pretty sharp
Rebecca writes: Today I watched a Malawian man climb to the top of a neighbor's wall and string razor wire BY HAND, without gloves or tools. I had assumed there must be a technical way to do that.

My doctor's appointment went fine. The clinic has no curtains or proper replacement coverings for the next patient, but it does have a fetal heartbeat Doppler. The doctor thinks the baby is small and that my dates are early. The timing is important for our travels. I have my dates, and I'm sticking to them! All is well; I'm thankful. God bless, Rebecca

It seemed this doctor and I were at odds for a due-date. I had my calculations and she had hers...and they did not add up. She insisted that my baby was too small for an April due-date and was instead due in mid-May. *My* dates put the baby's arrival around April 25. Ordinarily I would have shrugged and waited for nature's outcome. This time a flight of 10,000 miles hung in the balance. Rob's flights had been scheduled for April 21 through May 5. If my dates were wrong, Rob would travel around the world and back again for an unborn baby. I was a bit uncomfortable staking world travel dates on my personal calculations, but I left the situation in the Lord's MOST CAPABLE hands. After all, He is used to having the whole world in them!

Sent: February 11, 2005
Subject: this and that
Rebecca writes: Rob is in the bush again today. The Bartz family has thoughtfully offered to watch all the mission kids this coming Valentine's evening. Hannah wondered if we go to church on Valentine's Day, like at Christmas. I doubt many people think about church on February 14.

Hannah gave Rob a toy necklace for him to remember her by when she's gone. She got very emotional last evening. The separation will not be easy. Love, Rebecca

Hannah's assumption that Valentine's Day was a church festival truly warmed my heart—and not in a flimsy paper-Valentine way. She was right on. Oh, that on this special day we would put our earthly pining in second place and begin the day by celebrating our first love—*because He first loved us* (I John 4:19)!

Sent: February 12, 2005
Subject: A few answers
Rebecca writes: Rob finally went to an internet café today to delete a 5 megabyte message so we could continue to receive the other mail that was behind it. One incoming email informed us that Stephen's wife, Lenka, had a baby girl. We'll add our new little niece to our prayers!

Today I was thankful for my safe arrival at Bible Study. I had three close calls on the way there. It is CONSTANT defensive driving for survival here.

I recently received a note from my previous doctor in Milwaukee. She wrote saying that she'd be happy to deliver the new baby and that I should schedule an OB appointment. I'm glad she replied and gave me the green light. God bless, Rebecca

The reply from my Milwaukee doctor meant so much to me. She already knew me, my health history and about my move to Malawi, so lengthy explanations were unnecessary. Now I could look forward to this familiarity instead of being a new patient under a new doctor's care, right before a birth with unlimited unknowns. Thanks, Lord!

I also began to anticipate the chance to replenish our precious and depleted USA supplies. I began a major inventory of what remained from our last furlough, so I would have a realistic idea of how many deodorants, ointments, seasoning packets, mixes, pepperoni packs, chocolate chips, snacks, special batteries, vitamins, kid's shoes and clothes to buy while we were in the States.

Sent: February 13, 2005
Subject: church plans
Rebecca writes: I'm a broken record these days...but our phone is horrible. I'll write this email now and hope to send it another time.

Beautiful Savior's church dedication is next Sunday. The church ladies met to discuss the menu and logistics of cooking a meal for 30 honored pastors and guests and a "snack lunch" for 300 more. This church dedication deserves special attention and extra expense. The ladies suggested three meats for the menu, along with *nsima*, rice, potato dishes, many salads, vegetable dishes and desserts. It was difficult to figure out how to feed so many people and yet keep the costs manageable. To add to the logistical complications, there will be no tables, silverware (or plastic-ware) or plates available. The idea is to serve individual portions in small bags. Since the vast majority of the attendees will be traveling long distances by foot and public transport, a hearty meal would be culturally appropriate. The ladies in charge had thought over many details already. It was difficult for me to offer input, since I hadn't experienced a special Malawi church festival like it yet. I observed and learned a lot about the different cultures. Sadly, I will miss the dedication, since I will be attending the annual Bible Retreat in Zambia at the time.

Today I saw the men counting the church offering. There were only two MK500 bills (about $4.50 each) and all the rest of the offerings were mostly 5, 10 and 20 kwacha bills, which is pocket change. We definitely need to support one another as we continue to work together to tell others of the true Beautiful Savior! God bless, Rebecca

Sometimes it is hard to find a balance in supporting the national church. The church offerings that Rob and I had regularly and gladly set aside in the States would not be appropriate to put directly in the offering basket here. Between the cultural differences and the currency differences, our previous offerings would essentially hijack the national church's stewardship program. Here, we exercise our personal stewardship and help support the LCCA by contributing extra funds indirectly. Although it seems like our direct offerings would speed up the work and growth here, we are often able to help the church much more by giving private donations, by providing building subsidy (if additional supplies go beyond the allotted amount) and through scholarship assistance. We have contributed to a fund set up by Rob's grandpa, the E.H. Wendland Scholarship Fund, which assists the national pastors' families with their school fees. That assistance helps educate the children who may just be the next generation of called workers in the LCCA.

After observing the elaborate planning process for the church dedication, I asked Rob about food at church functions. He told me that honored guests at a church celebration often receive heaping portions of food as a show of respect. He noted that at one such occasion his plate had nearly two quarts (eight measuring cups) of cooked rice for him to eat, with *ndiwo* besides! The women and children often finish the leftovers on the plates once the honored guests have eaten their fill.

Sent: February 13, 2005
Subject: keep on truckin'
Rob writes: I've been quiet for some time. On the rare occasions when our phone has been connecting (sometimes only two minutes a day) I've been gone.

As for me, nothing extraordinary. My truck works. I've hit no cows, dogs or chickens lately (one pigeon, though). I've had no flat (or sabotaged) tires this week. The intense heat seems to have passed, so now it's only about 100°F in the valley, not 120°F. The Lord has blessed us with health. With all these factors in my favor, I was able to condense 2½ weeks of congregational work into one week. That means 800 miles traveled, 8 congregations and 1500 members visited, 3 confirmation classes examined, 27 adults confirmed, 14 baptisms, 3 days home after 5pm, about 14 rivers crossed (all at normal size) and a whole lot of blessing and strength from the Lord with the privilege to serve in His field. All this in preparation for next week, when Rebecca will be in Zambia at the Bible Retreat. The Cage Match: Dad vs. The Kids, behind bars…for days. The bigger work is coming.

It is great to hear from you all and certainly worth the phone angst. I am very thankful that Rebecca can get the word out while I get the Word out. Both are needful—on different scales maybe—but needful nonetheless. Blessings in Jesus, Rob

While Rob spread the Word with a capital "W," I spread the word by sharing informative updates. Little did I know that the many emails I wrote in an effort to stay connected would be used for bigger things in years to come.

In his email, Rob mentioned the possibility of tire-sabotage. After becoming a victim of the practice, Rob speculated that in the Shire Valley a group of locals must have once helped a stranded traveler change a flat tire. This traveler probably tipped the locals well—so well that they decided it was worth their while to try to make a living that way. That meant they needed more flat tires to fix on their stretch of the roadway. Rob found out how creative they were in arranging this. On one trip through the area, Rob hit an object. His tire blew out and he had to pull over. Immediately his truck was swarmed by locals who insisted they would change his tire. Suspicious of their sudden and eager appearance, Rob insisted that only HE would change the flat tire. The disappointed locals had to walk away empty-handed.

When Rob later took his tire in to be patched, the mechanics pulled out a three-pronged wire contraption that looked like it had been designed with the express purpose of rupturing tires. It had done its job. His tire was beyond repair. The cost of the wire to make that gadget: 5 cents. The cost of a new tire: $250. The outcome for the locals: heist-less.

Sent: February 14, 2005
Subject: Happy Valentine's Day
Rebecca writes: Rob made reservations at the "exclusive" (by Malawi standards...I'm anxious to see what that means) *Greens* restaurant in town. No young kids are allowed, so we have never gone. But since our Valentine night is kid-free (the Bartz family offered to watch them), we're heading there. We hope to enjoy a good meal. Happy Valentine's Day, Rebecca

Our Valentine evening was lovely. The waiter presented us with a business card, and there were red roses and chocolates on the tables (ooooh, this place *was* fancy). Rob and I enjoyed the food and ambience. We especially appreciated the special chance to connect over a quiet dinner before I left for Zambia and soon afterwards for the States.

Sent: February 24, 2005
Subject: "hi-jacked" again
Rebecca writes: Yesterday I arrived safely home **again** in Blantyre. I had a wonderful, spiritually-edifying time in Zambia for the study of Thessalonians. I do cherish the Christian fellowship with the Zambia missionary ladies as we serve the Lord hand-in-hand one country away. What a grand place heaven will be!

Our phone has been "hi-jacked" **again**. This time it was for hundreds of dollars' worth of calls to Pakistan. Yeah…we have so many connections there, you know. Rob said they disconnected us **again** for non-payment of the ridiculous bills. God bless, Rebecca

The Ladies' Bible Retreat in Zambia was once **again** a great time to refocus and grow in faith, so that I would be ready to wield God's Word in the face of trial and temptation. As Mom Wendland so meaningfully put it at the retreat, "Everyone falls in the mud. It is whether you choose to stay there or get up and get out of it that makes the difference." Our lives should show evidence of repentance as we strive to live anew because of His forgiveness; that is what sets Christians apart. May the Lord grant us all wisdom and patience as we live each day for HIM!

Where streams of living water flow,
My Savior gently leads me;
And where the verdant pastures grow,
With food celestial feeds me. (CW 375:2)

Sent: February 27, 2005
Subject: Greetings
Rebecca writes: Last week's dedication service at Beautiful Saviour had over 500 in attendance, including the minister of religious affairs who cut the ribbon before everyone entered the church for the service. There were people seated in all the hallways for overflow. The TV station filmed it. It was great that so many could hear God's Word!

Today during the service I found a tick crawling on my dress. I kept discreetly trying to capture it between two clothes pins (that I use to keep my music from blowing around). I finally smashed it.

Hannah wondered why some people have red dots on their heads. She came in the kitchen and showed me a picture of a group of smiling Hindu women with red *bindis* on their foreheads and inquired, "Why are they happy? Who could be happy if you don't know about Jesus and are going to hell?" I'm working with her on a softer approach to witnessing.

Hannah has also been looking through photo books and reviewing pictures of relatives with Nathanael. They'll be ready when they see you all again. Won't be too long now! Enjoy the week—living each day for HIM! Rebecca

Beautiful Saviour Lutheran Church

South-Asian *bindis* and *saris*. Arabic *burkas* and *niqabs*. Such attire is common in Malawi. To Hannah, these dress-codes are visible signs that the people follow a different religion than the Bible teaches. While over 80% of the population in Malawi professes to be Christian, Islam is the second largest religion in the country (about 15% of the population) and predates Christianity. Islam was introduced in Malawi in the early 1800's by Arab coastal traders who converted tribes along the lakeshore. Almost every village along the southern shore of Lake Malawi has a mosque, as does every major city in Malawi. There are also several Islamic schools throughout the country.

About three percent of Malawi's population follows a religion other than Islam or Christianity. This smaller percentage includes Hindus. In the last century, Indians were brought to Malawi by the British to help construct a railway line between Malawi and Mozambique. Many Indians remained and became an integral part of Malawi's business community. This Hindu group accounts for the red marks, or *bindis*, that caught Hannah's attention.

In general, the individuals of different religious groups with whom I have rubbed shoulders have been kind and friendly. I enjoy friendships with several ladies of different faiths, though there will always be a divide in our friendships. Sadly, that divide will be most evident on Judgment Day. Knowing this, I try to share what Bible truths I can in conversation and continue to pray that my friends will learn about our Savior Jesus, before their smiles fade for eternity.

Sent: March 6, 2005
Subject: dog days
Rebecca writes: Rob fed Shadow, our dog, two scoops of dog food before we left for a get-together. At the gathering we learned that the same dog food we are using (purchased from a vet clinic) may have been poisoned. Eighty dogs have died recently, including our German Shepherd's dad and (pregnant) mom. They tested the dog food and found poison. We were very thankful to find Shadow still alive when we got home.

I know the Staudes will appreciate how the Lord works through our actions with the next news item. The LCCA is currently having budget trouble. Congregations are finding it difficult to provide communion wine. This unfortunately coincides with a shortage of wine in Malawi. When someone asked Rob what he was doing for communion wine, Rob said he was using airplane wine. They kept waiting for the joke, but there isn't one. It is true! When the Staudes flew in to visit last June, they **all** kept their complimentary bottles of airline dinner wine. Those bottles (mixed about 50/50 with water) are currently supplying communion wine for 2 churches and over 600 communicants. Those little bottles are getting their mileage-worth! God bless, Rebecca

At first there were rumors that witchcraft had been involved in the dog poisoning. Here in Malawi it is not unheard of for someone to solve the "problem" of a rival business with a little supernatural intervention. As it turned out, the problem was simply the result of negligence. The food pellets had not been dried out properly during production, which allowed poisonous spores to grow. Now puppies were in demand.

I smiled at the way the airline wine turned out to be such a blessing during a Malawi wine-shortage. Before my family flew over, I had mentioned to them that they could have "free" wine with their in-flight meals. The surprise was on me when they lined up all their saved bottles on my kitchen counter when they arrived! Not one to drink much alcohol, I had tucked the bottles away, never imagining how the Lord would later use them! I would guess our lives are filled with similar small marvels.

"We know that in all things God works for the good of those who love him, who have been called according to his purpose." Romans 8:28

Sent: March 7, 2005
Subject: countdown continues
Rebecca writes: We are preparing for the upcoming USA trip. I realize we can purchase most anything once we arrive, but that could be a bit cost-prohibitive all at once.

It seems you're all going through way too many preparations for us. We appreciate your efforts…but don't overdo it! We hope to be pretty low-maintenance. (Rob has the idea that no one will need to cook when he comes, because he'll order from all the local pizza places on a rotational basis.) God bless, Rebecca

The excitement was building. The daily frustrations seemed to bother me less since I could think to myself, "In a week's time I won't be dealing with these things anymore." For that matter, the *nightly* disruptions were easier to shrug off too: the random gunshots, barking dogs and wailing alarms; not to mention the 4am *adhān* (Islamic call to worship) echoing from the loudspeakers of the local mosque with the assurance that "*Salat* (prayer) is better than sleep"… and followed shortly by screeching neighborhood roosters.

Sent: March 9, 2005
Subject: 3…2…1…
Rebecca writes: I'm almost done packing. I'm debating whether to put dust-covers on our furniture, or if Rob will feel like he's in a haunted house.

Hannah's latest observation is that, "When Mom was little she was a Staude. When Dad was little he was a Zambian. When Hannah is little she's an American."

We'll plan to see many of you on Sunday in person…Lord willing! Rebecca

One major decision of the new year had been made and acted on—in a few days the kids and I would be "homeward bound." I knew the cost of our early departure went beyond the price of our plane tickets. For the next six weeks, the kids would miss their dad. I would miss his daily interaction and help. He would miss his children and my support. We were thankful for emails that would bridge the distance until Rob

2005: A Birthing Decision; A Budget Decision

came to visit us in April.

Meanwhile, a major decision was being made on the mission-front due to financial shortfalls in the WELS. At a time when Malawi's harvest fields seemed to be multiplying, LCCA-Malawi would have to spread its missionary presence more thinly. Sadly, the pinch of mission field "belt tightening" would only get more painful as the years passed.

Sent: March 14, 2005
Subject: They're away
Rob writes: All the R.E. Wendlands are off except for one: the R.E. (me). I hope and pray all goes well. The phone is so terrible; I probably won't get this email out until long after they've arrived (or maybe never, if I attach pictures).

Paul Nitz called this afternoon. Due to Synod financial shortages, we will probably lose a bush missionary. It is difficult to cut any area of ministry here. I am not in favor of short-shifting our pastor-training institute, and the urban ministry has just gotten going. That leaves the bush-ministry liable. This comes when I have told 11 congregations with about 1000 potential members—who have been begging me to serve them and bring them into the LCCA—to write a letter to the LCCA president. Then the national church will have to discuss how they want me to serve, since I don't think I can serve 25 congregations effectively. We need more workers, a **lot** more; not fewer. Such opportunities abound here to spread the Gospel, if only there were enough workers in the fields. Rich blessings in Jesus, Rob

Relocating from the States to Malawi had been quite a feat with two children in tow. I figured that traveling in the opposite direction with those same two children would not be any easier. In fact, it would be slightly harder since the ratio was skewed: one (pregnant) adult to two children. I had never traveled overseas alone before, bearing the full responsibility of handling travel documents, flight schedules and children. However, I had been to plenty of airports before, I could read signs, and I was not afraid to ask questions. How hard could it be? As it turned out, the Lord blessed our trip from the very start to the very end.

The day we set off was bittersweet. We were all happy to be heading west but very sad to leave Rob behind. Not only that, Nathanael had awoken that morning with a fever. The ever-present possibility of malaria was now on my mind. I was frustrated at the timing. However, I would soon look upward and say a *thank you* prayer for that gift. Sapped by his fever, my busy and curious little boy sat at my feet during each check-in, napped beautifully on the plane and slept through the night on the 17+ hour flight. I was thankful for the added blessings that his fever did not persist and that five-year-old Hannah proved to be a capable and helpful little traveling companion. I had expected some eye-rolling when people saw a roundly pregnant mom carting two little kids around the world, but in fact many strangers were surprisingly helpful. Several assisted with heavy-lifting; others held my children's hands as we walked. I should have known better than to be concerned, since I know full well I am never alone. The Lord knows exactly what I need and how to help me!

> *"O LORD, you have searched me and you know me.*
> *You know when I sit and when I rise;*
> *you perceive my thoughts from afar.*
> *You discern my going out and my lying down; you are familiar with all my ways.*
> *Before a word is on my tongue you know it completely, O Lord." Psalm 139:1-4*

It was an overwhelming feeling to be back on USA soil. I nearly shook the first airport personnel man's hand when we disembarked—he was so friendly; I was so happy. HOME!

Sent: March 16, 2005
Subject: greetings
Rob writes: My Dear Sweeties; I am very thankful that everything went smoothly for your travels. It was my constant prayer from the moment you left.

The Johnston's yard worker, John, died of bacterial meningitis. Mark wanted my help to buy a coffin and sort out funeral arrangements. We bought a coffin for MK4,500 ($38), picked up the body at Queen Elizabeth's mortuary and transported everyone to his home village. We saw firsthand how a Malawian widow has no rights at all. John's family wanted to beat her up so that she would give absolutely everything she had to them—his last pay, food, clothes—everything. Mark stood up to them and announced, "No more. She's had enough grief." My job was to be the translator. We returned to the Johnston's by 3:30pm, where Jane had a wonderful meal waiting for us.

On Tuesday I went to Katunga. Many were attending a village funeral when I got there, and I doubted that we'd have a service. But have one we did, and by the end there were 36 adults and 21 kids—a good showing for the place. I love and miss you all very much. Rob/Dad

When you employ workers on your property in Malawi, you become responsible for the costs of all the workers' health issues and even any family-death expenses. The labor laws list the duties and obligations of an employer to a certain extent. Sadly, the laws of the land do not offer much protection for widows. As if dealing with a husband's death is not hard enough, many widows are commonly exploited by their in-laws and relatives. It is not uncommon for a widow to be left destitute after her husband's family (brothers, uncles, parents) claims all the deceased's possessions.

Sent: March 27, 2005
Subject: lone (Chichewa) soldier again
Rob writes: Paul Nitz informed me that the ACA has decided where the budget "axe" will fall. The Lemkes will return to the USA half a year sooner than planned. The ACA has asked Jim Bartz to take over Werner Lemke's vacated LBI position.

The area of Thyolo, where Jim Bartz had been planning to serve, has no current missionary supervision. They could use some assistance! When some Thyolo churches were visited a few months back, it was discovered they were serving Coca-Cola for communion. There has been a shortage of wine in Malawi—the people wanted communion, there was no wine, and somehow Coke seemed acceptable. There is work to be done. Love, Rob

I suppose if someone is accustomed to substituting ingredients in a regular meal, it might seem acceptable, even sensible, to substitute an ingredient in the Lord's Meal. However, we have more than a cookbook to warn against making Biblical substitutions. Millennia ago, Moses shared God's words with the Israelites: *"Do not add to what I command you and do not subtract from it, but keep the commands of the LORD your God that I give you"* (Deuteronomy 4:2). Those same words apply today, whether in North America or in rural Malawi. Certainly those Christians in Thyolo would benefit from a pastor's guidance and teaching...if only the manpower allowed it!

Kids listening outside of a packed church

*How can they believe in the one of whom they have not heard?
And how can they hear without someone preaching to them?
And how can they preach unless they are sent?
As it is written, "How beautiful are the feet of those
who bring good news!" Romans 10:14-15*

CHAPTER 12

A BABY; A BAPTISM; A BUSY FIRST FURLOUGH

*See this wonder in the making:
God himself this child is taking
As a lamb safe in his keeping,
His to be, awake or sleeping. (CW 300:1)*

God is good! Our six weeks apart from Rob/Dad went quickly; for *us* anyway. Family visits, amazing home-cooked meals, museum tours, toboggan rides, snow sculptures, Easter-egg dyeing and library trips made our days fly by. Meanwhile, Rob's time was spent eating my pre-made frozen meals, helping with funeral arrangements, conducting worship in the villages and dealing with repairmen.

My Stateside doctor became slightly concerned when I gained a sudden ten pounds (the time-span of which I will leave a mystery), so she encouraged me to cut out any snacking. What? I was *finally* in the land of snack food! Okay, for the health of baby and me I would cut out snacks. (To my delight, the doctor did not tell me to cut down on my mom's delicious meals.)

I actually celebrated my birthday at "home" again with my Mom and Dad that year. I couldn't remember the last time that had happened. Even better was the chance to celebrate Easter together. My Dad was currently serving a parish in West Salem, Wisconsin. The traditional Easter readings and the familiar hymns—sung in English and accompanied by a pipe organ—really meant a lot to me. It is true that you don't appreciate what you have until it is gone. The Easter readings brought tears to my eyes. I sat in the pew with the kids, who were stuck like magnets to their beaming Grandma, and took it all in.

The day we had been waiting for arrived: Rob flew safely across the sea to join us in the States. We were all very happy to be reunited. The next day I had a scheduled ultrasound. I was even more relieved Rob was there when the ultrasound tech turned the screen away from our view and called for expert evaluation. We were told to return home and await a call from our doctor. This was a new and slightly unnerving development. We went home and prayed.

When the doctor finally called, she told us the measurements of the baby were not proportionate. She told us the baby had stopped growing because of Intrauterine Growth Restriction (IUGR). My heart sank. What did it mean? The doctor said that "first thing tomorrow" I should head in for an induction. Lord, thanks for that timing. I could NEVER have planned it better. I had been so concerned that Rob would come and go with no baby being born. Instead, he had hardly stepped off the plane before we were rushed into the fast lane!

The induction went fine. We were thankful when our healthy baby boy, Caleb Stephen Wendland, was born on April 23, 2005. A week later, Rob officiated as Caleb was baptized at Calvary Lutheran Church in Thiensville, WI.

Miracle each time it happens
As the door to heaven opens
And the Father beams, "Beloved,
Heir of gifts a king would covet!" (CW 300:2)

We counted our blessings that Caleb's birth and check-ups fit neatly into our schedule. The IUGR was not apparent and his measurements out of the womb were "just right." Thanks Lord!

We seemed to blink and the two weeks we shared with Rob were over. It was time for Rob to board the plane to continue mission work in Malawi until his regularly scheduled June furlough.

Sent: May 9, 2005
Subject: **Ndinafiko bwinobwino** *(I arrived very well)*
Rob writes: My time with all of you Stateside came and went so quickly. It was packed full of amazing highlights, not the least of which was Caleb being born and baptized.

All went well during my air travels (having no kids tends to make it much easier). After clearing customs in Blantyre, I found the Johnston and Bartz families waiting for me in the crowded airport. I felt bad that I couldn't say much—I had started losing my voice while still in Johannesburg. Now I can only whisper.

I arrived at home to find everything in order. Sunday I conducted 2 services, 10 baptisms, 2 harvest-offering celebrations (where over 500 kg/1100 lbs of maize was donated) and the promised videotaping of Khanyepa's choir. I finally got home at 4pm exhausted…but no sleeping until proper times. Jet lag hasn't been bad. The key is to sleep when you are supposed to and be awake when you are supposed to. I find if you fight that battle for a couple days you avoid becoming cyclically jet-lagged.

Happy Mother's Day, Rebecca! I thought of calling and then realized that with my hoarse whisper you'd probably think it was a (very expensive) crank call.
I love and miss you all, Rob

It was a special Mother's Day to be sure, as I held little Caleb in my arms. Despite traveling through numerous time zones, Rob remembered to send special wishes from the far side of the sea.

While Rob was getting back into the rhythm of mission work in Malawi, the rest of us were finding our rhythm with a new baby in the family. I recovered enough to make some brief shopping trips for groceries and items on our furlough list. To my surprise, I discovered that it was rather difficult to shop for groceries in America. Before I moved to Malawi, I had been a decisive shopper. I knew my preferences and favorite brands and moved through the aisles quickly. A mere two years later, my shopping habits had altered drastically. I had become accustomed to Malawi where there is often only one "choice." Multiple brands and item-variety are not common in Malawi. There, my shopping philosophy is: "If the store has it—and it looks good—*buy it*." But that was not the best mindset in a USA store, where the prices were so reasonable and every kind of *everything* looked good!

Selecting packaged deli-meats was my first hurdle. I read all the labels, trying to figure out which flavor—*smoked or traditional*—and cut—*shaved or sliced*—and type—*turkey, ham, chicken or beef*—to buy. Then I priced all the different brands. After many shoppers had come and gone with their selections, I finally had to snap out of it and simply pick something. But it was that way with everything! A dozen different kinds of cereal, bread, buns, salad dressing, canned soup, snacks, pudding, cheese, crackers, pasta, juice, ice cream…the variety of food caught me off guard. Truly, if I could have, I would have selected one of everything!

I had clothes and shoe shopping on my furlough to-do list as well. However, I had been cautioned to make major wardrobe purchases toward the *end* of furlough, since my children would grow significantly over summer as they ate and drank all the rich, vitamin-fortified bounties of the States. Besides, I had to get a grip on grocery shopping before I tackled other merchandise!

Sent: May 26, 2005
Subject: halfway
Rob writes: I had a good day out to Tcheleni today, but I went to a new place first. They were happy and enthusiastic that I had come. We had a small service, introduced ourselves, talked with the people, ate a meal and were on our way to the next church by 11am. I took the digital camera along to get some pictures. They were all fascinated to see themselves on the camera. Some even needed

confirmation that it was indeed themselves that they were seeing! I guess that could happen with hardly any mirrors around. We got done with church and a special post-service meal at around 5pm and were on our way.

When I got home at around 8:30pm and got out of the truck, I heard one of my tires hissing but was too "tired" to do anything about it then. Sure enough, the tire was completely flat the next day. One lug nut was frozen shut, so I wrenched it until the bolt sheared. In town, the tire was repaired in 30 minutes.

At Nalipa they dug a foundation for their new church. I'll plan more supply-hauling trips out there soon. At home I've been working on an exegesis for the called worker's meeting, getting the NIV for Logos running and working on my deputation sermon. I have a lot of work to do before I return to the States for furlough. Love, Dad/Rob

I cannot imagine any person in the USA not knowing what they look like because they have never seen themselves in a mirror or a photograph before. Living in a third world culture has made me realize how blessed we are in ways that we take completely for granted. That is something to truly *reflect* on!

We would soon find ourselves reflecting once again on the blessings of Stateside medical care, when the results of baby Caleb's routine thyroid-screening test came back. We were informed that his thyroid levels were not in the normal range.

Sent: May 31, 2005
Subject: Happy Memorial Day
Rob writes: My prayers are with you as you deal with Caleb's skewed thyroid levels.

On Sunday, I went to Chizilo and Evangelist Master told me his wife was sick. They did some tests at a local clinic after church and confirmed that she had malaria.

On the way home I found that the traffic was backed up from the stop light all the way up to the Dairibord. I took a detour through Ndirande market. Mistake. The reason traffic was backed up on the main road was because the president was leading some political rallies in our area. One place where he was talking was right next to...Ndirande market. In the middle of the market I got swamped in traffic and people. The rally was finishing and people were still excited. Some were giving a hard time to whites and Asians on the road. Some people in the passing crowd stopped and began rocking my truck from side to side and even punched it a couple times. I kept calm and smiled. Others around me got it worse. When I got home, I found that the truck was fine—no damage from its misadventure. Since my adrenaline was pumping, I did my exercises.

After dinner, Mark and I went to an Ethiopian member's house. The member is putting together videos about Beautiful Savior and the LCCA that are broadcast on Malawi TV. Mark asked if I could take the member with me on Sunday when I go to Khanyepa, so he can videotape their choir. Next Monday he'll also do an interview with me for Malawi TV.

Last week President Gurgel informed me that all missionaries do a presentation at Synod Convention. I was not aware of that. I'm scheduled to split time with my Dad—he'll do half an hour on Zambia, and I will do a half an hour on Malawi. Love, Rob

It was difficult to hear of Rob finding himself in the middle of a mob. It was equally hard for him to hear the news of little Caleb's abnormal thyroid levels. We had breathed such a sigh of relief after Caleb's IUGR had seemed to resolve. Now the thyroid issue had hit the radar. We were told it could simply be the result of a residual hormone from my system, but that Caleb should get follow-up thyroid testing as soon as possible. We would deal with those ongoing tests for the rest of furlough. Wow. My mind was spinning from the news—many prayers ascended.

Far more tender than a mother,
Far more caring than a father,
God, into your arms we place him,
With your love and peace embrace him. (CW 300:3)

Sent: June 4, 2005
Subject: furlough preparations
Rob writes: I have been keeping you all in prayer. I will check around and see if there is a pediatric endocrinologist located anywhere in Malawi.

My computer started acting up today. About an hour ago I restarted it (for about the 10th time), and it still wasn't completely right. This isn't good timing as I try to prepare my furlough deputation work. With Caleb, the computer and summer work on my mind, I don't have much hope for a good night's sleep.

Tomorrow is church at Khanyepa and Balala. In addition to the regular service, there are those who want to be tested for confirmation and the choir will be videotaped for TV.

God's blessings to you and the kids. I love and miss you all very much. Dad/Rob

Discussing Caleb's thyroid issues with Rob over email was not ideal. I kept hoping I would not have to make any major decisions by myself—especially dealing with the sleep deprivation that is part of having a newborn. My parents were continually supportive. My mom made sure I kept my appointments straight and my nursing times on schedule. She helped me find time to rest, she interacted with the other two kids and—through it all—she kept delicious, hot, home-cooked meals on the table. Thanks, Mom!

Sent: June 9, 2005
Subject: early "hypo"thesis
Rob writes: I met with a German doctor at Queens Hospital. She noted that in Germany no action would be taken over Caleb's readings. She also told me that Mwaiwathu's lab can evaluate the thyroid tests, and they also carry thyroxin. She didn't know what quality their tests were and recommended that we test Caleb right before we leave the USA and again when we return to Malawi, in order to have a "control." This looks like good news.

It is under a week now before I fly out again. I've got two more places to go (Muhapokwa and Chizilo), deputation material to work on, cleaning and bug-spraying the house. I also met with Joaquin Ramsey. I printed out all the Bible Information Class lessons for him and Stephanie and went through another lesson. (They are the Peace Corps couple who are teaching in the Lower Shire, in Ngabu village.) They were glad for a small reprieve from Ngabu, since there are riots happening there. Love, Rob

I was glad that Rob would soon join us Stateside. I was also relieved that he could be with us for Caleb's ongoing tests. Shortly after Rob's arrival we were scheduled to take Caleb to Children's Hospital in Milwaukee for a full thyroid screening and evaluation.

I was also thankful that our family would have access to a furlough home and rental vehicle once Rob arrived. It had been a real blessing to spend extra time with Stateside family, but I did not want to overstay their gracious welcome. Having a proper furlough place would also allow us some privacy and room to spread out our growing family.

Rob's deputation plans were taking shape. He always enjoys getting the Word out and has a real gift for it, whatever continent he is on. Missionaries on deputation often travel with their whole family to speak about their work at various churches, schools and other mission-minded organizations. This time, the new baby meant that our family would not accompany Rob. He was scheduled to go solo for two weeks out West. Yet again it would be a necessary parting of ways.

Sent: June 12, 2005
Subject: update
Rob writes: My deputation is scheduled for July 6-19. You mentioned that several additional churches would like me to preach and speak. I'll also try to fit in

St. John's in Jefferson and Redemption in Milwaukee around that. Wow, it seems like furlough will be gone in a flash.

Only a few days left—I'm packing, cleaning and trying to get some final pictures for my deputation presentation. Love, Rob

When our family first moved to Malawi, we took many pictures and marveled at the new and unusual sights that greeted us each day. After a while, things were not as new anymore, and we did not always take the camera on our outings. Photographing the local people meant immediately being approached for money. It also seemed wiser to leave the camera equipment locked up at home to avoid theft—but we inevitably missed some great shots.

Many of Rob's bush experiences would also be great to capture, but regular trips on the Malawi roads would destroy any camera. On the occasion that Rob does have a camera along, remembering to use it is another matter. Usually his first thought when the tires are flat or full of thorns, or the truck is axle-deep in mud is, "How am I going to get out of this one?" Only later, after the Lord has seen him safely home, does the thought occur, "Oh yeah, I suppose I could have taken a picture of that." As furlough approached, Rob ventured into town with our camera to get some specialized photos for his presentation. He had a plan to visit the local *asing'anga* (traditional healers/witchdoctors).

Sent: June 13, 2005
Subject: witchdoctor
Rob writes: Attached is a picture I took today. I visited the witchdoctors by the clock tower roundabout. I purposely went without money. The guys let me take a few pictures but told me that if I fail to come and pay them, then the camera will break. Love, Rob

Witchdoctor with snakes and medicine

Although there is a high percentage of professed Christians in Malawi, many of these have no problem finding a way to blend witchcraft into their beliefs. Many Malawians believe in *mfiti*: evil witches and wizards with the ability to fly, become invisible and shape-shift into animals like cats, owls and hyenas. These *mfiti* supposedly use their sorcery to harm people out of greed or envy. Many common troubles are attributed to witchcraft, such as health ailments, business failures or relationship problems. Plenty of Malawians seek help for these problems from a *sing'anga*, or traditional healer. Although some of these traditional healers are simply herbalists, others specialize in divination and the spirit world. A witchdoctor is a type of healer who uses herbal concoctions, magic, and talismans to treat ailments believed to be caused by witchcraft. It is not uncommon, for example, to see a small talisman tied to a farmer's row of crops as "protection" from bad magic.

Many Malawians have such fearful respect for a witchdoctor's words that they would do whatever he asks. I asked Rob if he thought anything of the witchdoctor's threat. He told me, "No! The devil may be powerful, but Jesus has more power." (By the way, seven years and counting after the witchdoctor's dire prediction, our camera is still working!)

That phrase, *still working*, also sums up much of Rob's furlough. Two months away from a mission field sounds like a lot of time...especially if it is perceived to be one big vacation. Certainly, a furlough is many things, but a two-month vacation is not one of them! Rob made his second journey across the ocean safely, and we were once again glad to be reunited; although his deputation schedule kept him busy planning, preaching, presenting and traveling throughout the entire furlough.

For me, furlough is a most necessary opportunity to return to our home country and reconnect with family after an extended absence. We synchronized that first furlough with Rob's parents' furlough. We were blessed to live right next door to each other in the synod furlough housing in Mequon, WI. Those two months of seeing each other daily brought a wonderful closeness between the grandparents and grandkids. Furlough is also a special time to worship together—as a family, in English—an opportunity we rarely have in Malawi. As it turned out, our family ended up sitting together in the pew less frequently in the States than I had hoped, due to Rob's busy deputation schedule.

Furlough is a break from third-world life. It is a chance to experience and enjoy familiar American sights and sounds...and to observe all that is new in the USA within the past two years. Rob's parents have noted that every furlough there is a slightly different procedure to pumping gas and, unfailingly, a new toothbrush on the market. We also noticed a remarkable explosion of computers, PDAs, iPods and cell phones between 2003 and 2005. Furlough is an opportunity to stock up on necessities and scarce items, and to schedule endless doctor and dentist appointments for every family member.

Furlough is also a time to "fill up." During our 2005 furlough I was filled up with encouragement. It was heartwarming to know that countless people were praying for our family and supporting us; many of whom we had never met before. We greatly appreciated the support. We savored the fun furlough times and cherished the many memories made—as much as our hearts could hold. Then, before we knew it, our first furlough was over. Caleb's social security card, birth certificate and passport had arrived with time to spare, and a one-way airline ticket had his name on it. Our appointments had been completed and shopping items had been checked off the list. Rob's two-week deputation schedule to Colorado and Nebraska, the Synod Convention meetings and his interspersed preaching dates had served to spread God's Word and update people about Malawi. All too soon our bags were packed—yet again—to leave. Our time back "home" was up.

> *Here we bring a child of nature;*
> *<u>Home we take a newborn creature</u>,*
> *Now God's precious son or daughter,*
> *Born again by Word and water.*
> *(CW 300:4) [underlined emphasis mine]*
> See This Wonder in the Making **(sts. 1-4)**,
> text by Jaroslav J. Vajda © 1984 Concordia Publishing House.
> Used with permission. All rights reserved. www.cph.org.

Sent: August 29, 2005
Subject: Furlough thanks
Rob writes: We're back and our phone line is bad…so the battle resumes. I want to thank you all for a wonderful furlough. Thank you for your love and companionship. I know the time felt like a whirlwind, but it was so nice to see you all again. Thank you also for the help—for the babysitting, housing, delicious cooking, cleaning, packing, gifts and support. That is all so much appreciated (and kept us sane). Love, Rob

Rob wrote an earnest thanks to our family members. Each one of them made our furlough so special and supported us in such a caring and generous way. Now we dealt with missing them all over again as we faced the prospect of being apart for another two years. I wrote a follow-up email with more details. My family was waiting with bated breath to hear how the world travel went with a new baby! (Frankly, I had held my breath the whole time too.)

Sent: August 30, 2005
Subject: Return-trip from Milwaukee to Blantyre
Rebecca writes: Our phone sounds like a bowl of Rice Krispies, if it works at all. We'll send this later from an internet café in town. We are supremely thankful for

a safe return home, and for all your prayers along the way! I'll jot down highlights for those who were wondering how it went with a new baby.

To begin our return trip we woke at 2:30am, got the kids up, tried to eat breakfast and packed our last things. We saw the sun come up on the Milwaukee runway. We had a smooth flight and all napped. We saw massive cloud formations—compliments of the approaching hurricane Katrina—as we neared Atlanta. By the time we two luggage-laden-adults and three kids managed our way from the domestic area to the international terminal, the airport announcer made the last call for our Johannesburg flight.

The next 17+ hours went fine. The airline provided an infant bassinet that screwed into the bulkhead wall. We were cramped, but Caleb slept fine. We ate…though the meal consisting of fish in tomato sauce was not exactly kid-friendly. We arrived in Johannesburg the next day for a 24-hour layover, during which we all simply collapsed. The next morning we got to the airport at 8am. It was no picnic to board a plane by climbing tall, open-air stairways while carrying hand-luggage, a stroller and kids. I was happy for the help of Rob and the stewardesses.

The Blantyre missionaries greeted us warmly when we arrived at Chileka airport the next afternoon. Our luggage made it. The luggage straps were terrific. They held the pieces together well, helped us identify them and even made the customs gal hesitate to open them. In the end she only asked about the contents. I replied, "There are many diapers and clothes," and she waved me through. (I also plan to use one of those luggage straps in our car to rig up a seatbelt for Hannah. The Pajero is not equipped to seatbelt all of our children now.)

I fed Caleb around midnight and couldn't fall back to sleep. I lay in bed and decided to say some prayers of thanks—especially for our safe travels. I think at that very time we had thieves cutting our razor wire out in our backyard. Soon dogs were barking and the neighbor's alarm went off. Then our guard set off our alarm. We did not sleep well after that. The next day we ate our first meal at around 1pm—all very off-schedule. Rob was on "razor wire fix-it duty." He has many cuts as a result. He makes his tetanus shot worthwhile.

Today we checked in at Hannah's school. She is all set to begin standard one. Thanks for all the prayers and goodies you sent with us. God bless, Rebecca

We were so exhausted from the constant stimulation on furlough and from traveling that it seemed an "after furlough breather" would have been helpful. No such thing! Rob's schedule was packed solid with church work and home security. My schedule was about to get much busier making school trips for Hannah, homeschooling Nathanael and caring for Caleb.

Even more overwhelming, thieves were attempting to remove sections of our razor wire the first night we arrived back "home." Our raucous house alarm jolted us awake. Shortly afterwards, a security vehicle full of men with helmets and clubs came to secure the property. After that ordeal it was hard to go back to sleep, no matter how exhausted my body felt. Welcome home!

It may seem confusing how we use the word "home." When we embark on furlough, we head "home" to the States. After furlough we return "home" to Malawi. Do we know where our home is? Yes! Ultimately, it is no place on earth. Hymn 417 (CW) sums it up nicely:

> *I'm but a stranger here; Heav'n is my home.*
> *Earth is a desert drear; Heav'n is my home.*
> *Danger and sorrow stand Round me on ev'ry hand.*
> *Heav'n is my fatherland; Heav'n is my home.*

Sent: September 5, 2005
Subject: back in the saddle (Land Cruiser) again
Rob writes: I turned on the radio and heard this Malawian rap song:
"My Dad's a Bantu; my Mom's a Bantu;
When I wake up in the morning all I see are Bantus;
That makes me a Bantu! How would you like to be a Bantu too?"

I realized—as I dodged people walking everywhere, relearned to cope with a general lawlessness on the roads, drove on the other side of the road in the beloved Land Cruiser—that I was not in Kansas (make that Milwaukee) any more…and it felt good to be back. Malawi has given us the typical "rough" welcome home. Our phone line is dead, and there are serious water shortages throughout the country. Now people are lining up at the gate to have the missionary deal with this or that, from sick children to re-starting building programs.

The kids had a real bout of jet lag. They were all up and "not tired" from midnight until about 3am…and then cranky until about noon. Their jet lag did not help that of their parents. Gradually things are getting better. Tomorrow is a landmark for this family: our little girl heads to school. Her uniform is laid out and her backpack is loaded.

Today our phone line was fixed, so we can finally send an email from our house. Coming home from town I saw them stringing the new digital lines…so hope springs eternal. However, consider the timeframe: it was over a year ago that they dug ditches to lay the pipes for the lines, a year ago when they built brick joining-boxes, and 9 months ago when they actually laid the pipes. So, when will it all be hooked up? When will it all work as advertised? These are all questions that require a satisfactory answer before hope becomes justified. God's blessings, Rob

The jet lag finally subsided, and five-year-old Hannah broke new ground as she started formal schooling. She enrolled at Phoenix International School, a local school close to our home. Figuring out the British system of schooling meant that I was on a bit of a learning curve as well. Schooling at Phoenix begins as young as age 2. The class progression is as follows:

Pre-Nursery: age 2-3
Nursery: age 3-4
Reception (kindergarten): age 4-5
Standard One (age 5-6) through Standard Six (age 10-11)

When students enroll in Phoenix, they are assigned to be in one of three groups, or "houses" within the school. The houses compete with each other in sports and academics. Responsibility grows as the kids grow older. The school elects 8 prefects (4 boys and 4 girls) and house captains from the Standard 6 class to assist with various duties.

The school day begins early, at 7:15am, and ends around noon. Electives and sport practices take place each afternoon. Once a week there is a school assembly. A featured class performs a skit, the national anthem is sung and awards are presented for academic or sporting success. The school year in Malawi begins in early September and ends in early July. There are three terms, divided by half-term breaks. At the end of first term there is a one-month break from early December to early January. There is a two-week break for the Easter holiday, as well as public holidays celebrated by different religions.

The city of Blantyre is also home to Saint Andrew's International High School (SAINTS), which begins with Form One (ages 11-12) and continues to Form Six (ages 17-18). SAINTS is a day and boarding school that offers departmentalized subject areas and teachers, aimed at preparing students for further studies at international universities. Both Phoenix and SAINTS are filled with students from around the world, with up to 40 different nationalities represented and 21 different languages spoken.

Sent: September 9, 2005
Subject: lil Malawi update
Rebecca writes: Hannah is adjusting well to school. She has a back pack, a sports kit, a swim kit, a book bag and a snack bag to keep track of. I do love the school uniforms! They make it so simple to get ready each morning. They are also cheaper than a "stylish" school wardrobe.

The kids are used to constant snacks from furlough; they are asking often for special treats. We've told them that was fine in America but not anymore in Malawi. We cannot get fruit snacks, granola bars or munchies here like you can in the States.

The adjustment back is a shock, and not the most pleasant one either. After living here for two years, things did not seem quite so difficult. But after experiencing the ease of Stateside life again, the differences are glaring. On furlough I had enjoyed living without frequent power outages, locking a dozen locks each night, bed nets, periodic middle-of-the-night burglar alarms and shopping hassles. It took me three days before I was driving again, since it can be so confusing driving on the other side of the road. Our road is being prepared for something. Men with pickaxes are all over it; the pot holes are enormous now. We can only hope they are preparing to pave it.

I am thrilled with all the furlough goodies I brought and the time I spent packing them. Now we are enjoying our wonderful American foods, tools, supplies and clothes. It makes this initial adjustment more palatable! Thanks also for your notes. It definitely shrinks the miles into smiles! I'll end with Hannah's quote after devotion, "I love everyone in the whole wide world…and that is a lot of love to spread around!" God bless, Rebecca

Hannah's first day in school uniform

September 13 marked our second anniversary in Malawi. We had survived our first cycle of mission-field and furlough. Now we were back in the saddle again. Just when the readjustment seemed a little overwhelming, Hannah with her big heart reminded us why we were here. Her statement about loving everyone in the world was endearing to hear from the mouth of a five year old…and astounding to hear from the pages of Scripture about our Savior. He was punished for the world's sins so that we might be righteous in God's eyes. It was this love of Christ that compelled Rob and our family to be ambassadors in Africa…and to spread that love around!

>*"For Christ's love compels us,*
>*because we are convinced that one died for all,*
>*and therefore all died.*
>*And he died for all, that those who live should no longer live for themselves*
>*but for him who died for them and was raised again…*
>*We are therefore Christ's ambassadors,*
>*as though God were making his appeal through us.*
>*We implore you on Christ's behalf: Be reconciled to God.*
>*God made him who had no sin to be sin for us,*
>*so that in him we might become the righteousness of God."*
>*2 Corinthians 5:14-15, 20-21*

CHAPTER 13

YEAR THREE: LOADS OF CARES; LOADS OF PRAYERS

What a friend we have in Jesus, All our sins and griefs to bear!
What a privilege to carry Everything to God in prayer!
Oh, what peace we often forfeit, Oh, what needless pain we bear,
All because we do not carry Everything to God in prayer. (CW 411:1)

If there is anything we have learned in Malawi, it is to pray—frequently, fervently and faithfully! As we began our third year in Malawi our prayers included many petitions for health and safety, both our own and that of our members.

In September 2005, Malawi was in a drought and faced what some were calling the country's worst food crisis in a decade. That's saying something in a country that is almost always in a crisis cycle. Almost two-thirds of Malawians *regularly* live below the national poverty line and depend on maize as their main source of calories. When a drought shrinks the maize harvest, many people are left in desperate need. The widespread HIV/Aids epidemic doesn't help matters. HIV/Aids has infected nearly 15% of adult Malawians. Few of them have access to medical care, even supposing they could afford it—there is only one doctor per 100,000 people in Malawi. Many of these infected adults are too weak to grow food on their small plots of land. In 2005 this sad combination of factors meant that in a population of 12 million, nearly 5 million people faced starvation. The 2005 drought was particularly difficult for the villagers who lived in the Lower Shire area, where Rob's congregations are. Many people were eating only one poor meal a day. But as hungry as their stomachs were, their souls also needed to be fed.

We couldn't complain about our circumstances in Malawi when we considered how little those around us had. But our third year included a personal share of health trials that caused us to frequently carry our concerns to God in prayer.

Sent: September 16, 2005
Subject: Internal Adjustments
Rebecca writes: We took Caleb to Mwaiwathu hospital where they are testing his thyroid levels and sending them to South Africa. We paid $100 cash equivalent. They will call us next week with the results. (We pray our phone works when they try to reach us.)

The current drought in Malawi is major and affecting many members in the Shire Valley. Rob noted that his members don't have food, so they did not feed him.

This past week our digestive systems have all undergone an "internal adjustment." The kids have had runny tummies again. Two days ago I started feeling funny. I was dizzy; even bopped my head getting into the Pajero because I misjudged the opening. Then a terrible headache came. I was in awful pain if I squinted or put pressure by my eyes. I had minor stomach pain and was hot and cold all day long. I had numbness off and on in my arms and legs. By night I was in terrible shape. I read the stats on migraines in my medical book. It recommended establishing regular eating, sleeping, and exercise patterns, reducing tension and learning relaxation techniques. Hopefully what I had wasn't related to a migraine…but I can see why I'd be a candidate for one! With a new baby, furlough and now jet lag, the unpredictable scheduling threw me completely off-kilter. Whatever the cause, I pray the trouble passes soon.

The kids really miss seeing family. Not a day goes by where they don't ask for someone. God bless, Rebecca

Our "welcome back" unfortunately included lots of attention from the germ population! It took us a long time to re-acclimate. We were run down from the final push at the end of furlough. Our sleep patterns did not allow as much shut-eye as we needed. I was hit the hardest and had crazy symptoms. Fortunately, once I recovered there was no repeat performance. With a heavy sigh, I remembered how healthy we had all been on furlough. I knew there was no place on earth that was free from illness, but it was frustrating to return to Malawi and get hit so hard.

Sent: September 19, 2005
Subject: grass with that?
Rebecca writes: Thankfully we are all on the mend. Everything is covered in dust. We desperately need the rains to come for any dust-reprieve. Of course then the mold will come too.

Rob said that food is so scarce in the Valley that some people are eating grass. It really brings mom's old adage of "the starving people in Africa would love to eat what is on your dinner plate" to a new level. Our lawn is so parched that we would not even have any grass to eat. Everything is dry and brown.

Evidently Malawi police will confiscate a water-meter if they catch you watering, washing your car or wasting water. The whole city is on a water rotation. God bless, Rebecca

Living in the city has buffered us from the worst effects of Malawi's droughts. During hard times, many villagers gravitate toward the city in the hopes of finding food or work. Such a mass relocation often causes the city crime rate to soar. Rob saw the hunger firsthand as he ministered to the people in the Shire Valley. Church attendance was poor. The few wives that came explained that their husbands had rented plots of land near the Shire River to "try again" to plant crops. The men needed to guard the plots constantly against thieves and hippos.

Conditions in the Shire are so rough that the LCCA-Malawi will have to overcome difficult challenges to take complete ownership of the area in the future. The weather is terribly hot. There are many mosquitoes and a high risk of malaria. The people in the Shire are from a different tribe with different customs than most of our national pastors. They are also very poor and don't have much to pay their called workers. Heat, unfamiliar customs, disease...these are the concerns of our national called workers when they consider working in the Shire. It strikes me how similar those fears are to some of the comments we heard in the States when Rob was deliberating his call to Africa!

Although we were struggling with periodic health issues, electricity, water outages and terrible phone lines, I was thankful that our basic needs were met daily. Our gracious God has never failed to provide all that, and so much more!

Do Not Worry
"Therefore I tell you, do not worry about your life,
what you will eat or drink; or about your body, what you will wear.
Is not life more important than food, and the body more important than clothes?
Who of you by worrying can add a single hour to his life?
But seek first his kingdom and his righteousness,
and all these things will be given to you as well.
Therefore do not worry about tomorrow...
Each day has enough trouble of its own." Matthew 6:25, 27, 33-34

Sent: September 22, 2005
Subject: "awful" lunch
Rebecca writes: Today we had an "awful" lunch—according to Nathanael anyway, who can say "awful" easier than "waffle." I made a triple batch and will freeze some for another day.

Nathanael woke up with what looked like measles. It was a single vengeful mosquito in his bed net that inflicted 16 bites. The toddler had a red rainbow of welts on his forehead, neck and hands. I didn't want him to come along to school in case he looked contagious. Nathanael's latest remark at devotions (when he tries to answer like his big sister) is, "Jesus loves ME." It melts my heart!

Hannah won a pool race today. She says that she walks fast in the water and the others are pushed back by her waves. We get some great laughs from her reenactments. Love, Rebecca

When the power cooperated, and I felt well, and all the ingredients were at hand, I had learned to spend my time cooking in large quantities as I did for waffle day. That way I could pull out a frozen meal the next time the power went out, or I was sick or ingredients were scarce. I suppose it was also an economical way to feed the family, but I did miss the Stateside option of packaged dinners or "grabbing a bite to eat" on the way home!

Sent: September 23, 2005
Subject: "sick" of school
Rebecca writes: Hannah was crying after school today. She didn't feel well and seems to have a stomach bug. Rob and I haven't felt well either. At dinner Nathanael ate more than all of us combined. It could be new germs coming home from school.

Our road is still a disaster with large potholes. They are now covered in black oil.

Rob stopped at the diagnostic center to check if there were any results from Caleb's thyroid tests. We were supposed to get a call from them. It turns out they don't reveal results over the phone. (Why didn't they tell us that initially?) Caleb's levels were all in the normal range. Praise the Lord! This little glimpse into possible abnormality makes me extra thankful for our relatively good health. God bless, Rebecca

We were extremely thankful that Caleb's thyroid results seemed normal. We could avoid medicating him as long as his thyroid results were stable…and focus instead on recovering from our day-to-day illnesses.

At this time of year the *nsima* Rob is served by his village congregations is often grey. (It is supposed to be white—the color of the ground maize!) It is obvious the cooking water used is far from clear. It was therefore not surprising that Rob was struggling with health issues. Since the kids and I were not eating in the bush, I figured Hannah was exposing us to school germs. I wondered if there was a law of averages on how long it takes to acclimate physically to a third world country. Apparently longer than two years! Being sick AGAIN made the clock tick-tock so slowly. It was frustrating, but we could handle it with God's help—as He promised.

> *"For men are not cast off by the Lord forever.*
> *Though he brings grief, he will show compassion, so great is his unfailing love.*
> *For he does not willingly bring affliction or grief to the children of men."*
> *Lamentations 3:31-33*

Sent: October 3, 2005
Subject: I broke da house
Rebecca writes: Nathanael's quote for the evening is, "I broke da house." It seems that he bumped a hot-water pipe under the sink. The pipe broke and caused another flood in the office area. Hot water shot out of the wall—so hot that Rob ended up with blisters trying to fix the leak. To stop the water flow entirely we would have had to allow the geyser (a hot water storage tank) to drain. This would not have been a problem had it been the cold-water pipe, since there is no water coming in due to the water shortage. However, the geyser had plenty. We couldn't fix it…but instead used a tambala coin to temporarily stop the water. We were able to stop further dripping by winding a rubber arm band (from Caleb's Stateside blood draws) tightly around the coin.

Our power is so bad that we ended up with completely different menus all day. What I started for lunch had to wait…so I started it for supper. In the end that didn't work either. Since furlough I have forgotten how to cook in the dark. I will keep a few emergency meals in mind.

There is more news. Last night our alarm rang and the yard came alive. Shadow was barking like crazy and the guards were yelling. Rob spoke to one guard and noticed his eyes were HUGE! Thieves had returned to the same area of our backyard where our razor wire had been previously cut. This time they tried to pull the razor wire down. The team of "SWAT" men arrived in about 15 minutes. They think the thieves have a ladder.

This morning Rob and I surveyed the outside of our wall. Our corner posts have been fixed, so the razor wire is in better shape than last time. The thieves had uprooted all the newly planted sisal cactus bushes along our perimeter. There were stumps in one area, and we realized that they could easily be used as steps. Rob spent the day leveling the stumps with the chain saw. God bless, Rebecca

> *Have we trials and temptations? Is there trouble anywhere?*
> *We should never be discouraged—Take it to the Lord in prayer.*
> *Can we find a friend so faithful Who will all our sorrows share?*
> *Jesus knows our every weakness—Take it to the Lord in prayer. (CW 411:2)*

This hymn, "What a Friend We Have in Jesus" is beautiful. When I lie sleepless in the night, I often sing this verse to myself. It reminds me that the resources and people that God provides during troublesome times should not overshadow my reliance on God, who is my greatest help and comfort in times of tribulation and tiredness. Jesus knows my every weakness. He also knows every weakness of our guards, our security, and even of the thieves, who seemed to be visiting our neighborhood more and more frequently. It was not healthy for us to live in counter-attack mode. These words in 1 Peter also comforted me: *In this you greatly rejoice, though now for a little while you may have had to suffer grief in all kinds of trials. These have come so that your faith—of greater worth than gold, which perishes even though refined by fire—may be proved genuine and may result in praise, glory and honor when Jesus Christ is revealed." 1 Peter 1:6-7*

Sent: October 5, 2005
Subject: on the mend...
Rebecca writes: The thieves' Sunday night visit caused more of a breach than we thought. Monday evening the night guard arrived early and began patrolling as we sat down to eat supper on the *khonde*. I like to reinforce positive behavior, so I went out to share a part of our meal with him (food speaks loudly here). We walked with him to the backyard by the banana trees. He showed us that the thieves had cut all three of the supporting frames free from the razor wire. The actual razor wire was intact, though merely hanging there with no support. All the thieves would have to do is force something between the wall and the wire, and they'd have a nice easy spot to enter and exit. I couldn't believe it! We went back to our supper and I couldn't eat. All I could think of was how to fix it as dusk settled in. Rob got out our tools and repaired the supporting wires well into the darkness. I shone a flashlight on his work while the kids waited in the house. Pretty soon Hannah's voice called out that the power had gone out. The kids were in the dark and getting a bit spooked. I "passed on the torch" to the night guard and went in to take care of the kids. Rob got some cuts again. One is on his thumb right next to the burn blister from the hot water fix! What a beginning to the week! Love, Rebecca

That evening God sent to our assistance a thorough security guard who spotted a weak link in our line of defense. We were able to fix it and thwart invaders that night...although we wouldn't even make it to the end of the month before they made another attempt.

Sent: October 11, 2005
Subject: eating lily bulbs
Rebecca writes: Monday was Mother's Day here. We played some family games and afterward I stayed up until 11pm making tomato sauce with tomatoes Rob brought home from the village.

Malawi's food shortage was reported on BBC radio. The Nsanje district of the Lower Shire—home to several LCCA churches—has been hit so hard that people have begun to forage in the river for water-lily bulbs. Many don't make it out of the river because the crocodiles eat them. No famine for the reptiles. We sure are blessed having our needs met and continue to pray for those around us who don't. God bless, Rebecca

Many people were going hungry. I have learned that one definition of "not eating" is when local people cannot have *nsima,* boiled cornmeal, at a meal. Since the maize harvest in 2005 had fallen far short of the country's needs, many people were going without their usual source of calories. However, it seemed that the people in the Lower Shire literally had *nothing* to eat. The water-lily bulbs they were forced to rely on for food have little nutritional value, but in times of extreme need, locals pound them into a bitter-tasting porridge. One woman was quoted in the newspaper as saying, "The tubers are difficult to get as you must follow the stem of the lily down to the bottom, and you can only get one or two at a time as you run out of breath. You have to get someone to watch out for crocodiles and hippos, they are so dangerous. Two of my neighbours were taken by crocodiles last month, but without food this is what we have to do" (Bill Corcoran, *The Observer,* October 2, 2005).

Our mission wanted to help. A request for aid was made to WELS, and the Humanitarian Aid Committee gave a generous grant to provide maize to most LCCA-Malawi members at the end of 2005 and beginning of 2006. Both the LCCA and Lutheran Mission were extremely grateful for the needed assistance.

"Let us not become weary in doing good,
for at the proper time we will reap a harvest if we do not give up.
Therefore, as we have opportunity, let us do good to all people,
especially to those who belong to the family of believers." Galatians 6:9-10

Sent: October 17, 2005
Subject: Greetings again
Rebecca writes: Thanks for Nathanael's birthday greetings. Malawians often don't know their actual birthday. They "ask around" for a general consensus whenever they need a rough date for school or work. It is just another day in the grand scheme of their lives.

Today I was reading your letter, Mom, and you wrote how you would pray that rain would come soon. As I read rain began to fall—neat!

I've decided that driving down our road is as close to race car driving as I'll probably get. I feel like I'm playing Frogger (an old video game) by dodging all the people, animals and pot holes. My pony tail shook loose yesterday on my way to pick up Hannah from school. Nathanael wore his medieval helmet in his car seat. He was proudly narrating what he saw from between the visor slats. Maybe he's onto a good thing!

This weekend is our Ladies' Retreat in Lilongwe. I am really looking forward to the renewal in the Word. Rob will hold down the fort while I'm gone. Love, Rebecca

We were thankful for answered prayers for rain, although the rainy season wouldn't begin in earnest until closer to December. Until then, we could expect more hot, dry weather.

Rob's next email addresses some other situations—communication, health and security—that were not falling into place quite as cooperatively as those early rains.

Sent: October 30, 2005
Subject: Quite a week
Rob writes: Greetings! It has been quite a week. Sorry we haven't been able to communicate sooner, but our phone line has been pitiful.

Right before the missionary wives went to Lilongwe for retreat, Nathanael got sick with a 103°F fever for a few days. He was tested for malaria—thankfully it was negative.

Rebecca returned from the retreat on Sunday evening, and all was well... until Tuesday night. When we went to bed at about 9:30pm, Rebecca thought she heard something like metal wire being cut. I dismissed it for the sound of bugs hitting the metal screens. At 11:45pm we woke up to our alarm (for those of you keeping count, this is the 3rd time since furlough). The security team came and did a sweep of the property. They told us that the thieves had fled but had removed razor wire on top of our wall. I went out to look and found five meters (about 20 feet) had been cleared off. The thieves had managed to cut one end of the razor wire and then removed all the support wires that hold it in place. Then they pulled those five meters to the ground on the outside of the wall. With all of this accomplished by midnight, I figured they were planning on coming back the very same night. Good news: all the wire was still there. Bad news: five meters is a lot of razor wire protection gone for the remainder of the night.

More bad news: while the alarm was going off, Nathanael started throwing up all over his bed and mosquito net. So, we cleaned up Nathanael and started a load of wash. Since we were up and couldn't sleep anyway, I figured that I might as well fix the razor wire. That fixing took longer than I thought. Not only did I want to put the razor wire back up and fix all the breaks, but I also wanted to get at least one supporting wire wound through it all, so that they couldn't just cut one end and sling it down again. Finally, by 4am I had everything satisfactory. My

Year Three: Loads Of Cares; Loads Of Prayers

theory of the returning thieves was proven correct: at 3am we heard gunshots from one of our neighbors—the thieves probably saw us up and tried another location.

4 o'clock and all is well, right? Not quite. I was scheduled to go to a church service in the Lower Shire that day, and not any ordinary church service either; this was a dedication of their new church building. The congregation had been pooling its offerings for two months to buy food for this day, and even the chief of the village was invited. As a result, I didn't feel that I could skip the day. I had to go...but the place was Tcheleni and that meant a 12 hour day—out at 8am, back at 8pm. But before I would leave I wanted to make very sure that our security was tight again. What a conundrum! Who could help? As it turned out, all the other missionaries were out of town. I resolved that if we heard from the other missionaries before 8am, then I could go to Tcheleni. Otherwise I'd have to stay home and resolve things myself. Shortly after 6:30am we got text messages telling us that the other Blantyre missionaries were returning and could offer assistance. With that news I was thankful that I could go south.

The day at Tcheleni went very well. It was a wonderful, four-hour service. Rain poured for five minutes during the service, but the place was so dry that dust was still billowing as I drove home. The air was so dusty that I could not even see the escarpment, although the road travels right along its base.

I got home to find all well. Our security situation had been noted by the other Blantyre missionaries and more preventative security measures had been taken. Someone suggested we should possibly move out and rent. Meanwhile, the manpower issues on field might open up another mission house in the near future. We have more security lights up now; it looks like a stadium in part of our backyard. All we need is to clear away our trees and garden, put in a tennis court and we are "set!" Hopefully it should be safer. We pray these extra measures will be a deterrent to thieves.

But wait, there's more! On Friday Rebecca woke up and was not feeling well. She got worse and worse into Saturday—she could not keep any fluids in. Early Saturday morning she was so weak that she could barely even walk, and Caleb was too heavy for her to lift out of his crib. She thinks it is the sickest she's ever felt. Sunday morning came and Rebecca was still very weak. My stomach started to rebel too, but not as severely as Rebecca's. I went to church in Blantyre with Hannah and Nathanael (who themselves are not eating right—but no more throwing up at least). There we enjoyed a nice Reformation service and a Bible Class that was based on a Martin Luther video. Sunday afternoon has been a time of rest and recovery.

Now I thank all of you. For all your calls, emails, text messages and prayers—thank you! Most of all, thanks be to Christ who preserves His saving, wonderful, beautiful, sweet, and free truth of forgiveness from one generation to the next. It is in His Name that we work and serve, live and breathe. With Him on our side, any burden this world can throw at us is made light because His shoulders already bore the hard part. The victory is all that is left for us to "shoulder." Thank-you sweet Savior God! Our love, Rob

The events of that week are hard to describe. No words can really communicate the anxiety we endured. It was easy to feel alone in our self-defense. In Malawi, police do not routinely work after dark. Criminals are left to roam freely at night. It is a common "joke" in Malawi that instead of putting criminals behind bars, the law-abiding citizens put themselves behind bars. The more I ponder that, the more I realize the truth behind the dark humor. In the States, the only places I've seen surrounded by high, razor-wired walls are prisons. Here, nearly every decent dwelling place has a wall topped with broken glass, barbed wire, electric wire or razor wire.

Added to our distressing security issues, I was also sick again. I was so sick even my hair follicles hurt. That was a new symptom for me! I wrote a heartfelt prayer in my journal:

Dear Lord, help! Dealing with the attempted break-ins is draining. My poor health is draining. Each day is draining. I know You are in control of all things. Let me trust You. I confess it is easy to doubt and fear when the going is tough. Your Word has been a great comfort to me. I can count on You alone. Please continue to keep us safe; also protect fellow missionaries, friends, neighbors and family. I thank You for Your faithfulness and know that You will fulfill every promise. For that I am eternally thankful. May I glorify You in all things, whether I'm tired or not, and whether I feel like it or not. Please grant me rest. I ask this in Jesus' name. Amen.

Are we weak and heavy laden, Cumbered with a load of care?
Precious Savior, still our refuge—Take it to the Lord in prayer.
Do your friends despise, forsake you? Take it to the Lord in prayer.
In his arms he'll take and shield you; You will find a solace there. (CW 411:3)

Sent: October 31, 2005
Subject: take 2
Rebecca writes: Experiencing major malfunctions. Illegal operations performed. Malicious virus has spread: kids throwing up—me very ill. Shut-down required to salvage remaining data. Will write when there has been a chance to reboot. Love, Rebecca

Using imagery from the computer world, I touched base with my family and briefly noted the issues at hand. No matter what happened, I knew that the Lord was with me. I clung to that simple promise and, like a child, grabbed His steady hand as we walked together—one day and one step at a time.

Sent: November 18, 2005
Subject: dog days
Rebecca writes: I finally have a free moment to send my first real update since October. I think it has taken me almost a month to "reboot." Those were the roughest weeks ever.

Here are a few odds and ends:
- We have had beautiful sunbirds at our feeder lately.
- Our phone box was labeled yesterday. The new label: "24/7." I laughed so hard. Yeah, that is how often it <u>doesn't</u> work!
- It is HOT HOT HOT here. The rains are sporadic but seem to be coming. The grass is greening nicely, and we're trying a garden of sweet corn and pumpkins this year.

Samson, a puppy, is a new addition to our family. We hope he has watchdog potential since he is a Doberman, Rottweiler, and black Lab mix. I didn't exactly want another "baby" around, but we pray it is a smart move for security.

Eliza is another new addition. She is helping me clean three days a week. She speaks very limited English. God bless your week, Rebecca

The dog days of summer were here in more ways than one! We had added a second dog to our home in the hopes of beefing up our future security. In the meantime, we (and our German Shepherd) were trying to get used to having a spunky puppy around.

I was also adjusting to the idea of having house help. It was not something I was particularly comfortable with, but after a few years in Malawi I could see why so many people hired someone to help clean. Cleaning is a monumental task here, since there is a year-round battle against either dust or mold or bugs. Much of my time was spent tackling household duties that took significantly longer than they had in the States. We hoped Eliza would be a helpful addition to our family life.

Sent: November 20, 2005
Subject: confirmed in Christ
Rob writes: Today I did a confirmation—in English! Joaquin Ramsey is a Peace Corps Volunteer whose wife is WELS. The Ramseys came to Malawi shortly after we did, and their term of service is over soon. They live in Ngabu, which is about two hours south of Blantyre in the hot Shire Valley. He took confirmation classes with me during the times they could travel to Blantyre. It was a joy working with

Joaquin. I was very happy when the Spirit moved in our lessons and Joaquin agreed that WELS teaches as the Bible does. After the confirmation service we had a mission get-together at the Johnstons. The hot weather made the frosting melt off the cakes. Love, the Malawi Wendlands

It was very special to see Joaquin grow in his walk with Christ through the Bible information classes. That spiritual closeness, peace and joy will not only be shared in this life but also in the next.

Sent: November 24, 2005
Subject: we'll give thanks on Sunday
Rebecca writes: Happy Thanksgiving! We had our special meal/celebration planned for today. Unfortunately, Jayne Bartz and the Johnstons have been sick. I was added to the numbers last evening. We've postponed our celebration until Sunday. God bless your day reflecting on the myriad blessings we enjoy from HIM! Love, Rebecca

Thanksgiving could be easy to overlook since it is not a holiday in Malawi: there is no hype about it, school goes on as usual and it is not listed on the local calendars. This year, the actual date of our celebration became just another *minor* detail in how we said a *major* thanks to our God for His grace and care. Although our gathering had to be postponed, we took the opportunity to pray for the renewed health of the sick ones.

> *"Is any one of you in trouble? He should pray.*
> *Is anyone happy? Let him sing songs of praise." James 5:13*

Sent: November 25, 2005
Subject: I've fallen and can't get up
Rebecca writes: This morning Rob hired plumbers to repair once and for all the crummy pipe that keeps flooding part of our house. After what he hoped would be a quick fix, Rob had planned to buy cement next and take it to a congregation in Chiradzulu. However, the plumbers took much longer than expected. In the meantime, I was still making frequent bathroom trips because of a "runny tummy." It was 10am and time to feed Caleb. I first attempted to make a quick dash to the toilet. Out of the corner of my eye I noticed that Nathanael tried to follow me. I made it to the bathroom and heard a loud cry. I found lil N face down on the hardwood floor. He wasn't responding. His hands were curled up by his shoulders and he was going stiff. I called for Rob (who thankfully was still here because of the slow plumbers—not to mention God's providence). By the time Rob came, Nathanael's color was looking bad and he still wasn't

responding—but he was breathing. Rob took him to the hospital.

I met up with them after nursing Caleb. The hospital staff took Nathanael's temp, weighed him and did blood work. We waited over an hour in the lab room, watching workmen sand new paneling, varnish the paneling (glad I wasn't pregnant), attempt several times to line up the proper holes to screw the paneling into the wall, and then hammer in the screws (since they had no screwdriver). The grand finale was watching some men climb up a huge tree outside of the hospital in an attempt to cut it down by chainsaw. They used a blue rope and stood on a separate branch nailed to the tree.

We didn't get to see the tree fall, since the blood worksheet finally came. The results were normal. The doctor assumed Nathanael hadn't eaten breakfast; I'm sure many kids they see don't. We assured him that Nathanael had eaten a bowl of oatmeal and had no history of seizures. No signs of diabetes showed up either. After about an hour and a half, Nathanael began to act normal again. He has no bruising or goose egg anywhere. Nathanael says he "hit the house and fell down."

As we left the hospital, we noticed the workers had indeed felled the big tree… right on top of their new security fence—that is going to need repairs now. Love, Rebecca

We were thankful that Nathanael seemed unharmed by this mysterious incident. The Lord sure allowed the slow plumbers to be a blessing, since their delays meant Rob was still at home and could help. As it turned out, Nathanael had a similar "seizure" a couple of months later while we were in Lilongwe…but none in the years since.

Sent: December 2, 2005
Subject: yippee hooray
Rebecca writes: Hannah had an inter-house swim gala this week. School parents sat on chairs near the pool, drank tea and cheered while the kids raced in different events.

Nathanael's latest phrase is, "Yippee hooray!" We started new Advent calendars last evening. Sure enough, a "Yippee hooray" went up for that special event. Hannah was so proud to read her window all by herself. Thanks for sending those, Mom!

Our hired house helper, Eliza, is more of a frustration than a help. I would rather have an automatic dishwasher and skip the house "help." She is becoming problematic.

I'll wrap this up and get lunch going—German pancakes with fresh strawberry syrup. You can tell Grandma Staude I think of her every time I make them! The smell of them baking reminds me of her house. I pray she is doing fine. It is a comfort to know her health is in the Lord's hands and His timing is best.

Pineapples are in town now. 'Tis the season! Love, Rebecca

Grandma Staude was 95 years old and her health was failing. It seemed a very real possibility that the goodbyes we had exchanged on furlough might be our last ones on earth. I had become very close to Grandma Staude during high school: her home in Watertown, WI was my "home away from home" during the years I attended Northwestern Prep School. It was difficult to be so far away now and know that her days on earth were coming to a close.

Sent: December 7, 2005
Subject: update
Rebecca writes: Rob took Caleb to Queens, the local government hospital. There were hundreds of people waiting, coughing—probably dying—in the waiting room. He went to the desk and asked for a pediatric endocrinologist. They don't have one...but it sounded important enough that he was helped right away. Several doctors looked at Caleb's read-out of his thyroid levels, assessed his development and came to the consensus that he should be fine without meds. The medicine thyroxin, while easy to get, is tricky to administer at the correct dosage. They cautioned that Caleb would probably be worse off sitting in the waiting room at Queens catching junky diseases than dealing with a slightly elevated TSH level.

Hannah had her school Christmas concert yesterday evening. The content centered on Luke chapter 2 and they acted out the Christmas story. The unscripted entertainment was a snake that slithered into the crowd toward the end. As Rob put it, "You know you're not in America when there is a snake mingling in the crowd, a parent kills it, and the program continues as normal." You could see several parents turning their video cameras toward the snake as it became a temporary focal point. God bless, Rebecca

The snake at the Christmas concert might have made an exciting interlude in the midst of the Christmas story enactment, but it made me think to myself, "The serpent never stops trying to steal attention away from the 'TRUTH!'"

Sent: December 14, 2005
Subject: Christmas kringle-carol night
Rebecca writes: We had our first annual Christmas Carol-ice cream-kringle night at our house with the Blantyre and Zomba mission families. It is the first "annual" because it was a real hit; everyone would like to do this yearly at our house, since we have a piano. We began by singing carols and then ate Rob's homemade ice cream, which managed to feed all 23 guests. The kids especially went bonkers on the imported-from-furlough topping choices. As everyone went home, we sent along a braided blueberry-cheese kringle as our Christmas gift

Year Three: Loads Of Cares; Loads Of Prayers

(I decided this recipe was worthy of my single can of imported blueberries). I included a frosting squeeze packet so they could reheat it and freshly frost it when desired.

Today I found our house help sneaking out of our pantry. The pantry was supposed to be a "NO-GO ZONE"! This was in clear violation to our rules. Last week she was found looking through one of Rob's congregation's offering money bags. She's only been here a month, but it might be time to let her go.

Few kid-bits: Hannah is working on her lines for the church Christmas pageant. She has also been singing songs from school. One is, "We wish you a Merry Christmas, and a Happy New Ya." (Like a lamb says "baa," she sang "ya.") I told her the word was **year**—even though she hears it pronounced differently at school.

Nathanael has discovered that one present under the tree makes noise. Yesterday I saw him with his plastic hammer hitting all the gifts to see if any others made noise!

As for me, I seem to prepare food, feed everyone, nurse Caleb, clean things up and repeat the cycle all day long. Rob has been making breakfast for the kids, so that is a big help. I still wish there were "faster foods" here.

We put together food/pantry packets for our workers this Christmas season with *ufa* (maize flour), oil, sugar, salt, beans, nuts, *kapenta* (dried fish), fresh vegetables, matches, candles and sweets. I put John 3:16 on the card so it can also be a witnessing opportunity. God bless, Rebecca

The Christmas carol evening was enjoyable. Sharing food, festivities and fellowship with the other mission families was special. It was also great to sing familiar carols whole-heartedly with fellow believers…in American English! We filled the house with praise for our tiny King.

Sent: December 18, 2005
Subject: "par-annoyed"
Rebecca writes: When we got home from church today Hannah wrote this note:
Dear God.
A man toc my moms prs but we got it bac.
This is how it hapind.
I wus at Sunda School and the man toc it.
Mr. Felgenhauer got it bac.

During the church service today an unfamiliar man sat to the left of me in our pew. After Bible Class I was asked to accompany a Christmas hymn-sing. I went to the front of church and played several songs and then chatted with a member while everyone was leaving church. I noticed the unfamiliar man bending over the pew near my belongings. Then he rose, holding a small wallet (that looked like mine) and rushed out of church. After a few seconds of disbelief, I hurried back to the pew. The zipper on my bag was wide open and my wallet was gone. I shouted, "That man took my wallet!" Stefan Felgenhauer dashed out of church shouting, "Thief!" I ran down the flight of steps in time to see the thief nearly disappear into the marketplace. Thankfully, Stefan caught him mere seconds before he got too far. Without resistance, the man handed my wallet to Stefan. I think he figured that was the end of it. Another church member insisted that the thief needed to be taken to the police. I wrote a police statement and the man was arrested.

God is good and I am grateful for the happy ending. I got back my "travel wallet" (which was a useful gift from my brother), my Malawi driver's license (which is the most valuable item to me since it was torture to get it) and just shy of $100 worth of Kwacha. I had planned on shopping after church to buy some Christmas meal ingredients. So am I paranoid? More like par-**annoyed**!

Time to hit the hay. I hope to sleep until Caleb calls…or the dogs bark…or the alarms wail…or gunshots ring…or the guards talk loudly or blare their communications radio…or the daylight wakes me. I wonder which one it will be. Love, Rebecca

Between managing kids in the pew and playing keyboard, my attention isn't always on my pocket book. It isn't practical to keep it on my person at all times, but I didn't want to become a target again. Crime and theft is common in Malawi, and all the more so during seasons when food is scarce.

Shortly after this update, we found ourselves without a phone line for several weeks. Unfortunately my lack of emails did not mean a lack of action on the home front… including an accidental poisoning.

Sent: January 10, 2006
Subject: dipped and doomed
Rebecca writes: Christmas Eve included another bout of stomach trouble. Thankfully Mom Wendland and I had prepared a dinner the night before. The kids had a blast opening their presents despite their mother curled up on the chair.

Now that I am finally feeling better, I decided to redesign the kids' mosquito nets like teepees so they can get in and out of them more easily. My plan was to cut a slit from the bottom of each conical-shaped net for an entrance and hem the slits by machine. Then I would hand-stitch an outer flap over the new opening. Instead of un-tucking their net to awkwardly crawl under it, the kids would be able to lift the flap of their net and slip through the opening.

When I had finished the "teepee" flaps on the sewing machine, it was time to dip the nets in insecticide. The pamphlet directions for this process were all in Chichewa, but I managed to follow the pictorial directions. Although I had been told that mosquito insecticide net dip is relatively harmless, I made sure to wash my hands frequently. The dipping process went well. It was a windy day outside and the nets dried quickly.

All that remained was to sew on the outer panels and hang the nets before dark. I began the final hand-stitching and decided to use only five pins since they kept catching on the netting and were being flung around the room. Soon after I began stitching, Rob asked me a question. When I answered him, my mouth felt weird. I took a drink. My lips were numb. It dawned on me that because I was rotating a small number of pins and pinching them between my lips to keep track of them, I had been inadvertently poisoning myself with the net dip! I tried drinking some milk and flushing my mouth out, but nothing seemed to help. The tingling numbness spread from my lips to my nose, and they were numb for the remainder of the day. It felt like I was walking around with a jar of VICKS VapoRub strapped to my face. I was <u>very</u> careful after that! The bright side is: I wasn't bitten by mosquitoes on my face and maybe, just maybe, the poison helped kill my internal bugs!

The other noteworthy item is that our alarm went off a few nights ago. Thieves managed to cut through two more support wires in the backyard. The guard sounded the alarm and the team came to check it out. Rob fixed it the next day and nothing more has happened since.

Our water heater somehow got jolted into a "super hot" setting AGAIN (like last year). It sounded like it was raining **inside**…but it wasn't raining **outside**. Rob investigated. He found out that the water heater was boiling, causing heavy condensation in the crawl space. The drips have left ugly, rust-colored spots all over the ceilings—AGAIN! He is certain the thermostat was originally not set that hot. Our power surges are definitely altering it.

The phone people came to string a new line to our house (at our expense) for a different phone number. We asked them if they could fix our existing phone line instead. No, that wasn't their job. Currently our line isn't working well and internet is impossible. I don't like being disconnected, especially when we are paying for service. Love, Rebecca

The kids kept getting tangled up in the bottom of their conical nets when they got in and out of bed. My idea of sewing an overlapping panel over the entrance slit seemed like the perfect solution. However, I was hardly celebrating after I poisoned myself! In the end it was worth the time and effort, and others have even been inspired to do the same (redesign their bed nets, that is). Next time, I was convinced, I would be more careful not to poison myself. Little did I know that the "next time" I would end up poisoning my whole family!

*"The LORD will keep you from all harm—he will watch over your life;
the LORD will watch over your coming and going
both now and forevermore." Psalm 121:7-8*

Sent: February 3, 2006
Subject: fruitful "berry"er
Rebecca writes: Hannah LOVED her 6th birthday celebration and Barbie cake. She is currently singing in the yard wearing her new fancy shoes and silver crown. She recently told us that some kids at school were telling other kids not to go near a certain tree because a python was in it; such are the bullies in Blantyre!

Yesterday Nathanael asked me if he could help. I told him he could when he was older. Five minutes later he announced, "I'm ready now; I'm older."

Rob fell off his rocker. Really! His chair completely broke apart at a restaurant while we were waiting for our meal. Rob was holding Caleb since they do not provide child seats. Thankfully they were both okay. Because of the accident we ended up with a free pizza, as well as a few cuts and bruises.

Today at Bible Group I learned that within a year every lady that currently attends will be gone or transferred away. I used to like **turnovers**—apple ones, that is. I'm sad already to know they'll all be gone. We'll make the best of the time we have remaining.

I've begun to eat only cooked veggies to see if that helps my gut.

I've joined the church choir and find it challenging to learn the music by rote and "feel" when to sing. But I enjoy the fun rhythms and harmony. The Malawian director is cutting me slack. Often I'm the only one with the words, which are hand-written on a piece of paper. I'm thankful we are also singing some English songs. I've been typing the words out for each song so that we can begin to build a choir repertoire.

Two years ago I planted black raspberry starts against our back wall; they have become a terrific "berry-er." It would be difficult to cross that mess of thorns. They even have thorns on the leaves. Despite the prickers, I harvested ten cups of berries. I finally made a berry pie so I would stop dreaming about eating one.

Our gardener told us that it has been difficult to buy maize to make *nsima*. Recently he slept overnight in line to buy some. All I could think of was Americans who sleep in line for tickets to a big movie or show, not for survival. It would be hard to explain to a Malawian that unwanted food in America is often thrown away after every meal.

The house of Rob's church worker, Spider, collapsed recently because of the rain and wet conditions. It has rained nearly every day for about two months. Since village huts are made of bricks, and the bricks are mainly baked mud, excessive moisture returns them to their former state: mud.

Last but not little was the spider on our *khonde*...it was a huge tarantula! Thankfully Rob was here. I'll spare you the details lest I scare any potential visitors. Love, Rebecca

The new year was off to a challenging start: the maize shortage, houses falling down, Bible Group friends moving away and our non-functioning phone were all difficult pills to swallow. Also unwelcome was the tarantula within our walls. Malawians call them "baboon spiders" because of their hairy bodies and the thick black pads at the end of their legs that resemble baboon fingers.

Our attempt at a relaxing night out was foiled when Rob's chair broke beneath him at the restaurant. And that wasn't the only thing being broken on the premises—I saw some of the kitchen crew *licking* the ketchup bottles as they filled them. I guess it isn't a big surprise that we struggle with GI issues, considering our food will only be as germ-free as the kitchen staff at a restaurant.

Sent: February 10, 2006
Subject: on the mend
Rebecca writes: I'm starting this email (January 30th) to send whenever we have another connection. No hope of that happening soon...I saw the phone man sitting under a tree today waiting for the rain to stop. When the rain finally started to let up, it was 5pm and time for him to go home. So, we sit without a dial tone for yet another weekend. Our plan is to take Rob's computer to the Johnston's house to send and download mail. We've got to read and respond to some of the mail that is piling up. It's silly to haul around our computer to "keep in touch," but for now that is the plan. God bless, Rebecca
P.S. As of today I successfully made it ONE MONTH without being sick—yeah!

Soon after this email, I attended the Zambia Ladies' Retreat. It was not smooth travels! In my attempt to leave Malawi I was "deported" by the Malawi border official for not having the original Temporary Employment Permit (TEP) receipt with my passport. I was also told that Malawi didn't need "rebellious citizens" like me. I felt quite vulnerable since I was traveling with nine-month-old Caleb. Thankfully, a fellow missionary wife, Mindy Holtz, had driven to meet me from Chipata, a nearby city in Zambia, and she graciously helped me through the border issues. The man at the border window warned me that he would be watching for me when I returned. On my return trip, Missionary Paul Nitz met me at the border and handled things without incident. I had a final bit of action when I rode the local coach bus from Lilongwe to Blantyre. The bus overheated mid-trip and we were stranded. Thankfully it was a temporary stall and we finally arrived safe and sound in Blantyre.

When I reached home, I found that our phone still did not work. We were still toting the computer desktop to the other mission houses to download and send email. It is hard to describe how frustrating those months of poor communication were; we were unable to contact or update anyone easily, near or far. There had to be an easier way to stay in touch here!

Sent: February 20, 2006
Subject: African update
Rebecca writes: The other day I decided to call our house number from my cell phone. I wanted to see if it would ring, or if it would have some message like, "This number is spare" (a popular automated phrase here when a number isn't working). I dialed our number, and to my surprise someone answered! I was so shocked I almost dropped the phone. I blurted, "I'm trying to reach this number...what number did I call?" The lady's accent was so thick I couldn't understand her. Unfortunately, I got no other info before she hung up on me—my own number! The nerve. That is a preamble as to why I'm **not** sending this from our house.

Thanks for your help with our taxes, Dad. Thanks for the gift subscription to Taste of Home, Mom. Last evening I used one of the recipes for a Super Bowl party meal at the Bartz's house. The game had played live the day before at 1am our time, so Rob taped it. For the party I made two football-shaped "Quarterback Calzones." The power went out in the middle of the game...so we chatted for a while by candlelight until it returned.

Mom and Aaron will be proud to know I had my first Chichewa pun. With my limited Chichewa this was really something. Rob had a pip from a pineapple and mentioned that it was hard to chew, so I interjected, "*Pipani*." (*Pepani* means "I'm sorry.") I thought you'd like my multi-lingual progress in the pun world. God bless, Rebecca

Absence makes the heart grow fonder...even for football. For the 2006 Super Bowl, the mission families "tackled" the distance problem by having a Super Bowl party. We had taped it from a satellite service and enjoyed a fun get-together. We watched in suspense and waited in anticipation when the power went out, since none of us had peeked at the score.

Sent: March 8, 2006
Subject: don't get excited
Rebecca writes: The phone repair man, Mr. Moto, came to our house this morning. To make a long story short, today we have a working phone line in **half** of our house. At least the half that is working happens to be Rob's office. Love, Rebecca

Was the house half-full or half-empty if only half of it had a working phone line? Either way, I was thankful to access email from home again.

Sent: March 15, 2006
Subject: cold and rainy
Rob writes: So far we have had four days in a row with a dial tone! It will be interesting to see whether the "phone connection streak" or our "non-sickness streak" will last longer. The recent cold/flu has been bad in Malawi, with fever, diarrhea and nasal/aural infections among its various manifestations. It has attacked the rich and the poor alike.

Our rainy season continues. It has already lasted two months longer than last year. If it stops soon, we'll have a great harvest. What fickle things we humans are: "God, we need rain please; God, please no more rain!"

I enjoy the rains—although not the road destruction they bring. I have been told that when I go to Tcheleni in the Lower Shire it will take me about ten hours round-trip instead of six. They've had so much rain that the East Bank Road is one long river bed. When I went there a couple of weeks ago it was raining and very slow going. My travel time was doubled. I thought to myself as the Land Cruiser was in 4WD with mud flying everywhere, "How many people get paid to go five hours of "mudding" on a Sunday morning and still get to go to church?!" After plunging through streams, skidding through mud and dodging mini Grand Canyons, the Land Cruiser was brown—even on top—when I got home. Blessings in Jesus, Rob

Once Malawi's December-April rainy season begins in earnest, it rains almost daily. Six inches of rain can fall in a single day. Flash flooding occurs in the southern regions from time to time, and travel along the roads in all areas of the country becomes difficult and unreliable. The rains that we had so eagerly awaited back in October were now wearing out their welcome as the rainy season drew to a close.

Rural church parking lot

Sent: March 17, 2006
Subject: space invaders
Rebecca writes: Yesterday was hair-cutting day. When I took out the black comb, I saw white webbing on it. It was mold. Nothing like living in a tropical rain forest with all the baggage it brings. The mold will soon pass...and then dust will be invading every inch.

I found our house help "helping herself" to Rob's things on his dresser. I stood there until she sheepishly picked up her broom and continued to sweep. Tomorrow is her last day.

We had over a South African couple from Cape Town. They brought a Cape Town map and circled kid-friendly places to go. We have frequent-flyer miles that we'd like to use to visit there. Love, Rebecca

Although it was helpful to have someone assist with the weekly cleaning, it was NOT helpful to have her filling her pockets and "exploring" nearly every area of our house in our absence. We let her go without involving the police. Unless she had sold them, her house was full of our glasses, sippy cups, dishes, platters, silverware, knives, towels, clothes, stationary, tools and toys. Only after the fact (such as when company was coming and I wanted to set out spare towels and extra supplies) did I discover exactly how many things had been taken from under our noses. We had enough trouble with the thieves outside our walls. To PAY someone to come into our home and pilfer our belongings was too much.

One benefit of our international social circle has been the many insights we've gained about places around the globe. Neither Rob nor I had ever been to Cape Town. With our tenth wedding anniversary approaching, it was a place we hoped to visit.

Sent: March 29, 2006
Subject: Taste of America
Rebecca writes: Hannah was watching the Commonwealth games on TV with Rob. She commented that it was great that they all speak English! That is something none of us take for granted.

This evening at church Nathanael announced, "Jesus died on the cross..." (I smiled) "...to take away our germs!" One of Nathanael's recent, costly shenanigans was cancelling my USA stamps with our address stamper. I had all my stationary items out on the table while I was nursing Caleb. USA stamps are a rare commodity here and I was not happy to find them inked up by our own address stamper.

The two older kids had fun doing their own Olympic games in our backyard. I made "sleds" out of old potato sacks so they could slide down our drainage ditches. They were giggling for about an hour going around and around and up

Year Three: Loads Of Cares; Loads Of Prayers

and down. Cheap fun!

The weather has turned cool, so I decided to put Caleb in a footy sleeper for bed. When I tried to put his feet in, he began bawling. I can tell the kids are spoiled by the warm climate.

We have had it with the RAIN! It has been non-stop rain/drizzle for days. There is mud everywhere. The two dogs are moving mud blobs. Nothing is drying out. Our bathroom towels are as wet in the evening as when I put them on the drying rack in the morning. Every day I discover a new moldy object. Even our money molds! The rain by itself is one thing, but I am not fond of the mold or its smell.

At choir, a lady from Portugal was going on about the new Patriot Act in America. She and another member looked at me as if I was supposed to defend this new law "my government" had established. I responded that I wasn't aware of the new law. They kept talking and didn't involve me again.

God's blessings this Lenten season as we follow our Savior humbly to the cross and triumphantly to the empty grave! Love, Rebecca

During the 2005-2006 rainy season there was much more rain than during the previous growing season. The fields were doing well, but they couldn't take too much more rain or the crops would rot. There is such a delicate balance between rainfall, weather and life. I can only imagine what would happen if *people* were in charge of something as "simple" as when it should rain. Our city struggled just to regulate the water that was already on the ground!

It is interesting being an island, so to speak, in a foreign land. I am a mini-representative of my country. Some people almost assume I am part of the decisions that "my country" makes. Though I liked to stay informed, I am not prepared or willing to defend everything "my country" stands for. I can hardly keep up with the current price of USA stamps.

> *"All men are like grass,*
> *and all their glory is like the flowers of the field;*
> *the grass withers and the flowers fall,*
> *but the word of the Lord stands forever." 1 Peter 1:24–25*

CHAPTER 14

2006: A SEASON FOR EVERYTHING

*"There is a time for everything,
and a season for every activity under heaven:
a time to be born and a time to die,
a time to plant and a time to uproot,
a time to tear down and a time to build,
a time to weep and a time to laugh,
a time to search and a time to give up,
a time to keep and a time to throw away,
a time to tear and a time to mend,
a time to be silent and a time to speak."
Ecclesiastes 3:1-4, 6-7*

We were now in the thick of our third year in Malawi. I realized more and more that the "seasons" I often wrote about in my emails were very different from the neatly divided segments of summer, autumn, winter and spring I had known in America. Africa is so vast that our Malawian seasons do not even mesh with other countries in southern Africa, let alone those in North America. Two unmistakable seasons here in Malawi are the rainy season and the dry season. Additional "seasons" I've come to anticipate are: mango, guava, berry, *inswa* (flying termites), grasshoppers/katydids, moths and mold. These "seasons" are definitely cyclical, and for that I am thankful. Since the beginning of time, everything has had its season and time under the sun. *This* time is ours! We are living in the exact era that God chose for us from eternity. It is our time to go through the seasons of life. This is our time to serve as His witnesses. What we do with our time, how we live each day, how we use our resources and take care of the gifts we have been entrusted with (not the least of which is our children) is paramount, since our days are numbered and non-retractable.

Even as the 2006 season of rain finally drew to a close, across the ocean another kind of season was drawing to a close: I would soon receive news of a dear family member whose season of life on earth had given way to a heavenly resurrection. By the end of the year I would realize anew that there is indeed "a time for everything, and a season for every activity under heaven"…some of which were straight out of Ecclesiastes, and some that were uniquely Malawian.

A Time For Mold

Sent: April 7, 2006
Subject: guava bounty
Rebecca writes: It is currently guava season. Our backyard tree is loaded, so I juiced several dozen to make nutritious guava juice. I prefer the juice instead of eating them raw with all the seeds. I took a bushel to church on Sunday to "share the wealth."

It seems the mold season leads into the season of MOTHS! We have hundreds of moths in, around and landing on our house. Isn't there a Bible passage about "moth and rust destroy?" I hope the rust isn't coming. I already know what the Old Testament says about the mold!

Rob and Hannah's passports are expiring in a few months so we'll drive up to the capital city, Lilongwe. Our plan will be to go there and back in one day. The government offices don't make things easy with their sparse office hours and selective days for certain business.

My friend from Bible Group is returning to Germany and asked if we want to employ their reliable house worker. It seems she has proven to be trustworthy with their family. I am dragging my dusty feet on a decision, since we had such a rotten time with the last house gal. But considering how often I'm sick, it might be worth it to take another chance on hired help in order to stay on top of household duties. Love, Rebecca

P.S. Molding items of the day: card table and chairs

As I fought mold and juiced guavas, I was glad that the whole realm of nature was not mine. That responsibility is something only our omnipotent God can truly manage. Instead, I would simply try to be a good steward of what I had been given, whether great or small or from my own backyard.

> *Were the whole realm of nature mine, That were a tribute far too small;*
> *Love so amazing, so divine, Demands my soul, my life, my all. (CW 125:4)*

Dear Heavenly Father, allow me to take the gifts and time You have given me seriously, since You entrusted me to be the manager of them. I confess I often manage them selfishly instead of for the good of others or to further Your kingdom. May I see them as opportunities to show my love for You. Your Son showed sacrificial love by giving His life for me on the cross to take away my sins. Thank You today—through eternity—for that amazing gift. I want to be a good steward of the gifts and time You've given me and to use it all to Your glory in every season! Amen.

Sent: April 15, 2006
Subject: He is Risen in "D"
Rebecca writes: Happy Easter! A special, "He is Risen in 'D'!" from Nathanael. (Rob thinks it would be like Canon in D.)

We've been hammered with power outages lately. The electric company seems to take advantage of the holidays for repair work. That really throws a wrench into holiday meal-making. The power was out from 1pm to 8pm today. I had planned to make pretzel crosses for church tomorrow. That will not happen. Instead, I'll bring *naartjies* (tangerines) and guavas for a fruit medley.

Tomorrow the mission families will have a brunch (minus Rob who will be gone for the day). Speaking of Rob, his body sure took a beating during his last bush trip. His back was giving him serious pain. He couldn't even stand straight. It has improved but is still not great. Firing up the generator has been difficult for him lately with the torque needed to start it.

We recently got more support on the home front. We hired my friend's house worker. I appreciate the extra help in the house, but she will only work part-time as I also appreciate my privacy. God bless, Rebecca

P.S. Moldy item of the day: wooden hammer handle

Whenever special holidays approached, memories of "the way it used to be" crept in from past Stateside celebrations. It was helpful to anticipate celebrating with the other mission families. New memories would be made as we celebrated Easter—traditional trimmings or not.

> ***When I survey the wondrous cross On which the Prince of glory died,***
> ***My richest gain I count but loss And pour contempt on all my pride. (CW 125:1)***

Sent: April 23, 2006
Subject: Caleb's 1st birthday
Rebecca writes: Several days before Easter, the government declared that all the vendors should move to the allotted market area downtown. That was a major undertaking, since hundreds, if not thousands, of vendors roam every street and set up makeshift stalls wherever it suits them. All "illegal" vendors were to be moved by police force if necessary. The market area is across the street from our new urban church, Beautiful Saviour. It was rumored that our church could be a target for retaliation from the angry vendors. Thankfully, no trouble developed.

After Easter, we mission families gathered for a retreat and studied the book of Peter. It was enjoyable getting into the Word and empathizing with Peter's strengths and weaknesses. The mission kids enjoyed Sunday School lessons, made projects and sang a song at the closing worship service.

Hannah dreamt that she was at the Chinese embassy. (How many 6-year-olds have that for a dream venue?) She also noticed that the history channel was not in black and white and remarked, "Oh good, History has color!" (It sure *is* colorful!) Today she happily showed me a loose baby tooth in her mouth. Right behind her was Nathanael who announced proudly, "Look, I have a baby in my mouth too!" Speaking of our baby...Caleb turns one today. We are blessed! Love, Rebecca

P.S. Moldy item of the day: woven grass baskets

The decision to move the vendors from "illegal" spots in town was a good one. The timing, however, made for a very cautious trip into town for the Easter service. Much to our delight, the relocation of the vendors was not met with any obvious resistance or trouble. It was liberating to be able to park in town without local vendors swarming our vehicle. I did sometimes miss their end-of-the-day deals, but that was a small price to pay.

When it comes to paying a price, Easter defines the biggest payment of all. Christ paying for our sins and conquering death on our behalf cannot be celebrated enough. Sharing that celebration with fellow believers around the world is a joy. He is Risen INDEED!

See, from his head, his hands, his feet, Sorrow and love flow mingled down.
Did e'er such love and sorrow meet, Or thorns compose so rich a crown? (CW 125:3)

Sent: April 25, 2006
Subject: baker's dozen
Rebecca writes: Yet again, each day proves to be an adventure. I was doing some repairs on our back porch. I needed something heavy, so I grabbed two nearby bricks. I brushed some dirt off the first brick and put it into place. I grabbed the second brick and noticed it had a clump of moist mud on it. I looked a little closer and, lo and behold, there was a camouflaged mother scorpion with at least 12 babies on her back. Thankfully, they never moved while I held the brick. I was even brave enough to move the brick into better lighting to get a few pictures. Before the end of the day I found another scorpion on our porch. My heart is still pumping from the whole episode. God bless, Rebecca

P.S. Moldy items of the day: potholders

I inadvertently picked up this scorpion family

Rob was out of town for meetings during my scorpion encounter. I was thankful we had a gardener on the property to kill them—after I took a picture.

Having a gardener has made the whole Easter tomb scenario come to life for me. When Mary mistook Jesus for a gardener and asked where he put her Lord, I can easily picture the scene in an African context. Not only does history have color, but it is stirring when it comes alive!

A Time To Mourn

Sent: April 28, 2006
Subject: Grandma Staude in glory
Rebecca writes: Dad, sorry to hear the news of Grandma Staude passing away. I am glad that she is with Jesus and we will see her again in heaven someday. I can't imagine dealing with a family member's death if they didn't believe in their Savior from sin.

I entertained the thought that Caleb and I could fly back. Given the timing of the funeral, I physically cannot get a flight in time—so that is the answer. I obviously don't need to go, but the funeral certainly would bring closure and comfort.

Intermittent memories of Grandma are starting to make her death hit home. Grandma was such a blessing to me during my years at Northwestern Prep. Her house across the street was truly open any time. I have wonderful memories of walking to Tivoli Island to feed the ducks, sitting on her glider on the porch, her faithful weekend help with laundry, savoring Friday pizzas and cream sodas and having her warmly welcome any friends that I brought along. I am glad she kept the faith, and we know we'll see her again in heaven. Psalm 116:15: *"Precious in the sight of the Lord is the death of his saints."* Praise the Lord for Easter! Through tears of sadness we thankfully see the "Son"shine and rainbow of his promises. God will keep His promise of eternal life to us, thanks to Christ. Come Lord Jesus—quickly come! Rebecca

I was struck hard by the reality that I would never see my Grandma again on this side of eternity. The last good-bye that we had exchanged on furlough was indeed the *"last."* When I realized that I could not physically make the funeral service—even if I stepped on the next departing airplane—it was disheartening. That is the cost of living on the far side of the world. Praise our Lord that the cost of our sins has been paid, and we will be able to see each other again in eternity.

> *Be still, my soul; though dearest friends depart*
> *And all is darkened in the vale of tears;*
> *Then you will better know his love, his heart,*
> *Who comes to soothe your sorrows and your fears.*
> *Be still, my soul; your Jesus can repay*
> *From his own fullness all he takes away. (CW 415:3)*

Sent: April 30, 2006
Subject: 4-wheeling for Jesus
Rob writes: *Zikuyenda*, "things are going," as they say here. Our rainy season is winding down. People are starting to harvest their maize, and so it seems that the time of great starvation (Nov-Feb) in Malawi is over for now. We are thanking the Lord. Last year most people's crops failed.

The ministry work continues to go well as I serve my thirteen congregations. It was difficult reaching the village churches in southern Malawi during the rainy months, because many roads and bridges were washed out. A month ago, during heavy rains, I tried to reach the church in Tcheleni. At the normal bridge crossing, the river was moving fast and up to the level of the road. The bridge wasn't visible. Although I have sometimes tackled such bridges with my 4-wheel drive, this time it looked too risky. I turned around and went home. This proved to be a blessing, as I found out this month when I returned to the same area. The water in the river was down by 15 feet! The thirty-foot concrete bridge that had been covered by water last month, and which I considered trying to cross, was now entirely visible: it was lying with one end on the river bed 15 feet below. This time I simply drove down into the river bed and back up again. The water was at mid-tire.

Because most places in the bush have roads and bridges that are not yet repaired from the rains, I drive around a lot of downed bridges and across river beds that used to be roads. It means that my travel time is increased by about a third. I figured out that I spend about 50 travel-hours a month to conduct worship and confirmation classes in the bush.

Yesterday was a 10 hour day to the Lower Shire. The riverbed roads that I was "mudding" in a couple months ago have hardened up. In many areas it is like driving over a washboard; in other places it is like going over two-foot-high speed bumps with no option to go around; and in still other locations I have to make my own road through the bush since, where there used to be a road, there's now a five-foot-high cliff down to a brand new river bed. Concrete swales have been built in the past to enable vehicles to pass through most rivers. In a few places the whole concrete slab has floated downstream or crumbled, adding further rubble to navigate over. There were quite some flash floods. I am glad this Sunday is mostly on paved roads.

Many times, church members from Diwa want to ride in the back of my truck to the church in N'singano to "encourage" their brothers and sisters there. Yesterday I took the ladies' choir and the evangelist with me. On the way home they sang with all their might—kilometer after bouncy kilometer. We arrived back at Diwa under the light of a full moon, accompanied by the songs of the choir and the engine of the Land Cruiser. Jesus was sung out to the Lower Shire for 60 km.

Our phone line, which was cut just before Christmas, was fixed recently. We were almost three months without a phone! It worked for a total of 23 hours in January. We are thankful it is working now, and we appreciate every time we actually hear a dial tone. Love, Rob

A Time For Grasshoppers

Sent: May 5, 2006
Subject: grasshopper season
Rebecca writes: Hannah ran into the house to grab a flashlight, broadcasting that Nathanael's shoe was "gone forever." When I arrived, the kids were on their hands and knees looking down a big, empty ant hole. Nathanael had stepped on an anthill and broken through. His shoe fell to the bottom. Rob didn't want to stick his hand down a dark hole, so the kids were in a panic that the shoe was gone forever. When Rob was sure the hole was uninhabited, he brought the shoe back to the surface.

This afternoon Hannah was playing with play dough. The progression of her sculpted items was: bear rug (like Grandpa Staude's), *samosa* (an Indian stuffed pastry), and scorpion with babies on its back. Not exactly run-of-the-mill play dough sculptures. At school two of her classmates brought in idols of their gods for show-and-tell. She told me that she knows Jesus is stronger than all of them. Praise God!

We are now in the "season of the grasshoppers" (technically katydids). The Malawians collect and eat them. The katydids are <u>everywhere</u>. We extracted 50 from inside the house. In fact, when I looked in the mirror I saw I had one on my shirt, looking right back at me. They are literally lining our front door entrance. What I don't appreciate is when they hide in places like the underside of a car door handle! It's horrible to reach for the handle and feel a squirming surprise. They can

bite, but are mostly harmless. God bless, Rebecca
P.S. I returned to find that this was on the 203rd try to send. Now I'm offline.
P.S.S. Moldy item of the day: leather belt.

Katydid toothbrush surprise

Sent: May 20, 2006
Subject: busy week
Rob writes: Last Sunday I began working with a national vicar, Willard Chipembere, who has been assigned to work with me at Bangwe and Khobili.

On Monday I attended the monthly Bible Study with the southern area missionaries. I enjoyed studying the Word and discussing questions of casuistry with them. Next was a meeting with a man from another mission group. The man was interested to know about the curricula we are currently using to train our future pastors, which is the Theological Education by Extension (TEE) courses. Many of these TEE books were written by Grandpa E.H. Wendland in the late 60's and early 70's.

On Tuesday I drove to Lilongwe for LCCA Mission Board meetings. Fuel prices have escalated. I filled up the dual tanks on my Land Cruiser to the tune of $150! Blessings, Rob

Rob was perpetually busy with bush work, related studies, meetings and building projects. He shifted endlessly from one to the next, since they are all an integral part of the ministry here. In his email, Rob mentioned our Malawi pastor-training system.

In my opinion, the program that our future pastors follow is second to none, just as it is in the United States. Interested men must take the TEE course and then test to get into the Lutheran Bible Institute in Lilongwe, a three-year pre-seminary school. LBI graduates then spend another three years at our Lutheran Seminary in Lusaka, followed by a vicar year at a church. If they successfully complete all of the training, they graduate as pastors of the Lutheran Church of Central Africa. Since the early days, Lutherans have realized that to maintain a healthy church you need clergy that are well-equipped in God's Word. In the LCCA we are blessed to have such a firm foundation.

A Time To Weep And A Time To Laugh

Sent: May 27, 2006
Subject: conforming crayons
Rebecca writes: We are entering our fall season in Malawi, but the sun is still hot. I was recently preparing a Bible Group project and I left the crayon box in the sun. I returned to find them all melting into one another. Oh that we would spread our powerful "SON"shine that effectively and conform to God's Word so easily!

I was recently plunking out the hymn, "Go My Children," on the piano when I realized Hannah was in tears. I stopped and asked if something was wrong. It was the hymn title that bothered her: she was troubled that I would want my children to "go." I assured her that no one would leave any time soon. All day long she was sad when she thought of it! I comforted her with the fact that Jesus will never leave her, and all our coming and going is in the Lord's hands.

Our neighbors recently packed up and left. There has been no sign of them since. God bless your "Son"day. Love, Rebecca

P.S. Moldy item of the day: Our wooden carving of the Lord's Supper. I designated the man with the most mold on his head to be Judas.

I was surprised that our neighbors had unexpectedly moved, but I figured it was likely due to the thievery in this area—location, location, location! By June, more neighbors would follow; and before the year was out our own family would be slated to move too.

Sent: May 31, 2006
Subject: Mother Goose-egg
Rebecca writes: Today as I was picking a bouquet of bougainvillea flowers, a large paper wasp stung me right between my lip and nose. It was a painful sting and my head started to feel funny. Rob helped to apply various treatments, along with ice. It swelled for 45 minutes solid, in spite of the ice. Soon it was

the size of an egg…hence the subject title: "Mother Goose-egg." Ordinarily this incident would have been a minor inconvenience in the grand scheme of my day. However, I was supposed to teach a lesson for Bible Group within 20 minutes of the sting. Kathy Felgenhauer kindly helped out. My face was terribly puffy, my lip hurt, my teeth hurt and I didn't feel very good. By dinner my chest area was feeling tight and my breathing was affected. Rob gave me an antihistamine. When I swallowed the pill I could feel how tight my throat was. I will look into getting an EpiPen for any future incidents, since I have learned that my reaction could be WORSE next time. Oh, dear.

Anyway, you never know what your prayers are for. I appreciated any extra ones coming my way yesterday as it pained to breathe. I'm much better after a good night's sleep. Rob comforted me by telling me that puffy lips are "in style." Not **that** puffy, they aren't. In the end I used it as an object lesson for Nathanael—who stared at me in awe! I told him, "Be careful around poisonous things or this could happen to you!"

We took Caleb to Mwaiwathu this morning for another blood draw. They couldn't find his folder. He must have half a dozen folders there…somewhere! I encouraged them to keep the folders all together so we can effectively monitor his thyroid levels. We used the sheets I had along. After they weighed Caleb I asked if they could measure him to chart his growth. The nurse looked at me and responded, "No madam, it is impossible." I laughed inside. I think they lost the measuring tape—but that is the service on some days! (I recently saw someone downtown with a bathroom scale; they were charging 10 kwacha to weigh people. Maybe a measuring booth will be next.) Love, Rebecca

P.S. Moldy items of the day: music folder and hymnal stored on the bookshelf.

Have I mentioned that we never fail to have some action on the home front? At the time, my wasp encounter was not funny in the least…it was scary! But after the fact, it seemed a bit humorous. I thought I might even have stretch marks on my upper lip as a memento—maybe that's a stretch!

A Time To Uproot

Sent: June 9, 2006
Subject: "tree"ty
Rebecca writes: All three immediate neighbors have moved out within the last month. I think we should make a "tree"ty with the landlord, since every lovely tree on one property has been cut down since. Evidently they are selling the wood. Unfortunately for us, one of those trees was holding up our phone wires. (Lacking a proper telephone pole, the phone company had attached our wires to

the tree.) We now need to rig up some way to take up the slack, or all the various traffic in the neighborhood will continue to run over our wire. That is our newest phone problem.

I guess it won't matter who the new neighbors are, since we may not remain here long either. The mission has us slotted to move out of Nyambadwe in November. Some shifting on the mission field means that the mission house in Kabula Hill will be vacant soon, so that seems to be the most viable option. Time to uproot and MOVE ON!

You might want to "move on" from my next topic. Let's say (hypothetically) that we found a rather large worm, probably a tapeworm, in the toilet. Is there a possibility it came from our septic tank and not from one of us? Rob thinks it may have come from the worker's toilet, through the piping, and into our toilet. I'm skeptical; not to mention disgusted. We should all be treated for worms. It was (hypothetically—of course) thriving in the water and thrashing around with its tapered end looking for another host. Someone just might be exemplifying the "diet of worms."

Today at lunch Hannah was talking about what happens when people die. She said she hoped that she would go to Heaven when she dies. I told her we don't have to HOPE—we KNOW what Jesus promises when we die. We then recited John 3:16 together. At that point Nathanael interjected, "Yeah, if we go into the ditch we go to hell." (I'm not sure how deep he thinks the road-side drainage ditches are…but they aren't THAT deep!)

Rob called from the bush today. He was transporting a one-ton load of maize and got a flat tire. He used at least two jacks to attempt a tire change. That is the last I heard from him; I hope his return travels go smoother. God bless, Rebecca

Our "shifty" neighborhood, toilet worms, drainage ditches to hell, flat tires and an impending move gave us lots to think and pray about. We knew that moving out of Nyambadwe to a safer neighborhood would improve our security, but it would be a drain on our energy and time in the meanwhile. The bright side of moving was that it would force us to sift through our belongings, clean out closets and uncover other hidden moldy treasures.

Sent: June 20, 2006
Subject: White out please
Rebecca writes: I have been working on crafts with the ladies at church for our upcoming outreach event—a church "fayre." We are making handmade cards using banana bark designs. Some ladies hardly speak English, but it is enjoyable when we all work together to God's glory.

Rob went to Lilongwe for the Bible Institute's 25th Anniversary. While he was gone, I decided to paint the ceiling stains left by our overheated water heater.

After four coats I realized it was not going to be easy. I think my toothpaste has more whitening power than the local white ceiling paint! I used two ladders to position myself in the 10 locations needed and moved the ladders countless times. I applied 12 coats of paint to the spots, and in the end I had to scoop up blobs of paint and plaster it on to cover the stains. Ridiculous! I don't mind hard work. This time it was literally a "pain in the neck!"

The current water shortage means that some village ladies have quite a task to bring water home. One of our members gets up at 2am to walk to the water borehole. Even at that hour she has to stand in long lines, hoping to leave with a full bucket of water on her head, her newborn baby on her back and still make it to work by midmorning. It is hard for me to imagine that added burden to the family schedule. It makes boiling and filtering our water seem easy, since I go from the tap to the stove to the filter…all in one kitchen. God bless, Rebecca

Our church, Beautiful Saviour, was planning a "fayre" (it took me a while to get used to that alternate spelling) for October. The community would be invited to visit our church for information, services like blood-pressure checks, games and fun. The Ladies' Group was making crafts to sell. I was in charge of designing several Christmas cards, gift tags and star ornaments, using the local paper products.

We were experiencing major water shortages again. Even though we had enjoyed good rains and the reservoirs were still plenty full, breakdowns at the water plant and in water-supply pipes caused the difficulties. As a result, some Malawians were getting up in the middle of the night to walk to any place that had water. There were such long lines that many people couldn't get water and make it to work in the same day.

Communication breakdowns have been evident in the Malawian government also. Once, without warning, a government official declared a 3-day holiday around Malawi's Independence Day (July 6). Nobody knew if stores would be open or if any official business or banking could be done. It was frustrating for employers to deal with this spur-of-the-moment declaration. After day two, it was announced on the radio that the holiday was over and people should go back to work.

Sent: August 10, 2006
Subject: ministry update
Rob writes: On Thursday I made my monthly visit to two congregations that were part of recent building projects. Apparently, constructing buildings is a good evangelism tool: before the buildings were erected I had 17 communicants at one place and 30 at the other. Now they are both over 60.

I had 20 baptisms on Thursday! I was also informed that I had another 40 people to confirm. I was skeptical about this, since I had just confirmed 40 adults when I visited the month before. I had never even met this class of 40. How could the church elders have taken the class through the five confirmation books so quickly? When I asked the elders this, they laughed and told me that this class asked to meet every day—seven days a week for one hour. That would do it! At this rate they'll outgrow their new buildings in a year. Thankfully the churches are designed to hold 2-3 times the amount of people that they used to have! Love, Rob

A Time To Mend

Our days were certainly eventful, but August wasn't all business for our family. We also enjoyed a trip to South Africa and a visit from Rob's family…wonderful days that helped to restore our energy and mend any lingering frustration over the day-to-day grind.

Sent: August 21, 2006
Subject: backtracking
Rebecca writes: Our phone is back. We've covered a lot of ground since I wrote last. Our family took a trip to Cape Town for our 10th wedding anniversary and had a fantastic time. Nathanael wanted to live there.

About a month ago we enjoyed a visit from Rob's parents and some Stateside members of his family: his sister Naomi, his brother Stephen, Stephen's wife Lenka, and their daughter, Makayla. Our family drove six hours to the Malawi/Zambia border and then endured an additional three-hour, pot-holed road trip to meet up with them at South Luangwa Game Park. We saw a monitor lizard a few feet away as we got out of our vehicle…and that was only the beginning of our wildlife experience.

We stayed at a chalet that was nestled among hippos wallowing in a lagoon and crocodiles sunbathing on the banks. The dining area overlooked the river basin. The hippos were several feet away, snorting all night long in the lagoon. It was an awesome experience to be "at one" with the wildlife…but I kept an eye on the kids at all times. Once it was dusk, we HAD to be escorted to our rooms by an armed guard with a flashlight.

The next day we spotted a resting pride of lion. On our night drive we saw lion, hyena, porcupine, genet cat and other smaller game. One lioness was calling her twin cubs very nearby. And we heard lions outside our camp area in the night. That was something! It was almost hard to sleep at night with all the wildlife activity and sounds.

Not only did we sleep among the wildlife; we also bathed in their midst. The bathtub/shower area had shutters that opened up so that we only had a screen between us and the hippo lagoon. The kids had a blast taking their baths. A big, thick rope hung down to help bathers hoist themselves from the bath. The kids of course pretended they were Tarzan—swinging on it and giggling away.

After our amazing taste of wild Africa, we continued on to Malawi. We ran into a difficult official at the border who gave us trouble. Our hearts were beating rather quickly, since we were completely at this man's mercy and the sun was setting. Thankfully, the issue resolved.

Our travels brought something new to our attention: Malawi started speed traps. The new speed limits are: urban areas–50 kph, public roads–80 kph, highway–100 kph. The city sent out a warning that although they have posted only a few speed limit signs in the whole country, it is no excuse for not knowing. "*Takulandirani!*" (Welcome!) God bless, Rebecca

Wendland safari breakfast in the bush

Malawi is reported to have the highest number of traffic fatalities in the Southern Africa region. Speeding is common, despite the many roadway obstacles. Fatal accidents are frequent, and emergency services are basic at best. In an effort to curb the frequent fatalities, speed traps were set up. By 2008 road radar would be introduced on many of Malawi's major roads.

The family visit was a boost. The kids found it hard to say goodbye when the fun was done. They also found it hard to say goodbye to the special American *snacks* that our guests had brought along for the trip. It amazed me to watch how snack-food options turned them so picky, so fast. Normally when a meal is served they don't have much of a choice other than: 1) To eat or 2) Not to eat. They adjust.

Some creatures that aren't picky are the ants! There were no ants in our house when we returned from our trip. I waited. It took them only three hours to detect food in our kitchen and return in full force. (These are critters whose powers of detection cannot be underestimated: once I made a pumpkin dessert in a large pan. There was no room in the fridge so I stored it on the stove, sealed with its "airtight" plastic cover. In the morning I lifted the lid to find hundreds of ants scurrying every which way across my dessert!)

Sent: August 22, 2006
Subject: "tired"
Rob writes: On Sunday I failed to reach my village congregation for worship. I had two flat tires on the way. I was very glad for the two car jacks I now carry. After the second flat tire I had to get one tire fixed. I was helped at a nearby bicycle shop. After the tire was repaired and replaced, I arrived at Nalipa…but everyone had already worshipped and was gone. I pray all of your services went better than mine.

On Monday I got new tires. I was trying to make the old ones last a few more months, because it's about $1,000 to get a new set. Four flat tires in five trips finally convinced me that it is time. Blessings in Jesus, Rob

In an effort to be a good steward of mission money, Rob tried to make his tires last as long as possible. That effort tended to "tread" a fine line, since it was also costly in time and efficiency to get stranded with flat tires. The rough roads here can destroy the tires before their tread is worn down. Sometimes it's "a time to mend"… and sometimes it's just "a time to replace."

A Time To Shine Our Lights

Sent: August 25, 2006
Subject: thinking outside the box/bars/grate
Rebecca writes: The kids all sat separately with church families while I played keyboard for today's service. Nathanael sits like an angel with the Ntambo family. His halo falls off after church when he sees his brother Caleb and begins to pester him.

Speaking of pestering, Friday night there were thieves outside our wall in a tree near our bedroom. The security light in that area had been frying light bulbs. The last time Rob put in a bulb it sizzled the whole assembly. That area outside our bedroom was completely dark, and that is where the thieves made their attempt last night. Thankfully, our guards pressed the panic button and the thieves did not get over the razor wire. Since the fix-it people do not work on the weekends, we needed another solution to light up that area before nightfall. In the end I rigged up our reading lamp by stringing the cord past the screen, window and first set of burglar bars and resting it on the second set of burglar bars. The repair guys had a good laugh when they saw my "out of the box" solution. It worked: the thieves didn't attempt a second breach in that area.

I'm thankful this incident happened **after** Rob's family had come and gone. A team of armed response-men trampling through the property in the wee hours might count as a vacation highlight—but not a positive one! Love, Rebecca

Security lights by any means

The thieves that frequented our property would not give up. Even though they had not yet managed to enter our house to steal anything, they were certainly robbing us of our sleep! We were tired of the unending dead-of-night scenario of prowling thieves, screeching alarms, scrambling guards, barking dogs and the sun rising on a new slate of duties that awaited us, despite our weariness.

Be still, my soul; the Lord is on your side;
Bear patiently the cross of grief or pain;
Leave to your God to order and provide;
In every change he faithful will remain.
Be still, my soul; your best, your heav'nly friend
Through thorny ways leads to a joyful end. (CW 415:1)

Sent: September 4, 2006
Subject: draining
Rebecca writes: Recently our night guards turned in their "torches" (flashlights)

to be refilled with good batteries. The last time we changed the flashlight batteries, Rob had marked our name on each one. Yet when he opened up the flashlights this time, only one battery had our name on it. The guards have been removing the powerful batteries and using them for their own purposes. They replace the good batteries with cheap, dead ones and then tell us they need to be changed. Rob patiently explained to them that the gig was up. And we PAY for this service! Love, the Blantyre Bunch

Sometimes the thieves outside the wall were only part of our security problem. The guards were often a source of grief too. We wanted the guards to have flashlights to illuminate any trouble in the dark, but we couldn't allow them to steal from us in the meantime. Lord, help me *shine* in spite of it all.

Sent: September 12, 2006
Subject: furlough opportunity
Rebecca writes: Rob set off for Nalipa this morning for his first wedding. He had the entire Blantyre choir in the back of his truck. Hope the tires hold up!

Our 2007 furlough dates are slightly up in the air. Rob just received an invitation to speak at the LWMS Rally in Detroit from June 22-25. That is a special invitation. Hannah doesn't get out of school until July 5, and our original furlough plan does not have us Stateside by June 22. We'll talk to the coordinator and see if we can reconcile the dates.

Today we were stopped at an intersection. There was a car with flashing lights (very rare here) and six additional cars behind it. I pointed out the procession. Hannah exclaimed, "Oh, it must be rush hour!" The big city dwellers can stop laughing now! Love, Rebecca

Rob's first wedding in Malawi turned out to be a "no show." He had been so looking forward to it. He had worked hard on the service and was prepared to conduct it in Chichewa. However, a local funeral trumped the wedding...so maybe next month.

Rob was honored to receive an invitation to speak at the upcoming LWMS rally in Detroit, MI. I was glad we had been notified early, since our furlough plans would need immediate adjusting and Hannah's school would also have to be notified.

Sent: September 20, 2006
Subject: Bumping ghosts
Rob writes: I bumped a donkey with my truck yesterday—the animal just stood in the middle of the road and wasn't going to move without some encouragement. I was glad I even saw it. How can you miss a donkey standing in the middle of the road, you ask? It was nighttime, and a truck had passed by not long before,

casting clouds of dust into the air. A pale donkey standing in a haze of fine, white powder exacerbated by the gleam of headlights on a pitch-black night seemed only a ghost in the mist. I nearly tested his "ethereal nature"…and my bull-bar would have judged him wanting.

Yesterday went well with my congregations in the Lower Shire. The bulk of my time was spent at N'singano where I had 20 people who wanted to be tested to join our church. When the dust cleared (this time metaphorical), only 1 person passed. The evangelist quietly told me that I should encourage the people. So there was a lot of "*Musataye mtima*" (don't lose heart) and "*osakhumudwa*" (don't be discouraged) because "these things are important." I was pleased when the chairman backed me up by saying, "Sure you can go to another church where it is easy to join, but doesn't it make you think when you ask their members who Jesus is and they can't tell you? There is no doctrine and no salvation there."

Tomorrow it's back to the Shire, this time on an exploratory trip. Several weeks ago one of our national pastors told me that he had visitors from Maraka in the Lower Shire who want a *nthambi* (branch) of the LCCA there. After thoroughly searching a map, I finally found Maraka. It's as far south as you can get in Malawi without entering Mozambique; about four hours one way. So they will have their special visit. It is bittersweet. Any Christian would be crazy not to jump when someone asks to be told about Jesus. On the other hand, I don't know how they could be served. I don't know what their future could be in the LCCA. I have 6 other "prospect" congregations (not part of my current 13) in the Shire that have waited two years for an answer from our *akulu* (national church leaders) as to how they can join the LCCA. No decision has yet been made for how we can serve all these places, or whether a national pastor can be assigned to the area. Those 6 prospect congregations are at least close enough to existing LCCA congregations (within 15-30 km) that the evangelist can visit them once in a while, and their elders can worship with us when I come down. Maraka is a different story—they are an hour removed from the closest LCCA congregation and at least three hours beyond where the Evangelist lives (who is our only national called worker in the entire Valley)!

Added to that, our mission plan is to phase out rural mission work in the coming years. So even if I would serve them, could the LCCA continue if and when I leave? I am quite skeptical, since I see the reluctance of our national church workers to live in Chikwawa, much less Nsanje. We must take it a day at a time and see what happens—*pang'ono, pang'ono* (little by little).

Since the LWMS has asked me to be the preacher for their opening service at the Detroit convention, our new furlough dates will tentatively be June 16-August 27. Those dates depend on a) approval by our MMC/ACA and b) ticket availability. It looks like the tickets will be double the price of our last furlough. Prices are going up, up. Love, Rob

It was exciting to hear of a group of people in the Lower Shire who wanted the LCCA to shepherd their flock. But with no national pastor in the entire area, any new congregations would by default go to Rob. Rob was eager for the national church to look into the requests further and come to a viable decision. If manpower prevented the LCCA from serving this group, their request, exciting as it was, was also discouraging.

Sent: September 24, 2006
Subject: "Game" viewing in Blantyre
Rebecca writes: We recently learned that Malawi is the fifth poorest country in the world. Malawi also has some of the most inflated prices in the world. Our Malawi tax is 16.5%. To help research that statistic we went "Game" viewing. How will that help you ask? This past week there was a grand opening of a new South African chain store named "Game." The lines of people wanting to go "viewing" were out the door. Earlier in the week people had waited hours in lines that stretched down the block merely to *look* at the merchandise.

On Friday we were shopping around town for hardware for the mission house we will move into. We saw that the line at Game had finally subsided, so we ventured in. I immediately found some nice drawer knobs to replace some broken and nonexistent ones. We also found replacement light fixtures to cover bare wires in several spots at the Kabula Hill mission house. The store is wonderfully stocked with goods from South Africa. How long those stocks will last remains to be seen. So we bought the light fixtures, hardware, another ladder and a rubber bath mat. Game also sells decent disposable diapers, sports equipment, food, electronics, gardening equipment, toys and small appliances. In general their prices are gouging. But if you want availability and are willing to pay the inflated costs, it is the place to go. We have been told that they only get their first shipment duty-free, so once this stock is gone…then the real prices will hit (oh dear). This merchandise availability has brightened our spirits over our upcoming move and house repairs. It will be helpful to find many of the needed supplies under one roof.

I have about 20 boxes packed—slowly but surely! God bless, Rebecca

It was official: we were moving to Kabula Hill area in Blantyre, a much safer neighborhood than Nyambadwe. I was already packing and preparing to relocate. It was just as well that I didn't know that the move—slotted for November—wouldn't actually take place until April.

Sent: September 25, 2006
Subject: where is it?
Rebecca writes: Rob pulled out of the driveway today, carpooling with other

missionaries and heading for Lilongwe. We pray they have safe travels and that the LCCA Synod Convention meetings and decisions can be carried out to God's glory.

Our temperature has been fluctuating. Yesterday I mentioned to Nathanael that the temperature had dropped again. He calmly replied, "Well, where is it?"

We are having serious water shortages here. Most people are commenting on the hardships they face without a constant water supply. Cloth diapering can be the pits. One couple remarked that only one of them can take a shower a day (if that). Then—if possible—they fill their bathtub and water jugs with water for the rest of the day. Often the water comes on around 3am, so people can do a load of laundry at that time. The water shortage reminds us to keep proclaiming the Living Water to all who are thirsty in this sinful world! God bless, Rebecca

There are so many things that a person can live without, but water isn't one of them. I was extremely grateful for our water storage tank, which helped to buffer the impact of the frequent water outages.

Sent: September 29, 2006
Subject: dowry daze
Rebecca writes: Yesterday Hannah asked me about a dowry. I explained that it meant paying a bride-price to get married, such as a number of cattle (which they still do on occasion here in the villages). She said, "Oh, I can do that when I get married." I told her we have no cattle. She replied confidently, "Yes, I'll give them our dogs."

The other day I was sitting outside at a friend's house. Suddenly a dust devil swept through the area. My friend had her infant in a seat; she had to dust him off after the gust. There was a THICK layer of dust over all the items in my basket, on everything and everyone. We all sat in shock for a few seconds, wondering how things in Africa can get THIS dirty this FAST?! Despite the lack of rain, the Jacaranda trees are beautiful. There are canopies of beautiful purple flowers as you drive through Blantyre, which is a refreshing sight in the midst of the blowing dirt and dust.

Rob made it home safely from synod convention today. He will head to the bush again tomorrow, along with a guest preacher and choir, to dedicate a new church building. There is expected to be about 600 for communion and goat for lunch—Rob's "favorite!" Love, Rebecca

Tradition! Longstanding customs like bride-prices are still carried out in Malawi. It is not as commonly practiced in the city, but in some villages cattle exchanges are made as surely as wedding vows are.

Sent: October 3, 2006
Subject: I want to be cool
Rebecca writes: It turns out one of the guards at Kabula Hill (the mission house we are moving to) was tampering with the lock to the storage room during the week. When the lock didn't give, he decided to spend his time chipping away at the outside caulk that holds the windows in place. He successfully removed the caulk, took out the window and stole everything that was being stored in that room. It was several $100's-worth of household items. Now any thoughts I had of moving boxes ahead of time or leaving items unattended on the property (even in a locked room) are out of the question. Mind you, we are *paying* for these people to be on the premises to stop thievery—and they are the very thieves.

Stefan Felgenhauer met with the security company's head manager today to have a talk with them about their untrustworthy personnel. At the very least, that window will have to be replaced. We should add burglar bars now before we move in: ONE MORE HEADACHE!

A few kidbits: Hannah was concerned that the tooth fairy might forget to come, since she lost her tooth early in the morning. The big question at nightfall was, "Do I give her kwacha or dollars?" I decided to give a small denomination of both. That will get her excited to save American money for furlough. Nathanael was running around with his shirt off and a lightning-shaped pen scribble on his belly. I stopped him and asked what it was. He replied, "I want to be super… (pause)…I want to be COOL!" With the hot weather officially here, we **all** want to be cool. God bless, Rebecca

How different my life on the mission field would be without children! Guiding them and spending time together filled my days. Their innocent statements gave such insight and kept me smiling. I was looking forward to our next furlough when I could share a glimpse of their growing years with our families. In the meanwhile, the "Kidbits" email section played a vital role in keeping our Stateside family knowing and growing with us.

Jesus, lead us on Till our rest is won;
And although the way be cheerless, We will follow, calm and fearless.
Guide us by your hand To our fatherland. (CW 422:1)

A Time To Plant (The Gospel)

Sent: October 4, 2006
Subject: Eager for the Word
Rob writes: On Sunday morning I picked up my guest preacher for the day, Renard Kawelama, and the Mpemba Beni choir to go to the church dedication at Muyere.

It was a wonderful event. The new church building was filled to overflowing: people sat on all available spaces in the church and in shaded areas outside the church. Five choirs sang and Pastor Kawelama had a great sermon: "This is the LORD's house." The service lasted an enjoyable four hours. Afterward, food was given to the honored guests. I expected goat to be served for lunch…and it was. Since I was the most honored guest, I got the most special parts of the goat. I lifted the cover from my bowl to find goat liver, goat heart, and some delicacies from the nether regions of the goat's digestive tract…reserved just for me. No dodging! I did what I could to sample here and there but mostly ate the nsima with the oil/gravy from the cooked delicacies. Goat is not my favorite and—to me—even the special parts of the goat aren't really that special. But I greatly appreciated the gesture and did what I could to show it.

You may remember that I visited southern Malawi in mid-September to meet with a group that wants to join the LCCA—they were as far south as one can go. Actually, I ran out of Malawi. I was told I was in Mozambique (standing on the hills I could actually see the Zambezi River)! The congregation was about 50 yards on the "wrong" side of the imaginary border line. Five congregations (four in Mozambique and one in Malawi) were asking to join us, representing about 130 adults in all. Their request went to Mission Board, but I am not optimistic. These places are far from Blantyre.

Recently, I drove south again to meet with another group that wants to join the LCCA. Have I ever mentioned that the Lower Shire is hot? Wow, when I opened my truck door it felt like opening the door of a furnace. Summer arrived *mwadzidzidzi* (suddenly)! We were greeted by over 100 people who "warmly" welcomed us as we met for a couple hours underneath some trees. Then it was off to Katunga for my regularly scheduled service there. There is a large minority now worshiping there who were previously members, then left to attend another church for a few years (since those congregations were temporarily handing out free maize) and now have returned.

Furlough note: After the LWMS convention, I will do another two weeks of deputation in July. I'll intersperse other preaching dates for congregations that have special interest in our mission and have supported us so wholeheartedly. Blessings in Jesus; Rob

There is so much potential for church growth in southern Malawi. Rob thinks that if you shot an arrow as far as you could in any direction, you would find people eager to start a congregation in the spot where it landed. Lack of manpower is the greatest issue… and there is no easy solution on the horizon to change that.

Rob has struggled with aid projects funded by donor countries. They are *so* difficult to do effectively. Many such projects plant a church, hand out aid/food, and then leave.

Without a sustained spiritual connection, the short-term aid can create serious jealousy as people lie and cheat to get more. The "congregation" that is left behind inevitably flounders without leadership. The LCCA has often been approached by such groups who desire to belong to a lasting church.

A Time To Be Tested

Sent: October 5, 2006
Subject: jacked
Rob writes: I had a good day in the village at Muhapokwa. After the service I made shut-in calls to several ladies who are very sick. The members of the congregation went with me to the ladies' houses. They set up chairs for me and Spider on the *makhonde* (porches) while they carried the ladies out on straw mats. There we had our private communions.

Back in town I checked the mail. I locked the truck and checked the mailbox. There was a note that a package had come. (Thanks Mom and Dad Staude for the package with Nathanael's birthday gifts.) I went to the room to pick up the package. I waited about five minutes, got the package and left. When I got back to the truck, that terrible, sick feeling hit me in the chest when I saw that the truck's passenger door was open. I looked inside the truck—my "office" bag, which I take to all my appointments, was gone. It had my Chewa Bible and hymnal, some orders of service, two dictionaries (Eng-Chewa and Chewa-Eng), a compact umbrella, some hand wipes…and my PDA. Most of the items are replaceable, except for my notes written in my Bible. The item that really will cost me is the PDA. I used that palmtop computer for all my work—from expense sheets for building projects, to worship statistics from each service and contact information. Of course no one in the parking lot saw anything. Neither did the two security guards on duty. Police and authorities in the post office could only say, "Sorry." *Eeh, koma "pepani" alibe makhwala!* (Yes, but there's no medicine for "sorry!")

So that's that. Some were wondering what to get me for Christmas. I have a suggestion…then again, maybe just coal. The beat goes on (*zikuyenda*)! Love, Rob

P.S. It's hot enough here that our cheap local taper candles can't stay upright—they are gradually bending out of their holders, without even being lit.

Our post office was conveniently located in the middle of town, but that made Rob a convenient target too. The post office was aware that thieves were a problem, so they hired guards…but beneath the veneer of security there was still trouble.

If the way be drear, If the foe be near,
Let not faithless fears o'ertake us; Let not faith and hope forsake us,
For through many a woe To our home we go. (CW 422:2)

Sent: October 6, 2006
Subject: "car"ry on
Rebecca writes: It was not a fun day for Rob yesterday with the theft. The most sickening is that the thieves were able to break into his locked truck. On the bright side: his truck wasn't stolen, he did NOT have his spare truck key in his bag, he wasn't mugged for the bag, and the actual briefcase was quite tattered anyway. I can still identify with that sick feeling from when my wallet was stolen at church.

At the LWMS convention they are encouraging the wife to speak also. I'll have to think of what would be fitting to share. Thanks much for your encouragement and prayers. We appreciate them as we find ourselves at a rather challenging time. God bless, Rebecca

Some days it seemed that there was no safe haven. Our old house was a target, our new house was a target, our vehicle was a target and simply *being who we are*—comparatively well-to-do foreigners—made us a target.

Lord, You too were a target. Let me never forget that You willingly endured that suffering to pay the debt of sin I could not. You are so amazing to do that for even me. I confess I fall far short of Your holy expectations and would be lost without Jesus. Please grant me and my family the patience, wisdom and love to follow the calling that You have for us in Malawi. Amen.

> *Be still, my soul; your God will undertake*
> *To guide the future as he has the past.*
> *Your hope, your confidence, let nothing shake;*
> *All now mysterious shall be bright at last.*
> *Be still, my soul; the waves and winds still know*
> *His voice who ruled them while he lived below. (CW 415:2)*

Sent: October 10, 2006
Subject: out again
Rebecca writes: I am writing this even though we have no dial tone. I feel a bit vulnerable at home since our cell phone was recently stolen and the land phone lines are burned. It is the season for burning, with smoke and haze everywhere. Malawian subsistence farmers still practice slash-and-burn to create or clear their fields. Fires frequently spread beyond the field they were meant to clear. This time, our ground lines were collateral damage.

Interestingly, the phone faults number can only be reached **if you call from a land line**, not a cell phone. That is quite a restriction. Malawi Telecom doesn't seem to get the irony. If our land line worked, we would not NEED to use the number. When our land phone is out, how CAN we use the number? According to Rob, that question is always met with silence then... *"Ah, azungu ali otopetsa."* ("Ah, white people are tiring.")

For Malawian Mother's Day we enjoyed a nice lunch at a restaurant in town. While we were waiting, Hannah noticed some handcrafted tile pictures on the wall. The pictures (a lion and an elephant) were made up of six tiles each. She commented that the tiles weren't right. We looked more closely and saw that they had inadvertently switched the sixth tile from the elephant picture and the sixth tile from the lion picture. The lion had elephant legs, while the elephant's back legs were hidden in a clump of grass out of which a lion's tail protruded. Why am I not surprised? God bless, Rebecca

The mixed-up handcrafted picture tiles at the restaurant somehow seem like a metaphor for Malawi. God's loving handiwork is apparent here: there is so much natural beauty; the people are eager to hear the Word of God; the weather is lovely; the pace of family life is healthy. But at the tail end of all these blessings, a "mixed-up tile" sneaks in. Thieves lurk, alarms ring, nights are sleepless, days fumble along with no water, no power, no electricity, no phone, big bugs, big dust, big mold and daily misunderstandings. On this side of eternity, the last tile is forever in the wrong place. That isn't all bad: we are left longing for the time our frustrations will be gone, when God will make all things new in His presence.

Dear Lord, Please help me long for YOUR peace and contentment on this side of eternity. The world is disappointing. My life has many disappointments. You alone promise to help. You alone keep your promises. Keep my eyes off myself and direct them heavenward instead. You are forever worthy of praise. Amen.

Sent: October 12, 2006
Subject: Noah experience
Rob writes: I went out to Mpira in Chiradzulu to test a confirmation class there. Missionary Mark Johnston was present too, since he is staying with Evangelist Chikwewe for the week to pick up some language and culture. Mark shared that it has been a great experience. He told me that Ev. Chikwewe has been very gracious to him; he and his wife let Mark have the one and only bedroom in the house, while they moved into the room with the chickens and goats. Mark noted that he could have endured the "Noah experience"...but is glad he didn't have to. For one dinner, Mark was served a chicken head with his *nsima*. He learned that he had to break the head open to eat the "meat" inside. Last night Chiradzulu got rain for three hours, 8-11pm. Mark noted that it took some

adjusting to sleep with rain clattering on the tin roof. Blessings in Jesus, Rob

Our urban pastor/missionary Mark Johnston got a real taste of Malawian culture, even if he did manage to bypass the full blown "Noah" experience. But he couldn't avoid the rain that fell mainly on the plain…huts of Malawi!

Sent: October 14, 2006
Subject: some like it hot…
Rebecca writes: We had a party for Nathanael's birthday. He was all smiles playing games, one of which was mini-golf—hitting a ball down our water drainage ditches with croquet mallets. He loved his race-car cake, birthday gifts and attention.

Thinking of this month makes my head spin. I'm on the docket for crafts for the church Faith, Family, Fun Fayre; I'm cleaning and preparing to move; I'm researching and working on a Bible study for the upcoming Ladies' Bible Retreat; and the ACA will be visiting soon. That only takes up a few lines in print…but it will be all-consuming throughout the next month.

Driving home recently I noticed a man wearing bowling shoes and selling about 50 colorful ladies' bras on each arm. Any shape, size, color or design; you name it—it was at his fingertips.

"Some like it hot" is a nursery rhyme, but was also the advice from our mechanic concerning mice. I've seen many footprints on my engine under the hood, so the mechanic advised me to sprinkle curry on the engine. Evidently mice don't "like it hot." When I carpooled for choir yesterday I warned everyone that if they smelled curry it was my engine baking! I have such a HOT car and a SPICY life, hey? Love, Rebecca

As Nathanael celebrated his fourth birthday, I couldn't help but think back to when he turned one. We had only been in Malawi for a month. Our phone didn't work. Nathanael was so sick with malaria-like symptoms. Happily, this year everyone was healthy; we enjoyed a special cake and celebrated with lots of friends. We had come a long way since those early days…although our phone still wasn't working. Some things never do change!

Sent: October 19, 2006
Subject: odds and ends
Rob writes: On Tuesday I was in the Lower Shire at two congregations. I confirmed 22 people and baptized 8 new members. Goat and fish were on the menu. If I ever say they are not my favorite, it is from experience.

Listening to the radio, I laughed all the way back home to Blantyre. Madonna was in the country (in Lilongwe) to adopt a little boy, Davie Banda. This has caused a commotion among those who say that only residents of Malawi should be able to adopt Malawians. The radio DJ argued, "How many Malawians could have given the boy a $1.3 million rocking horse? Let him go." All the way home I listened to the Material Girl sing the best of the '80s and '90s while the DJ manipulated the message of the songs to fit the current situation. It was done tongue-in-cheek and very funny.

Thanks in advance for the packages that are "in the mail." We are still waiting and check for them daily. Third world living can be a great lesson in patience. Love, Rob

Hanging goat meat for sale at market

I think the term "Material Girl" is the polar opposite of "Malawi Girl." Our family had to make cultural adjustments when we moved to Malawi. I cannot fathom the culture shock of a Malawian boy being taken from his home village to live a Hollywood lifestyle.

Years ago in school I recall talking at length about the "American dream." It was a hard concept to grasp while sitting in a nice desk, at a reputable school, with all my needs met—including the blessing of a wonderful Christian upbringing. Now that I had lived a handful of years in a third world country, I was starting to understand what the American dream really means. I could see the obvious positive aspects of "living the dream" for the Malawian boy. David Banda will certainly have his daily needs met, albeit in a very unfamiliar way. I'm sure he *won't* have *nsima* at every meal, chickens running around in his yard, a kickball made of plastic bags, tattered dirty clothes, questionable drinking water or an empty tummy at bedtime. That seems to be "better" for him, of course. Though I would guess, from time to time, his spirit will hunger for the heart of Africa—his homeland, culture and people. I also wonder if he will get ANY spiritual food. Without Jesus, even the American dream is hollow and fading. There are so many things money cannot buy, even if you are living with the Material Girl.

A Time To Be Sick And A Time To Heal

Sent: October 22, 2006
Subject: I've fallen and I can't...
Rebecca writes: We all got sick with the runny tummy. I walked to the kitchen to drink some apple juice; without warning my limbs went numb and I collapsed. I needed the toilet but couldn't walk. Thankfully, Rob was within earshot and assisted me. When he got me a drink I couldn't even hold the cup. It was a scary feeling. I asked Rob if he thought I should go to the ER. We know the care there is unpredictable. The thought of going to the hospital drove me to drink—more juice of course. For all we know, they would give me an aspirin and send me home. I ended up sleeping on the bathroom floor for a few hours. Our health is still a work in progress. I plan to see a doctor when I'm feeling better (a bit of a paradox, I know). God bless, Rebecca

We were still struggling with troublesome bouts of poor health. My symptoms were becoming scary. With each episode, my physical reaction was worse. I could not seem to bounce back the way the others did, nor develop immunity. Time to get to the "bottom" of it! Ha.

> *When we seek relief From a long felt grief,*
> *When temptations come alluring, Make us patient and enduring;*
> *Show us that bright shore Where we weep no more. (CW 422:3)*

Sent: October 24, 2006
Subject: picnic with lions
Rebecca writes: Thankfully we're all feeling better. We were surprised to find out that today is Eid; a declared holiday that marks the end of the Muslim celebration of Ramadan. Eid fluctuates each cycle. (I'm still caught off guard by the non-Christian holidays here.) We made the best of the "surprise" holiday with a picnic at the nearby Michiru Wildlife Park. When we arrived at the picnic area we were almost deafened by the sound of cicadas. We enjoyed a lunch, followed a walking path until we reached a bridge that didn't look safe and turned back.

One highlight was when Rob dug up antlion larvae and let them crawl around on the kids' hands. They also had fun watching the larvae catch ants. Nathanael is now full of stories such as, "We ate lunch with the lions! Some were so big their homes were like volcanoes and they catch rhinos to eat." God bless, Rebecca

Michiru Park was a "park" in true Malawi-style: no colorful swings, spiral slides, teeter-totters or zip lines…just the rugged outdoors and real wildlife. It was a 4WD trip to the picnic area, where we found a few cement tables, a fire pit, a small *chimbudzi* and several hiking trails. Thrill-seekers could hire an armed guard at dusk to follow one of the trails past nearby hyena caves. For our kids, the antlions proved to be enough of an attraction. Hey—with entertainment like that, who needs playground equipment?

Sent: October 28, 2006
Subject: Nanny massage
Rebecca writes: I went to the doctor about my gut troubles. He told me my current symptoms were from a previous intestinal virus. It is his opinion that I simply didn't give my body time to recover. After I had described my whole ordeal, the doctor sat back, put his hands behind his head and mused, "You should write your symptoms up for a medical journal article. You have a textbook case for tropical diseases related to this intestinal virus…right down to the muscle numbness and loss of function." I told him that each cycle of sickness is worse and asked him what I could do. Everything he suggested, including drinking apple juice and oral rehydration solutions, I had done. His final recommendation was that I should, "Go home, take an aspirin, rest, and have your nanny give you a massage!" Yeah, I'll have all of my nannies get right on that! The expat community here hardly believes I have three children and no nanny.

We've been lighting candles as the sun goes down. Our power has been bad. Meals are tricky. In addition to outages, we are getting power spikes up to 275 volts (supposed to be 220).

The members of the ACA arrived and we host them for supper tomorrow. I gave them a heads-up on the power trouble. They assured me, "We don't mind eating by candlelight." (I hope the power cooperates so we can have *hot cooked* food with our candlelight.) God bless, Rebecca

I've heard of laughter being the best medicine, but this was the first time I'd been recommended a nanny massage. I got a kick out of the local train of thought. I was also relieved that someone could describe my symptoms "to a T." My system was apparently showing a natural reaction to tropical living. The doctor never said what to do if my symptoms kept getting worse, so I planned to rest and pray that this was my "time to heal."

A Time To Search...And A Time To Give Up

Sent: October 31, 2006
Subject: Reformation Round-up
Rebecca writes: I've stopped packing since no moving date is set; we've been told it may not happen soon. I feel loopy when I reach for something and realize it's already packed.

Since we will remain here for a while, we finally sprayed our house for bugs. There have been too many scorpions, roach sightings, unidentified bugs and mosquitoes on the move. Today there were piles of dead bugs at almost every door entrance. Now I have to make sure we don't poison ourselves. Don't laugh; it isn't hard to do.

Rob left today for several days of meetings in Zomba. Some of the discussions are about the recent exploratory work in Mozambique.

After naps today I organized a Reformation Round-Up (aka: trick-or-treating). The kids rounded the house a few times and then told me to go around. Hannah handed out one fruit snack piece to me at each door. I was surprised she would use her own fruit snacks, since they didn't get that many items. It was fun...and they got extra snacks for exhibiting such good sharing.

I'd better get moving on my project list, which includes dipping and hanging the bed nets as well as preparing the guest room for Rev. Steve and Sally Valleskey. They are visiting as part of the Mozambique exploratory team. Love, Rebecca

There is no such thing as neighborhood trick-or-treating here in Malawi. Reformation Round-Up was an in-house alternative and a fun way to "search" for treats. Little did I know that a less innocent round-up was being plotted at Kabula Hill, where we were slated to move. The guard there was claiming all sorts of "treats" for himself...but soon the search would be on for him.

Sent: November 5, 2006
Subject: un-Safetech
Rebecca writes: Lots transpiring lately. We were informed by Safetech management that the night guard at the Kabula Hill property had left the premises, taking with him the remote panic-button, the company radio and charger, a wheelbarrow, the generator and an empty drum, which they figure he filled with water before departing. He even left a note behind, claiming that he was "borrowing" these things and would be back soon. We suspect this was an attempt to buy time, so he could get as far away as possible before we blew the whistle.

The next day, a Safetech investigator asked us to go with him to the police to make a report. He paused and told me that he used to work for us, and he really appreciated the Christmas gift we gave him that year. He also appreciated that we called him back when he went astray. (I'm guessing I caught him sleeping?) Wow, that was a ray of sunshine in the storm. Rob went with the investigator and the police to the Kabula house and did the necessary reporting. The police told Rob that the house is probably a big target now since there is no remote panic-button or radio.

Today I came home to find that our own guard has lost our keys to the gate lock. He claims he lost them when he ran to see what a dog was barking at. I told him to find the keys before his shift ended. About 15 minutes later I found him sitting under the mango tree…**without the keys**. God bless, Rebecca

There is a time to search and a time to give up. When it came to searching for our lost gate keys, our Nyambadwe guard was more inclined to *give up*. We finally gave up too, and changed the lock on our gate that very night. That guard wasn't our only source of trouble: over at Kabula Hill a second guard in the span of a month had abused his position and stooped to robbery. The investigator who thanked us for our past intervention was a rare exception in our experience with hired guards.

Thank God that *His* ever-attentive eyes and ears are never closed in sleep; that His hands work to protect us, not plot against us. He knows our troubles and delivers us from them all, according to His mercy and love.

> *"The righteous cry out, and the LORD hears them; he delivers them from all their troubles.*
> *The LORD is close to the brokenhearted and saves those who are crushed in spirit.*
> *A righteous man may have many troubles, but the LORD delivers him from them all; he protects all his bones, not one of them will be broken.*
> *The LORD redeems his servants; no one will be condemned who takes refuge in him." Psalm 34:17-22*

A Time To Give Thanks

Sent: November 6, 2006
Subject: a week to remember
Rob writes: Here's an update on last week's meetings. Our first meeting was with the leaders of the LCCA-Malawi, the Malawi Mission Council and the ACA. The question that guided our discussions was, "What does the LCCA-M see the role of the WELS Mission in Malawi as being?" Through a series of directed studies and tasks we pondered this question together for six hours. We didn't come up with final answers, but important relationship steps were taken and the nationals continue to discuss the issue among themselves. In my humble

opinion, this question is absolutely vital to our Malawi work. Without the national church discussing it, we (on the mission side) can plan all we want, but the work will be for nothing. Hopefully we are getting on track together.

We also discussed the report of the Mozambique Exploratory Team (Bill Meier, Rev. Steve and Sally Valleskey and Prof. Ken Cherney) after their two weeks in Mozambique. The exploratory team did an excellent, thorough presentation. They made 30 contacts in different regions and positions in the country, did pages and pages of reporting and were able to answer every question they were asked.

We then spent much time making a proposal plan of action for WELS. Mozambique is ripe, the harvest is waiting and the door is open—as it has been for about 17 years since our first exploratory trip in 1989. Now more than ever the conditions are right for us to try proclaiming Christ in that field…but the opportunities might not remain for long. The government has indicated some frustration at all these groups coming into their country now and "abusing the system." They hinted at tightening things up in the future.

On Sunday I resumed my regular rotation of work in Khanyepa and Balala. 300 communed and 20 baptisms—a good day (thanks Lord)! Blessings in Jesus, Rob

Progress on a mission field is sometimes hard to see. Yet even small, slow steps gradually can lead to bigger things when God's people work together to save souls by spreading the Word of Christ.

It is difficult for me to re-read these emails and recall the excitement and effort that went into the plans to enter Mozambique. These plans continued full-steam for several years. Two men were called and immersed in language training; spring of 2009 was their goal for residing in Nampula, Mozambique. But larger events were at work. By 2009, a downturn in the global economy was showing no signs of easing. The economic slump in North America had resulted in the loss of significant gifts to WELS and a decrease in Congregation Mission Offerings. Synod Convention delegates had to find a way to drastically reduce the synod budget. Many heart-wrenching sacrifices were made across our WELS mission fields and in Synod administration; Mozambique was one of them. It was certainly not easy to turn away from that open door and ripe harvest, but we knew that God's promise to bless the spread of his saving message had not changed. Where human hands had failed, God's hands would find another way.

Mission work in Mozambique originally started around 1990 as former refugees of the Mozambique civil war (1977-1992), who had fled to Malawi, returned to Mozambique. These refugees had become LCCA members during their years in Malawi and now wanted to start LCCA congregations in Mozambique. When the

WELS was unable to send missionaries to Mozambique, they instead focused on continuing to fund the cross-border work being done by Malawi's LCCA pastors and lay people.

> *Faith comes from hearing the message,*
> *and the message is heard through the word of Christ.*
> *But I ask: Did they not hear? Of course they did:*
> *"Their voice has gone out into all the earth,*
> *their words to the ends of the world." Romans 10:17-18*

Sent: November 14, 2006
Subject: weekend report
Rob writes: Last week I went to four places in Chiradzulu. I had 35 children to baptize, 12 adult baptisms and 20 confirmed. I'm thankful for the numbers, and continue to encourage the adults to remain faithful members of their congregations after their confirmation.

Our electricity is catawampus again. The voltage is too low to power our electronics. Thankfully our lights and stove still work, just dimmer and slower. I contacted ESCOM and told them that we were the same house they had recently visited for too high voltage. The man on the line sighed, "Oh, that's bad." They haven't been out again to fix it. The beat goes on. Love, Rob

Our unreliable electricity was annoying and inconvenient, but it served as a good reminder to never take for granted our true "power source": our Savior. What a contrast between our faithful Lord and the fickle things of this earth. *He* is as consistent a power source as they come!

Sent: November 24, 2006
Subject: we did the dorkey
Rebecca writes: Happy Thanksgiving! We appreciate you all as a special blessing from God! Thanksgiving morning we woke up "in the dark." The power returned mid-morning, so I got busy preparing food. The power held throughout all my cooking and went out again as we left our house for Thanksgiving dinner at the Johnston's place. We had a lovely time. Rob started it off with a devotion and ended with Psalm 136. The meal was terrific. In the words of Nathanael, "We did the dorkey." We figure he must mean the "turkey"—which we didn't have, or even miss. The main course of chicken was a lovely complement to all the side dishes.

I've been trying to fill out an online overseas resource compensation survey, which determines if we get any salary deducted or added depending on the local prices in the country in which we live. I am frustrated by the rapid inflation here. I wanted to fill it out with local feedback. Since our phone line, internet and power were all working at the same time, I typed away. Suddenly the power went out. Rob came in the office wearing a headlamp. He had been in the attic retrieving a recently sprung rat trap—with the rat still attached. Happily, his attic headgear had inadvertently prepared him for the power outage. Love, Rebecca

Sent: November 28, 2006
Subject: latest info
Rebecca writes: Rob finally received the renewal for his TEP that he applied for last November! This employment permit allows us to exit and enter the country legally, and it is theoretically good for two years. Now that we finally have it in hand we need to start applying for a new permit, since less than a year remains on the existing one!

A lil update from the Kabula thefts. The investigators traced the thief (their own guard) to Lilongwe, where they discovered that his family is prominent in the Malawi Revenue Authority. Not surprisingly, the family wanted no further investigations. They have offered to pay out of their pockets, hundreds of dollars-worth, for all the items and damages—if the investigators quit pursuing the felon, their son. Is that really justice?

The kids cannot wait until furlough. Thank you in advance for your willingness, Mom, to help out and take vacation time to assist with the kids during the LWMS convention. Love, Rebecca

A Time for Water Surplus And A Time For Water Shortage

Sent: December 10, 2006
Subject: The sun was a hammer
Rob writes: ...and the earth its anvil when I went to the Lower Shire a week ago. It is at Katunga in Southern Malawi that I have experienced some of the hottest temperatures in my life. At times I have needed two communion cloths: one to wipe the chalice and one to wipe my forehead. Tuesday was going to be another one of those days. The sun blazed down, causing the corrugated iron sheets on the church to radiate pure heat and transform the building into an oven.

I had traveled down to Katunga with quite a crew. This month I have been taking some of the elders of Lutheran Women's Organization (LUWO) with me to my congregations to encourage the members. I picked up Spider and 5 LUWO ladies in Blantyre. Then, at the Valley entrance, I took a 40-minute detour down the East Bank Road to Chikunumbwi to collect 11 more ladies and Evangelist Master, so they too could encourage the members at Katunga. All told, it was about four hours to get there—and the heat nearly smacked me back into my truck when I opened the door to get out. As I sat preparing for service with sweat springing up all over, the thought came to mind: If you complain, be careful...the Lord might do something about your "problem."

A few minutes before the service, one of the ladies announced that the rain was coming. I looked out of the window and saw a wall of brown darkness. It was not rain. It was wind (a *chimphepo* they call it—"a great wind") and, borne on the wind, dust and sand. The wind began to blow so hard that I feared that the corrugated iron sheets would be ripped off the building. Thankfully they weren't, but they rattled viciously. For an hour that wind blew. At times the dusty, sandy gusts were so hard that I couldn't see my truck just twenty feet away from the church. We began the service; what else could we do? (As it turns out, I was happy I did my part of the liturgy/preaching during the wind...it was quieter than what came next.) Dust covered everything. Every time I looked down to read I had to dust off my Bible/hymnal—that is how much was accumulating. With all the sweat we had been exuding, the dust stuck to us too. I noted that my skin darkened a couple shades, while that of my congregation lightened by a couple.

I was just finishing my sermon when the rain came—in sheets. Now the corrugated roof was a metal drum; a deafening one. Both Spider and Master had messages to share. They had to shout. I don't think they were heard beyond ten feet. We proceeded through the rest of the service and communion that way: shouting. Outside I noticed rivers forming—torrents three feet deep. Village kids were wading into them and then sitting for a "ride" downstream. By the time the LUWO ladies got up to speak, the rain had died down a bit. After the service the congregation had prepared a nice meal of chicken and nsima. Even though the service had been quite eventful weather-wise, this was one of the best services I have had there. Through it all we had close to 100 people in church.

After four hours of worship, presentations and a meal, it was time to return. It was still pouring, and the ladies had no other option but to get back in the open bed of the truck. The LUWO "uniform" includes a white blouse. The roads were now a muddy mess. Every time we passed another vehicle, mud splashed all over the truck. With our lights on and windshield wipers flapping, we slip-slided three hours back to Chikunumbwi. My vehicle had mud on the roof—just imagine the condition of the ladies in the back. With the storm, the temps had fallen by about 30 degrees. It was still probably in the 80°s, but sitting in the rain and traveling in the back of a truck had everyone shivering.

The experience wasn't quite over. With the remaining five Blantyre ladies in the back, we headed back up the escarpment through thick fog. We meandered slowly to the top of the escarpment, where the fog left us as suddenly as it had gripped us. About 12 hours after setting out, I finally dropped the LUWO ladies off in Blantyre. I thought that this might "dampen" (I know, I know—couldn't resist) their spirits. Not so. Right away on Thursday they joined me on a trip to Muhapokwa.

Maize has been planted here and is about a foot high. We pray that this can continue. Everything is very green and we hear all the "new" sounds of this season—crickets and frogs.

Before I sign off, I'll include the quote below. I ran across it in Logos doing sermon research: "Preaching of the Word in the pulpit has too often been replaced by the entertainment of the world on the platform. Dr. Donald Coggan, Archbishop of Canterbury, has said of Christian pastors: 'It is their task to feed the sheep—not to entertain the goats.'" Advent blessings in Him, Rob

It is not uncommon for passengers in Rob's truck to throw up or relieve themselves as they bounce over the rough bush roads. Passengers in the cab of his truck have sometimes broken the unfamiliar truck door handles in an attempt to exit the vehicle quickly. It was conceded by this particular group of passengers that the trip to the Lower Shire was tough. The national vicar's wife even had a special prayer for Rob when it was over. She didn't realize the missionaries' travels were so difficult.

Jesus, still lead on Till our rest is won.
Heav'nly Leader, still direct us; Still support, console, protect us
Till we safely stand In our fatherland. (CW 422:4)

Sent: December 14, 2006
Subject: carols and cookies
Rebecca writes: Yesterday we enjoyed our "second annual" Christmas carol evening. We all shared Christmas cookies, treats and carol singing. Mosquitoes made an appearance too. Tonight we'll take some cookie plates to the neighbors along with a card, ornament and invitation to our Christmas services at church. Every time it is a trick to make it past the walls, dogs and guards to actually meet the neighbors at home.

I recently asked a local lady about her Christmas traditions. She likes to eat chicken (and the bones), rice and chips (French fries) for Christmas. She goes home to her village and her family stays at church for a few days, sleeping on the floor at night and singing and worshiping during the day.

Unfortunately, our water is still a problem. Our tank has a leak and needs to be repaired. We have been allowing water to flow into the tank daily for only 15 minutes, which is enough for flushing toilets, showers, and dishes—and then it runs out. The tank needs to be dry when the repairmen come. They have promised for ONE WEEK now that "We will come this afternoon." So we play this ridiculous daily game of "how much water should we fill?" It is frustrating: once we realize they aren't coming to fix it that day and we turn on the tap, we find there is no water coming from the city, so then we are truly high and dry. That happened last evening—how festive! I would like that fixed before Christmas. God bless, Rebecca

Whether you are a missionary or a local, making special Christmas traditions takes some creativity and effort here in Malawi. Many Malawian Christians celebrate the season with a decidedly non-Western twist. Their preparations begin a few months before Christmas by setting aside a live chicken, which will become the main course. As Christmas nears, they buy special items like rice and soft drinks. Some people will not drink a soda all year and will save extra money or even work an extra job so they can afford such food specialties for their families.

It is also customary to bake for the season. That's not surprising…until you consider that there are no ovens in the village. Village women start their baking preparations with a large, lidded pot. They oil the pot and fill it with a basic baking-powder cake batter. They place the pot on top of hot charcoal, place a flat lid on top of the pot and place more hot charcoal on the lid. This homemade "oven" bakes over the coals for about 40 minutes. A long thin stick is inserted it in the middle of the cake to check if it is finished. The cake is then flipped out of the pot and cut into squares for serving. This is one of the few times all year that women bake in the village.

Carrot cake baking on *mbaula*

In a typical Malawian village, the Christmas Day celebration begins with a local church service. After church, relatives gather at a designated house. Each family unit contributes a live chicken. The Christmas meal is so special that it consists of mainly meat and rice. I'm told that if separate vegetables are served, no one will eat them! Not even traditional *nsima* is prepared. The meal requires boiling a huge amount of rice, so that each person will have between four to eight cups of rice heaped on their plate. Served over this mountain of rice is fried chicken with an oily onion and tomato sauce. It is seasoned only with salt. Any additional seasonings are claimed to cover up the taste of the chicken. Generous portions of goat or beef are also prepared and enjoyed. Everyone celebrates by drinking a soda. The family eats until they are very full, leaving leftovers on their plates—as a sign that they have had plenty to eat. Leftovers cannot be easily preserved in the villages, so they are either eaten for the next meal or given to beggars or animals.

In the village there are no Christmas decorations. Houses are simply cleaned in preparation for visitors. Traditionally there are no gifts exchanged, although occasionally a family will give practical gifts to children such as needed clothes and shoes. Attending church and sharing a meal and fellowship are the focal point of a village Christmas. What a great reminder for all Christians to keep our Christmas focus on Immanuel, God with us. Indeed His presence is with us…and that is the greatest present of all!

A Time For Tarantulas

Sent: December 17, 2006
Subject: the itsy bitsy spider went up the water spout
Rebecca writes: Lately we've had issues with both a spider (but it wasn't itsy bitsy) and our water spout. We found a tarantula, or baboon spider, making a web/nest in our hallway this morning. And our water system has been disassembled, which means our water troubles are worse before they can get better. The catch is, if we don't fix it by this Friday, many stores and businesses close for the entire Christmas holiday…which is a month long. Dandy!

We have been patiently waiting for our water tank to be repaired. Finally, right before lunch on Friday, the repair truck pulled up. Simultaneously, the sunshine faded and the sky grew ominous. The repairmen disassembled the water pipes, tried to fix the tank, made the cracks worse and left in the pouring rain. We were entirely cut off from our water supply for the weekend. In anticipation of this, I had set aside spare buckets of water and bathed the kids. Rob spent much of Saturday rigging up a garden hose from one spigot to another to bypass the tank and bring some city water into the house—if and when the city water is flowing. By 5pm he had managed to direct the water through the pipe and into the house, but it leaks profusely from one side of the hose. So we only run it enough to flush the toilets, shower and bathe.

Last night Hannah woke up to use the bathroom, apparently got disoriented and wandered to the couch, where she fell asleep. Rob came in later and locked the bedroom-area grate for the night without realizing where she was. Around 2am Hannah was pounding on the hallway door. She was locked out, had several mosquito bites and was a bit frantic. God bless! Rebecca

Sometimes it was a real circus trying to keep the good in and the bad out. On this occasion, our six-year-old daughter was accidentally locked *out*, while an unwelcome tarantula somehow found its way *in*.

Sent: December 18, 2006
Subject: hey, that is NOT a WALL spider
Rebecca writes: The title is yesterday's quote from Hannah as she spied the gigantic legs of the tarantula through the hallway transom window. The spider was big enough to cast a shadow. Rob wondered if something was up when he walked through webs the night before. But that's not all: after finding the tarantula nesting in our hallway yesterday morning, we had a second encounter last night. Our power had gone out. I had grabbed a flashlight and was walking toward the stove. I came within 12 inches of stepping on **another tarantula** with my bare feet. I couldn't believe my eyes. It ran fast and stopped by the sink. Rob trapped it with a broom…but then its long, hairy legs began crawling over the top of the broom! Rob finally squished it and took it outside. I swept up two legs that were left behind. As I brushed them into the dust pan they sounded like rocks, reminding me of an exoskeleton of a crab! They are TOUGH!

As a side note—I've noticed there haven't been many ants lately. Rob wondered if I'd rather have ants or tarantulas. Ants, hands down! Even the big, feisty, biting ants or the ones that come out at night would be better. (Time to move, hey?) God bless, Rebecca

I had to remind myself that tarantulas, too, are part of God's amazing creation. And, despite their menacing fangs, their bite is only painful, not fatal. (Small consolation when almost stepping on one with bare feet!) A tarantula's dinner-fare includes ants, cockroaches, *solifugae* and scorpions. Larger tarantulas also prey on small rodents and reptiles. I realized they probably had a great place in the food chain of creepy-crawlies—OUTDOORS!

Sent: December 19, 2006
Subject: Arachnid 4 B ya (aka: arachnophobia)
Rebecca writes: Dad Wendland arrived at the airport safely last evening. Shortly after he arrived, Samson started barking at a tarantula on the driveway. We all

went out to admire it in the beam of the security light. It became aggressive when we got too close. That was the first tarantula that Dad had ever seen in the "wild." Today the tarantula's skeleton is being dismantled on our lawn by ants. I looked at it with a magnifying glass. The skeleton is not unlike a crab. It is smaller, but the hollow joints are very large.

Rob called around 2pm and had not even finished with the service at the FIRST church. He and his truck of LUWO ladies were still slotted to eat and have a second worship service elsewhere. I doubt he'll return home before dark.

The repairman came this morning to fix the tank. He came to the door asking for an extension cord, a cable and a pipe wrench. The repairman proceeded to tip our heavy metal water tank on its side on top of its high brick platform. He put a rock on one side so it wouldn't roll off the edge of the platform. Minutes later, rain came down in buckets. The workman abandoned the tank and went for shelter. All of a sudden I heard thunder. No, it wasn't thunder. It was the sound of the tank rolling off the platform and smashing to the ground. A BIG crinkled dent is now on the top. I will be astounded if it doesn't leak now. It was a comedy of errors all afternoon long. "Oh, don't worry," he consoled me, "I will come back tomorrow!" I can't wait. God bless, Rebecca

Gravity proved to be a bad thing for our repairman and our water tank. The complete lack of competition in the repair field was a good thing for this company though—it was the only reason they were still in business. What could a customer do? If we did not supply them with the tools they needed at that moment, they would sit under a tree until they were picked up by the company truck…and then promise to come back another day. In the end, we tried to make the metal water tank work as long as possible—for months. As critical as our broken water tank situation had become, it paled in comparison to what happened next.

A Time To Tear Down And A Time To Build

Sent: December 21, 2006
Subject: OH, SMASH!!
Rebecca writes: Oh dear. It is 5:30pm and a big dirt-hauling truck just smashed through our back wall, creating a 15-foot gap. Rob isn't home yet from the bush, so I called Mark Johnston to see if there was some protocol that I should follow. I am collecting details of who owns the truck, who they work for, etc…but that is proving difficult since the driver of the truck ran away. Please pray for our safety and a quick remedy to this problem. TERRIBLE TIMING—right before Christmas (AKA, "The Time of Thieves")! I am thankful that we have guards on the property for such a time as this. When it rains—it pours. God bless, Rebecca

Truck-sized breech in security

I can't put into words the feeling I had when I heard the sounds of shattering glass, crunching metal and crumbling cement—and looked out to see a truck stuck on our property. Our wall was now breached very near the area that local thieves had made repeated break-in attempts. It was a most disturbing and frightening sight. The wall and razor wire were our safety net against trouble. The protective barrier was down, Rob was gone, the sun was setting...Lord, help!

Jesus, lover of my soul, Let me to thy bosom fly
While the nearer waters roll, While the tempest still is high.
Hide me, O my Savior, hide, Till the storm of life is past;
Safe into the haven guide. Oh, receive my soul at last! (CW 357:1)

Sent: December 22, 2006
Subject: yet another aftermath
Rob writes: "On the sixth day of Christmas my true love (?!) gave to me:

4 feisty, webbing tarantulas,
3 days without water,
2 weeks with repairmen,
2 power outages and a hole in our wall,
1 smashed and leaking water tank,
1 flooded bathroom,
and a dump truck in a Persian Lilac Tree!"

That would be "Melly Clismasi," Malawi style.

Q: How come most of this fun happens when I'm gone? I arrived home at around 8 last night after another exploratory trip to the very southern edge of

Malawi, to find the aftermath of another exciting day.

We had an uneventful night; though when the electricity went off twice, all sorts of conspiracy theories entered my head. I found one guard sleeping when the power went off at 11pm. I told him when the thieves come he'll be killed for his laziness—he replied, "Yes, sah!" All things were safe. We thank the Lord for his tender care and your prayers.

S.R. Nicholas is the General Contractor of the building site behind our property and responsible for the truck. (I guess if someone is going to bash your wall in, it might as well be a major building contractor!) One of the consulting engineers came over this morning. He suspended their building project so that his team could work on repairing our wall. A bulldozer has already extricated the truck. Due to the Christmas holiday, all other builders are closed, but this guy knows the owners of the area companies; he was able to call around and see about getting materials. The engineer even asked if they owed us for any extra security measures.

Just to bring back our recent spider-theme, one of the barefoot workmen fixing our wall was bitten by a spider. It turned out to be a wolf spider, which inflicts a painful bite. Merry Christmas—with "spiders, thieves and trucks, oh my!" Blessings in Jesus, Rob

It was a week of extreme action. All the crazy, pre-Christmas upsets kept us occupied and praying. It turned out that the nearby building project was not only upsetting tarantula nests; the truck driver delivering supplies to the site ended up upsetting *our* home in a horrible way. We blocked the smashed wall with plywood from our shipment crates and posted our night guards by the breach. We left the remainder of our security in the hands of our capable Lord.

Shortly after all of this, a friend called me, "You have had too many troubles to deal with all at once. This is too much for you!" My head wanted to nod in agreement. My heart knew differently. In 2 Corinthians 12:9-10, God reminds me: *"'My grace is sufficient for you, for my power is made perfect in weakness.' That is why, for Christ's sake, I delight in weaknesses, in insults, in hardships, in persecutions, in difficulties. For when I am weak, then I am strong."* Though I wasn't exactly on the edge of boasting about my troubles, I realized that God can and does use trials to bring us closer to him. I knew He loved me, and I trusted that the recent string of troubles was under His control and could be a growing experience. My hands were clasped and my head was bowed as my thoughts drifted unceasingly heavenward for the needed strength to carry on, come what may.

Other refuge have I none; Hangs my helpless soul on thee.
Leave, ah, leave me not alone; Still support and comfort me.

*All my trust on thee is stayed; All my help from thee I bring.
Cover my defenseless head With the shadow of thy wing. (CW 357:2)*

Sent: December 22, 2006
Subject: Where's a Wall-Mart when you need one?
Rebecca writes: It would be nice to have a **WALL**-Mart here! As of 2pm today, St. Nicholas brought our presents—oh, that was S.R. Nicholas unloading the concrete wall slabs! Same thing! The trench is dug and the crew is plugging away. I do believe with their constant work the wall could be repaired in a day or two; for sure before Christmas. Wonder of wonders. Thank you to everyone for the heartfelt prayers that were sent up on our behalf. It seems they are being answered rather quickly and visibly!

I want to wish you all a very blessed Christmas celebration. May the Savior's birth remind us again this year that our witness here on earth is not in vain, our God certainly loves us, and He has made eternal joy complete in Jesus. Rebecca and family

The rebuilding of our wall was a miracle happening before our very eyes. I'm sure the company wanted the wall repaired before Christmas as much as we did. To my complete astonishment, it was repaired in a mere two days. One baffling statistic—which could only be a gift from above—was that it did not rain for the two crucial days that they dug, built and cemented the wall and secured razor wire on top. It rained the day of the crash, and it rained again the day after the wall was rebuilt. Thank You, Lord! "Jesus loves even **me**! He knows my needs and well provides for **me**! The Bible tells **me** so!"

*"God will meet all your needs according to
his glorious riches in Christ Jesus." Philippians 4:19*

Sent: December 26, 2006
Subject: Merry Christmas
Rob writes: Merry Christmas! Our wall is fixed! It is record time even for the States; here it is a miracle. In 48 hours we went from "wall to wall." We are very thankful it is repaired.

You are all in our thoughts and prayers. We pray that you too are having an enjoyable remembrance of our Savior's birth. God's blessings to you! Our love, the Malawi Wendlands

Thank You Lord! Thank You for keeping our family safe. Thank You for the people that You have used to bring about solutions to our troubles. Thank You for allowing us to rest at night and feel refreshed as another day dawns. Thank You for the days without rain so repairs could continue. Each day is a gift. Sadly, I don't always use what You have given me to the best of my abilities. Let me not miss opportunities to witness, even if it is to the workmen building our wall. Help me shine each day with Your light, and make me a good reflection of Your love. Your perfect love is amazing. Amen.

Be still, my soul; the hour is hast'ning on
When we shall be forever with the Lord,
When disappointment, grief, and fear are gone,
Sorrow forgot, love's purest joys restored.
Be still, my soul; when change and tears are past,
All safe and blessed we shall meet at last. (CW 415:4)

CHAPTER 15

2007: LOCKED OUT, ARRESTED, POISONED—TIME FOR FURLOUGH #2!

Oh, for a faith that will not shrink, Though pressed by many a foe
That will not tremble on the brink, Of poverty or woe… (CW 405:1)

By God's grace we finished the old year all in one piece, in spite of things crumbling to pieces around us. Those difficulties were an excellent lesson in patience and trust. We weren't always overflowing with energy or health or patience, but God *always* gave us the strength needed to endure each day and to face the next. His provision for us reminded me of Elijah at the Kerith Ravine. In 1 Kings 17, Elijah was at the mercy of the birds of the air for food. Through them, God gave Elijah one morsel at a time. I generally tend to appreciate *spare* items, "just in case." I feel better prepared with extras, such as *several* diapers in the diaper bag or a few *extra* liters of fuel in the tank. But when it comes to the Lord's promises to provide, He is all-sufficient. There is no need to rely on extras. Like Elijah, I was learning a lesson in trust and sustenance—one day, one event and one moment at a time.

Sent: January 1, 2007
Subject: ministry update
Rob writes: Blessings this New Year! We enjoyed a wonderful holiday with Grandma and Grandpa Wendland from Zambia. It is extra special to celebrate our Savior's birth together.

The service of the Lord continues here as I serve 12 rural congregations in southern Malawi. I visit each one once a month. Change might be in the works for the New Year. I may be given outreach in the Lower Shire region of Malawi, in addition to my congregations. There are 8 groups in that region that want to join our church body. I also serve on the Board of Control for our Lutheran Bible Institute in Lilongwe, which deals with the operation and planning of our first-stage pastor training school. As we plan for the national church to take over

2007: Locked Out, Arrested, Poisoned—Time For Furlough #2!

more and more, the planning aspect of this board becomes greater. The Lord is keeping me busy in His service. Love, Rob

Of course, beginning a new year didn't mean that life would slow down. In fact, Rob anticipated becoming busier and traveling greater distances with the additional outreach in the Lower Shire. And our family was still anticipating a move in the future. By February our preparation would intensify, and we would need all the energy and patience that God would provide, since—as you have probably noticed—nothing is straightforward here! For a little while, though, life was blissfully UN-eventful. (By Malawi standards, anyway.)

Sent: January 3, 2007
Subject: berry nice
Rebecca writes: Rob is gone for meetings in Lilongwe. Recently, he experimented by adding some cocoa to his homemade ice cream. Wow, that makes his ice cream go from "good" to "great!" Now you all have to come back and try it! We're hosting a cake and ice cream afternoon for Hannah's birthday.

Hannah and I picked five cups of berries from our "berry-barrier." That section of the wall is well-protected: it takes the precision of a surgeon to extract some of the berries without getting caught on the prickles and thorns.

We have had no thieves lately. That is good, since we found two guards asleep on Christmas and another guard doing somersaults and headstands for a crowd of onlookers as our wall was being repaired. Our dog Samson has cuts from the fallen razor wire. Love, Rebecca

Outreach to the Lower Shire was often discussed at Rob's Mission Board meetings. Despite the huge opportunity for growth, it is a very difficult area to serve. Aside from the challenges of distance, climate and customs, the LCCA was also concerned that they would not be able to support or serve new churches in that area.

In the end, Rob's workload did not increase much in the Lower Shire. Adding new outreach to his existing 12 congregations would have been too much for one man to serve on a regular basis. The best-case scenario would be to have a Lower Shire resident trained and installed as a national pastor in that area; as of 2013 this has not yet happened.

Sent: January 11, 2007
Subject: half a mind to pig out
Rebecca writes: Or should I say a "Half a pig?—my mind is out!" We got a call from the Meiers in Zomba asking if we wanted to buy a half a pig from their friend. It isn't butchered, but the price is right compared to the ridiculous prices of

locally processed pork/ham. Do I want to buy a half a pig? No, not really! We are cleaning **out** the freezer and trying to pack. On the other hand, it will certainly be an adventure and we'll have a pocketful of change for buying it wholesale! Ever since we heard the proposal, I've had dozens of ham recipes floating through my head. On January 24, when we go for a missionary Bible study in Zomba, we'll come back "hoggin" the road. The Bartz family will buy the other half.

Recently, Rob heard a noise in our guava tree and discovered a small green snake with big eyes. He was tempted to "leaf" it alone if it was a harmless grass snake variety—but the fact that it was in the tree and had big eyes led him to suspect it could be a boomslang (very poisonous). The guard flicked it out of the tree with a stick. When it landed in the thick grass it was nearly invisible. Thankfully the guard didn't give up until he found and killed it. God bless, Rebecca

As a stay-home mom in Malawi I did not spend a lot of my time bringing home the proverbial bacon, but I did spend a lot of my time cooking it. I had big meal plans for our pig purchase, but my dreams of bacon and ham dinners disappeared as my education of pork and ham became clearer. Pork is meat straight from the pig. Ham is made after a curing process. I know my cooking skills over the years have also gone through a similar curing process!

Malawi is home to a number of venomous snakes, including black mambas, green mambas, puff adders, cobras and tree snakes. A boomslang is a slender, green tree snake with unusually large eyes. Its venom works by deactivating the body's natural blood-clotting mechanism, causing internal organs to bleed. Rob was not about to take a chance on the wide-eyed tree snake in our midst; we were thankful for the guard's determination to get rid of the potential threat. When it comes to snakes, Malawians rarely follow a "live-and-let-live" policy. They are inclined to kill every snake they encounter and ask questions later. Many Malawians seem to regard snakes as not just dangerous but evil; they even have an aversion to snakes once they're dead. Once, when our guard and gardener's teenage son had killed a snake I came out to investigate the commotion. They showed me their "black mamba." Black mambas are named for the black lining inside their mouths. When I got two sticks to open the dead snake's mouth to try to identify it, the men were aghast. As I suspected, it was *not* a black mamba. It didn't even have venomous fangs. It was a harmless snake that ate skinks and lizards. I tried to point out its identifying characteristics, but this didn't seem to interest them as much as watching the *mzungu* (white) lady handle a dead snake.

Sent: January 12, 2007
Subject: I'm tayad ("tired" in Malawi English)
Rebecca writes: These sure are long, draining days trying to pack a little each day and start repairs at the Kabula house. Nothing is easy. Our water ran out

2007: Locked Out, Arrested, Poisoned—Time For Furlough #2!

again, and there is no water at the Kabula house either. Some days we are literally high and dry.

Today I was wanted at our gate. So, in the rain and under my umbrella I went to the gate. Two young Malawian men—with a basket in their hands—greeted me with big smiles. My first thought was, "Typical vendors!" It turns out they were from next door and had brought a gift-basket full of fruit to say a neighborly thanks for the cookies and Christmas card/ornament we gave them! I was astounded. That is a first!

Last night there seemed to be quite the bit of action outside the wall. The dogs were going back and forth and the guards finally buzzed the alarm after 30 minutes of seeing people look over the wall in several places. My concern is that the razor wire and support wires might not be pulled tight enough after the recent wall repairs. We still await our move to a safer neighborhood. God bless, Rebecca

When I heard that two young men were waiting for me at the gate, I was nervous. The big question is always, "What will they want FROM me?" Instead I was pleasantly surprised that they brought a gift FOR me. I guess our neighborly efforts and Christian witness hadn't gone unnoticed. To God be the glory! How special that He chooses to work through us.

"For we are God's workmanship, created in Christ Jesus to do good works, which God prepared in advance for us to do." Ephesians 2:10

Sent: January 15, 2007
Subject: party done!
Rebecca writes: Thanks for the many wishes for Hannah's 7th birthday. We had a lovely "royal" party with the mission families. Hannah's castle cake turned out nicely. For the party I also made a mountain-berry *kuchen*, which we ate with Rob's delicious chocolate ice cream. It was unanimously declared the best ice cream around!

The girls arrived in fancy ball gowns. The kids did an educational treasure hunt while the parents enjoyed the Cowboys vs. Seahawks game. It's that time of year for USA football. We ate our "royal snacks" during half time. The ladies picked berries afterward. We were blessed with a gorgeous day. I am ready to hit the royal hay! Rebecca

On furlough, Aunt Melissa had made special birthday cakes for Hannah, Nathanael and Caleb, and my family had celebrated their birthdays for the two years we would be apart. It was a touching way to acknowledge the kids' birthdays despite being worlds apart on the actual day. For Hannah's real birthday we organized a royal bash. She invited "fellow heirs of the heavenly kingdom" (missionary families) to the Nyambadwe castle for a royal "joust-of-the-ball game" (football), a hunt for "kingdom treasure" (a treasure hunt for the kids and berry picking for the ladies) and royal refreshments. Our royal reminder from above:

> *"But you are a chosen people, a royal priesthood,*
> *a holy nation, a people belonging to God,*
> *that you may declare the praises of him who called you out of darkness*
> *into his wonderful light." 1 Peter 2:9*

Sent: January 18, 2007
Subject: tap, tap, tap
Rebecca writes: Tap, tap, tap is the sound of rain outside but also the good news that we now have water at every tap. For much of this week the water pressure was low, which meant we had no water in the kitchen and the toilets wouldn't flush. This has been a fun, stinky, waterworks-waiting-game for months on end.

Last evening I stepped on a snake when I was getting Caleb out of his car seat. I think someone had hit it earlier. It is still eerie to step on a snake in the dark.

Rob carpooled with Mark and Jim for mission meetings last week. On the return trip, one of the engine belts on the truck shredded. The men were stranded. They ended up getting sunburned playing cribbage by the truck until a mechanic arrived. Love, Rebecca

The stranded missionaries couldn't find a good shade tree, but thankfully they did have a good mechanic. Mr. Eugene Murphy drove to their location and repaired the truck. The men appreciated his helpful service, which has come in many shapes and sizes over the years as he "goes the extra mile."

Sent: January 22, 2007
Subject: no secret
Rebecca writes: Apparently it is no secret that we are most likely moving from Nyambadwe to Kabula Hill. Today I was told that Paulo was at the gate. Paulo had heard that we were the new people moving into the Kabula Hill house. (In which case, he knows more than we do, since we do not have the clearance to move there—or anywhere—just yet.) He wanted us to give him transport money to rent a truck to deliver manure to the Kabula house. Considering we do not even know the guy, that would be a resounding <u>NO</u>!

We've had rain and more rain. Rob noticed that the kitchen cupboards and counters at Kabula are all full of mold. I can't decide which I'd rather deal with: mold or moving. Now it is both! AGH! God bless, Rebecca

The fact that Paulo had managed to locate us in Nyambadwe was *not* a comfort to me! If the word was out that we were moving, security would be a troublesome issue on both ends. We weren't sure how the rumor had spread so fast. We had only told a few, select people that this move was even a *possibility*. Oh, that the Gospel would travel that quickly! And oh, that people were as eager to seek us out for *that* purpose!

Sent: January 25, 2007
Subject: this lil piggy went to market
Rebecca writes: Yesterday, we Blantyre mission women carpooled to Zomba for a Bible study on the Apostle Paul. We also picked up our pig. Half the pig managed to fit in my cooler. I ended up with the tail, so I paid $5 extra. Jim Bartz found a place in town that would butcher the pig for a fee of MK60/kilo. God bless, Rebecca

I was quite relieved to pass on the task of butchering half a pig. I knew packaging it would be hard enough. Rob, on the other hand, was slightly disappointed to put away all the carving knives we had prepared that morning.

Sent: January 26, 2007
Subject: this lil piggy stayed home
Rebecca writes: We picked up our frozen pork chops. It took me 3 hours to trim and package the meat into 15 bags of 6 chops each. The man at the butcher shop wondered if we were having a party or if we were planning to eat pig until Jesus comes. Why, as a matter of fact we might...do BOTH! Love to you all from weee 5 weee, weee, weee, all the way home!

I had several delicious family pork recipes that I had not yet made here. It was not often that I had seen pork for sale at the local shops AND found that it looked fresh all in the same trip. Now we had a freezer full of fresh pork, and we could eat to our hearts' content!

"For health and strength and daily food we give you thanks, O Lord!"

Sent: February 6, 2007
Subject: sticks and stones may break...
Rebecca writes: The Kabula house is taking LOTS of work. The attic is being

cleared of dirt, crud, bugs and leaves. The debris was enough to fill Rob's truck bed a few times. The original roofing tiles, of overlapping clay, are from Nyasaland (predating the country of Malawi). Because the joints aren't air tight, a LOT of crud filters past the tiles and onto the attic floorboards. Any strong gust of wind sends a shower of black particles through seams in the kitchen ceiling all over the kitchen counters and stove. I plan to caulk what I can since this situation is not sanitary.

I had packed a lunch for the kids, which they ate while I scraped paint. When I went to join them, I saw that Nathanael was at the gate instead of by the house. Evidently some kids at the gate told him to hand over his sippy cup and, being the sharing kid he is, he gave it to them. They took off running with his cup. The guard ran all the way to their village to retrieve the cup…which by then had already been pawned off to other family members. Nathanael was crying about the whole episode. It is difficult to teach them when to share and when not to.

Recent action on the Nyambadwe front—we awoke two nights ago at 2am. The dogs were barking, but there was another noise too. Rob guessed it was stones hitting the razor wires. Within a few minutes we could hear very large stones, about the size of a shoe, being thrown over our wall. They were landing on the roof of the house and scattering in the yard. (It's a blessing we have no windows on that side of the house.) The guards were hiding but they pushed the alarm. As the alarm blared, the perpetrators kept pelting our yard and house. I was nervous since they seemed unfazed by the alarm. Right up until the armed response came, about ten minutes later, we heard rocks being thrown. We had quite a "rocky" night's sleep after that.

The latest kidbits: I asked Nathanael if he had slept well. He whispered, "No, I heard scratching on the drapes." I asked, "What do you think it was?" He told me—with a straight face—"A kangaroo!" He recently marveled at a toaster that he saw at someone's house and wondered if it cut things. He also told me he needed Hannah's sweater to wipe his sweat on! There will be quite a learning curve come furlough! Love, Rebecca

Pelting large stones at our house was a new tactic for our neighborhood miscreants. In the morning we saw that the stones had landed in an arc *around* our vehicle and hadn't damaged anything. I wondered if our angels had a few dented feathers.

Oh, for a faith…
That will not murmur nor complain Beneath the chastning rod,
But in the hour of grief or pain Can lean upon its God… (CW 405:2)

2007: Locked Out, Arrested, Poisoned—Time For Furlough #2!

Sent: February 7, 2007
Subject: a bit flushed
Rebecca writes: I am soooo tired as I sit this evening. I spent the whole day at the Kabula house scrubbing and cleaning. At least the water came on today, so I didn't need to bring some for cleaning. A scorpion was waiting for me in the bathroom sink.

I noticed the porcelain toilet had cracks and was leaking from the bowl. So we have toilet fixing, installing burglar bars (where the guard broke into the storage room) and fixing the damaged glass window on the "To Do" list yet. Rob is teasing me that what I've packed already is probably molding in the boxes. I'm not laughing. His leather watch (which he hasn't worn for a few weeks) was fuzzy green and white with mold this morning. This time of year is not exactly ideal for packing and moving. Love, Rebecca

Is *any* time of year ideal for packing and moving? Regardless, we needed to leave. A recent incident by the nearby railroad track made this especially clear. Someone got a flat tire in the area and they were mugged and beaten up. We were warned not to stop in our area, not even for a flat tire, but to continue driving even if it meant ruining a rim. It seemed to be only a matter of time before more trouble came knocking. Time to go—and we would not look back.

Sent: February 23, 2007
Subject: wall of refuge
Rebecca writes: We took a trip to Lilongwe to the Zambian High Commission to get multiple entry visas for our family. That was not straightforward. In the end they charged $100 per person for 5 of us. They wouldn't take US dollars, only Malawi kwacha. We didn't anticipate it would cost that much, so we had to go back into town to change more money. The whole ordeal took several hours.

During devotions this evening the power went off, and we heard an unusual crash near the bedrooms. The hallway light fixture was on the floor. The light bulb had shattered in the hallway, leaving shards of glass all over. Oh what fun it is cleaning up glass by candlelight! The power fluctuations and continual outages take their toll.

Two neighborhood brick walls have fallen due to the continuing rain. Currently our neighbor to the west is building a higher brick wall. Thieves had climbed trees to get over their existing wall. When the group of thieves finally got over their wall, all SIX neighbor's guards came running to **our** gate for help! We're such a safe haven you know. God bless, Rebecca

We realized that it would benefit our family to have three-year multiple-entry visas for Zambia. We did our best to jump through all the proper hoops to ensure a smooth application process: we made phone calls ahead of time, did email research and finally drove to the capital city. Despite our preparations, the visit was an unorganized fiasco. After all was said and done, we paid $500 for our whole family. Later we found out that the kids did not even *need* a visa. Our total should have only been $200. I guess it was our gift to the country next door!

Sent: March 24, 2007
Subject: rained out
Rebecca writes: Yesterday was one of those days. It started with one workman showing up drunk. Rob sent him home. That set the tone for the whole day. We had the welder lined up to begin the burglar bars at the Kabula house, but he never showed. The electricians were supposed to come at 7:30am to fix some problems; they didn't show up until 1:30pm. Then they broke their drill, so they couldn't finish the job. They asked to borrow Rob's drill.

On the way home we saw one of the most beautiful rainbows I've ever seen. It completely framed Mt. Ndirande. It was a double rainbow and the colors were vibrant and spectacular. I was glad to pause and turn my thoughts heavenward. That evening the sunset was red and I told the kids the ditty (which is even referred to in Matthew 16:3), *"Red at night, sailors' delight; red in the morning, sailors take warning."* The next day, as we waited at a stoplight, Nathanael told me, "Green in the morning means GO!" Love, Rebecca

We had finally received the "green light" to move into the Kabula Hill mission house. Before we moved, several major security repairs were required. We spent the entire day at the Kabula house, anticipating that some of these repairs would be checked off the list. We were mistaken! Everything seemed to be going wrong. I was starting to wonder if a move was worth the hassle after such an unproductive day with the local workmen. The stunning rainbow on the way home rightfully took my thoughts heavenward. It was a good reminder that God had promised to help me through any difficulty. I could look at the difficulties as a test, and strive to shine through them with a God-pleasing attitude, like a beautiful rainbow after a stormy day.

Another analogy came to my mind as I considered our frustrating day. I reflected that my life is similar to a container carried on the head of an African lady. Passersby can't see what is in her container. The content is hidden from sight. It could be water, maize or produce. Only if the lady stumbles does anyone get a glimpse of what is inside her container. Similarly, many people do not know what *I* am filled up with at first glance. It is when I'm bumped and tested that what is inside me spills into plain view. May I always be brimming with God's Word and His Spirit, so that when I am jolted by trials I overflow with God-pleasing contents that glorify Him!

A common way to carry goods

Sent: March 25, 2007
Subject: dem bones
Rebecca writes: If all goes well, we hope to move in early April. Meeting that goal directly correlates with the speed and sobriety of the remaining repairmen, not to mention the weather. The movers will not come if it rains.

Last evening when the electricity went out, Nathanael was glowing. He was wearing his new glow-in-the-dark dinosaur-bone pajamas from the Wendland grandparents.

Hannah dreamt there was "Oatmeal Special" for breakfast, but not enough chairs. She sat on the stairs until builders came and built chairs. (Our oatmeal has been dotted with weevils lately, which might explain the menu item in her dream.)

Rob got within 7 km of his congregation, Chizilo, and got totally stuck in mud. 4WD did not help. Thankfully, he returned in one piece—sadly, no worship for anyone. Love, Rebecca

Nathanael's glow-in-the-dark bone pajamas reminded me of the song, "Dry Bones." As I pictured Ezekiel connecting "dem dry bones" in the valley, I felt like I could relate. I was in a valley of boxes and trying to connect our lives from Nyambadwe to Kabula Hill. Not to mention, I felt *lifeless* at the end of each long day.

Sent: March 28, 2007
Subject: doubles out
Rebecca writes: Today's Scripture reading from Exodus was meant for me. It

started out, *"The curtain was hung with clasps..."* That is how I spent my afternoon. After the drapes were cleaned and ironed, I spent several hours hanging drapes at Kabula. What a job. I did glean more from the text and sermon than that, but that part in particular was "fitting."

Another "exodus" is affecting our field. Here in Malawi we are losing some of our missionary name-doubles. These are the doubles scores as they stand:

Currently on Malawi field:	Leaving or left Malawi field:
Paul Nitz	Paul Wegner
Mark Johnston and Mark Panning	Mark Wendland
Susan Nitz	Sue Pontel
Kathy Felgenhauer	Cathy Meier (likely)
Jane Johnston	Jayne Bartz
Rebecca Wendland & Rebekah Johnston	Rebekah Bartz

In the realm of singles, Rob will be the single remaining bush missionary in Malawi if the Meiers head to Mozambique. God bless, Rebecca

Families on a mission field become a unit similar to an extended family of aunts and uncles and cousins. Just like a regular family, a mission family experiences great joy in welcoming new members. Just like in a regular family, it is unpleasant for a mission family to say goodbye to those leaving. The drop in world mission funds meant that we could not anticipate new mission arrivals in the near future. For now, we could only bid a sad farewell to each departing family.

Sent: March 29, 2007
Subject: I am so buff
Rebecca writes: This morning while I was in the shower Nathanael raced in shouting, "Come quickly! There's a striped snake by the garage!" Simultaneously I heard Caleb scream. In a flash I wrapped myself in a towel and peeked outside to see this snake. Turns out it was a harmless blind worm "snake." They ordinarily live underground in ant and termite nests. This one was feisty. It moved like a sidewinder snake but was otherwise similar to a worm. It was shiny grey with tiny stripes. It responded to any loud sound, so the boys were kept giggling and occupied for quite a while. After I was dressed for snake-handling and our observation time was over, I put it onto a shovel and set it by the plants far from the house.

I got the parquet wood floors at Kabula sanded this week and machine-polished/ buffed today. The sanding helped, but the floor still isn't exactly smooth. I still trip occasionally on the uneven sections if I am not watching carefully. Love, Rebecca

There is nothing like being on the "snake-patrol-squad" at any time of day! My well-thumbed book on local snakes helped me to identify the creature the boys found as a harmless blind worm. We did not need to keep many pets; there were plenty of unique critters that made drop-in appearances for us to marvel at.

Sent: April 1, 2007
Subject: white-washed tomb
Rebecca writes: Happy Palm Sunday. After church we unpacked our kitchen items at Kabula. The top of the curtain box above the kitchen stove felt... unusual. Our kitchen had been freshly painted but this surface had obviously escaped a paintbrush. I climbed up for a closer look. Collected on the surface was a thick layer of brown, moldy goo. I assumed it was a collection of years of mold/dirt/grease/gecko poop and kitchen grime. Since this house dates back to Nyasaland, that adds up to many years of grime indeed! I scraped off over a quart of muck. The scenario reminded me of the passage of the white-washed tombs! One more step forward with "this old house" that we are trying to call home. God's blessings this Holy Week. Love, Rebecca

Even though the kitchen looked crisp and newly painted, I knew that one hidden area was soiled. I suppose we eagerly compartmentalize our lives in that same fashion. We can put on a crisp, clean, friendly exterior, but our true thoughts lurk filthily in the corner, undisturbed. We might even convince ourselves that our hidden filth is harmless. But like a searching hand, God's law reveals our grime: sin that no human elbow-grease and effort can remove. God could turn from us in disgust; instead He gives us a gift. He bleaches clean all our hidden surfaces with Jesus' blood. He empowers us through Word and Sacrament to face each day wearing a fresh new layer of "paint"—our lives of sanctification. In appreciation for Jesus' sacrifice, we strive to keep ourselves clean—both on the surface and within—lest we resemble a white-washed tomb.

"Blind Pharisee!
...You are like whitewashed tombs, which look beautiful on the outside
but on the inside are full of dead men's bones and everything unclean.
In the same way, on the outside you appear to people as righteous
but on the inside you are full of hypocrisy and wickedness." Matthew 23:26-28

Dear Lord, thank You for refurbishing our tarnished lives by your Sanctifying Spirit. Lead us daily to expose our hidden grime through prayers of repentance. Then help us joyfully rely on the cleansing we have in You, and to live in a way that reflects Your beauty in us. We are truly blessed every minute of every day through You. Amen.

INCOMING EMAIL: April 02, 2007
Subject: Happy B day
Joel writes: Lord's Blessings on your Birthday! We read your emails wondering what you will do today! Franny mentioned that you should give classes on how to take care of three children, school two of them, sand and polish floors, clean bugs and grime from colonial times, paint, and finally deal with sick children! I know I have not even touched the surface for all you do! You are a very special person and a blessing to us all. May you have a wonderful day! JJ and his crew

My brother-in-law, Joel, wrote me an encouraging email. Somehow, seeing a written list of all my recent efforts and activities made them seem inspiring. How could someone get all those things done? Wonder of wonders, what the Lord could all do—when the time and talents *He* gave me were donated back to *Him* on this Malawi mission field!

Sent: April 4, 2007
Subject: sunny day; time to move
Rebecca writes: It is moving day. So far it is a beautiful, sunny day—praise the Lord! This morning the moving company's small truck broke down...but in the end they got it repaired and came late. The manager of the moving company told me to take up the harmonica instead of the piano! Don't be fooled—he didn't lift a finger as he directed all the workers! The Lord is blessing the move and keeping us in one piece among all the pieces. Love, Rebecca

Sent: April 5, 2007
Subject: dawn at Kabula
Rebecca writes: Happy Maundy Thursday. We finished unloading at 8pm last night, right as the Johnstons dropped off our kids after graciously watching them for the day. We still had to plug in the appliances, assemble the beds and locate bed nets and pajamas, but we were thankful for a place to put our heads down.

We wish you a Blessed (early) Easter. May we humbly follow our Savior to the cross and triumphantly to the empty tomb! Love, the Kabula Klan

Soon after we celebrated Easter in our new home, we were off to the annual missionary Easter Retreat, this time in Zambia. Our Sunday departure was a bit of a fiasco. After church we planned to grab a quick lunch at home before we began our trip. That was when we realized we had left our keys inside our locked house. What to do? We knew the bathroom window did not lock properly. Seven-year-old Hannah climbed through the burglar bars, one shoulder at a time, onto the bathroom sink and retrieved the misplaced keys from inside the house. Haste makes waste...of time!

2007: Locked Out, Arrested, Poisoned—Time For Furlough #2!

Sent: April 18, 2007
Subject: back in Malawi

Rob writes: We made it back safe and sound from Zambia. We did accidently lock ourselves out of our "new" house (an hour before we wanted to leave) since we are still in the key-disorientation-phase of things. The trip to and from Easter Retreat went well, the kids traveled nicely, we enjoyed time in the Word, fellowshipped with the mission families, and despite one arrest we made the trip home in good time. We... hey, wait a second—what is this about an arrest in the previous line? Yeah, I had hoped to slip it in there, but you're too quick for me.

Just north of Dedza I passed a slow minibus, only to find a police officer waving me to the side of the road about a kilometer later. After I rolled down my window and exchanged pleasantries he asked, "Can I have your driver's license? Thank you. We're going to arrest you now."

I went to the rear of the car to find two other officers there. They told me my offense. I had passed the minibus where there was a solid line painted on the road. I was guilty of "Inconsiderate Driving." From where we stood we had a clear view of where I had committed the offense. (Why was there a solid line painted where there is a clear view of a kilometer of road? Let's not get distracted by such trivialities.) The facts were these: there was a solid line and I had crossed it. By those facts, I was guilty.

The officers told me that I would have to go to traffic court and await the judge's sentence. The problem was that I could not be processed in time for court on Tuesday since it was after 3pm, so I would have to answer charges on Wednesday. I wondered aloud if I could work anything out here and now since Blantyre was three hours away, and to come back would waste precious time and fuel. They said that in former days when they traveled with a cashier they could have taken care of any fines on the spot. Now they don't; so I needed to come to the Dedza courthouse on Wednesday.

Just then they saw "Lutheran Church of Central Africa—Malawi" on the side of the car and asked if I was a reverend. I concurred (though not feeling so "reverential"). I stood there, silent. I was resigned to throwing Wednesday away in court. Finally, the man who had been talking to me said, "No, you can go." I didn't get it. Was I being dismissed to return on the morrow? They repeated, "No, you can go."

"What about my offense?"

"It is between us—you can go."

With that, they handed back my license and we went on our way. Whew! Thanks, Lord.

Today I returned from a long day in the Shire Valley. It was eight hours on the road, a flat tire, a squished wedding ring (fixed by pliers when I got home), a nicked windscreen, and a rooster—given as a gift to me. Blessings in Jesus, Rob

Home, sweet home! We had lived in our new place a mere two weeks and had already locked ourselves out, traveled out of the country and been arrested. Must be time for some real action...like poisoning ourselves!

Sent: May 3, 2007
Subject: poison in the pot
Rebecca writes: Things are super busy here. I've made little deadlines for myself to keep progressing. Meals have been quick and simple in order to maintain my goals. Today I scrubbed potatoes. When I peeled them, I saw there were green specks on the inside. I cut out as many green spots as I could. Hannah helped me slice them into the crock pot. We added carrots, pork chops and a garlic-parsley seasoning packet.

As we began eating supper, Hannah mentioned it tasted weird. Caleb, however, cleaned his entire bowl and wanted seconds. We ate on. Soon Rob was asking about the seasoning packet. He wondered if it might have had a tear that caused it to harbor mold. That was a possibility. When I got up to check the packet, I felt sick. I actually got a bucket since I felt like vomiting. I had to lie down. My mouth was tingling; soon Rob agreed his mouth was too.

Rob did some internet research and figured out what had happened. I had poisoned us all with solanine—a toxin that is found in potatoes under certain conditions. When we moved houses, the table that I keep my potatoes on was put in the washer room. Unknown to me, the table had been sitting in direct sunlight at certain times of the day ever since our move. Those locally-bought potatoes were possibly older, had been exposed to UV light daily and had a reaction that caused the solanine toxin (potatoes are part of the nightshade family) to build. Cooking does not lessen this poison and can even intensify it. Thankfully our dosage wasn't deathly. Our symptoms of a tingling mouth and itching throat indicated a "moderate overdose." I suppose we should have seen a doctor, but with our web research I figured we knew more than the ER people anyway. All in an unsuspecting day's work! Rebecca and her sack-o-tatoes

Had we been Stateside I might have made the headlines: "Mother of Three Poisons Family Dinner." Here in Malawi, I'm not sure anyone would have guessed the cause if we had all been found dead the next morning. A little further research revealed that potatoes in the USA are checked for solanine levels. Potatoes with high levels of solanine are deemed unfit for consumption. This is a clear example of the benefits of USA safety measures and high standards. Thankfully we lived to tell the tale. Obviously the Lord has more work for us to do!

2007: Locked Out, Arrested, Poisoned—Time For Furlough #2!

Sent: May 4, 2007
Subject: I live in a zoo
Rebecca writes: After breakfast I heard the dogs barking and a high-pitched noise. I went outside and saw a family of monkeys using our trees to cross the yard. They were squawking away at the dogs and vice versa. I got a few shots on the camera and some video footage. This evening I saw a Spotted Eagle-Owl perched on our roof.

Bill Meier accepted the call to Mozambique. Portuguese, Nampula, maiden voyage—there they go! Love, Rebecca and the zoo

A family of monkeys lives in our area. One of our neighbors had to cage their kittens because the monkeys had been killing them. As neat as it was to see monkeys swinging in our treetops, I was grateful that our dogs kept them at a safe distance.

Sent: May 15, 2007
Subject: Working while it is day!
Rob writes: Yesterday I was at Khanyepa and it was their grain-offering day. I had offered to buy their maize to get a down-payment (*masika*) for a new church, so the people brought maize today—3,870 lbs of it! That's a new record. I didn't bring enough bags, so people just dumped their offerings at the front of church. It was like walking in a grain bin up there. Finally, enough members went home to get bags that we were able to store it all—35 bags full. I feared that I could not haul such a load in my Land Cruiser without breaking it. I gave several bags to Evangelist Chikwewe and our gardener. That lightened things enough for my return trip to Blantyre. I plan to give the rest to other called workers. In case you are wondering what 1.7 tons of maize is going for these days…about $350.

Today I tried to complete more Muhapokwa building project tasks. I bought the iron roofing sheets for the church but didn't get home until 7pm from delivering them. I was glad I got home **that** early. I had ordered the *malata* (iron sheets) in the morning, and they told me to pick up my order in the afternoon. When I got there, the sheets weren't made and they had to put on a new spool of metal sheet. Each metal spool is about 10 tons, so that took a while. I didn't get started out to Muhapokwa 'til about 3:30.

I made it fine along the paved road, but about 10 km down the dirt road (15 km from Muhapokwa) I heard a bang and saw all the metal sheets slide off the back of my truck. The metal stand on the back of my truck had broken off. It turns out the weight of the *malata* and the huge potholes in the road were enough to shear the two bolts and bend the metal braces that were holding the stand in place. Now I was in a pickle. Thankfully, no vehicle was following me to ruin $650 of iron sheets, and no people were hit by the razor-thin metal. Within minutes, a "village" of women and children had gathered around the truck. I decided to lean the *malata* on the front rail and brace them on the bottom of my tail gate. The women and kids helped me put the *malata* back on, two at a time until all 52 sheets were on. No one was cut, everything got loaded, and I started out very slowly to get to Muhapokwa. The final 15 km took me an hour. When I arrived it was past 5pm, and no workers were at the site to help me unload. I went to a member's house nearby. He helped me, but it took a while. Those sheets are heavy. Thankfully they were delivered and I could journey home. Love, Rob

Sent: May 23, 2007
Subject: Get ready 'cause here we come!
Rebecca writes: We're gearing up for furlough. I'll get out the suitcases and begin to pack (YET AGAIN) for our time Stateside. The kids can't wait. If they could burst, it would happen soon. I plan to dress both boys in a white dress shirt with a bright orange T-shirt over it. It should help me spot them instantly at the airport.

Mom, thanks for lining up all of our medical appointments. Now we can hit the ground running and hopefully have enough time for any necessary follow-up appointments. God bless, Rebecca and "just plane" antsy children

Our moving in and unpacking had melded right into our furlough preparations. It was an organizational puzzle to put items on the right piles and keep order among the boxes and suitcases.

Sent: May 30, 2007
Subject: no hippo food
Rebecca writes: No stoplights are working throughout all of Blantyre. In a way it is better, since they aren't properly synchronized anyway. But it makes for a real mess on the busy intersections where you need some guidance—especially during school hours.

We all bundled up for church today. WOW—it hasn't gotten much above 60°F. Time to head out of these tropics for Wisconsin, hey? I went over rules concerning strangers today. Nathanael told me he was excited to eat the meals on the plane. Then he added, "I hope they don't give me hippo food! It is dirty." God bless, Rebecca

We traveled safely to the States and spent a few days getting reacquainted with family members and falling into the rhythm of our long-anticipated furlough. Being surrounded by the normalcy of a first-world country made the following email from Africa all the more strange to read. My father-in-law in Zambia sent an article from his local paper. Maybe you have sometimes wondered whether you can believe everything you read, even in a credible USA newspaper. Now you can enjoy an example of the tangled web of truth and fiction that counts for some African reporting. Apart from being entertaining, articles like the following one from a Zambian newspaper give great insight into what is considered to be "for real" in a community where so many people cling to superstition.

INCOMING EMAIL: June 15, 2007
Subject: news, kind of
Dad Wendland sent: *Dead Woman Resurrects* TIMES OF ZAMBIA June 14, 2007
A woman, who died four years ago, has reportedly resurrected. The woman, identified as Rebecca Fumbelo died on December 18, 2003 after delivering a baby boy. The woman has reappeared and is at her relatives' village in Zambezi district. Zambezi district coordinator confirmed the incident yesterday and said he had received a report that a woman had resurrected and that relatives rightly identified her on June 8. Her father took his found daughter to his uncle, under the care of a traditional healer. She is unable to speak but can hear and see. She was buried the same day she died. The relatives said the woman was mysteriously turned into a cow and lived among livestock until she was sold to a businesswoman in Angola. When the businesswoman wanted to slaughter the cow, the animal turned into a human being. The businesswoman sold the woman as a maid to a rich businessman. After two days as a maid, she lost her speech and was confused, prompting the businessman to call in a diviner who put some herbs on her head and she disappeared. On arrival in Zambia, she was taken to the police.

Even though there are not many local public libraries, Africans do not seem to be at a loss for intriguing stories. Take your pick: fiction or non-fiction!

"The big dance" –an aspect of witchcraft

Our 2007 furlough schedule was full. Three days after disembarking in Milwaukee, Rob and I were on our way to Detroit, MI for the LWMS convention while our kids stayed with my parents in La Crosse, WI. Being part of the LWMS rally was a very special June highlight and a grand way to kick off our furlough. The sessions, worship and fellowship were amazing. It truly was a time to fill up after being drained in so many ways prior to furlough. The encouragement, prayers and support of thousands of Christians boosted our spirits to continue spreading the Word in Malawi. The rest of our furlough was crammed with doctor appointments, deputations and shopping, as well as cherished family time.

Each furlough I thought I had a sensible and manageable shopping list of truly necessary items. *Then we went shopping.* Suddenly, dozens of great new products were available. These products were not extraordinarily expensive, the shelves were stocked full of them, and soon our cart(s) began to fill up! It was very hard to escape the clutches of the "materialism monster"—especially when we could put so many of those items to good use in Malawi! State-of-the-art electronics, top-of-the-line supplies and flashy toys were hard to ignore. Most enticing for me were the kitchen gadgets that could make meal preparations easier and faster. It was hard to stay content in these conditions—HELP!! Needless to say, cramming two years of shopping into the space of two months was definitely not healthy for our pocketbook!

Two things particularly struck me during our 2007 furlough: the first was that, despite my frequent health-woes in Malawi, I was healthy *every day* that I was in the States. The second surprise was how I found myself dealing with Stateside "inconveniences." Situations that had once been very annoying and easy to complain about—like freeways congested due to construction and detours—I now saw in a new light. I viewed those activities as positive evidence that the country was taking care of needed maintenance.

In a flurry, another furlough came and went. Each day spent with family and friends on USA soil was a cherished blessing. I wished it wouldn't end. I wasn't exactly counting down the days until we could return to the routine struggles and trials in Africa. Still, I knew that it was in those challenging surroundings that I was more mindful of God and His will for me. In contrast, when I was surrounded by family it was easy for my thoughts to become centered on "us." Part of me wished I could disappear into the comfort and security of our family sphere; another part of me realized that this wasn't where true contentment could be found. I struggled with this dichotomy. And I longed for heaven where we would have the best of the best for all eternity.

Oh, for a faith…
…A faith that keeps the narrow way, [That trusts the guiding hand,]
And with a pure and heav'nly ray Lights up the [path ahead.]
(CW 405:5) [alternate words my own]

2007: Locked Out, Arrested, Poisoned—Time For Furlough #2!

Sent: August 29, 2007
Subject: back in the Warm Heart
Rob writes: We're back. All in all, it was a smooth trip; for that we are very thankful. Our plane was delayed an hour in Johannesburg, as the ground crew had "lost" 20 pieces of luggage. I was convinced that our pieces were among those missing since they spent the night unattended at the notorious Johannesburg airport. Our plane ended up heading to Blantyre without the luggage being found.

As we began our descent to Chileka airport, the plane was rocking all around. We got lower and lower, with grass zooming by the window, and it seemed we were coming in too fast. Sure enough, with mere feet to go until touchdown, the engines powered up and we flew back up into the sky. The pilot explained that the winds circling in the hills around the city were causing his instruments to tell him to use one runway and then another. A family in front of us commented that last month a SAA pilot had tried landing three times before he aborted and went to Lilongwe. For us, the second attempt worked and we were down.

When we disembarked, we found that much of the Immigration and Customs hall was under construction. As a result everything was pure chaos. Bags were emptied on the tarmac, Immigration was in a small room behind a narrow corridor, and Customs was set up around the corner behind a door that was inaccessible to luggage trolleys. The good news is: our luggage made it—all 10 pieces! More good news: the Customs lady did not even want to look at our suitcases and kindly waved us through.

And so life in Blantyre begins again. The kids are shot—up and crying in the middle of the night—but hopefully that will soon pass as we get back to business in the Warm Heart of Africa. Thanks for all your support, gifts, fellowship and love. We already look forward to the "next time." Our love in Jesus, Rob.

Departing for Malawi after furlough is a good reminder that we are merely transients on this earth. As we exchange family good-byes, we each realize that these could very well be our last farewells before we meet again in glory. Our times are in God's hands. We leave the details of our lives in God's hands too, as we continue to put *our* hands to the work he has called us to do.

> *Lord, give us such a faith as this, And then whate'er may come,*
> *We'll taste e'en now the hallowed bliss Of an eternal home. (CW 405:6)*

Sent: September 18, 2007
Subject: a lil brief
Rebecca writes: Things here at Kabula are normal. Although that is hard to say, because before we left for furlough things were not normal. All I've been doing

since we returned is unpacking.

A few kidbits: Hannah is happy to be in Standard 3. Caleb's new word is "FILFY." Nathanael is still fond of bugs. The other day there was a *chongololo* (centipede) in the bathroom. I called to Nathanael, "Come and see. We have a visitor!" He came running, asking, "Is it Auntie Stephanie?"

It tugs at my heart when the kids keep asking when the grandparents, aunts, uncles and cousins are coming to visit. They also miss the fancy food (like chicken nuggets). Evidently this is in contrast to what I was making for supper. Nathanael walked in the kitchen and asked me, "Are you cooking dog?" Without hesitation Hannah piped in, "I hope it is tender!" (For the record—he thought I was cooking the dogs' *food* since the dogs eat a cooked, mushy meal.) At least the minimal variety here makes for healthier snacks. Both boys ate two pieces of whole wheat bread for a snack this morning!

I shopped yesterday for yogurt, some veggies, rice and milk and my bill was $150. Money doesn't seem to go very far here, since there are rarely sales and never coupons!

Rob bought a bale of milk yesterday (milk comes in 500 ml bags; these can be purchased in a large bundle of 20 bags, called a bale). ALL 20 BAGS were sour. He called ahead to the store to make sure they would exchange them. They told him they would do a "bacteria test" to make sure they were sour. I laughed and hypothesized, "The guy will turn around, drink a swig and then declare it good or bad." Sure enough—that is what the employee did. It was all sour so they replaced them.

I don't like turning off the kitchen light. After it has been turned on and off a collective five times, it shuts off the electricity to the whole house/yard as well! Then I have to round up a flashlight and stool to flip up the offending breaker. Rob has been playing electrician. He fixed the front door light and our gate light (evidently prowlers were noticing the dark area).

The jumping spiders are out of control here. We have killed at least five a day EVERY DAY since we have returned. That is way too many for my liking. I had one nearly descend on my head and barely miss my dinner plate. They are better than tarantulas at least. God bless, Rebecca

Life in Malawi has a way of illuminating the ease and blessings and convenience of life in the States. Certainly I missed the Wisconsin dairy products already! The longer that I live in Africa, the more I notice the contrast in flavors when we return to America. The USA flavors taste great—the way they are "supposed to." In Malawi, the same food often suffers from "box essence." Products often sit in packaging for months on end, since the majority of goods on our grocery shelves are shipped in from South Africa or somewhere else around the world. Expiration dates aren't even on some packaging in Malawi. It is a good reality check. We realize "there is no place (or taste) like home."

September 2007 marked our fourth year in Malawi. We knew from experience that if we wanted something done right, and quickly, it was best to do it ourselves. Besides repairs, it seemed that moving into a previously vacant house meant we needed to get the population of spiders and bugs under control—even if it meant removing them one at a time.

Sent: September 25, 2007
Subject: beauty and the beast
Rebecca writes: The Beauty: nine gorgeous Jacaranda trees on our property. They are absolutely lovely! Their falling flowers also provide a beautiful purple carpet to cover over the dust for a while. It is our version of fall. Nathanael is sure to bring me one purple flower each morning—a real sweetheart.

The Beast: a few days ago I encountered an enormous hunter/wolf-type spider in the kitchen. Its front legs were about 2 inches long. It was smaller than a tarantula, but it was the biggest spider I EVER want to see in this house. I thought I was leaving behind those gargantuan arachnids.

Rob is at meetings in Lilongwe. Love, Lady Jacaranda and her purple petals

I cannot get enough of the beautiful jacaranda trees. Their vibrant purple color against the blue sky and dusty landscape is striking. Even when the flowers fall to the ground, they make a lush purple carpet to walk on. As my mother-in-law often points out, "It's amazing what beauty God puts right under our feet." Remarkably, this purple brilliance appears in the depths of the dry season. These trees must draw from a stored energy-supply in order to bloom. To me, they seem to symbolize how we Christians should also stand out against the backdrop of this parched world. When we hear God's Word, we must soak it up and store it for future use. When tough times arrive, we can then draw on our "living water" reserves to bloom in spite of the deprivation around us. These trees are an inspiring reminder to me to bloom where God has planted me, in spite of any unpleasant conditions or challenging locations.

Sent: September 30, 2007
Subject: latest buzz
Rebecca writes: Last night our house alarm rang. Some men were trying to climb a tree by our front wall. The guard pressed the button. It was total punishment to be wide awake at 1:05am (with Rob still in Lilongwe), waiting for the armed guard team to come, waiting for the dogs to settle down and knowing that the rest of the night would be rocky and robbed of sleep—in spite of being so tired.

Church, choir, keyboard playing and crafts all went well at church today.

About a dozen ladies helped for crafts. We made several-dozen handmade cards.

Hannah has a plan for chicken strips tonight, so I have an appointment to cook with her. Lately, the boys' idea of fast food is eating raw oatmeal as a snack.

I am finally done unpacking from furlough and our move. God bless, Rebecca

The year had felt like an endless cycle of packing and unpacking. Pack for moving; unpack from moving. Pack suitcases for furlough; unpack suitcases on furlough. Pack and unpack while traveling on furlough. Pack our purchases and suitcases for Africa. Unpack suitcases from furlough. Finish unpacking boxes from moving. I didn't want to go ANYWHERE for a while by plane, train or automobile if it meant more packing!

Sent: October 2, 2007
Subject: Cherry valley
Rebecca writes: As Nathanael put it, "Dad is in the Cherry Valley again today!" Yes, he is down in the Shire Valley, conducting church and probably really "cooking" as I write this, since the weather is hot and very dry.

Kidbits: Nathanael found a rusty tack outside today. He told Caleb to eat it. Caleb obediently bit into it. So it goes. It is a wonder we all survive as we do. (The Lord is good!) At supper Hannah announced that she has found two new uses for her left hand: she can use it to play the recorder and to hold her hockey stick. Rob and I hardly eat supper for the food; we just fill up on all the latest kid comments and antics.

Thieves broke into a neighbor's house twice last week. Our guard pushed our alarm too while they fled. God bless as you live each day for HIM! Rebecca and cherry gang

Our furlough trip to Door County, Wisconsin had Nathanael thinking "cherry." I couldn't blame him. Picking cherries, eating cherries to your heart's content, staying at "Uncle Bob Doneff's" in Egg Harbor near the cherry orchards and touring a cherry factory all did make a lasting, tasty impression. No cherries are found here though, not even in the Valley. We would have to wait patiently for another two years to eat cherries again…which was kinda the pits!

Reading the local paper sometimes seemed to be a glimpse into the "pits" of Hades. An article in our newspaper revealed that witchcraft continues to be a stumbling block in Malawi, even for city-dwelling business owners.

DAILY TIMES October 1, 2007 By Wanangwa Tembo
"Clapperton Phiri, 39, found himself on the wrong side of the law. He is

alleging that three months ago he asked a witchdoctor to help him boost his business and get rich. Apparently, the witchdoctor gave him three options. He was told to either kill one of his children, convince his wife to carry herbs around her waist wherever she goes or lastly to sleep with one of his daughters. Three months after the incident his daughter was found pregnant. Phiri has been charged with incest."

Indeed there is still work to be done! This article was a timely reminder of why we are here in Malawi: to spread the message of truth and freedom from sin in Jesus Christ.

Sent: October 3, 2007
Subject: Are you Chicken?
Rebecca writes: As I was showering this morning a large wall spider began climbing on the inside of the shower curtain. I thought, "No need to panic. I'll finish and take care of it." It stayed put for most of my washing, but then things got slippery. I suddenly lost sight of it. As I scanned the area, the spider jumped from the height of my head and landed near my bare feet. Our shower isn't big; I wasn't amused. I quickly grabbed the conditioner bottle and squished it.

Q: Why did the spider climb down the shower curtain?
A: To get a little conditioning.

Rob sprayed for bugs today. That should make a dent in the bug population trying to access our home. Extra effort was taken to keep the kids away—although they tend to bug one another.

Q: Why did the chickens ride in Rob's truck?
A: To be an egg-cellent addition to our empty coop.

Since there is an existing coop in this yard, we bought some hens to occupy it. The boys (and dogs) were beside themselves with glee over the new chicks. Rob also brought home a dozen tomatoes, 200+ pounds of sweet potatoes, bananas, and other live chickens as part of the offering/gift from Katunga yesterday. God bless, Rebecca

The congregation at Katunga was so thankful for Rob's return after furlough that they sent him home with a truck-load of wonderful gifts/offerings. He took the live chickens home and put them in our coop, along with the seven layer-chicks we had already purchased. As a fledgling chicken owner, I was on a learning curve. Evidently, layer chicks are raised for laying eggs and broiler chicks for eating. There are even different feeds for the two types of chickens. So many things I didn't learn during my years of being "cooped" up in the city!

Sent: October 6, 2007
Subject: Say "Uncle" for Ant
Rebecca writes: I think the phrase, "Say Uncle!" is used when someone makes somebody else give up. I've never used the phrase before...but it is time I "Say Uncle" for ANTS.

We sprayed for bugs none too soon. There have been several-dozen dead roaches outside...but the ants! This morning there were 50 dead ants in the bathroom. I am not talking about small sugar ants. These babies are 1½ inches from antennae to hind leg. We found at least 100 prior to today. They were making a nest under the tub in a hole in the tile. I would've caulked it shut, but the opening was too big. Rob sprayed the poison directly into the hole. Now the ants keep crawling out and dying on the bathroom floor. Caleb sees them, grabs a shoe and starts hitting the ground for all he's worth.

Our neighbor's alarm was ringing again a few nights ago. The dogs were going bonkers, frantically barking around 3am. The thieves must have been close to our house. These nighttime disruptions are fewer and farther between than our Nyambadwe issues, but we're not out of the woods. Love, Rebecca and Kabula bugs

Nyambadwe or Kabula Hill—no matter where we lived, we still had issues to contend with. My dreams of moving away from hordes of bugs and nights filled with ringing alarms and barking dogs were quickly fizzling into reality: we were still in Malawi...and life anywhere in Malawi isn't exactly "dreamy."

Incidentally, some years later I learned that the family of one of Hannah's classmates had moved into our Nyambadwe house after we moved out. The property had been purchased and put up for rent, and the new family planned to move in on a Saturday. They moved all their belongings into the house a day early, but they spent the night elsewhere. That night thieves came. They locked up the guard, broke into the *khonde* and then smashed through the living room window. They stole everything the family had dropped off (still in boxes); but they didn't stop there. They also seized anything removable, including the toilet cisterns (causing an indoor flood). The family replaced some belongings and completed their lease, but they never felt safe and never slept very well. The incident highlights several things: the mission was certainly pro-active in getting us out of there...and the Lord protected us from the day we came to Nyambadwe to the day we left.

Sent: October 16, 2007
Subject: Mzuzu robot
Rebecca writes: The kids' latest source of entertainment is hundreds of dying moths that have suddenly appeared. It is that time of year. They especially like

it when the moths fly in circles on the floor. Caleb giggles, "airplane!" He also thinks we live in "Africata."

Hannah's statement yesterday was, "I think they forgot to put flavor in this cookie!" She was eating the local quality-<u>un</u>controlled "biscuits."

I tried making my own tortilla chips the other day. They aren't bad. Not quite like the real thing, but with all the salsa I have been making they have been a delicious treat.

Yesterday was our Faith, Family, Fun Fayre at church. Thankfully the rain held off. We set up our craft tables while others manned a snack station and grilling area. Activities included a jumping castle, church tours, Christian movies, kids' crafts, and family games supervised by the church president. Jane Johnston took blood pressures and weighed people. Most visitors came because they see our church's TV program with Pastor Johnston during the week. The fayre was also great to strengthen the fellowship of the members and allow them to use their various talents.

Toward the end of the fayre I asked Martin Ntambo to save two pieces of grilled chicken for Rob, who had stayed home with a napping Caleb. Martin asked if I wanted them medium or well-done. I replied, "Oh, Rob likes his things well-done!" Martin laughed and responded, "Yes, just like his sermons!"

A friend told me that the first robot (stoplight) had been recently installed in Mzuzu, a city up north. This robot was causing trouble because the crosswalk signal had a green-lit man for "walk" and a red-lit man for "don't walk." When the crosswalk man went from red to green, all the *male* pedestrians crossed the road. The ladies, however, stayed behind and waited for the green-lit lady to show up. So it goes in the heart of Africata. Rebecca

I had to chuckle at the story about the new stoplights in Mzuzu. I think those ladies will be waiting a looonnnggg time for a lit-up lady in a *chitenje* to appear, carrying a baby on her back and a water jar on her head.

Sent: October 22, 2007
Subject: tree/house
Rebecca writes: Rob is out to Muhapokwa with the builder, attempting to deliver a load of cement. There has been a serious cement shortage for months. Evidently the "big" companies were told to leave the country to give the little companies a chance. Well, the little companies could not meet the demands, so now no cement is available. It is bad timing, since the builders are getting paid whether they have cement or not. Since they can't continue without cement, they are being paid to sit around and do nothing. Just today some cement was available, so Rob is making a quick dash to buy some and deliver it. Hopefully the building

can continue before the money runs out.

We had some action around the house again. I was in the kitchen and heard a loud thud, thud, thud. That noise was accompanied by the sound of many things pelting our roof. All I could see from the window were large billows of dust. A rather large tree near the top of the property had collapsed and tumbled down three terraces in our backyard. It stopped shy of smashing into our house. (I hadn't had any idea it was rotting, since it was still producing large seed pods. Nathanael has collected a dozen of the seed pods and stashed them in a corner by the house as "bombs, in case the enemy comes"—so he told me.)

Rob came home from the bush with about 100 tomatoes, cabbage, cassava, maize, bananas, eggs, small soap bars and rice (shelled and unshelled) as gifts. I'll prepare salsa tomorrow. God's continued blessings as you live each day for HIM! Rebecca

It is humbling every time Rob comes home from the bush with gifts from his church members. We have many more worldly goods than the average member here in Malawi. Those villagers needed the produce more than we did. But since their gifts had been given to God's representative to show their love and trust in God, we intended to appreciate each gift, use the produce and think of our fellow believers as we enjoyed it. Their generosity was a good reminder of why we give gifts to God—not because *He* needs them, but because *we* need to give them as an exercise of our faith. Joyful, generous giving is a spiritually mature response that reveals our trust in God and our gratitude to the Giver of all good things.

> *"Out of the most severe trial,*
> *their over-flowing joy and their extreme poverty welled up in rich generosity.*
> *For I testify that they gave as much as they were able,*
> *and even beyond their ability.*
> *Entirely on their own, they urgently pleaded with us*
> *for the privilege of sharing in this service to the saints…*
> *But just as you excel in everything—*
> *see that you also excel in this grace of giving…*
> *For God loves a cheerful giver." 2 Cor 8:2-4, 7, 9:7*

Sent: November 1, 2007
Subject: sinking feeling
Rebecca writes: Today we left early for Bible Group. I pulled onto the main road and saw traffic was seriously backed up. There was an oversized **boat** in the road! Cars were beginning to back up, turn around and go back the way they had come, right past us. In the end I had to turn around too. Hannah exclaimed, "The

2007: Locked Out, Arrested, Poisoned—Time For Furlough #2!

boat sunk into the road because it was too heavy." Who could guess we would get stuck in traffic behind a huge sunken boat in the middle of Victoria Avenue in Blantyre?

Kidbits: Hannah is thrilled this week because she was chosen to be Mary in the upcoming Christmas play. She told us that everyone at school is calling her Mary now. Nathanael responded, "It is better than calling you Joseph." Caleb walked around the other day with a "Patent pending" sticker on his arm. I'm wondering if there are any royalties associated with that? Really…the Lord deserves them all!

Rob saw a washing machine ad in the paper. It stated, "Washing machine with cycles including: Fuzzy, Heavy, Speedy, Blanket, Wool." Not your typical selections—they sounded more like a sequel to *The Seven Dwarfs*. God bless, Rebecca

I don't usually have a sinking feeling going downtown; at least not until we got stuck behind a boat in the road, "sunk" more than 2,700 feet above sea level! It is so easy to be late in Malawi for a multitude of crazy reasons. Hardly anyone keeps strict time. In fact, it is not uncommon for an invitation to read: "Starting at 3pm to begin at 3:30." It seems there is sort of a built-in "lateness buffer." If someone actually arrives on time, it is noteworthy and will often be commented on.

Sent: November 8, 2007
Subject: Did I Twinkle?
Rebecca writes: I've been busy painting and caulking again. There are so many cracks in our ceiling boards that my bathroom cup often has a layer of dead bugs, dust and debris in it in the morning. I need gallons of caulk!

Last night I began wondering if the caulking was for nothing. At 3:45am we had an earthquake. Our whole house shook for about ten seconds. It was the talk of the town. A few items fell off our shelves. Many village people evacuated their houses—afraid they might fall apart. I was also wondering about ours. It wouldn't take too much shaking to cause all of our clay roofing shingles to ccrumble tto ppieces!

A few kidbits: Out of the blue, Nathanael asked, "Did I twinkle?" I wondered if he needed to use the toilet. Turns out he was trying to wink. Later he inquired, "What do you call a ladybug when it is a man?" Caleb is quite the toddling problem-solver. A door was shut and he couldn't reach the handle. Undeterred, he returned with his toy chainsaw and tried to saw the door open! Love, Rebecca

In Malawi it does not snow, we do not have tornadoes, we will most likely never have a tsunami and major flooding is unlikely in Blantyre. Being on the Rift

Valley does, however, allow for some infrequent earthquakes. This quake caused some shantytown houses to collapse, and several people were killed. I had been rudely awakened in the middle of the night for a multitude of reasons but never before for an earthquake. With my head still fuzzy, I thought for a split second that maybe it was the end of the world. No blaring trumpets or bright lights, though. I wondered how unbelievers must feel about such a powerful encounter. It must shake a person's very core to know of—but not believe in—the true God. I was given a fresh resolve to work while it is day and pray for those who are not yet of the family of believers.

> Dear Lord Jesus, what a blessing it is to know You and be able to come to You in prayer. Thank You for Your unfailing protection and care for my family. Please continue to keep me safe under Your wing when any unexpected events come during the night or day. Please also keep other family members, fellow missionaries and believers around the world safe and in Your unshakable care. Help me always to trust Your promises and commit all things to Your Will, even when I am tempted to doubt. I also pray for those who do not yet know You, Your peace, Your love, Your faithfulness and Your will for them. May You use me and all believers as Your witnesses daily, so others can learn of You, come to faith, and one day enjoy eternal life with You. Amen.

Sent: November 17, 2007
Subject: floating away
Rebecca writes: During a downpour today, I looked out the window to see the dog dishes had floated from our backyard to our front yard. The rain is simultaneously greening things up and creating brown: lots of mud.

After some stomach trouble last week, I've been feeling fine. I'm on a mission this week to get sewing and mending checked off my "darn" list. (ha ha!)

A new friend, Tertia, and her daughter are coming over today. I met her through the paint store and she has been coming to Bible Group ever since. She is very musical, teaches piano, has a beautiful voice and has produced several Christian CD's. Love, Rebecca

The silver lining of moving into a fix-up house on Kabula Hill was finding a new friend. While researching paint, we met the manager of a local paint store. When I found out he and his wife Tertia had a little girl, I invited them to Bible Group. I connected with Tertia on many levels and looked forward to a deepening friendship. Sadly, a few months later their family unexpectedly moved back to South Africa. I was happy for them, but it gave me the blues saying good-bye to yet another Christian friend.

Sent: November 25, 2007
Subject: call me "MOTH"er
Rebecca writes: We celebrated Thanksgiving yesterday at the Johnston's house. Jane bought two frozen turkeys imported from Brazil. The directions were in Portuguese. We enjoyed them together with all the fixings. After our feast we ended the evening with a mini-service and singing.

We've been melting in Blantyre. Our temps in the shade have been about 100°F. It is terrible timing for the current water shortages. If Blantyre is hot, the Lower Shire is sweltering! Rob came back super sweaty from his trip to Chizilo. He saw members periodically exiting church to sit under a tree for relief from the heat. A full church with a tin roof isn't exactly cool.

It is still "the time of the moths." Outside it is almost like walking in a snowfall, because the moths are fluttering around by the thousands. The birds are hitting our windows trying to catch them. Last year around this time it was "the time of the tarantulas" and wall repair at Nyambadwe. A better scenario all the way around this year! The "MOTH"er and flighty ones

November in Malawi is neither autumn nor harvest time, but it is as good a time as any to be thankful. In fact, with the water shortage and hungry season upon us I almost felt guilty as I gave thanks for our family's abundant blessings, both physical and spiritual. I knew that many people around me did not enjoy these same blessings. I was determined to be the best steward that I could be with what I had been given and to look for ways to give back to the Lord what he had entrusted to me.

> *We give thee but thine own, What-e'er the gift may be;*
> *All that we have is thine alone, A trust, O Lord, from thee. (CW 485:1)*

Sent: November 28, 2007
Subject: GOOD NEWS
Rebecca writes: GOOD NEWS: our backyard wall (constructed of old roofing sheets) is done!

GOOD NEWS: the temps have dropped over 30 degrees since I wrote. There was a thick fog today as a result. Thunder is rumbling—we could use the rain and cool temps that might follow.

GOOD NEWS: Rob finally fixed the boarded-up broken window from when thieves got into the storage room about a year ago. He's the plumber, the electrician, the carpenter, the window fixer and of course, the only Malawi bush missionary, all wrapped up in one! BUT not for too long, because…GOOD NEWS: the Lawrenzes will be arriving in Malawi next week!

The water shortage this time is worse than ever. The Water Board sent in two students to see what was wrong with the dam. Well, they went "in"—and both died. Then their friends went in after them, and also died. In addition to water-fixing, they'll have to sort out the dead bodies. We are thankful again for our water tank on these hot days when we go through water quickly.

May your Advent season be blessed as we ponder the coming of our amazing Savior...the best GOOD NEWS of all! Rebecca and good news gang

Our recent Malawi manpower loss meant we had several positions to be filled. The Spirit led the ACA to call Rev. Steve Lawrenz to Blantyre. He and his wife Lori had been serving in Zambia since 1986. His new role would be to assist the national pastors in southern Malawi. Another Zambian missionary, Rev. John Holtz, was given a call to serve in the northern region of Malawi. He and his wife Mindy had served in Zambia since 1997. Their African mission experience, familiarity with the Chichewa language and added manpower would be welcome additions to our field.

Sent: December 4, 2007
Subject: Mary/merry termites
Rebecca writes: Today Hannah was Mary in the school Christmas play. When it was almost time to leave for the play, I discovered that the boys were filthy from head to toe. They were too dirty to go through the house to the bath. First I swept them off with a brush and then hosed them down. Finally, much later, they were at least clean enough to get into the car. They told me they had been playing and rolling in the sandbox. Then Caleb had discovered a termite mound nearby, so they both had been playing in the muddy termite mound. No wonder they'd had several multi-colored layers of mud crusted on them (like elephants). So it goes. I **knew** it had been too quiet! Evidently they wanted to be "merry" too. God bless, Rebecca and band of "Mary"/merry ones

The school Christmas play went very well. Almost-eight-year-old Hannah played Mary beautifully and spoke very loudly. To God be the glory! Meanwhile, my nature-loving boys were involved in a different play altogether: dirt play! Five-year-old Nathanael and two-year-old Caleb had turned a shade of brownish-grey. I reflected thankfully that this was only superficial dirt—their sin-soiled insides had been washed clean in Christ. For that we could all be merry!

Sent: December 14, 2007
Subject: Kabula Caroling
Rebecca writes: We've had over seven inches of rain in a few days, and things are NOT drying out. I have every fan we own blowing like crazy. It is like living in a wind tunnel. In other Blantyre news, we learned that the minibus drivers are on

2007: Locked Out, Arrested, Poisoned—Time For Furlough #2!

strike. That is affecting countless people.

Yesterday we had our Christ-Child carol night. It was a lovely evening spent in song, fellowship and food with the Johnstons, Rachel Kionka and the Lawrenzes. Rob made an outstanding batch of his chocolate ice cream for the occasion.

Kidbits of late: Caleb was caught putting my favorite, imported mint chapstick on Shadow. Not his shadow—our dog! He is a little adventurer; he enjoys climbing up our burglar bars and swinging on the vines that hang from our Kachere tree. Nathanael loves filling his bug house (sent as a gift from a church care-package) with many creepy crawlies. He has also taken up the task of catching bugs and feeding them to the chickens. I often find him with a beetle or *inswa* clutched in the palm of his hand—even while riding his bike. Hannah is counting down each day until Grandma and Grandpa Wendland come for Christmas.

Tomorrow we will take a Christmas card, ornament and food gift to our neighbors. We hope to meet some of them, let them know who we are and "let our light shine" at Kabula Hill. Advent blessings, Rebecca

We only have to drive an hour to visit an official rainforest. During the rainy season in Blantyre, the rainforest comes to us! When the bath towels need to be dried in the dryer to prevent them from molding in the bathroom, then I know it is seriously damp.

Downtown spirits were also dampened when the minibus drivers went on strike. The drivers were protesting a recent law that limited the number of passengers they could carry at one time. Ordinarily, it was to the drivers' financial benefit if they jammed as many passengers as they could into one minibus. Luggage didn't even count; it could hang out the back of the minibus. Fish or chickens were often tied with wire to the side mirrors. I think the new law was for the good of everyone. (I wish they had a seatbelt law in the works too—our old Pajero didn't even *have* seatbelts in the back.)

Sent: December 19, 2007
Subject: all around the neighborhood
Rebecca writes: Ever since we moved, I've wanted to meet our Kabula neighbors. As you know, it isn't exactly a piece of cake trying to get past the gates, guards and dogs to meet people at home, but we wanted to make the effort again this Christmas in our new home. We spent much of the day walking around our neighborhood. We even went up and around several blocks to get to the neighbor directly behind us. Many of them already knew we were with the Lutheran church. Every neighbor expressed their gratitude for our effort to say "hello;" may it reflect well on the name of Christ!

One lady who lives down the road is the grandma of one of Hannah's classmates. She was most hospitable and invited us in. She sent us home with a whole bag of candy and chocolates—saying it is their custom to make sure the gift-giver goes home with more than they came with. Our kids were all smiles.

The neighbor across the street from us is an Indian businessman. His brother happened to be visiting. The brother recognized both of us from coming to his shop downtown. The neighbors that live behind us are Canadian. They were hosting a United States Agency for International Development Christmas party. They also used to live in Zambia and knew Mom Wendland right away. They recognized us from the family picture on her desk at the Health Unit. Love from the friendly neighborhood "Round *Robins*"

Sometimes I wonder why I feel compelled to do certain things. It would have been so much easier to have enjoyed a quiet day at home, rather than preparing gifts and cards and traipsing around our neighborhood. In the end it was worth all the effort; we made some wonderful connections. What were the odds of the backyard neighbors recognizing us from a family photo on a Health Unit desk in Zambia? It's a small world after all!

Sent: December 20, 2007
Subject: mini update
Rebecca writes: As we look back on all the blessings of the past year, we are thankful for the privilege Rob had of helping to build three new churches with offerings and donations from the USA. We are so thankful for the generosity of our brothers and sisters in WELS whose offerings allow projects like these to be completed here.

We are gearing up for Grandpa and Grandma Wendland to join us again for the Christmas holiday. We are certainly blessed to celebrate Christ's birth with them. The special family time is a glimpse of what heaven will be like, with the whole family of believers worshipping our Lord, forever. What a wonderful reason for us to keep spreading that Word to many in Malawi. May your light shine brightly to those you meet in your corner of the world. God bless, Rebecca

For God, who said, "Let light shine out of darkness,"
made his light shine in our hearts
to give us the light of the knowledge of the glory of God
in the face of Christ. 2 Corinthians 4:6

CHAPTER 16

2008: A VISIT; A CALL; A FEVER; A DEATH

I hear the Savior calling! The gospel comes to me.
My eyes once closed in blindness Are opened now to see
That I myself was helpless To live eternally,
But, dying, Christ did save me, And now he calls for me! (CW 560:1)

Christmas 2007 had come and gone, but we were soon to receive one more thrilling gift. South African Airlines was promoting a buy-one-get-one-free special on round-trip tickets from the USA, for trips completed before Easter. My parents decided that the offer was too good to pass up, so they made February travel plans to Malawi. They would be here in one month! What an unexpected blessing!

2008 in Malawi would also stretch us in unforeseen ways. Rob would wrestle with a divine call. He would wrestle with a health crisis. We would wrestle with the usual shortages of grocery items, electricity and water; and with the usual overabundance of pests. There would be more than one death in the course of 2008, but one in particular that resonated with our family. The sudden death of a young United Methodist missionary acquaintance was a reminder that sometimes the Savior calls us to serve on earth; sometimes he calls us Home.

Sent: January 20, 2008
Subject: snail mail
Rebecca writes: Our church is hosting a weekly segment for TV Malawi. Last Sunday, Dad Wendland was the featured speaker. He taped the show during his Christmas stay. Rob is taping for this week's program. Such Christian "anchors" we have in our family.

Caleb's mischief is getting more creative. During Bible Study he took a lady's umbrella and used the hooked end to unlatch the door so he could escape. The other morning when I pointed out a broken wheel on a toy car, he told me, "Superman broke it!" (I marvel at the fact that Jesus was once a little boy, but I marvel even more at the fact that HE NEVER SINNED!)

The kids got a metal swing set as a Christmas present. Ever since, they spend the better part of the day passing the time like a pendulum.

We have had daily rain for three weeks—often several inches each day. The damp conditions create the perfect habitat for huge snails. These snails grow a shell about six inches long and are destroying many plants. I plucked off a dozen baby snails and am hoping the vegetation can make a comeback. Such is life in the tropics. Love, Rebecca

The Giant African land snail is one of the largest species of snail in the world. They are mesmerizing to watch, but they wreak havoc on gardens. These snails eat almost any type of plant in their path; they can cause structural damage to plaster and stucco on homes; and they multiply faster than bunnies, laying over 1,000 eggs a year.

Hannah holding a giant snail

Sent: January 29, 2008
Subject: Humpty Dumpty—wait—the wall fell down
Rob writes: Part of our wall fell down from the saturated ground. All attempts to contact brick-layers have failed. With the daily heavy rains the repairs will have to wait until things dry out.

Last week we accumulated almost 8" of rain. Our January total was 19". Streams have sprung up all over our back terraces. The sidewalks/pavement/steps at our house are getting treacherous because slime is starting to form. It is like living on the bottom of a river. Our rain total for the season is somewhere around 36 inches! I am a fan of the rainy season, but this one seems a little out of control (but not out of **His** control). I have not been to the village churches for over a week, since all my scheduled congregations in the Lower Shire are either blocked or underwater.

Our hens have started laying eggs. Only 220 more eggs to go and they'll have paid for themselves. Love, Rob

It was so wet in early 2008 that we had a semi-permanent stream flowing through our yard. Our terraces and stairways created mini-waterfalls. In theory, we now had several fun, free water features for our yard...never mind that the stairways and walkways were so slippery that they were hazardous to use. The slimy stairways fed into a little stream through our yard, which was soon occupied by frogs and tiny creatures. I was amazed at how quickly an ecosystem could emerge. The kids loved it!

Sent: February 4, 2008
Subject: Whiteriver, AZ
Rob writes: Wow—a shock out of the blue. I received a telephone call from Rev. Dan Rautenberg to inform me that I had been called to be the director of the Apache Christian Training School (ACTS). The call is to further develop and teach prospective pastors in the ACTS program (which is the pastor training program on the Apache Reservation.) It sounds interesting. My head is spinning. If you have any thoughts, I would be grateful. Blessings in Jesus; Rob

A few weeks after Rob received his call, my parents arrived safely in Malawi. The timing of their visit was an extra blessing since we were able to discuss Rob's deliberations with them. We also looked forward to sharing part of Lent with them and celebrating a special birthday milestone with my dad.

Sent: February 21, 2008
Subject: Super 60!
Dad Staude writes from Africa to family back in the USA: It's 2am in Malawi on my birthday and I'm wide awake. Maybe it's jet lag; maybe it's the excitement of a little kid on his birthday. We celebrated yesterday. What a party! Rebecca made a tiered brownie cake, they sang for me, I blew out candles (several times), opened presents, drank delicious cherry-plum soda, and Rob served his great homemade ice cream.

I went with Rob and Spider around town today to get building materials for a village parsonage. People are everywhere! We miss hitting them on the road by ½". We drove from place to place. Either they didn't have what we wanted or it was very expensive. We ended up with creosote for the wooden beams (for termites) and a box of nails. We ordered custom-made corrugated roofing sheets. When they're done we'll deliver them to the bush. I can see why the building projects here run over the cost estimates/limits. I can see why projects can easily be left undone.

Rob is incredible with his language ability and adaptability to the customs here. He's certainly in his element. However, after discussing his call, I can see why they called him to Apache ACTS. Here, a lot of his time is spent doing "general builder contractor" work. In Arizona he might put his theological training to better use. He would be the complete seminary there! He is struggling with this, and I can appreciate why they called him.

Now it's 3am and I should probably try to get some shut-eye (just heard the first rooster). Or I could talk with the night guard—except he can't understand my English. (I can't *versteh* his Chichewa either.) In summary, I am humbled to have Ruth as my good wife and all of you as my wonderful God-given children. God bless you in everything you do. All my love, Dad.

Sent: March 1, 2008
Subject: week two of Staude visit
Rob writes: We enjoyed a wonderful scenic drive around the base of Mt. Mulanje with Mom and Dad Staude. On our homeward drive, the skies opened up. A huge storm is now passing overhead, with massive thunder and lightning. Amazingly, we've kept our electricity today. We lost power both on Tuesday (3am-10am) and Thursday (3am-5pm). We're told thieves are stealing the electrical wires.

Mom and Dad have been given the full Malawi experience this time. Dad went down to the Lower Shire with me, to Chizilo. After the service I was served *nsima* and chicken. Since I had told them that Dad would not be able to eat that meal, they went out and bought him cookies and a coke. He tried some *nsima* on his cookie. (I've never seen it eaten that way—points for ingenuity.) Last week Dad helped me out on my building project trips. We hauled cement, iron sheets and paid salaries. Tomorrow we'll go to Khanyepa to worship together. Love, Rob

Sent: March 7, 2008
Subject: one week to go in Africa
Dad Staude writes from Africa to family back in the USA: Rob left with other missionaries for a conference in Lusaka (about 16 hours on the road, one way). We continue to keep him in our prayers concerning his calls. The timing is difficult since there are many village vacancies. Meanwhile, we're busy doing necessary odds and ends: fixing and changing the oil on the lawn mower, replacing wood-rot boards and sawing down a tree.

It's still the rainy season—every day. Last night Rebecca saw water coming down the kitchen wall right before we left for the Lenten service. She scrambled into the attic to pinpoint the leak so we could fix it—another project.

A big project for Ruth and Rebecca was successfully making cheese. They made a pound of mozzarella, plus ricotta from the whey. It was delicious! Speaking of cooking, Rebecca has really developed into a culinary expert. Considering everything is made from scratch and staples are hard to find, she puts out some fantastic meals. Pineapple every day is nice, too! All the meal preparation is very time-consuming. God bless, Dad

Making mozzarella with Grandma Staude

I had already learned to turn our sour milk into a soft white cheese that could be used as a substitute for cream cheese, sour cream or cottage cheese. While mom was visiting, we made mozzarella together. I was pleasantly surprised to learn that the by-product is ricotta cheese. Since we could not purchase either mozzarella or ricotta in Blantyre at that time, they were a delight to have in the refrigerator, and they inspired some lovely Italian meals.

Sent: March 13, 2008
Subject: they're off
Rob writes: In case you were wondering why you haven't heard from us recently, it is because a tree fell on our telephone line while I was in Zambia. Recalling our Nyambadwe problems, I resigned myself to waiting weeks before we were back up again. But the repair men got us back online again after only a week off.

My missionary meetings in Zambia went well. However, since my return I've felt sick. Sunday night I had chills and woke up with a 103°F fever Monday I was drained, but no fever. Tuesday night I had chills and 103°F fever. Wednesday, drained but no fever. Accompanying the fever is lethargy with stiff shoulders and neck. I used a malaria test kit on Tuesday evening; it was negative. In the past few weeks I've been from Lake Malawi to Lujeri to Lake Kariba, eaten across two countries, and scratched up my legs in beach volleyball.

Mom and Dad are off. We greatly enjoyed our time together. Many events were packed in and memories made. We pray they travel safely home. Back to lying low for me. Love, Rob

My parents' visit was lovely, even though it was a much lower-key visit than their safari-tour in 2004. Much of their time was spent at our home in Blantyre, experiencing daily life. That included cooking from scratch, dealing with downed telephone lines, and growing increasingly concerned about Rob's malaria-like symptoms. We also used the time to talk over Rob's calls, his gifts and where he felt needed for the ministry at large.

Sent: March 14, 2008
Subject: Call to ACTS decision
Rob writes: Dear Loved Ones; I have been led to return my call to serve on the Apache Reservation as ACTS Director and Lead Professor. It has not been easy to weigh these two missionary calls against one another. Thank you so much for your prayers and input! Please spare some prayer time for our brothers and sisters in Apache Land and the vacant ACTS position. Blessings in Jesus, Rob

God had called Rob to the ACTS position in Arizona, but at the same time He was still calling Rob to Malawi. Two calls—two areas in need. It was difficult to evaluate where God might be able to use Rob's talents best, but finally the decision was made. For now God wanted us to remain in Malawi, Africa.

> *I hear the Savior calling! He gives this charge to me:*
> *To serve the best I'm able, What-e'er the call may be.*
> *Thus hand in hand with others Who share the gospel key*
> *We spread the gospel tidings—My Savior calls for me! (CW 560:3)*

Sent: March 15, 2008
Subject: Blantyre bout
Rebecca writes: Greetings. We got 2" of rain yesterday in one hour! It is rumbling now.

The kids are fondly remembering the fun things they did with Grandpa and Grandma. Mom and Dad aren't nearly as much fun—especially since we're under the weather. A doctor informed us that 30% of Blantyre is sick. Rob got a full blood, urine and malaria work-up yesterday. Nothing is glaringly out of place. The bilharzia and typhoid results aren't in yet. God bless, Rebecca

Now that my parents had left and Rob had made the decision to remain in Malawi, life was gradually returning to normal. Sad to say, that normalcy included health struggles!

Sent: March 16, 2008
Subject: illness
Rob writes: My fever came back again last night. It was the worst yet—up to 104°F. I felt okay during the day, apart from fatigue and an incessant headache. I woke up at 11pm with a temp of 103.7°F. I went to Mwaiwathu to see if they might detect malaria during the fever. The malaria result was negative. After I returned home I went to bed, but I woke up at 2:30am with a temp of 104.2°F. I took a cold shower and held ice cubes for an hour and went to bed at a much more comfortable 102.2°F. It could be that the illness is viral and then nothing can be done. What I have brings a recurring fever every other night. Hannah had Pastor Johnston pray for me in church today. Love, Rob

Despite Rob's sickness, he carried on with his normal schedule as best as he could. I kept finding unusual diseases listed in my medical books that resembled his symptoms—but nothing was a perfect match.

Sent: March 17, 2008
Subject: still troubled
Rebecca writes: Steve Lawrenz came over to have a devotion with Rob. Afterward Rob made a trip to the doctor and diagnostic lab again, but neither test showed signs of malaria. If no malaria shows up tomorrow after more testing, then the doctor will assume it is NOT malaria. If the typhoid returns negative on Friday, then it must be viral. It is a bit scary to wait and see what happens, since his fever keeps rising with each cycle.

I consulted the <u>Where There is No Doctor</u> reference book, since it is full of descriptions and pictures of illnesses. It gives helpful info on illnesses (like typhoid), lists the symptoms and suggests possible treatments. I happened to page through the diarrhea section. There were eight pages on diarrhea! Malaria didn't even take up two pages! A fever can be an indicator of several things. However, a **recurring** fever points to malaria even when the testing doesn't. Please keep Rob in your prayers. God bless your Holy Week as the Holy One became weak for sinners' sake. Love, Rebecca

Rob's fevers had been recurring predictably for over a week. Although the lab tests kept indicating that there were no malaria parasites, the more I paged through my medical reference books the more I suspected that Rob's cyclical fever pattern pointed to that dreaded, anopheles-borne infection.

Sent: March 17, 2008
Subject: under the weather
Rob writes: Today the doctor sent me to the Malaria Unit where they look at malaria all day long. He said they will find it if it is there. He told me to get tested between 4pm and sundown (in his opinion that is the best time to catch the malaria in the blood).

The Malaria Test Clinic followed a different lab procedure than my previous blood tests. They put my blood directly on a slide and took it to the lab for examination. After 20 minutes they gave me a note: "malaria ++." Still skeptical, I went to talk to the technician and he claimed, "Yes, positive. I saw it." I called the doctor who responded, "Ha, I knew they would get it." He prescribed the medicine Co-Arinate. I took the first dose immediately to try to interrupt my scheduled fever tonight. Thanks again for all your prayers. Love, Rob

When Rob's malaria test came back positive, my main reaction was relief. Now we knew what the problem was. He could start medication and hopefully be on the road to recovery as soon as possible. I had never seen Rob so sick before; I'm not sure how much longer his body could have coped with those ever-increasing fevers without sustaining long-term damage.

Sent: March 18, 2008
Subject: Holy week/weak
Rebecca writes: It has been quite a week in the health arena here. Yesterday we made it a family outing when Rob went for his malaria test. As we sat in the waiting room, we learned one lady finally got a positive result after three weeks of intermittent testing. I think I know why: mosquitoes were flying all around us as we sat there. So even if you came without malaria, theoretically you could go home with it! I had sprayed everyone ahead of time.

In the waiting room there was a picture wall of the staff. I recognized several "medics" from the Music Society choir, including the head doctor and lab-tech. I went to choir last night and got some helpful information from them. The head doctor even offered to check Rob's slide and find out specifically what type of malaria he has.

We are hopeful that the Co-Arinate will solve Rob's prolonged sickness… but it has not been an overnight answer. Last night the fever returned with a vengeance: his temperature crept over 105°F. He spent a crummy night taking a cold shower and wearing ice packs to try to cool down. Your continued prayers are most appreciated. By Wednesday his meds should be done and hopefully the fever will not return. Normalcy is not appreciated until it has been upset.

The kids are healthy. I hope to dye some of our own eggs for Easter with them. I got four pumpkins from our garden today—in time for Easter Pumpkin pie! Love, Rebecca

A recurring, seriously high fever is a telltale sign of malaria. I was frustrated that all prior tests had not caught it. Rob's doctor felt he should wait to treat anything until a positive reading had been found. It made me sympathize with the early explorers of Africa who were exposed to malaria with no known treatment. It would have been a horrible way to die. Even in our present times, 500 million people worldwide are infected with malaria every year. Two million of them, mostly children, die from it. There are four known types of malaria parasites that infect humans in Africa. They all cause similar symptoms: fever, headache, chills and vomiting. Severe malaria can lead to kidney failure, hemorrhage, jaundice or even a coma. The most lethal strain often leads to death if not treated within 24 hours.

Sent: March 20, 2008
Subject: fever gone
Rob writes: After 10 days I've finally made it longer than 12 hours with my temperature staying under 100°F. Last night I did miss my appointment with the malaria bugs. Thanks for all the prayers. I thank the Lord for His mercies which are new every morning! Even though the parasites seem to be gone, I still have a road of recovery to walk after those grueling fevers. I am still "weak and weary."

Thanks again for the support from afar! May you have wonderful Easter with the Lord. How awesome is God's mercy and grace that though we are so rebellious, yet for the sake of His own Son we are His children. *Chikondi chodabwitsatu!* (Amazing grace indeed!) Love, Rob

Thank you, Lord, for modern medicine and for Rob's health recovery. It was one more reason to praise our amazing God at Easter time.

Sent: March 28, 2008
Subject: Easter Retreat
Rob writes: I did make it out to my congregations for Easter worship. Our family also made it to the Easter Missionary Retreat, where I presented on the topic of Third Culture Kids (TCK). At first, I wasn't sure I'd be up to it. I had been working on it during my illness and as much as I could in between some hefty power outages.

For my presentation I talked about my experiences, gave a summary from the TCK book, and then finished with the "solid foundation," which is what floated me through and kept me sane during my cultural adjustment to the USA—our wonderful victory in Christ. The first passage page included a progression from the Cross, through the grave and into our hope in Christ. I asked the group to find *zinthu zodabwitsa*, (amazingly wonderful things) in each of those passages (Ro 8:28-39, 1 Cor 15:17-21, Matt 11:28-30, 1 John 3:1-2, Heb 11:13-16, Phil 1:20-26, Eph 2:19-22 and Rev 7:13-17). The second Bible passage page included a small study in weariness (a different word translated as "weary" in every passage—figure out what aspect of tiredness is being talked about). We also looked at passages about hope and strength in the Lord (Is 40:28-31, Is 50:4-5 and Ps 119:27-28) and others about encouragement to walk and talk in that strength (Heb 12:1-3, Jer 20:9 and Rev 2:3). My presentation went well. Several families have kids around high school age. I hope the Lord is able to bless some through my presentation; it was the tip of the iceberg.

The venue was Senga Bay by Lake Malawi. We enjoyed Bible Studies, VBS, presentations, missionary "Olympic Games," great fellowship, encouragement and a special closing communion service. Every family wrote a new verse for a hymn or prayer and used it as part of our closing devotion. Our family wrote a new verse for "Now the Light Has Gone Away":

> *"Jesus send us on our way, Safely traveling all the day,*
> *As your people worship true, May we give our hearts to you."*

I had worried about getting run down, but thankfully the opposite happened: from Wednesday on I felt better and better. Blessings in Jesus, Rob

We were so thankful that Rob had recovered. To prevent any further health issues, I had taken lots of mosquito spray and 20 liters of our own boiled and filtered water for our family. I was astonished that in three days we nearly drank all of it. Our family returned home safely after being spiritually—and physically—refreshed.

Sent: March 31, 2008
Subject: stuck in the mud
Rebecca writes: Rob's bush work has been slower the last few months due to much rain. The wet conditions make it hard for him to reach the rural congregations. Last month he tried to reach Tcheleni church. He traveled 3 hours on rain-soaked roads and was within 1 mile of his destination when he realized the mud was getting thick. It was almost up to his truck doors. As he attempted

to turn around, the truck was sucked even deeper into the mud. It took 20 men and 2 hours to go about 10 feet. They literally lifted his truck up and turned it around. Thankfully, Rob was freed from the muck, but unfortunately he had to return home without conducting the service.

The LWMS-sponsored building project for the Khanyepa parsonage in Chiradzulu is scheduled to be completed this March/April. Despite the rains and cement shortage, supplies are in stock again and it is near completion. God bless, Rebecca

Rob's farthest congregations in the Lower Shire are in an area called the Elephant Marsh. His recent "truck stop" in the area gave validity to that name.

Sent: April 4, 2008
Subject: cookie contest
Rebecca writes: Rob has been busy running errands. He also got a call for help from a national pastor. Rob immediately took him to the hospital. They discovered he has an enlarged heart.

Hannah started her first piano lesson this week. She also has been enjoying a nice week off of school for the second term break.

Yesterday I stirred up some cookie dough for a *Taste of Home* cookie contest. I saw the contest ad in their recent magazine (which actually came on time, before the contest entry deadline) and I want to enter it. God's blessings, Rebecca

Sent: April 9, 2008
Subject: Malawi blog
Rebecca writes: Now and then I send in my updates to the WELS World Missions for the website or for Malawi PR in general. Nikky, the missions promotions lady, recently posted my blog article from our Easter Retreat. God bless, Rebecca

Rob and I had suddenly become the blogging couple. Rob submitted the following blog with condensed information from his Third Culture Kid (TCK) presentation at the Easter Retreat.

A TCK Thinks of Home

Have you ever had the disheartening feeling that even though you are surrounded by people, you are very much alone? It is a feeling that I felt most acutely in the fall of 1986, when I left "home" (Zambia) for high school. As a child and grandchild of WELS foreign missionaries I was born and had spent the vast majority of my life in Zambia, Africa. When my parents gave me the option of going to high school in the States, I was excited about the opportunity. I considered myself an American, had done some studies on U.S. government and culture, had relatives who all lived in the U.S., and had really enjoyed our family furloughs there. I thought I was prepared for life back "home" in the United States. I was wrong.

Years later I would find out that there is a special classification for people like me: a TCK, or Third Culture Kid. One definition of a Third Culture Kid is "a person who has spent a significant part of his or her developmental years outside the culture of his/her passport country. The TCK builds relationships to many cultures, while not having full ownership of any."

But in '86 I knew none of that. I figured that there would be some adjustment—hey, I was living away from "home" for the first time—but little did I know. It soon became apparent. While I looked like an American at first glance, my clothes (and how I wore them) certainly were not the fashions of the mid '80's—and the soles of my shoes froze hard outside at the first sign of winter! Though I spoke English, my accent wasn't quite right. While my classmates were all excited about the fall sports and using vocabulary like "JV" or "Varsity," I had no idea what they were talking about—I didn't even know how to hold an American football, much less how to throw one or play the game. In class I found that my education didn't quite line up: in some subjects I was ahead, in others I was behind. I was finding that my whole culture was completely different than that of my schoolmates. We had different ideas on what makes a joke funny, what things to talk about at school, what language to use (at my public school in Zambia, swear and curse words were few and far between; not so at this Christian school), what is good music, what are popular trends, and on and on. After the curiosity of being the "kid from Africa" wore off, it was hard for me to be seen at all. I was different and didn't fit in; I didn't even know how to start. Alone but surrounded by people.

It took a few months, but soon the temptation was very great to give up and go back to what now felt like "home"—Zambia. However, I couldn't get a ticket any earlier than the one I already had for Christmas, so I stuck it out. Thanks be to God that my parents had laid the foundation in Christ while I was with them. There were so many times during my adjustment to the USA that I ran to the refuge of the Word, so many hours walking alone, crying out to Him in prayer…and hearing His gentle whisper through His Word. "I am with you always, you are never alone. Rob, I already loved you so much that I died for you. If I loved you like this, could I ever leave you or abandon you? Bring your heavy burdens to me and let them be gone. Let me wash you in forgiveness daily and remind you that you are my child for whom I've got a plan and a purpose; let me lift you up and give you the strength to carry on. Oh yeah, and **heaven** is your home. So set your heart there."

Looking back I see how marvelously the Savior drew me close during those years. In fact, my experiences in 1986 played a great part in leading me into the ministry. In a world lost and dying, hurting and confused, what better thing could I do with my life than to tell others of the peace, hope, forgiveness, eternal life of Jesus the Messiah? In Christ we are never lost or alone…forever. The Lord strengthened my faith, but he also blessed me in other ways. He helped me adjust, gave me friends to help with North American culture, allowed me to enjoy greatly twelve years in our pastor training system, and gave me a call to serve His grace. God is good indeed!

Getting acclimated to a different culture may seem like a minor inconvenience; something to check off the "To-Do" list once you arrive in a new place. It is not that simple. In fact, sometimes it takes years, decades, or even a lifetime to sort through some of the issues and adjustments that accompany learning to live in multiple cultures. It is easier for some and harder for others. The longer our family lives in Malawi, the closer our children come to wrestling with this cultural transition—and the deeper the impact will be on them. As parents, we can't always protect our children, but we can do our best to prepare them. One way to prepare them is to lay a foundation of faith. That faith will assure them of the Lord's invitation to carry all their burdens to him in prayer. That faith will equip them to bloom where they are planted, no matter how many times they might be uprooted. Thanks be to God for His love that transcends all cultures, barriers and baggage!

Sent: April 22, 2008
Subject: Tidbits from Blantyre
Rebecca writes: Here are some recent tidbits. Monday we learned that our gardener's wife gave birth to her 9th child (all living). Our gardener went back to the village for the week. He took his wife some cotton balls and an umbrella as a gift.

Last week our house worker called. She reported that she was in the hospital and she didn't know why. When she returned this week, she told us that she'd had cerebral malaria. Apparently, on her way to work last week her heart started racing, her ears started ringing, and then she blacked out. Someone found her, knew who she was and took her by minibus back to her village. From there she was taken to the Lunzu hospital. They did some tests, discovered the malaria and treated her. She could have died.

I went to Shoprite the other day and there was absolutely no butter, salt or yogurt to be had. OK, yogurt is sort of a specialty item—but butter and salt? That is our best shop in town! Thankfully, my pantry can hold me through many of these frequent shortages.

Our water went out. It was a bad day to make chili. The only water around was what I could drain from the garden hose and five liters that remained in our water filter. So, with that we washed up, boiled the various beans, made soup and rinsed out all the chili bowls and pot. It was a bad day for the kids to play in the sand box. They should have bathed. Instead they got about a quart of water and a bar of soap to get clean.

Some kidbits: Nathanael was doing school work, and one problem asked which animal doesn't eat meat. Nathanael answered correctly—the elephant. Then he asked me, "Is it because they are Muslim?"

Hannah enjoys writing. This is a special poem she composed:

"Dear Grandpa and Grandma,

I hope everything's fine in America. Is it snowing? Nathanael is praying for you and so am I. Here is a poem I wrote for you:

Still Wishing

Still wishing through winter, spring, summer, fall
That you could come to Africa
But not to go to the mall
Sill wishing every day
From dawn till night
But still in bed I lay
STILL WISHING
LOVE, Hannah Margaret Wendland"

God's blessings from our family to yours, Rebecca

Eight-year-old Hannah's poem was a poignant reminder that we are constantly separated from dear family. We think of them often and miss them daily. We have every reason to keep wishing to see them here and now, but we also have the solid confidence that an eternity of togetherness awaits us because of our bond in Christ.

Sent: April 24, 2008
Subject: Hear ye, hear ye…
Rob writes: Dear one and all; no, we're not announcing *that*…but we do have a new addition. Rebecca now has her own email account! Her computer is now online and she can be reached at her new email address. Blessings in Jesus, Rob

This was huge! I no longer needed to sit in Rob's office chair in order to correspondence. That might not seem like a big deal, but when working around power outages, nap schedules, cooking obligations, school runs and Rob's computer usage, my personal computer time was very limited. Our internet was also upgraded from dial-up to broadband. Now I could maximize my time and know that when I had a spare moment, my computer chair would be waiting.

Sent: April 27, 2008
Subject: "Son"day
Rebecca writes: This Sunday Hannah had a 103.5°F temperature. Rob stayed home with her until the boys and I returned from church; then he went to his congregations. On the way home we saw a minibus literally wrapped around a light pole. The bus was vacated but it was a sickening sight, with glass everywhere.

Hannah was talking in a British accent at the table the other day. Nathanael tried but couldn't copy her. He sighed, "My English isn't working!" Love, Rebecca

I got a sinking feeling each time the kids were feverish, especially after Rob's serious bout of malaria in March. We kept a close eye on the little girl and were relieved when her fever later subsided with no further malaria symptoms.

The sight of the mangled bus was sickening. The thought of the people inside reminded us to continue to pray for the safety of those around us—especially those who must entrust their lives to minibus drivers.

> *I hear the Savior calling! His call has urgency!*
> *Each moment souls are dying; Soon comes eternity.*
> *And so, my precious Savior, This is my humble plea;*
> *Prepare me for my mission For you are calling me! (CW 560:5)*

Sent: May 2, 2008
Subject: prayers
Rebecca writes: Hello—just a prayer request for a safe night here at Kabula Hill. A few minutes ago our alarm went off—thieves have smashed down part of our temporary wall (where the brick wall had fallen during the heavy rains). Rob is gone!

This is one unanticipated but MAJOR BLESSING of having had my own email account installed last week. Now I can use my computer AND have Rob's office locked up. The breach in the wall is mere meters away from his office door. Love, Rebecca

> *Abide with me; fast falls the eventide.*
> *The darkness deepens; Lord, with me abide.*
> *When other helpers fail and comforts flee,*
> *Help of the helpless, oh, abide with me! (CW 588:1)*

Sent: May 3, 2008
Subject: safe in the night
Rebecca writes: Thanks for all the prayers. We had a quiet and uneventful night after the alarm went off. The guard told me a section of the bamboo grove on the neighbor's property had been recently cleared away. Now a path is leading straight to the hole in our wall. However, the Lord kept us safe. I managed to sleep great until midnight; after that, every little sound interrupted my sleep until morning. Rob returned this afternoon.

Today I was one angel-wing away from hitting a man with my car. The man was hunched over next to the road. I thought he was tying his shoe. By the time he stood upright, I realized he was drunk. It was almost too late. He lurched into my lane as I approached. I knew if I veered to the other shoulder, I would most likely hit another pedestrian or 20. Everyone on the sides of the road watched in disbelief as he weaved uncontrollably across the road. Time to hit the hay. God bless, Love, Rebecca

There was no dismissing the knowledge that thieves were scouting our residence. My head struggled to give the complete burden of that information over to the Lord in prayer. In Rob's absence I kept rehashing plans to deal with every possible scenario. I kept thinking that *I must do something more* to ensure our safety. It was truly a challenge to leave what was outside my control in the hands of our capable, omniscient, almighty God. It helped me to picture God sitting on His throne in heaven and leaning over for a bird's-eye view (like Google Earth) of the thieves and their location. He could also see our guard at his post (hopefully awake), us in our rooms, Rob at his out-of-town meeting and even the angels that He had assigned to each of us. I know it is a fanciful visualization of how God operates, but it put everything in perspective for me. His promise in Psalm 91 was also a tangible reminder and comfort. Then I could sleep.

> *"For he will command his angels concerning you*
> *to guard you in all your ways." Psalm 91:11*

Sent: May 23, 2008
Subject: one-night-sit
Rebecca writes: Autumn is in the air! Temps are dipping down to 50 degrees at night.

The fallen wall on our property is finally fixed. Before the builders left, they commented that Nathanael has the makings of a pastor. He was very friendly with the workers, watching and interacting with them.

Rob is recovering from a second malaria bout; the doctor thought it was a relapse of his first infection. The three-day meds have done their job, and he is feeling better.

Thursday we had repairmen in for our water system. They replaced three major parts and it is STILL not right. So we play games with the water and have repairmen around again. We've also had no electricity in the bedrooms and no outdoor security lights since last week. Our circuit-breaker switch won't flip back on. The electricians came but could not find the problem.

Yesterday I heard the buzz of approaching bees and told the kids to go in the house quickly. Suddenly, African bees were swarming in our yard by the thousands. They eventually made an evening nest (conglomeration) high up in the tree next to our picnic table. I got some pictures and footage. I was a bit nervous that they were scouting out a permanent dwelling. I hoped this was merely a "one-night-sit." They were still there after lunch today. Then all of a sudden the kids ran in, claiming that the bees didn't like Caleb's loud shouting. Sure enough, the bees were gone. I can still hear them buzzing in the area but not on our property.

Sending our love from this land—where the temps are getting cooler but one can still pick a vase full of roses and calla lilies. Rebecca

Cluster of bees in tree

The sound of thousands of African bees buzzing in the distance was unmistakable and unforgettable—especially since I had experienced it up close and personal a few years before. They were amazing to watch…but only from a distance. This time the bees were not interested in making a home in our home. Instead they created a ball around their queen as they rested in our tree. The next day they sojourned on…just "bee"cause.

Sent: June 23, 2008
Subject: EIEIO
Rebecca writes: The title stands for Ebony-Ivory-Ebony-Ivory-Over! What a demanding last few weeks it has been. Much of my time was spent learning to play accompaniments for the British music exams at the high school. About a dozen violin students had requested my piano assistance. Each student had three pieces for me to learn for duets. I had been practicing with each student weekly for the last month. Despite the large time commitment I met some neat people, and I was glad my musical abilities were helpful.

Saturday we drove to the Lower Shire to Nyala Park for a home-schooling outing. We learned there are about 30 pythons in the park. The animals in the park love to eat the tops of the sugar cane that are discarded by the sugar plant. The park trades and sells their Nyala, since the antelope are a unique variety found only in the park. We toured the park on foot to admire the giraffe up close, and enjoyed a picnic while watching the wildlife.

Hannah played during the church offering on Sunday and did a very nice job. Love, Rebecca

For the past year we had been active in a local home-schooling group, since I was home-schooling Nathanael. The group organized fieldtrips so that the children could interact with each other on a monthly basis. On our outing to Nyala Park we also interacted with the local wildlife!

I was also keeping active in the WELS Malawi mission public relations. I kept our field information current, kept the pictures of the missionaries up-to-date and posted blogs. One article that I wrote for the Malawi website was about "going green."

Going Green – Malawi Style

"Going green" and being environmentally friendly is a topic on many people's minds lately. Here in Malawi, Africa, "going green" is a way of life. Generally, Malawians do not have many material possessions. When they do acquire something, the product serves its intended use as long as possible. The person then finds alternate uses for it, and the item is discarded only after it has genuinely worn out.

Here are a few examples of Malawian resourcefulness:

Plastic bags: these are cut into strips and crocheted into handbags; stretched over wire to make a toy kite or decorative flowers; woven into doormats; gathered and rolled into a ball for a child's toy.

Broken glass bottles: these are cut in half, sanded down and used for drinking cups.

Rubber tires and inner tubes: these are cut into thin strips and used as strapping to secure loads on bikes and minibuses, or to secure bamboo fences; cut into chunks and wired together to make doormats; used for slingshots; fashioned into sandals.

Soft drink bottle tops: these are strung together with wire to make musical instruments to shake or strike; fashioned into earrings, toys, baskets and wall decorations using wire.

Tin cans: these are pounded out to make cooking pots or pans; used for bug-proof food storage.

Scraps of wire: these are used for assorted musical instruments; made into children's toys, such as a wire "*galimoto*" car, motorcycle or gecko; strung with beads and woven into baskets; used to make beaded flip-flop thongs.

Reusing products here in Malawi is a way to prolong their usefulness. Disposable cups, plates and silverware are rarely tossed. Disposable communion cups are cleaned and used indefinitely. A worn out farm implement can make a serviceable church gong…one might even see an old trailer hitch being used to strike it. A pair of safety pins can serve as a shiny set of earrings. Plastic strapping is turned into a durable all-weather basket. An old truck bed may become the new ox cart someone has been waiting for.

As I write this, I realize how blessed we are. Our family isn't wanting for anything. In fact, we have never even had to *wait* for anything we truly needed. Malawians' adeptness at recycling makes me think of God's Word and the reason we are here as missionaries in Africa. Isaiah 55:11 says, *"So is my word that goes out from my mouth: it will not return to me empty but will accomplish what I desire and achieve the purpose for which I sent it."* God's Word is one product we will want to use, reuse and recycle again and again for the benefit of all who hear it!

"Going green" is in vogue in North America, but the "reduce, reuse, recycle" mantra is really a non-issue here in Malawi. Most nationals follow a green lifestyle out of necessity—not because of their environmental awareness but because of their limited resources. However, there are certainly ways the Malawian lifestyle could be greener. In the cities there is no penalty for littering and very few public waste-receptacles. If someone is finished with a wrapper, bag or banana peel, they toss it in the street. In time, the wind might blow it away or a city worker might sweep it up. Local streams are dotted with slowly decaying plastic bags of all colors, and the streets are often lined with debris. That is life in Blantyre city.

Sent: August 21, 2008
Subject: just one flea
Rebecca writes: It seems we've encountered yet another annoying pest. Our chickens have been such a blessing, but we have discovered that they are harboring

something called a sticktight flea. This pest is very similar to a regular flea, but once it bites it stays attached to the host for 2-3 weeks. It is often transmitted by rats—oh goody. I contacted the poultry farm owner and he recommended a pesticide. He also suggested that we rub oil around the areas where the fleas attach, to suffocate them. Like mosquitoes, this flea is partial to certain people. This has been one more thing to make my skin crawl! I now stay away from the chicken coop and pray the treatments take care of these fleas SOON! Love, Rebecca

If I were given a choice to pick one pest over another, I don't even know if I could do it. I certainly didn't want the tarantulas, but I'd also had enough of those minute fleas. Of course, I *didn't* have a choice: from big to small it seemed we had them all! Variety is the spice of life—and right now my life was EXTRA SPICY! I guess our moderate weather has that price tag attached. We do not have a ground-freeze, so a variety of pests can keep on "pesting" all year long. I am thankful that these pests are a temporary earthly nuisance and that someday my heavenly mansion will be bug-free (or, if there are bugs, they will not bother me). As for the rats that may have transmitted the fleas…well, eventually they would show up too. That's Malawi's way!

Sent: August 22, 2008
Subject: ministry update
Rebecca writes: Our "winter" temperatures have dropped to mid-40°F at night. Without indoor insulation or heating that feels quite chilly. Recently the kids got out the few hats and mittens that we own and happily ran around the yard—wondering if it would snow.

Rob continues to serve 12 congregations. He was recently assigned a vicar to help out with his large congregation, Khanyepa, in Chiradzulu. As Chairman of the Board of Control, Rob had the privilege of attending the recent June graduation from the Lutheran Bible Institute in Lilongwe. There were 13 graduates. They will now spend a year in the field as vicars, gaining firsthand experience and learning congregational work. There are many vacancies. It is great that more men are in the process of becoming pastors to help fill the needs in the congregations. Please keep the pastor training program in your prayers as the next generation is equipped to become shepherds and church leaders.

It is our dry winter season here, so the rains have not been a factor in Rob's travels to the village churches. However, now that the rains have stopped so have the crops. In the Lower Shire Valley area one church member went fishing for food. Sadly, that member, Mr. Dixon Clemence, became the target of a hungry crocodile. In an instant, the crocodile lunged out of the water and clamped down on his thigh. Other villagers beat the crocodile so that it released him. They were all relieved when the creature retreated into the water. But the damage was done. The bite was substantial, and it claimed Mr. Clemence's life within a few minutes. The church is mourning the loss of a faithful member and lay leader. Yet amid the sadness it is joyful to know that he hungers no more. John 6:27 says, *"Do not work for food that spoils, but for food that endures to eternal life, which the Son of Man will give you."* Mr. Clemence's quest for perishable food has ended, but because he had the spiritual and enduring food of faith and forgiveness, he now rejoices with his Savior Jesus in heaven.

In July our family traveled to Zambia to visit Rob's parents in Lusaka. It is about a 16-hour trip one way, over some very crummy roads. We decided to drive straight through. When we reached the capital city of Lilongwe at about 8am, we discovered that there was no diesel fuel anywhere. After stopping at four gas stations to no avail, we wondered how to proceed. People were commenting about the lack of diesel in the whole city. A few minutes later, Rob spotted a fuel tanker truck pulling into another station. He pulled in behind it. Amazingly, it was coming to unload a tank of diesel. Three hours later, we had a full tank and could proceed to the border. Thankfully, we had no trouble for the remainder of the trip and enjoyed the time spent with Grandpa and Grandma Wendland. In Lusaka we were able to go to a local zoo, a reptile farm, shop and enjoy big city life…including a pizza delivery dinner. The delivery man arrived two hours late. Apparently a tire had blown out on his bike, so the pizzas needed to be scraped off the top of the boxes. No discount, refund or raised eyebrows. Simply scrape the food off the box and reheat the pizzas. That is life in Africa!

As our Malawi weather cools, I find myself reminiscing about a North American fall season. The changing leaves, the pumpkins, hot apple cider, hay rides and Indian corn all come to mind. Despite the seasonal differences we experience here on the other side of the world, it is a comfort to know that we have something that will never change: the Word of our Lord. Isaiah 40:6-8 declares, *"Men are like grass, and all their glory is like the flowers of the field… The grass withers and the flowers fall, but the word of our God stands forever."* May we together share the Word of our unchanging God to the ends of the earth. God bless, Rebecca

Python pillars at reptile farm

My heart went out to the family of the fisherman taken by the crocodile. The death of Mr. Clemence was also a blow to the church in the valley. It can be hard to trust that God's timing is best when it seems to us that it would have been better to allow that faithful church elder to continue serving here on earth. But what can we know about what is best for anyone in the grand scheme of things? Thanks be to God that He *does* know and upholds everything in His hands.

> "If we live, we live to the Lord; and if we die, we die to the Lord.
> So, whether we live or die, we belong to the Lord.
> For this very reason, Christ died and returned to life
> so that he might be the Lord of both the dead and the living." Romans 14:8-9

Sent: August 26, 2008
Subject: land line living
Rebecca writes: Last week our land line was out because wires had been tampered with. Rob saw repairmen welding the underground access covers shut. I think it will mean fewer wires being stolen. (On the other hand, it will take them extraordinarily longer to make future repairs.)

We welcomed in some warmer weather by taking a hike at Michiru. Hannah ran ahead of us for a while, until a monkey scared her and she let out a shriek.

I'm happy to say that our outdoor security lights are now fixed. It is reassuring to have the light shining into the darkness! God bless, Rebecca

What a sense of security a mere light can be. How much more so our Lord who came to be our eternal light!

> *"In him was life, and that life was the light of men.*
> *The light shines in the darkness,*
> *but the darkness has not understood it." John 1:4-5*

Sent: September 5, 2008
Subject: school daze
Rebecca writes: It is the first week of school. Hannah enjoyed her first French class. She and Rob counted in French at lunch. As we ate, Nathanael announced, "Every day 'til Judgment Day I can't stop thinking about chicken!"

Rob returned after two flat tires again on Tuesday. He only carries one spare tire on his truck, so mathematically that was not good. His second flat happened within walking distance of a side-of-the-road bicycle repair stop. He made it back okay, but much later than usual. One tire was totally blown out. As a result he got a new set of tires for the upcoming rainy season.

We think of you often (in addition to chicken) and pray you are well. Love, Rebecca

Having kids in school added a whole new dynamic to life. What the kids learned, how the classrooms were run, the accents they brought home and the stories they told were all educational. Our lunch-time discussions had now become a special time to reconnect as a family with American accents, Midwest roots and a Lutheran heritage.

Sent: September 9, 2008
Subject: license to drive
Rebecca writes: The government declared ALL Malawi driver's licenses invalid at the end of 2008, whether it is time to renew them or not. Yippee. My experience in the transportation building is my worst memory from our first year. It should be better having Rob along to secure our personal space in the half-dozen or more unorganized lines.

'Tis the season for tomatoes again. Rob came home with a generous bunch of produce from Khanyepa on Sunday. Construction on the parsonage there is almost finished. Rob took his tools to help drill holes and fix up some unfinished details. He says their new vicar is doing a great job. After sharing some produce with the vicar, Rob still brought home a bushel of tomatoes, several-dozen eggplants, onions, an unidentified green vegetable, cabbages and two bags of prickly greens. Many of the tomatoes had been squished or split. Rob helped me process one stock pot of sauce and one of salsa that evening after the kids went to bed. Love, Rebecca

Renewing my driver's license with Rob was manageable but still chaotic. People get so tired of disorganized lines that they try to maintain their own order. We could hear people clarifying, "I'm two in back of the white guy," or threatening, "I will beat you up if you skip in line." Needless to say, the lack of method and poor signage "drive me crazy" on a good day.

I am ever so grateful for my teacher colleague, Doris Koeller, who years ago brought a jar of salsa as a welcome gift to our home in Milwaukee. Her salsa is legendary. Doris not only shared her salsa and recipe, but she also invited me and fellow teacher, Amy Buege, to join her for a day in her farm kitchen in Jackson, WI. There she gathered her home-grown produce and showed us how to make and can salsa. The ingredients for salsa are plentiful in Malawi. It has become a family favorite and a requested item for social functions. When Rob brought home bags of tomatoes I did not regret the time that would be required in the kitchen; instead I had visions of salsa to share and fond memories of days gone by!

Sent: September 14, 2008
Subject: share around the neighborhood
Rebecca writes: Yesterday I made fortune cookies with religious messages inside for several new neighbors. They were successful, so I made extra for a Bible Group treat.

Beautiful Saviour is having a meeting today to call a national pastor to work with Rev. Johnston.

Recent kidbits: Nathanael told me, "I am going to exercise now, but I will sweat later." Hannah wondered how bats go to the bathroom when they are resting, since they rest upside down. (Do we "guano" know?)

I finally tried to hook up our webcam and look into Skype. Let me know if it could work on your end. Love from Kabula Hill, Rebecca

I have fond memories of my mom spending special time with my brother and me in the kitchen. Once she made fortune cookies with us. Now that it is my turn to head up the kitchen projects, I figured fortune cookies with Bible passages and friendly messages inserted would not only be a fun treat, but also a way to let our light shine around the neighborhood.

In spite of being far away, we valiantly tried to keep up with the times as we connected with our loved ones around the world. Happily, the webcam and Skype worked pretty well in spite of our slower internet speed. It was surreal to see our family members sitting in their homes across the ocean and just as surreal that they could see us back.

Sent: September 17, 2008
Subject: Kabula action
Rebecca writes: This morning at about 8am there was some action down the road from us. I heard what sounded like stadium cheering, lots of firecrackers and then a siren. I wondered what was happening. Evidently two brothers were fighting over a property barrier. One brother got mad and killed the other one. Then the family of the murdered man started throwing stones. They were stoning cars that were going by. Then the police came and started shooting off a gun. It seems there is always something to write about here. Love, Rebecca

> *Swift to its close ebbs out life's little day;*
> *Earth's joys grow dim; its glories pass away.*
> *Change and decay in all around I see;*
> *O thou who changest not, abide with me! (CW 588:2)*

Sent: September 23, 2008
Subject: update from Kabula
Rebecca writes: Health-wise we have been struggling again. Rob is still a question mark. Last night he woke with a fever of 102°F. We pray it is NOT malaria related.

The kids and I watched a few online church services. That takes some getting used to: we would listen for a few seconds, wait for more to download, listen to the next few seconds, wait… One positive side to that method is that during the pauses I could interact with the kids and make sure they were getting it. We got to see Uncle Aaron preach, which was a nice bonus.

Nathanael asked me the other day, "Why can't I run faster than a rat?" I asked him how he **knew** he couldn't. He replied, "Oh. Yeah. Can you get one so we can race?" (The answer was no.)

Recently I burned my finger while cooking. The burn was bad enough that I tried a remedy with a comfrey plant. I took a dried leaf, pounded it into a pulp, added burn cream, pasted it on my burn and put a band aid over all of it. At first the paste didn't do much for my pain, but by the next day I had forgotten all about it. I glanced at my hand, saw a faint red mark and realized—that was all that remained of my burn! I'll keep some dried leaves "on hand" from now on. Love, Rebecca

Apparently, comfrey has been used for centuries as a topical treatment for many ailments, including burns, scrapes, bites, bruises, sprains and arthritis. It is amazing to go outside and find a burn salve, cooking herbs or a beautiful flower arrangement without visiting a pharmacy, spice rack or floral shop!

Sent: October 1, 2008
Subject: undiagnosed fatalities
Rob writes: Thanks, Mom, for the recent medical heads-up and article:

A fourth person with viral hemorrhagic fever symptoms has died. The virus has already claimed the lives of three people at a clinic in Johannesburg.

I was thinking about hemorrhagic fever on Sunday. I conducted my regular services at Khanyepa and then had a funeral at Balala. When we got to the funeral the elders were saying, "Short service; the body is not in good condition and there's blood coming out all over." The man had died the day before, but that's the worst condition I've seen a corpse in after such a short time. It has been in the mid 90°s, and the man was not in good health even when he was alive, so maybe that all contributed to a quick onset of decay. The family had to use a *chitenje* to tie the coffin lid on because he was starting to bloat. As they brought the coffin outside of his house for the service, blood was dripping from it and you could smell the decay. I was asked to transport the coffin to the grave site. There were drops of blood left in my truck after the coffin was taken out. According to tradition here, the man's clothes and the mat he was lying on while sick and dying were placed on top of his coffin after it was put in the ground. His clothes and mat had dark blood stains all over. After the services I saw that someone had taken sand and scrubbed the bed of my truck "clean."

Anyway, it was probably a combination of an old man being in poor health and the high temps—but I did think of Ebola as I observed the loss of blood. I can see how a disease like that could spread like wildfire here. The whole village gathers around the deceased's house right after death and keeps a 1-2 day vigil. People stream in and out to see the body. The deceased's clothes and possessions are divided among the people (around 1000 at this funeral) and the ladies of the church kneel around the body and the coffin while singing hymns. Love, Rob

Hearing about the member's death and profuse bleeding was creepy. Coupled with the recent hemorrhagic fever news, I was on alert. We disinfected as much as possible. The rest was in the Lord's hands. Thankfully there were no further reports of similar symptoms.

Come not in terrors, as the King of kings,
But kind and good, with healing in thy wings,
Tears for all woes, a heart for ev'ry plea;
Come, Friend of sinners, thus abide with me. (CW 588:3)

INCOMING EMAIL: October 2, 2008
Subject: thanks for the update
Lenka writes: Hi Rebecca. Thanks for the great update again. One day you will have to write a book from a missionary wife's point of view. I think people would find all your stories totally fascinating. Love, Lenka

My sister-in-law, Lenka, wasn't the first to encourage me to put my emails into book format. Someday, I figured—when I had more spare time—I could seriously consider writing a book. For now, I was writing updates merely to keep my family informed. I considered myself fully "booked" with the business of raising kids. Another year would pass before I was convinced that a book was something I could tackle. Looking back, it was probably best that I didn't have a public book in mind while I was sending private emails, or I might have been more selective with what I wrote, or left out the ugly highlights. Instead I continued to honestly and openly record my impressions on the good, the bad and the ugly of life in Malawi.

And, as it turned out, I wasn't *fully* booked with kids…there was room for another one!

Sent: October 20, 2008
Subject: family update
Rebecca writes: We've had a few sporadic rains, but nothing substantial since last February. People are preparing to plant. Food is running short since the last harvest was months ago, and we are again in "the hungry time."

We are happy to announce that a little Wendland #4 is on the way. I am currently struggling with heavy morning sickness, so things have slowed down accordingly. Our three kids are excited. I'll be excited once I start to feel better. God bless, Rebecca

It had been such a blessing to be healthy for much of the past year. Now I would have to wait an extra few months to feel good again, since morning sickness had struck with full force. It would take all my effort to stay on top of things at home; even emailing wasn't such a priority for a while.

Meanwhile, Missionary Steve Lawrenz had been accompanying Rob on various bush trips. He forwarded the following email about a trip he and Rob took to Katunga.

INCOMING EMAIL: November 17, 2008
Subject: South to the Lower Shire Valley
Missionary Lawrenz writes: There is only one missionary in Malawi who still serves as an official pastor of congregations. He is Rev. Robert Wendland, the

son of Rev. Ernst R. Wendland of Zambia and grandson of famous pioneer, Zambia missionary and Seminary Professor, Rev. Ernst H. Wendland. Among other places, Rob serves the Lower Shire (SHEE-ray), the most southern part of Malawi where it is beastly hot.

Recently I went with Rob to his most distant congregation in the Lower Shire: Katunga. I observed. Rob speaks Chewa incredibly well for being in Malawi only five years. Rob speaks a clear, fluent and grammatically correct Malawi Chewa.

After Rob preached, a layman, Mr. Spider Chinyanga (chee-NYAH-ngah), preached a sermon also. At one point Mr. Chinyanga needed to explain Goliath's size, so he pointed to me. Malawians are small people and I am, well, large. After the service, the children were interested in me, so I put little bits of duct tape on their foreheads. None removed the tape; they wore it like a crown.

The members had a harvest offering for our Malawi Synod. Rob received many bags of sweet potatoes and even a guinea fowl. I enjoyed the experience.
Love, Steve

Missionary Steve Lawrenz is known to draw crosses on the kids' hands and use this as a visual springboard to teach them what the symbol means. Malawian children, like children across the globe, are alive with curiosity. A large white man in a sea of dark faces is still a novelty deep in the African bush, and Steve has a knack for capitalizing on this as he makes connections for Christ!

Sent: November 19, 2008
Subject: mini update
Rebecca writes: The kids have all been sick. I'm not feeling great either, so I made an early prenatal appointment. The doctor did a blood test for anemia since she thought I was so pale. I'm sure I looked extra pale to a doctor who ordinarily sees dark patients!

We've had a hard rain and the weather has cooled. We also have one BIG brown puddle mark on our living room ceiling. Don't look up, Mom and Dad Wendland, when you come for Christmas. I'm sure it will still be there! Also, don't forget earplugs! The nightly noise from neighborhood dogs is out of control.
Love, Rebecca

I think I shall stop expecting to acclimate to Malawian germs. Sickness is a part of life here. At least my current sickness had an end in sight…sometime after the first trimester. Or so I hoped and prayed, anyway!

Death, as I have mentioned before, is also a part of life in Malawi. After five years in Malawi, we had experienced the reality that many lives here are cut heartbreakingly short. But this reality was about to impress itself on us in a very vivid way.

Sent: December 2, 2008
Subject: quick prayer request
Rebecca writes: Around 8pm our American missionary friend, Jen Willson (with the Free Methodist mission), called. Their fellow missionary was heading back to Lilongwe, and he had an accident. Apparently he is at the Balaka hospital, severely injured. Jen was wondering if Rob would accompany her husband, Ryan, to Balaka tonight to help out. So Rob grabbed his Bible, a jug of water (the essentials you know!) and met up with Ryan to drive to Balaka. I don't expect him to be back before midnight at the earliest. So, if you read this any time soon, a few prayers for travel safety at night and for the missionary in the accident would be appreciated. Thanks, Rebecca

> *I need thy presence ev'ry passing hour.*
> *What but thy grace can foil the tempter's pow'r?*
> *Who like thyself my guide and stay can be?*
> *Through cloud and sunshine, oh, abide with me! (CW 588:5)*

Sent: December 3, 2008
Subject: re: quick prayer request
Rob writes: I've got a sad update. We found out when we got to Ntcheu (halfway between Blantyre and Lilongwe) that the missionary in the accident had been killed instantly. Jen called saying the doctor at the District Hospital in Ntcheu confirmed that their friend was dead. We continued on. I drove and Ryan began contacting their fellow national pastors, other missionaries, and superiors in the USA. While we were traveling north from Blantyre, a group of Methodist missionaries was heading south from Lilongwe. In that group was the wife of the missionary in the accident. She only knew that her husband was in the hospital.

Shortly after Balaka we passed the scene of the accident. The missionary had been driving a three-ton truck and it was completely mangled. The car that hit them looked like a crumpled piece of paper.

We got to Ntcheu at 10:30pm—before the group from Lilongwe arrived. The doctor on duty led us to the morgue. We waited in line as the family of the other driver claimed the body of their relative. Then it was our turn. With great sadness, Ryan identified his dead friend/fellow missionary. We walked back to the front of the hospital. There we saw the vehicle from Lilongwe pulling through the gate. As we walked toward them, Ryan asked, "What do I say, Rob?" I could only reply, "Bring them to Jesus, Ryan." In that parking lot in the middle of the night, Ryan had to tell the missionary's wife that her husband had been called home to the Lord. Her husband was 37 years old and leaves behind 3 daughters. Wracked with sorrow and with tears streaming down her face, the widow's difficult question was, "How do I tell them?"

I went with another of their colleagues to fill out death certificates at the hospital and then to the police station to pick up any personal effects from the accident and to get their report. The missionary was the innocent party in the accident. A man heading south was travelling at a high rate of speed, lost control of his vehicle and veered into the oncoming lane, right into the truck. Besides the missionary, there was a national pastor in the truck. He survived the accident but had to have both legs amputated and is struggling for his life.

It was a tough return trip to Blantyre at 3am. Throughout the night I was mindful to keep the focus on Jesus, since He alone gives us hope in death. Not only was the dead missionary the same age as I, but his children are the same ages as ours, and he and his wife graduated from high school the same years that Rebecca and I did. It encourages one to be prepared in Christ at all times. *"But Christ has indeed been raised from the dead, the first-fruits of those who fall asleep in Him."* (Paraphrase of 1 Corinthians 15:20) Blessings in Jesus. Love, Rob

> *I fear no foe with thee at hand to bless;*
> *Ills have no weight and tears no bitterness.*
> *Where is death's sting? Where, grave, thy victory?*
> *I triumph still if thou abide with me. (CW 588:6)*

It was impossible *not* to relate to the family of the American Free Methodist missionary who had died so suddenly, since we shared so much in common as far as age, family and calling. Although we did not personally know the victim, we shared a mutual friendship with his fellow Methodist co-workers, Ryan and Jen. We grieved for their loss. Our shared hope in Christ assured us that the earthly loss was for heavenly gain. John 11:25 brings the comfort of Jesus' promise: *"I am the resurrection and the life. He who believes in me will live, even though he dies; and whoever lives and believes in me will never die."*

> *Hold thou thy cross before my closing eyes;*
> *Shine through the gloom and point me to the skies.*
> *Heav'n's morning breaks, and earth's vain shadows flee;*
> *In life, in death, O Lord, abide with me! (CW 588:7)*

Sent: December 20, 2008
Subject: Christmas "NEWs"
Rebecca writes:

Christmas greetings. The theme this past year was the word **NEW**!
"Sing to the Lord a **NEW** song, for he has done marvelous things...The Lord

2008: A Visit; A Call; A Fever; A Death

has made his salvation known and revealed his righteousness to the nations."
Psalm (98:1,2)

Our Blantyre urban church, Beautiful Savior, recently received their first national pastor, Rev. Bright Pembeleka. He is a great **NEW** addition to the ministry in Blantyre, and we are thankful to have him working alongside Missionary Mark Johnston.

Our mission field is blessed to have a **NEW** mission family at the LBI in Lilongwe: Missionary Peter Martin, currently in Zambia, accepted the call to begin ministry there.

We have surpassed 21" of rain already this season. Sure signs that we are in the middle of a **NEW** rainy season:
- 4 inches of rain fall in a single hour
- any incline becomes a mini-waterfall
- the flaps on my stationary envelopes get pre-sealed by the moist air
- our paper money gets moldy
- the fridge is sweating and leaving puddles on the floor
- giant snails, roughly 6" long, have appeared in the yard
- everything outside is very green, including moss-covered rocks and bricks
- the dog-food bowls float away "downstream"
- earthworms take up residence in the garage since the ground is too wet

In family news, my dad, Rev. Steve Staude, accepted a call to a **NEW** ministry. He will re-locate from La Crosse area to work as a WELS Christian Giving Counselor near the Twin Cities, MN.

Our family has a **NEW** addition on the way. Lord willing, in June of 2009 we'll add baby #4 to our Wendland household.

I had some fun **NEW**s in the mail recently. I received several copies of the Dec/Jan *Taste of Home* magazine. The magazine had published a picture I submitted of our kids making one of their recipes. Our kids were absolutely thrilled to see themselves in print and will now each have a copy for their scrapbooks. My mom sends me that magazine as part of my birthday gift. This year it paid for itself: in February I entered their cookie contest and received the prize for taking second place!

May God richly bless your **New** Year 2009! Missionary Robert & Rebecca Hannah (8), Nathanael (6), Caleb (3) & baby Wendland

"My sheep listen to my voice; I know them, and they follow me.
I give them eternal life, and they shall never perish;
no one can snatch them out of my hand." John 10:27-28

CHAPTER 17

2009: HEAVEN SENT—HEAVEN BOUND (FURLOUGH #3, BABY #4)

Christ is our corner stone; On him alone we build.
With his true saints alone The courts of heav'n are filled.
<u>*On his great love Our hopes we place*</u>
<u>*Of present grace And joys above.*</u>
(CW 528:1) [underlining added for emphasis]

The blessings we have in this world and the joys we await in the world to come are ours, not because we have earned or deserved them, but because of God's great love through his son Jesus Christ. By God's grace, I had three healthy children and one on the way. By God's grace my husband had safely traveled over countless dangerous miles since our arrival in Malawi in 2003. By God's grace we knew that our blessings were heaven-sent and that, no matter what trials and losses we might endure on earth, we were heaven-bound.

It is this great love of God that gives our lives one real purpose, expressed in the words of Jesus in John 9:4-5: *"As long as it is day, we must do the work of him who sent me. Night is coming, when no one can work. While I am in the world, I am the light of the world."* These words were so vivid to me as we closed out 2008, and they were a focal point for the year ahead. While it is still day—while I have opportunity and while I am able—it is my calling to continue to spread God's saving message to those who may not live to see tomorrow.

As 2009 began, we had some major events on the calendar: our third furlough was approaching and baby #4 was on the way. Trying to pin down a departure date and order plane tickets was no easy task, since we had to mesh my projected delivery date with Rob's furlough dates and with the school calendar. We decided to work around the kids' third-term school break as a natural time to pack up and head across the ocean.

Sent: January 14, 2009
Subject: furlough planning
Rebecca writes: This morning we looked into airline tickets. The recent ultrasound information we had was necessary since the airline's first question to me was, "Are you high risk?" Thankfully, everything looks good so far. Wow, the ticket prices are higher than last time—even with a missionary discount during low season! Love, Rebecca

The kids and I planned to fly back in May in preparation for the baby's June birth. Rob would join us in June. My ultrasound had ruled out the possibility of twins and any other high-risk situations that might prohibit airline travel. Little did I imagine at the time how close the airlines would come to denying me passage due to health concerns.

Sent: February 7, 2009
Subject: me and my amoeba
Rebecca writes: Lately there have been local political rallies. It made traveling yesterday nearly impossible. The kids and I were driving downtown when suddenly we found ourselves heading into a crowd a thousand strong. People marched around us and took up the entire road ahead. I quickly maneuvered out of there before we were gridlocked. We did get to our destination, but the trip took an hour longer.

I am happy to report that for one year now I have not had that recurring gut trouble. I think my resident amoeba was evicted once and for all with the powerful meds. God bless, Rebecca

I was grateful that the gastro troubles which had plagued me between 2003 and 2008 seemed to have disappeared. That was a heaven-sent blessing—especially with my pregnancy. It was amazing to be free of serious health-concerns for ONE YEAR STRAIGHT. Good health had allowed me to be so much more productive. Thank you, Lord!

> *Enter his gates with thanksgiving and his courts with praise;*
> *give thanks to him and praise his name.*
> *For the Lord is good and his love endures forever;*
> *his faithfulness continues through all generations. Psalm 100:4-5*

Sent: April 1, 2009
Subject: odds and ends
Rebecca writes: A piano tuner from Zimbabwe flew here to tune pianos. We

haven't had ours tuned recently, so we were happy for his services. At lunch Nathanael quipped that a piano tuner's favorite meal is a "tuna" melt (British accent required).

My doctor checkups are fine, although my health statistics are fluctuating. I can tell I'm transitioning into the third trimester since my energy is waning and swelling has begun. I pray it doesn't go crazy like it did with Nathanael's pregnancy. The Lord knows! I decided to take my rings off now while I still can. I'll keep them in the safe while I puff up, so my fingers don't turn purple.

Glad you were able to buy a house this past week in Lakeville, MN, Mom and Dad. We were able to see it via virtual tour. God bless, Rebecca

It was odd having my parents move. It meant I could not go "home" again. In fact, I wouldn't even know how to get to their new house on furlough. As it turned out, the timing of my parent's move was heaven sent. It meant that my mom was not currently working outside the home, so she would have more freedom to help out our family during furlough. God foresaw how critical her extra help would be in the months ahead due to problems brewing with my pregnancy. My doctor was becoming concerned with my increasing blood pressure and the steady swelling I was experiencing. I did my best to take things easy and lay low, but this was the first hint of trouble to come.

Despite my email about removing my wedding ring early, in the end I couldn't bear the thought of traveling alone and pregnant without it. I put it back on. How was I to know that in a short time it would become not just a matter of comfort, but imperative to remove it? It would take the help of a nurse in Milwaukee as well as lots of cold water and grease to do so! My decision to leave on my wedding ring was merely the beginning. In the weeks to follow, we began to question many of our best-laid plans.

Take the world, but give me Jesus! In his cross my trust shall be
Till with clearer, brighter vision Face to face my Lord I see.
Oh, the height and depth of mercy; Oh, the length and breadth of love!
Oh, the fullness of redemption,
Pledge of endless life above! (CW 355:3)

Sent: April 29, 2009
Subject: Easter info
Rebecca writes: We had a wonderful Easter service here. We decided not to travel to the mission Easter Retreat due to my swelling. In a few weeks the kids and I will be Stateside preparing for the baby's arrival at the end of June.

While we prepare for our new arrival, we have been told missionary departures

2009: Heaven Sent—Heaven Bound (Furlough #3, Baby #4)

will happen on the Malawi field. We pray that the decisions can be made without a large negative impact on "Word" work. It is a fitting time to reflect on what we have been given and to keep our focus on the giver of all good gifts. I have been mulling over the hymn, "When I Survey the Wondrous Cross," verse 4: *"Were the whole realm of nature mine, that were a tribute far too small…love so amazing, so divine…demands my soul, my life, my all."* That puts things so clearly into perspective for me. We are mere stewards of all His unending gifts—great and small.

Since our rains have subsided (we had over 50 inches this wet season!) more birds are visiting our bird baths. A Purple-crested Lourie took a bath right outside our dining room window recently, and a sunbird hovered at our window looking for our feeder. Recently we've also spotted a paradise flycatcher, hoopoe and kingfisher perched on the kids' swing set. It is amazing to wake up to such beautiful representatives of God's creation right in the yard.

Caleb put a spoon horizontally in his mouth at lunch, tilted his head back and forth and announced, "I'm an airplane!" Our approaching world travel hasn't gone unnoticed in his little head. Ready or not, we're coming soon! God bless, Rebecca

At this point, I wrote no more emails for a while. The last trimester of my pregnancy was taking quite a toll on my body. At my last doctor checkup I had pronounced swelling and my blood pressure was sky-high. The doctor was sure I had preeclampsia. I was given a steroid to assist the baby's lung development in case I would need to be induced soon. The steroid added to my swelling. I was also put on a blood pressure medication and bed-rest. This turn of events did not fit into my plans very neatly. How was I supposed to pack for furlough on bed-rest? How could I keep the household running and prepare for things ahead? However, it was obvious that my body needed to rest as the days ticked onward, so rest I did. Jane Johnston's nursing background was a blessing; she came to take my blood pressure often. She also took the kids frequently, and she and Lori Lawrenz left meals at our doorstep often. That helped me abide by bed-rest restrictions as much as possible.

I did leave my bed to attend Bible Group, but I must have looked particularly poor one day. A friend wanted to be assured that I had medical assistance lined up on my flight to the States. I responded that my assistants were Hannah, Nathanael and Caleb. News that I "looked like a pumpkin" traveled to our field coordinator, who encouraged us to reconsider our current plans to travel separately. After much discussion and research, we arranged for the whole family to travel to the States at the end of May. That way Rob could manage the luggage and kids, and I could take it as easy as possible on the 30+ hours on airplanes and in airports.

It turns out I was more high risk than anyone could have predicted. It frustrated me that my health was deteriorating so quickly, and that I wasn't already in the States preparing for the birth. In January when we sat at the airline desk, our travel schedule had looked fine. But now my health statistics were not so fine. By May it appeared that I might have any number of difficulties. One thing bed-rest did allow for was ample prayer time…prayers that God answered with grace and wisdom in the following weeks.

We were within days of boarding a plane when the following letter was sent from the States:

> *INCOMING EMAIL: May 22, 2009*
> *Subject: FW: Dad/Ernie—an unexpected turn*
> *Dad Wendland writes:* Great Grandpa, EH Wendland, is on his way Home. We pray that his departure will continue to be peaceful and without pain—and that the Lord would continue to uphold dear Kathie as she accompanies him along the way. I have very mixed emotions as I write this—rather sad that I probably will not get to see Dad again in this life, but so happy that he will finally get to be with his Father in heaven, an event that he has been awaiting for a long time. May we all have such an end—even as our living Hope of Heaven keeps us going in this lifetime! Much love, dad/mom

At Chileka airport, the boarding personnel took one look at my swollen form and nearly refused me entry on the plane. In a country of small, slender people I looked ominously large. Most of that long overseas trip was an uncomfortable blur, but thankfully all went well. The day after we arrived in the States we took a trip to Two Rivers, WI to visit with Grandpa EH Wendland. Rob and I were able to visit and have a devotion with Grandpa and Kathie. A few days later, Grandpa died—heaven bound.

Four generations of "Ernst Wendland"

2009: Heaven Sent—Heaven Bound (Furlough #3, Baby #4)

Here may we gain from heav'n The grace which we implore,
And may that grace, once giv'n, Be with us evermore
Until that day When all the blest
To endless rest Are called away! (CW 528:4)

It was God's hand that we were on the west side of the Atlantic Ocean, so Rob and the children could join the Wendland family as they said farewell to this veteran soldier of the cross. With sincere disappointment, I could not go to Grandpa Wendland's funeral, since I was back on strict bed-rest. It had been confirmed that I indeed had preeclampsia, a pregnancy complication that causes a rapid rise in blood pressure and can lead to seizure, stroke, blindness, multiple organ failure and even death of the mother and/or baby. Despite this diagnosis, I was at peace. I knew God was completely in control of whatever might happen. He had been in every event up until now. He will be until the day I am called home.

It pained me to be in the States physically and still miss such events as Grandpa's funeral, family reunions and special parties. However, I was grateful to be on bed-rest rather than hospitalized. My doctor was keen to see my health statistics improve, but preeclampsia is only resolved by delivery. I wanted the little one inside me to "bake" and mature as long as safely possible. Thankfully, I could assure the doctor that my mom was staying with us in the furlough house, and that I was resting in bed and doing nothing more. My mom was a huge blessing for our family throughout our furlough as she helped with the kids, cooked meals, cleaned and helped manage our full calendar of events and medical visits. The morning that the baby was 37 weeks old, and not a day more, I went to the hospital and was induced. Mere hours later, baby Bethany was born—heaven sent.

Sent: June 9, 2009
Subject: Baby Bethany is born
Rob writes: We thank the Lord for a healthy baby girl, Bethany Ruthann. She was born on June 8, 2009 and baptized on June 14, 2009 at Calvary Lutheran Church, Thiensville WI.

We gave Bethany the middle name "Ruthann" after my mother, who played an integral part in the beginning months of her life. Bethany was healthy—PRAISE THE LORD! I was healthy—PRAISE THE LORD! However, my road to recovery was long. My blood pressure was slow to level out and I was easily fatigued. It would be six months before I felt relatively normal.

In the meantime, it was wonderful to be in the States…but the time went way too quickly. In July, Rob began his deputation tour. He visited South Dakota, Minnesota and Wisconsin. When he preached and presented at Christ in Eagle River, WI, we drove up to join him. That is where Rob had vicared 13 years before. It was quite special to visit with many members again and drive around the town and notice all the changes.

Even as Rob traveled to congregations around the Midwest to share his mission work, the 2009 Synod Convention delegates were making a difficult decision that would affect Malawi and mission fields across the world. The global economic downturn had made its pinch felt in North America and in the WELS. Somehow the synod budget had to be drastically reduced. Many painful sacrifices were made across our WELS mission fields and in Synod administration. In our corner of the mission world, plans and preparation to enter Mozambique with two missionaries were terminated, and we would return to a Malawi mission field that had shrunk by one family.

More joyous highlights of furlough included family reunions and birthday parties, Bethany's baptism and the birth and baptism of cousin Joshua Staude. We also enjoyed sharing the furlough months with Grandma and Grandpa Wendland in Wisconsin. Before the furlough concluded, we made a special trip to Grandma and Grandpa Staude's new home in Lakeville, MN. The kids had a blast taking a canoe ride right in their backyard. We captured lots of fun moments on video and on camera, so we could enjoy the memories throughout the next two years. Once I was off bed-rest and feeling stronger, I managed to fit in a handful of shopping trips. In an attempt to make up for lost time, I was often seen pushing two carts through the aisles.

Each day was maxed out with special things to do in America, along with caring for a newborn and packing for Malawi. Thankfully, we got Bethany's birth certificate, social security card and passport in a timely manner, so we could order her a ticket for our return trip.

Here, gracious God, do now And evermore draw near;
Accept each faithful vow And all your children hear,
And more and more On those who pray
Each holy day Your blessing pour. (CW 528:3)

Sent: August 29, 2009
Subject: we arrived from furlough '09
Rebecca writes: What a blessing to share many wonderful memories with our family during furlough. Many accolades to mom for donating her time and effort to help us out!

We had a terrible, turbulent descent amid thunderstorms into Senegal. I had the barf bag ready. It didn't help to hear others heaving away. Amazingly, the pilot had a great landing in the dark, and everyone clapped. Nathanael kept looking for water fountains in the Johannesburg airport. He wouldn't believe me that they don't exist there. The time we spent shrink-wrapping our luggage paid off.

2009: Heaven Sent—Heaven Bound (Furlough #3, Baby #4)

Johannesburg airport is notorious for crime, but all our bags arrived in Blantyre still wrapped and unscathed.

Don't give up the prayers for our security and safety here. Thieves came while we were gone—about eight, according to the yard worker. We found areas chipped away on at least three burglar bars, one screen pried loose, punctures every few feet in our washroom screened area as they tried to find entry (sorry dad—all your hard work on patching up the previous holes), one security light removed and the back door broken into. We had quite a number of items stolen. We are grateful that our yard worker pressed the alarm. The guard was nowhere to be found.

Rob will be gone to meetings this coming Monday. The kids start school on Wednesday. They have been very sad in the evenings as they think about America and family, and they go to sleep crying.

Lori kindly left several meals in our refrigerator. She also salvaged most items in our fridge/freezer when the power went out for nearly a week while we were gone. Supposedly our neighborhood transformer was recently rewound. God bless, Rebecca

It is always a blessing to complete international travels without any major troubles. We had returned to Malawi safely, but we were very tired, off-schedule and faced with a huge emotional and physical adjustment. The older our children get, the more difficult it is for them to leave our relatives behind. They realize how long it will be before they will see those dear family members again. As a parent, it is one thing to bear up under your own conflicting emotions; it is another thing to guide your children through that struggle.

The physical contrast from life in America to life in Malawi is stark. When we live in Malawi for months on end, the third-world way of life begins to feel normal. But when we return to Malawi after a prolonged absence, the disparity is clearly evident. Malawi's dry and dirty conditions, security issues, third-world ambiance, tattered clothes, broken windows, peeling paint, dilapidated houses, crumbling roads, worn-out vehicles and foreign way of operating (or being inoperative) are more than striking. These things are a wakeup call reminding me where we are and why we are here.

Sent: September 8, 2009
Subject: kidbits
Rebecca writes: Every time I turn around I'm nursing, cooking, staying on top of homework, home-schooling or changing a diaper. Slowly but surely things will return to normal and I'll have some free time again—someday!

We've been back in Malawi for a week, and I'm glad to say that the new school year has started well. One comment on Hannah's report card was that she is very gifted in languages! She must get that from "Grandpa Einstein," as Nathanael called Grandpa E.R. the other day. (That *is* what the "E" stands for, correct?)

Kidbits: Caleb told me that someday he would like to ride a motorcycle with training wheels on it! I gave Caleb some new shoes from furlough. He tried them on and replied, "These don't fit at all: my big toe doesn't touch the front!" (The poor kid was overdue for some new shoes.) Bethany is cooing and smiling for everyone. Nathanael referred to the "Alfalfa and the Omega" the other day. Furlough farm knowledge creeping in.

I am adjusting slowly. I have eaten only one breakfast since the airplane. Usually, after nursing throughout the night and with my residual jet-lag, I wake up and eat an early lunch. I've lost 7 lbs already in 7 days. I knew Africa would naturally trim me down...but I had no idea it would be that drastic. Most of my shoes don't fit since my feet are still swollen. Love, Rebecca

The adjustment from furlough was not easy. Getting the family back on schedule, not to mention a nursing baby, was an ongoing effort. The school schedule helped, but there were no shortcuts to acclimating our bodies. We tried to stay awake when the sun was up and went to sleep when the sun went down. Some days that was easier said than done.

On our first Sunday back at Beautiful Saviour, one mission field change was very apparent. Our pastor, Missionary Mark Johnston, was gone; synod/mission cutbacks meant his position had been terminated. He and his family had returned to the States while we were on furlough, and Pastor Johnston had subsequently accepted a call to New Jersey. We missed their mission family presence in Blantyre, and it was a difficult loss for Beautiful Saviour. We were thankful for Pastor Bright Pembeleka, who was now our fulltime shepherd.

Sent: September 21, 2009
Subject: along came another...
Rebecca writes: Rob has successfully cemented in the compromised burglar bars, I've washed and dipped the bed nets and washed, hung and ironed most of the drapes. I won't install a wash line below a palm tree again; it becomes a bird lavatory!

I was feeling good about getting the dust under control until the other night. Soon after the kids went to bed, Hannah shouted for me to come. I found her standing on her bed. On the floor below her was...you guessed it...a spider of large proportions. Rob came armed with the dust pan and smacked the thing dead in its tracks. Hairy hollow legs, shiny black fangs...yeah, it was a tarantula. That accounts for my lack of free time. Ever since, I've been cleaning, sorting and taking

2009: Heaven Sent—Heaven Bound (Furlough #3, Baby #4)

apart the house to see if we have any other unwanted guests that made themselves at home while we were on furlough. I only found one web with a daddy long leg spider. Nevertheless, Hannah now checks under her bed every night to make sure it is "safe." (The worst part is nursing in the wee hours at night and hearing creepy crawly noises…and wondering. I've decided it is better to use that time to pray.)

Caleb asked the other day, "If Jesus hadn't died on the cross would there be lots more monsters?" (A profound statement in its own right.) God bless, Rebecca

Within the month, we found a second tarantula in our utility room. Rob took care of that one too, although it charged at him before it was killed. We also found the molted skin of a tarantula, which Hannah took to school for show-and-tell. Her teacher had been skeptical that there were tarantulas in Malawi. He changed his mind after seeing the molting…and after supervising Hannah's class on an overnight field trip to Majete Game Park in the Shire Valley. The outing was to encourage the class to learn about the animals in the park, their conservation and the threat of poaching. Hannah had a little more action than anticipated while she was there. Here is the field trip account she wrote:

"I rode down to the Shire in the mini bus. A game ranger told us the rules of the game park, the history of the park and showed us a display of poacher weapons. The highlights were seeing rhinoceros, sable and a family of elephants on a game drive. The male elephant was trumpeting and almost charged the vehicle. We could see in the distance the water's edge and lots of animals drinking since it was very hot. It was so hot there that my roommate, Ridhi, fainted from heat exhaustion.

After supper we went to our chalets. Ridhi went to sleep quickly. I sat down on my bed. As I was taking off my slippers I dropped one. When I went to pick it up I saw a baby tarantula crawling across the floor with his hairy legs. Then I saw more hairy things. Under my bed were about 50 newly-hatched baby tarantulas, about the size of a penny. They were being watched by their mother. The teachers called the gardener and he killed all the tarantulas. As I lay on my bed I heard monkeys chattering on the roof. Then I went to sleep to the buzzing of various bugs in our room."

I hope never to see that many tarantulas in my lifetime, much less all at once under my bed. Hannah is such a good sport about the inconveniences of life here. I am glad she can keep a smile on her face and let her light shine through it all.

Sent: October 20, 2009
Subject: truck trouble
Rebecca writes: It's after 10pm here and Rob is not yet home from the Shire Valley. Apparently he had one too many (three) flat tires. He has been stuck

since 5pm. Rob doesn't have too many options in his predicament. He is with Evangelist Master and his wife. Ev. Master does not think it is safe for them to remain in the vehicle for the night. It is possible they will have to abandon the vehicle to keep the people safe. That is not a preferred option either, so they may see if a friend in the next town, Mkate, can repair the tire yet tonight.

I called Steve Lawrenz, who has gone to the rescue. He is taking an LCCA member along to help; they should be able to meet up with Rob in the next hour or two. Prayers for everyone's safety tonight would be appreciated. Love, Rebecca

*Now the light has gone away; Father, listen while I pray,
Asking you to watch and keep And to send me quiet sleep. (CW 593:1)*

Flat tires are common during Rob's bush trips. The odds finally caught up with him this time when three flat tires left him stranded overnight.

Sent: October 21, 2009
Subject: truck trouble
Rob writes: Well, well; usually rolling in at 5:30 from the Lower Shire means I made good time on my return trip. That was the time on the clock as I came home today...only it was *5:30am!* I have had two flat tires before. This time I had three!

The first flat tire was on the way to the church; I changed it quickly. The second happened on my way home, around 5pm. The good news is that we were about 500 yards from a place that could fix a tire. The bad news is that the place had no electricity and had to pump up the tire with a hand pump. In fact, they had to pump up the tire three separate times, after fixing and resealing holes. We waited about four hours. I feared the patches wouldn't hold. Sure enough, a mere 20 km later the same tire gave out—this time far from any options to fix it. I called Rebecca and she called the Lawrenzes.

Steve and his helper arrived around midnight. Mrs. Master, the helper and I began our night vigil in the truck. Steve and Ev. Master drove the tire to a member to repair. Three punctures were found in the tube...so it was another four hours before we finally had a tire back on my truck. Thankfully this time all went well, and we arrived in Blantyre around 5:30am. Hannah and Rebecca were already up. Thanks for all the thoughts and prayers—all's well. Love, Rob

All night long I listened for the sound of Rob's diesel truck pulling into the driveway. All night long the noises kept me guessing. As the first rays of sunshine made an appearance, I heard the diesel rumble, the gate open and the truck door close. Rob was home safe and sound: Thank You, Lord!

2009: Heaven Sent—Heaven Bound (Furlough #3, Baby #4)

Keep me safe, O God, for in you I take refuge. Psalm 16:1

Sent: October 27, 2009
Subject: Kabula klan update
Rebecca writes: Rob is in the Lower Shire again all day today. We are praying this time it isn't all night, too. He has built a small wooden box behind the passenger's seat to house some of his necessary items, in place of the cardboard boxes and woven baskets that he used to take. They shook to pieces. **Everything** shakes to pieces, which makes it hard to maintain a nice supply of gear. His glove box door shook itself free once and fell on the floor along with all the contents. Even his two reflective triangles (often necessary to show at police checks) are in pieces from the jolting bumps and pot holes.

Kidbits: Caleb told us that sometimes in his dreams he goes in the washer. (Maybe it is because he is SOOO dirty all the time.) Recently Nathanael asked dad before he left for the bush if his necktie played music. I suggested "*On the Road Again.*" Hannah has been a big help. She has learned how to make a shepherd's pie, she can whip up a salad, and she puts Bethany to sleep by practicing piano.

Shoprite currently has absolutely no cold items: no cheese, yogurt, butter or margarine; no frozen goods or any meat. So it goes. Love from the Kabula Klan

Sent: November 4, 2009
Subject: "I saw the sign"
Rebecca writes: As of today there is NO DIESEL in all of Blantyre. You can be assured that this is not an exaggeration, since Steve Lawrenz dedicated his whole day searching (in vain) for it.

We are thankful that all the Malawi mission ladies traveled to and from the annual Ladies' Bible Retreat with fuel in the tank last weekend. The retreat was held in Chinteche (about 450 km north of Blantyre). I was sweating it on the way back since it seemed the diesel shortage was spreading—fast. (Literal sweat too: the heat made it seem like we were in a slow cooker.) On the way home we **tried** to fill up in Salima, but there was no fuel. I sat in the car while Lori talked the situation over with the police, who were sitting in the shade. I noticed a metal sign posted on the Petroda wall. It read: "400 VOLTS - DANG." I laughed to myself, musing that the sign painter didn't allow enough room for the whole word "dangerous," so he clipped it to a mere "dang." It inspired these thoughts of the dangers/"dangs" we faced:

No diesel to be had = dang
This weather is so hot = dang
Traveling with an infant is difficult = dang
Why are all the trees cut down so there is no shade = dang

I am so thirsty but I don't want to drink much
because we still have half a day of travel with no good toilets = dang
I hope we don't get a flat tire = dang
Diesel from "Uncle Alex's drum" costs MK199.60 a **liter** ($1.40) = dang

I enjoyed the signage—though too much danging could be dangerous. After all the danging, I counted my blessings. The Lord smiled upon our journey, allowing us to return home without incident. We did not have a flat tire. At least we found fuel. At least we had a vehicle. At least I could cool off and take a clean drink of water when I wanted. The Lord had renewed and refreshed us as we studied His Word together.

Rob mounted a second spare tire on his truck while I was gone. We pray that will help the "next time," whenever that may be. The current fuel shortage means Rob's truck isn't going anywhere for now. Love from Kabula, Rebecca

When we first moved to Africa, fuel shortages were stories from an era gone by. Missionaries' tales of waiting in long lines throughout the night were just that—stories. Not anymore. Now we faced the reality of this commodity shortage. There are not too many options during a fuel crisis. Either you try to find fuel somewhere, or you don't go anywhere. On our way home from Ladies' Retreat, Lori and I took a chance that an off-the-road-drum-on-stilts was a legitimate place to fuel up to get us back to Blantyre. Whew, it worked.

Sent: November 13, 2009
Subject: Diesel daze
Rebecca writes: This evening our power went out just as I was getting supper going. Rob finally called the faults line to ask when the power might be restored. They told him, "When they extinguish the fire at the station they will tell us." That did not bode well. Thankfully, the power returned that evening.

Our diesel situation is hopeless. Rob has meetings in Lilongwe. He hopes to catch the local coach bus leaving here at 7am tomorrow. The bus depot *thinks* they will have enough fuel to make the trip. Love, Rebecca

The fuel situation was definitely uncomfortable. It is not a good feeling to watch the needle dip into the red area and touch the word "empty" with no hope of refueling any time soon. There wasn't much we could do but stay put as much as possible, patiently wait, and hope diesel tankers were on the horizon.

Sent: November 15, 2009
Subject: Blantyre update of late
Rebecca writes: Hello from "wee" Blantyre folk. It is only the kids and I, which

always creates an interesting dynamic. Rob is still at meetings.

The diesel shortage has continued. Rob saw some fights at the gas stations. Bribes for fuel are rampant.

Game store is on strike. Between the strike, Shoprite not having cold food items and no diesel, it is a wonder ANYTHING gets done around here. I saw a bumper sticker on a truck that read, "Please take a time." I think it was trying to say, "Please be patient with my driving." One MUST learn patience to cope.

This afternoon I saw a jumping spider attack and kill a black ant while I was taking out the compost. Some days I feel like I'm right in the middle of a National Geographic show…or maybe the Twilight Zone.

Bethany has awakened; that's all for this episode. Love, Rebecca and "wee ones" or "ones that wee" or "we wear onesies"

INCOMING EMAIL: November 16, 2009
Subject: Blantyre update of late
Dad Wendland writes: Dear Rebecca, Thanks for all the interesting news "bites"—as usual. I DO hope that you are keeping a file of all your writings—the good, the bad, and the ugly. I mean that—you write well and it would be a shame to lose all these reflections and insights on "life on the mission field" from a wife's perspective! Love to all—GpaW

Encouragement like this was beginning to sink in, and I started to sift through old emails and think about formulating them into something bigger. My parents had printed out every email I had written through the years and sent them my way. With toddler toys at my feet, baby cereal stains on my shoulder and race car stickers on my keyboard, I began the task of condensing my emails. In many ways the timing seemed crazy. In other ways it seemed like as good a time as any to put my thoughts into writing. Being on bed-rest for a good portion of the past year had allowed me plenty of time to think and reflect. Nursing a newborn also affords many an hour of sitting, pondering and praying.

Sent: November 26, 2009
Subject: Happy Thanksgiving
Rebecca writes: Our fuel situation is not better. Rob talked to a man who waited in a fuel line from 10pm until 3am, hoping to fill up his truck. He only got 10 liters.

The kids have school today, on Thanksgiving. EVERY YEAR, without fail, we have a power outage…so I baked ahead this morning. The Lawrenzes are joining us for dinner. Our families toyed with skipping a celebration (and conserving diesel), but it is special to keep the American holidays in mind. That's especially true of Thanksgiving, since God has truly blessed us without measure. Love, Rebecca

It is part of our sinful nature, I'm sure, to only appreciate things to the full when we can't have them to the full. Family is far away; we appreciate them fully. Fuel is far away; we appreciate a full tank. Heaven is far away; I appreciate that blessed future when all emptiness will be filled and topped off for all eternity. This Thanksgiving we focused not on what we lacked, but on our heaven-sent blessings and our heaven-bound "travel plans." At least our journey to heaven doesn't depend on diesel!

Let my near and dear ones be Safe with you eternally.
Oh, bring me and all I love To your happy home above. (CW 593:3)

Sent: November 30, 2009
Subject: Wall came tumbling down
Rebecca writes: A section of our wall came tumbling down. We'll have to fix it soon.

This evening Hannah drew a Christmas tree with eight presents under it. One present looked like a wrapped-up water pitcher with a long, curved spout. I asked what it was. She looked at me sincerely and whispered, "Mom that is a container of diesel fuel." Bless her heart—it is something we really could use for Christmas!

At church yesterday I was discussing the fuel shortage with a pregnant Malawian lady whose baby is due anytime now. She said her drive home from church will probably be her last trip with fuel. I asked her what she would do if she went into labor and had no more fuel. She answered, "Well, I will walk to the hospital then!" (Which is what most women here do.)

Nite from never-never land, where the rain pours down, the sun beats down, no fuel downtown and the walls come tumbling down. Rebecca

Whenever I'm tempted to complain about my pregnancy difficulties or the woes of traveling around the world with a newborn, I am brought back to reality by daily life in Malawi. Pregnant Malawians get no pampering! Many don't even receive what North Americans would consider basic support. In the years following 2009, the economic and political situation in Malawi deteriorated, resulting in chronic shortages of medicine, food and fuel. By 2011, government hospitals were (unofficially) demanding that birthing women bring along five liters of diesel to run the hospital generator! Also on the list of requirements for women to bring when giving birth:

- A plastic sheet to deliver on (to prevent spread of infection)
- A razor blade (to cut the umbilical cord)
- A cord clamp (to clamp off the umbilical cord)
- Painkillers
- Disinfectant
- 1 liter of paraffin or 1 candle (to provide lighting in local birth clinics)

Further complicating matters for pregnant Malawians is the male-centric society they live in. Tribal custom demands that decisions about when and where to seek obstetric care are made by the *uncle* of either the pregnant woman or her husband. Without the uncle's consent, the woman and her relatives can do nothing but wait. If the uncle lives in a distant village or is travelling, the pregnant mother will approach her due-date with trepidation. Ladies have died because they did not get permission from the uncle to go to the hospital at the needed time. Some have attempted to finally seek health care as their delivery became imminent and have suffered terrible complications—or died—along the way. Fortunately, the modern technology of cell phones has allowed an ancient custom to continue with easier communication and fewer sad endings.

Sent: December 2, 2009
Subject: Malawi news
Rebecca writes: I thought I'd forward to you the latest news here:

> **Fuel crisis cripples transport sector** THE NATION NEWSPAPER Dec 2, 2009
> The Road Transport Operators Association of Malawi says the country's transport industry is on the verge of collapse, warning that commodity prices could increase any time if the fuel crisis is not resolved urgently. The fuel situation is so fragile that the country's economy is under severe threat. Businesses are in danger of collapsing. Some drivers said they had been waiting for a week for what has become the most scarce commodity in the country.

Things have deteriorated. The fuel situation is terrible. All modes of transport are affected. Rob cannot get to his village churches. Some kids cannot get to school. Most minibuses are not running and transport trucks continue to wait in huge lines to attempt to refuel. People have tickets to fly out of Lilongwe for the holidays and now they can't even get to Lilongwe. We have no plans to go anywhere in the near future. I have 15 kg of flour, 1 kg of butter, canned veggies, some boxes of long-life milk and our chickens to get us through for a while if things get even worse. The upside is I'm making homemade rolls again. Love, Rebecca

Sent: December 4, 2009
Subject: fuel update
Rebecca writes: It seems a fuel tanker or two has come into town. There are so many cars waiting in lines that the roads look like a parking lot. I wish I had captured a picture of about 30 guys sitting on their fuel cans right in front of the

pumps, with cars parked at least two deep for as far as you could see.

My friend sent her gardener to get 25 liters of petrol in a tin. He waited all day and into the early evening. At dusk, police arrived and announced it was illegal to collect more than 5 liters in a jerry tin. Thus, all the people with large tins were obviously (according to them) planning to sell it on the black market. So, the police confiscated all the containers—full or not—"in the name of the law."

Rob's truck has spider webs on it from lack of use! That is a first. Love, Rebecca

It is difficult to do the right thing when the police are known to make up rules on the fly. You might easily break the law even if you don't intend to. I appreciate the fact that God, by contrast, has laid out His laws clearly. I also appreciate the fact that He has perfect justice. (Okay…I only appreciate *that* fact standing in Christ!)

Sent: December 10, 2009
Subject: December update
Rebecca writes: It is beginning to look like Christmas with the tree up and stockings hung. The kids all have small things to say for the Christmas Day service this year.

Here is what today's paper has to say about the fuel situation:

Fueling corruption, not vehicles THE SUNDAY TIMES Dec 10, 2009
The current fuel crisis the country is going through is fuelling other engines: corruption. On Capital Radio, callers are reporting of filling stations closing at 5pm only to open after 2am to sell to those that have paid an 'extra charge.'

Rob has been driving around with our fuel tin for several weeks now—without success in filling it up. Yesterday he **finally** found a station with fuel. He filled up his vehicle and jerry tin with diesel. Now we have some fuel for the holidays, and in case Rob's parents need it for their journey to and from Zambia at Christmas.

At recess Hannah's classmate, Aliah, presented her with a challenge, "Let's race. Muslims versus Christians. Whoever wins means their God is the strongest." So Hannah agreed to race. Aliah's friend, Kadijah, gave the cue…after an extra wink to Aliah to give her a head start. Hannah caught up and won the little competition. Kadijah asked Aliah, "So now Hannah's God is the strongest?" Aliah's only answer was, "Well I was **supposed** to win."

Hannah is currently working with me on several duets to play for the Christmas Candlelight Service…in praise of our God who is the strongest, yet who—for our sake—chose to become weak and take on human flesh. Love, Rebecca

2009: Heaven Sent—Heaven Bound (Furlough #3, Baby #4)

While some poor folks had their hard-won diesel arbitrarily confiscated by police, others were getting away with bribing gas-station attendants. Life isn't fair. Rather than stew about the corrupt state of affairs, we strove to train our eyes and hearts on the heaven-sent Son of God in this Advent season.

Sent: December 13, 2009
Subject: **Te Deum** *time!*
Rebecca writes: Here's a fuel situation update—since many of you are sending up prayers on our behalf. ("Tank" you!) Today I heard there was fuel in Nyambadwe. In the distance I could hear heavy rain approaching. I decided it would be worth being caught in the downpour to have a full tank. The older kids came with me. That worked well, since they both had to hold the yard gates open against the strong winds.

As we approached the station, the scene looked good. No traffic was backed up onto the road; in fact, there were only five cars ahead of us. We waited patiently and were finally waved forward. The man told me they did indeed have diesel and he would give me a full tank. (This was great, since they had been restricting the amount of liters you could have in one stop.) Hooray! I unlocked the fuel door and saw a large bolt of lightning out of the corner of my eye. Seconds later, a big boom sounded, followed by lots of rumbling. The man checked inside the station. He told me he would have to wait for them to turn the pump on. After some time the man reappeared and announced that the main switch for the pump was burning from the lightning strike…and I would not be able to fill up today. SOOOO close!

The kids and I ventured to another station. No diesel. Then the road was blocked and we waited again and watched as the president and his caravan of cars drove past. Onward. We tried again at another station; they did have diesel. Despite the heavy rains, the lightning, the waiting (and more waiting), we **finally have a full tank**! It has been about a month since we were last able to fill up. We have been thankful school is out, to minimize driving. I plan to do a major shopping trip soon and hope they have SOME of the things on my list for the upcoming Christmas baking and cooking.

Icing on the cake today is that Bethany finally slept a nice stretch last night. As the title expresses, indeed, it is "*Te Deum* time!" (Borrowed from Uncle Paul's usage: when the kids go to bed—it is time to offer up a *Te Deum*!) We praise our gracious God who even cares about the small things that seem so great to us at times. Love, Rebecca

The timing of the lightning strike left me speechless. We were within seconds of getting a tank-full of the elusive diesel. I nearly laughed at the absurdity of the situation. I took it as a lesson in patience and perseverance. Romans 5:2-5 has a good reminder: *"And we rejoice in the hope of the glory of God. Not only so, but we also rejoice in our sufferings, because we know that suffering produces perseverance; perseverance, character; and character, hope. And hope does not disappoint us, because God has poured out his love into our hearts by the Holy Spirit, whom he has given us."*

It often seems our praise and thanks to God is most sincere *after* adversity! Sometimes it requires a difficult struggle before we fully appreciate God's hand in restoring normalcy. And sometimes the abnormal struggle becomes the new normal! Unfortunately for Malawi, the severe and chronic shortage of fuel that began at the close of 2009 did not have an end in sight. Years later, Malawi was still struggling with a lack of foreign exchange currency and fuel. These shortages had a domino-effect on other facets of life, causing inflated prices and shortages on staples like bread, meat, milk, butter and oil; along with erratic power supply, job losses, tourism cancellations and deadly riots. Concern over government mismanagement caused many international donors, including those based in the UK and the USA, to either freeze or terminate assistance to Malawi, a country which relies heavily on foreign aid.

More than ever, each day in Malawi has become an exercise in trust that God will provide exactly what is needed for that day: heaven-sent blessings that we cannot take for granted!

Gridlocked for scarce fuel

Sent: December 21, 2009
Subject: and to all a good night…
Rebecca writes: There have been several earthquakes in Malawi leaving hundreds of people without proper homes. Many people were injured and some were killed.

2009: Heaven Sent—Heaven Bound (Furlough #3, Baby #4)

ESCOM has been on strike. Fine thing to do, especially since we were recently told that power prices will triple in the next month!

It is that "hungry time of year" again, which escalates the crime level. The rains are not steady yet...which means the crops planted early may dry out too soon.

Hannah and I went shopping for lettuce today. Of course they HAD lettuce until someone bought 30 heads right before me, so it was all sold out! UGH. Frustrating when I can't get a-"head" on my shopping. While we were at an import store, Hannah saw a display of boxed Barbie dolls (which sell for about $100). She noticed that there was a spider web with a big black spider **in the box** by Barbie's hair.

Despite these earthly difficulties, soon we'll celebrate the best thing that has ever happened to the earth: the coming of the newborn King. Christmas blessings, Rebecca

The past year seemed cluttered with ways in which Malawi had "struck out." We'd had ongoing problems with fuel, food supplies, workers, government inefficiency, law enforcement and thieves. I kept reminding myself that *Jesus left **HEAVEN*** to come to earth. Leaving the States to come to Malawi pales in comparison!

As 2009 drew to a close, we focused our eyes instead on the undeserved gifts that God had seen fit to send us: four children, our health, our wealth. Every one of our needs had been met. Not a day had gone by leaving us hungry or without shelter or provisions. And always at the top of our list of blessings is the tiny Baby who was heaven-sent to be our Savior! It is in His coming, dying and rising again that we rest all our hopes while here on earth. It is because of Him that we are heaven-bound.

Now my evening praise I give; You once died that I might live.
All your precious gifts are free—Oh, how good you are to me! (CW 593:4)

CHAPTER 18

2010: MINISTERING IN MALAWI WHILE IT IS DAY

Take the world, but give me Jesus! All its joys are but a name.
But his love abides forever, Through eternal years the same.
Oh, the height and depth of mercy; Oh, the length and breadth of love!
Oh, the fullness of redemption, Pledge of endless life above! (CW 355:1)

2010 marked our seventh year of living and doing mission work in Malawi. It capped a period of acclimation to life in Malawi: from those whirlwind first days in Nyambadwe, through the births of two more children, to settling into our routines and a new home in Kabula. 2010 also marked a subtle turning point for me. The newness of life in a foreign culture had worn off. The details of daily struggles weren't often worth writing home about anymore. Instead, my emails began to focus only on significant events and news related to the children.

And so our seventh year seems as good a time as any to conclude what is an ongoing story. My family is not in the final "chapter" of our lives in Africa. For now Malawi remains our ministry, forms our experiences and has become our life. We remain at the mercy of our Lord, who knows the ongoing economic and political woes that Malawi is suffering. We continue to live with inconvenient fuel and food shortages, intermittent health crises and invasive bugs. We continue to live in the midst of Malawi's cycle of harvest and hunger. We continue to rejoice over Malawi's hunger for the Word and our privilege in sharing it. Each year that passes allows us to experience and learn new things. More "chapters" will be written: in 2014 we will, Lord willing, send Hannah to high school on the far side of the sea—to Luther Prep School in Wisconsin. We will learn in a new way to entrust our children to the Lord, even as we send our first child out of reach of our arms, our phone range, our continent…but never out of reach of our prayers. We will have to let go, but God's right hand will hold her fast.

Many people have encouraged me to write this book and I feel compelled to put these writings into print while they are still fresh and the memories seem like yesterday. It is a gift to our children who someday may want to connect to their past, and who might ask questions of yesteryear and "the way it used to be." Perhaps as you read it you will find a special place in your prayer life for missionaries on the far side of the sea...and for the souls to whom they minister with the Word of Life.

> *"If I rise on the wings of the dawn,*
> *if I settle on the far side of the sea,*
> *even there your hand will guide me,*
> *your right hand will hold me fast." Psalm 139:9-10*

Sent: January 10, 2010
Subject: the latest here
Rebecca writes: On New Year's Day we took a scenic drive down toward Mulanje to buy pineapples. They are so delicious this time of year. Pineapples are the smell of Christmas in Malawi!

We had an unexpected visitor last night. Another tarantula. Hannah will take it to school tomorrow for show-and-tell.

Recently Caleb came in the kitchen crying, "Nathanael opened the bedroom window and now the stars will come in—boo hoo." Rob thinks they are inventing reasons to fight.

Me? It dawned on me that I've played the organ for church for 25 years now. Here are my reflections—roughly to Golde's expressions in the tune "*Do You Love Me?*" from Fiddler on the Roof:

For 25 years I've practiced the hymns, learned each liturgy, preludes and postludes.
For 25 years I've awoken early, gathered my music, accompanied the choirs.
For 25 years I've spent countless hours in dark, cold churches,
Paper-clipping pages, warming my fingers.
For 25 years I've played for many weddings and funerals, even college morning chapel.
For 25 years I've bought lots of music, learned many pieces, struggled with the pedals.
For 25 years I've sat on the bench, kept alert for each pastor's words.
For 25 years I've heard each sermon twice, ok, even thrice.
For 25 years I've made every error, covered many too.
For 25 years I've become sometimes nervous, sometimes distracted.
For 25 years I've valued the talent, recognized the gift and opportunities that I've been given to glorify the Lord.
After 25 years I love to play the piano, but I guess I love to play the organ... too! Rebecca

Sent: January 16, 2010
Subject: birthday girl
Rebecca writes: Thanks for Hannah's birthday wishes. Turning 10 was mighty exciting for her! She is happy to be two digits—old enough to get her ears pierced.

One of Hannah's school friends had been throwing away her PBJ sandwiches every day at break, so the school called the parents to report the offense. (Should I even ask if they would do that Stateside?) Another classmate thinks Hannah wears a wig. Maybe Hannah's long hair seems unbelievable—it is at her waist. Hannah's other friends are vouching for her, saying that at sleepovers Hannah does not take off any wigs at night. (I love their solid logic.)

Our fuel situation has temporarily stabilized, allowing Rob to visit some of his village churches. He baptized a kid last week who has the unique name of "Faver Fraction Fack." Quite the alliteration.

There is a meeting after church tomorrow, so I'd better pack some snacks for the "bottomless pits" that accompany me. Love, Rebecca

Sent: February 5, 2010
Subject: Oh Rats
Rebecca writes: The local mosque must have installed new speakers. Now at 4am we can hear more clearly their "calling" to the community.

All the crops have failed in the Lower Shire due to inconsistent rainfall. The members there are saying the church should help them. The last time Rob distributed "humanitarian aid" it was frustrating. All of a sudden EVERYONE far and near was a LCCA member. The real members were reluctant to tattle on the pretenders for fear of repercussions. As a result, several legitimate members ended up without the aid. What a conundrum. If fellow believers are in need, we want to help. But there isn't enough to feed all of Southern Malawi.

We received a notice explaining that the ESCOM men would be trimming trees in our area, so our power would be out ALL Wednesday from 8-4pm. I spent Tuesday cooking the next day's meals ahead, so I could reheat them on the gas burner. On Wednesday the power went out…but for only four minutes. Now what? All day Wednesday I didn't turn on my computer and didn't make a hot lunch, thinking any minute the power would go out for the duration of the day. It never did. That ended up being worse. Did they get the day wrong? Didn't they get the repairs done as planned? Does that mean the NEXT day it will be out all day? I have kept meals simple. So far there have been only a few minor outages this week.

When Rob went into the chicken coop today, about a dozen rats came scurrying out. One ran over Rob's foot trying to escape the investigation. Now the rat population is something to be reckoned with. Yippee.

According to Rob's latest phone text message, he had a terrible day in the bush. In addition to one flat tire on the three hour drive down, the church members were not there when he arrived. The man in charge of relaying the message that Rob was coming, forgot...and went fishing instead. To cap it all off, Rob is having truck trouble on the way home. God bless, Rebecca

Changing another flat tire

Sent: February 6, 2010
Subject: Kondi come to life
Rebecca writes: Recently we had a WELS *Kids' Connection* interview via Skype. It went well and the connection was amazing for the occasion. This encouraging follow-up note came from a lady at the Synod Administration Building:
I was deeply touched and thoroughly enjoyed your family interview. I was so impressed with your children and the entire family's fervor for where God has placed you. Thanks for letting us see a glimpse of your ministry. Kris

This week Nathanael has the main role in his class play, *Galimoto*. (That is the Chichewa word for "vehicle.") He plays the boy named Kondi. (Aunt Lenka may recognize the title...she sent Nathanael that book as a gift after meeting the illustrator, who based her work on the Lower Shire.)

Galimoto is a story of a Malawian boy who searches and trades things for scrap wire. He then makes a toy *galimoto* (car) out of the wire so he can play with it with all his friends. For Nathanael's costume his teacher told him to find his most worn-out clothes. I debated **making** holes in something. What a demonstration of how blessed we are!

Our yard gate broke. The metal gatepost rusted through. I've talked with the welder; he'll try to get things fixed. Love, Rebecca

Sent: February 22, 2010
Subject: welded shut
Rebecca writes: On the home front we've been welded in. A welder came to fix our fallen, rusty gatepost. He got a late start due to the rain but got it fixed. In order to keep it in place, he had to weld it shut until the next day. We'll have him return to weld cross-bars to the burglar bars on our bedroom windows. I can only imagine our heavenly mansions with delight: no gates, grates, burglar bars, razor wire, guards, electricity issues, mosquitoes, dust, spiders and mold to deal with. Someday! God bless, Rebecca

The rainy season complicated our welder's work…but he continued welding in the daily deluge. He operated with the very basics. His welding machine didn't even have a plug—merely bare wires to be inserted into a socket! His long cord was spliced, with only electrical tape wrapped around the splices. I cringed when I noticed that the spliced sections of his cord were draped in the running water of our drainage ditch.

Sent: February 23, 2010
Subject: kidbits of late
Rebecca writes: Hannah's latest news is that she got her ears pierced! I took her to a salon called "Weedles." An Indian lady pulled out a sample card of earrings for Hannah to choose from. There were several dozens of designs on the display. We began looking at all of them… until the lady pointed to the whole bottom section and told us those were unavailable. Hannah thought her birthstone would be nice. The lady then waved her hand over the birthstone section and told us she didn't have any of those either. I asked her to show us which ones she *did* have. There were two choices: a large gold ball or a 3 mm fake diamond stud. Okay, the 3 mm diamond stud it would be. I had already put a dot in pen where the hole in her ear should be. As the lady took the gun, I asked her if the pen marks looked right. She noted, "I'll grab my glasses." Anyway, it went well.

I must get dinner going. Electricity is on, Bethany is still napping, and everyone is getting hungry. Love, Rebecca and family

Sent: March 2, 2010
Subject: looking up!?
Rebecca writes: Lately it feels like I'm riding on a yo-yo that is in the hand of an amateur. I'm dangling at the end of a string with a few jerks here and there in an attempt to begin an upswing.

Rob has had a flat tire every time he has gone to the Lower Shire this month. This week was no exception; this one went flat overnight.

It is pouring outside. More rain has fallen in the last few weeks than in all of this rainy season previously. I thought we were going to escape the moldy, soggy, muddy, damp, rainforest-ambiance this year. I was wrong—dead wrong. I've had the fans on almost non-stop to help things dry out as much as possible. I am thankful that we have a clothes dryer during conditions like this! Nothing can help the outside conditions until the sun and wind make an appearance. Until then we have many snails coming out.

After the drapes were opened this morning Caleb exclaimed, "It is raining sugar—I'll go check." Unfortunately for him, it was the same rain as always. Of course a sweet rain would create a bug problem. And speaking of which, a certain small black ant that I dread found our dining table earlier this week. They have been active during this very wet time. Last week they found the kids' school snack bags. When they find something they cover it by the dozens and eventually by the hundreds. Yesterday, Bethany's baby cereal bowl wasn't collected right away. By the time I went back to the table after nursing, the bowl was black with ants. We have found some of their entry points, but the poison isn't doing the trick…yet. We keep trying!

Our house worker recently told us she has a serious bedbug infestation in her home and needs help. This is horrible news. It seems problems here are only addressed after the situation is already out of control.

When I picked up the kids from school, it was pouring buckets. As I walked to the classroom, the water in the courtyard was up past my ankles and touching the bottom of my skirt. Soon my skirt was drenched and clinging to my legs. Each step that I took tugged at the elastic waistband, which began to inch downward. I had Bethany on one hip, so she anchored the left side. However, the right side kept slipping. Every few steps I had to let go of my umbrella to pull up my skirt waist and shake the bottom of the soaking skirt off my legs. I was a sight to behold. Needless to say, Bethany doesn't like the rain.

On Sunday I found out JUST how wet things were. I had driven past our property after seeing a suspicious man loitering by our gate. When I returned he was gone, but it meant I had to do a three-point turn to get into our angled driveway. When one back wheel went on the grass, it immediately sank. The wheel spun and spun. We sank deeper and deeper. The kids were shocked.

They were afraid that we'd slide down into the neighbor's wall. Once I enabled the 4WD we climbed out easily. Many prayers of thanks followed. That was a terrible sinking feeling that had a happy ending.

Today we had another sinking feeling with an unhappy ending. Our house worker was an hour late because her property wall had collapsed on a small boy as he walked by her house this morning. When she rushed out to help, she could hear a faint cry under the bricks. Everyone walking by helped to lift off the bricks, and they took the boy to the hospital. At the hospital they confirmed he was dead. I couldn't believe it! After they took him to the hospital she rushed as fast as she could to our house to work. I told her to go back home to sort things out.

Her family owns the property, so it is their responsibility. She lamented that they will have to move out tonight since they can't secure the property with a broken wall. Thieves come rain or shine! She was shaken to the core. Love, Rebecca

The extra-long 2010 rainy season was troublesome, and not only for us. Between flat tires, getting stuck in the mud, walls falling down and a boy dying, we spent a lot of time in prayer. I had to remind myself that while I may have *felt* like a dangling yo-yo with no momentum, I wasn't flopping around in the hands of an amateur but securely held by a mighty and loving God. Our times are surely in HIS hands.

Capping all these other issues was our house worker's struggle with bed bugs. She told me that her family was being bitten every night and finding the bugs still on their bodies in the morning. They needed help. HELP INDEED—AGHH! I had recently been waking up with unusual bites around my torso. After hearing about our house worker's bed bug infestation, I became absolutely paranoid. I went on the internet and began researching bed bugs. Even as I read, my skin was crawling (it is similar to someone mentioning lice and then your head itches). It soon became apparent that we had our own problem with bedbugs. Without checking price tags, I did everything possible to rid our house of the parasite. I even allowed a wall spider to spend the night a few feet above my pillow to catch any infiltrators! Bed bugs were the latest addition to my "creepy crawly loathing list," especially when I read that they could live over one year without feeding. It took several months before we finally eliminated them.

Bed bugs are a physical nuisance to be sure, but they are also psychologically taxing—as only someone who has struggled with them can empathize. God certainly made the little critters very efficient. Whatever original purpose He had for them has obviously been corrupted by sin. That is true of my existence too. My efforts to eradicate the bed bugs were a good reminder that the parasite of sin that lives in me should "bug" me too. I should no more comfortably co-exist with sin than I would with bed bugs. My purpose as a redeemed child of God is not to live as a corrupt creature destined for eternal destruction but to live for Him who died for me and set me free from bondage forever. Thanks be to our liberating God!

I consider that our present sufferings
are not worth comparing with the glory that will be revealed in us.
The creation waits in eager expectation for the sons of God to be revealed.
For the creation was subjected to frustration, not by its own choice,
but by the will of the one who subjected it,
in hope that the creation itself
will be liberated from its bondage to decay
and brought into the glorious freedom
of the children of God. Romans 8:18-21

Sent: March 6, 2010
Subject: Hannah playing for church
Rebecca writes: Brief update on our house worker whose wall collapsed and killed a little boy: she shared that the child's family isn't giving her grief because they realized it was an accident. They all went to the home village for the funeral.

I'm on deck to play for church tomorrow. I will play until the sermon; Hannah will play the last two hymns and two "Amens" to finish the service. Rob's church service in the Lower Shire was cancelled because the roads are under water. Thankfully, he can sit with Bethany and the boys. Love, Rebecca

It probably sounds incredible to readers in North America that no litigation was pursued against our house worker whose wall fell and killed the small boy. Malawi is a society with few safety laws; accidental deaths are common. Litigation, on the other hand, is uncommon. Accidents between fellow Malawians rarely result in a lawsuit; they are often willing to concede that an accident is an accident and leave it at that.

Sent: March 21, 2010
Subject: Dreadlocks?
Rebecca writes: Hannah has had a high fever for several days. She asked me if her hair would turn into dreadlocks. We did not make church today. Nathanael wanted to lie down after breakfast, and Hannah's fever was still hanging around. We listened to some sermons via the internet and watched the *Kids' Connection* video that came in the mail. Later Hannah began throwing up. I took her temperature: it was 105.5°F. She is really getting hit. Tomorrow she'll get a malaria test. Your continued prayers are appreciated. Love, Rebecca

Sent: March 30, 2010
Subject: By the light of a full moon…is it Harleys?
Rebecca writes: Thanks for your prayers for Hannah—her malaria test was negative and she has recovered nicely.

We have a beautiful full moon here that lights up the night in a neat way. The downside to a full moon is that the thieves can see too well. On Saturday night our neighborhood transformer was vandalized. Thieves drained the oil out of it to use for cooking or to sell it. We heard two huge banging noises and then it quit working. We have had no power since then. It has been quite the adventure to do without power that long. Thankfully, our small generator has powered us up enough to keep the refrigerator and freezer cool. The neighborhood sounds like a Sturgis motorcycle rally with generators sputtering along throughout the days and nights. Our generator cannot seem to keep my computer battery backup running. I'll sign off. Rebecca

Sent: March 31, 2010
Subject: By the light of a full moon the repairmen worked
Rebecca writes: Last night new poles were sunk into the ground. By the light of the full moon, the rewound transformer was hoisted up onto tall poles—out of easy reach of the thieves. With the return of electricity our water pump can pump water up to our house again. Our generator could not manage the task. We took very short showers and used water sparingly from our spare water tank.

We had rain all day long. It rained so hard at one point that it was literally pelting leaves off the trees. *"It's raining, it's pouring—and now the mold is growing!—I cringe inside to look outside—and see more rain is falling."* The veggie lady lamented that there are no carrots for a while because of too much rain. Love, Rebecca

Sent: April 10, 2010
Subject: Post Easter blessings
Rebecca writes: Our Easter celebration was nice; I always enjoy playing for Easter! Beautiful Saviour hosted nearby congregations for a joint Easter service. Several hundred members gathered to worship together. A meal of *nsima*, goat meat, beans and cabbage was provided by the women of our church. Sadly, the water was out, so the facilities struggled to support the large crowd. (Several toilet seats were broken, since many rural people are unfamiliar with flush toilets: they stand on the seats.)

On Easter Monday the Malawi and Zambian missionaries gathered for a Bible Retreat. We met at Salima (near Lake Malawi) and had a nice time being in the Word and strengthening friendships with the other missionary families. The weather was hot. We were ALL hot! To avoid bilharzia exposure, we did not cool off in Lake Malawi. We have enough sicknesses to deal with without knowingly exposing ourselves to more.

It was a nice time, in spite of the hot weather and rustic facilities (saving money you know). Someone in another room plugged in a hot pot and it shut off the power to several rooms. We had no shower curtain, no hot water, bats lived loudly above the bathroom, and mice roamed above our bedroom and visibly ran around during our meals. Our food was periodically peppered with grit that fell from the thatched roof. I got such a dousing of grit from the roof that I jumped out of my chair thinking something had fallen on me. We weren't there for luxury accommodations.

We had Bible classes, Sunday School, daily devotions and a special closing service (led by Rob with a liturgy from the new Worship Supplement), all to the theme of "True Wisdom." The kids all had fun during Sunday School and family games. Hannah cried as we left because she was sorry to leave Christian friends behind. I'll include our group picture for you to see.

We were happy that our power was on to welcome us back home! I went to bed at 8pm, thoroughly exhausted. Traveling in Africa with kids and a baby is so draining it requires recovery time! God bless, Rebecca

Zambia and Malawi missionary families 2010

INCOMING EMAIL: April 10, 2010
Subject: Re: Easter Retreat update
Grandma Kathie Wendland writes: Your description of Salima brought back many memories. ALL that you described is what Linda Phelps Golembiewski

and I lived for over two years as registered nurses with Central Africa Medical Mission in the late 70's. Just think if you couldn't go home to get away from the "wildlife" because that WAS home—and hot and humid! As we came over the knoll to get down to the house after a long clinic day, the temperature went up about 7 degrees. The material in my clothes didn't wear out so much as it rotted and fell apart. Yes, I did make a dress on a treadle sewing machine out of a tablecloth. I felt like Scarlett O' Hara.

Not only was there no shower (only a tub); hot water only came after a wood fire was built in the Rhodesian boiler outside. The electrical set-up was another story. We had to use a wringer washer that had a SERIOUS electrical leak. I wore rubber shoes at all times while in the laundry shed. I used a wooden stick to get my laundry out of the water and put it through the wringer. It was more than a little challenging.

We had similar problems with mice in the ceiling causing the whitewash to drop into our meals. I was happy to note that all of a sudden the mice disappeared, only to find the reason why a short time later: a family of pythons was living in our ceiling. The yard workers killed the mother, which was easily eight feet long.

And bats are good. They eat mosquitoes so we let them alone. We had one that regularly used our toilet to deposit his droppings. No, I didn't look over my head when using the toilet. There was a frog that lived in the toilet for some months too.

Did I swim in the lake? Yes, because we were told it was safe at that point. I did have severe diarrhea that lasted a decade after leaving the country. Ah yes, memories. Interesting place to visit, challenging place to live! Thank you so very much for your updates. I look forward to them. Love to you all, Kathie

Sent: April 12, 2010
Subject: painting job
Rebecca writes: We stopped at the post office to check the mail and couldn't get the box open. All the boxes had been painted…SHUT! Rob went back to the post office today with his multi-tool and was able to pry the box open. Then it took some tweaking to get it to lock again. How can it be that a painting-job is NOT an improvement? I wish they'd left the boxes alone, rust and all. Somewhere in between these extremes, I'm confident, lies progress. Love, Rebecca

Sent: April 13, 2010
Subject: bugs me
Rebecca writes: Rob returned from a long day in the valley—seven hours of driving.

This morning I was nursing Bethany and I didn't have my glasses on. I saw a large shadow mixed in with the terracotta crown-molding on the other side of the room. I couldn't make out exactly what it was. I pointed across the room and asked the kids, "What's that?" Hannah replied, "It's a spider descending from the lampshade." She was correct...but not looking high enough. Caleb pointed out another spider...but on the neighboring wall. Finally, Nathanael looked right where I was pointing and told me it was a moth. I laughed that we had enough "life" on our walls that my finger-pointing ended up being only a vague guide. Enough to bug a person!

Here is a list of my recent musings. <u>You know you are living in the tropics when</u>:
- You grab the flyswatter before you turn the shower on.
- You occasionally have to bend that flyswatter back into shape after use.
- "Spring fever" means malaria.
- You instinctively **don't** kill an ant found indoors. You follow its meandering trail to locate every possible entry point into the house before taking action.
- The rain comes down so hard that it leaks through an umbrella
- The kids play with seasonal toys such as *chongololos* (a large millipede), *inswa* (flying termite) and ant lions.
- You ALWAYS look for bugs or debris in the bottom of a cup before filling it.
- The kids take a tarantula to school for show-and-tell.
- You find a mosquito perched on your toothbrush in the evening and in the morning a praying-mantis is lurking beside the toothbrush holder.
- You determine how wet the rainy season has been by how fast the current is in your backyard, or whether any part of your wall fell down.
- The kids' music teacher keeps cymbals by her door to scare away the monkeys.
- The kids' Easter baskets and eggs are only hidden after they are enclosed in ziplock bags.

Love, Rebecca and family

Sent: April 18, 2010
Subject: I dream of...BP!
Rebecca writes: I will share Rob's latest dream with you. I laugh each time I think of it. Rob dreamt that he needed to obtain a short green tie from a British Petroleum (BP) attendant for an upcoming deputation in the States. One BP attendant told him it would cost MK1,200. He didn't have the money. He returned the next day and bought it. At home he looked at what the attendant had sold him: it was a heavy green curtain with a hair-tie scrunchie around it instead of the BP symbol. His dream ended with him thinking that MK1,200 wasn't a bad price for a heavy green curtain.

I think it gives such insights to the inner workings of life here in Malawi. Good night and sweet silly dreams! Love from BP land, Rebecca

Sent: April 25, 2010
Subject: sickness ends
Rebecca writes: We are so thankful to be healthy again, particularly after the sad story Rob told me after returning from Chizilo today. Evangelist Master's grandson, his only one, was sick last week. He was about Bethany's age—almost a year old. He got quite sick with vomiting and diarrhea. (This was a flashback of Nathanael's struggles after we moved here.) They were told to keep pushing oral re-hydration salts. It turns out the grandson died on Thursday. It is a recurring paradox: death is such a part of life here. All the more reason to keep spreading God's Word and to look forward to the joys of heaven, where we will join with the African choirs in praising our amazing God.

While Rob was gone, a chicken flew into his office. It bedded down under his desk until the neighbor came looking for it. Thankfully it didn't leave a mess. Love, Rebecca

Sent: April 30, 2010
Subject: So gingerly
Rebecca writes: For over six years I've been wondering about the identity of a particular plant. A few days ago I went online and discovered it is ginger! The leaves were beginning to wilt and the flower stalks were turning color. That is the signal that it is ready to harvest. What a pleasant surprise! So, I read up, dug up, and have been making ginger delicacies ever since. I've been using my micro-planer like crazy—I feel so professional! I have shared many and also replanted several shoots so we can harvest more again next year.

Today we celebrated Caleb's Baptismal Day so he felt extra special. He told me, "I just love Jesus so much!" That is a sincere gift indeed! Rebecca

Sent: June 2, 2010
Subject: Are we living in paradise?
Rebecca writes: If you would have asked me, "Are we in paradise?" at the turn of the year, I would have replied emphatically, "NO!" However, the vibrant bloom on our beautiful flowering bird of paradise is my latest reminder that God's beauty shines through all our troubles; and frankly, it is awesome to behold. If that is how He "dresses the lilies of the field," we are blessed abundantly!

I am happy to report that several troublesome issues have resolved in the last months. The horrid black ants that covered our kitchen by the hundreds during the last few months have vanished. It was to the point they were all over the garbage can, occupying kitchen appliances and living in our water filter tap. They even maneuvered their way past the refrigerator seal and got into the food. That crossed the line! Their absence is one reason to give thanks. The bed-bug issues also seem to have cleared up—hooray! The local filling stations currently have had some diesel—hooray!

Rob's bush work is a bit more involved, as he is taking along a national pastor to the Lower Shire. It has been a blessing to have a national pastor work with him. He is slotted to go out tomorrow again, but this afternoon his truck was dead. He popped the hood and discovered that the entire battery connector, which is brass, had snapped off! He simply could not get the connecting bolts off to see what could be done. So, plans for tomorrow will be changed. Such is life in Africa. Time to hit the hay, Rebecca

P.S. I don't say, "Don't let the bed bugs bite" anymore!

Sent: July 18, 2010
Subject: Life around the yard
Rebecca writes: Today church went fine, but we are all under the weather again. Hannah has been playing the keyboard every week after the sermon. It is not 4-part yet, but she is doing a great job and has an upbeat attitude about helping out with her talents.

Yesterday, when I was feeling especially sick, Hannah handed me a paper and told me to write down any jobs that I wanted done and she would do them. That included chopping veggies and making a chicken divan dinner nearly all by herself this evening. What a dear one!

I tried to get cheddar cheese today from the Dairibord. They told me their cheese won't be ready until the middle of August. Great. I noticed a Halaal sign posted. It seems they are now certified by the Islamic center (for the little they actually produce).

I will not be baking much for the kids' school parties anymore. I recently baked some yeast treats and sent along homemade sweet-potato crisps for the kids' class parties. Nathanael's class didn't eat any of it. It turns out that many kids in his class are Muslim and they only eat Halaal foods. That had NEVER crossed my mind. I will send a pack of store-bought cookies next time.

Speaking of food, we found shu shu (*choko*) again, and I will try to plant one to grow at Kabula. It is a lime-green vegetable with a consistency somewhere between a squash and a potato. It has a big pit in the middle. It also has little prickers toward the bottom and makes my skin peel if I don't wear rubber gloves when handling it. Despite its unusual characteristics, we really enjoy it sautéed with some onion. Love, Rebecca

Choko, more commonly known as "chayote" (also "mango-squash" or "vegetable-pear") in North America, is a Central American plant once eaten by Aztecs. It is now grown throughout the tropics. The pear-shaped *chokos* grow on a vine; they can be prepared as a savory side-dish or included in a dessert.

Sent: July 23, 2010
Subject: neighborhood going to pot
Rebecca writes: Rob went to town to buy replacement sink parts and met our neighbor, Satish, at the hardware store he owns. Satish mentioned that new neighbors/tenants had moved in next door. He informed us that one day the new tenants had a celebration. All of a sudden, a pan came flying over his wall and landed about a meter away from his car. He suspected that one of the neighbor's house workers was throwing things over the wall to take them home after work. Satish went straight to the neighbor and explained the scenario. The new tenants assured him it wasn't foul play, but rather their European custom to throw a pan over to the neighbor's yard. Satish replied, "What if I already have enough pans and I don't want it—what should I do?" The tenants suggested, "Throw it back!" Love, Rebecca

Sent: July 31, 2010
Subject: Cooking in the rain
Rebecca writes: Rob returned from week-long classes interspersed with meetings in Lilongwe. Professor Sorum from Mequon's Lutheran Seminary taught a class on 1 Thessalonians. Rob enjoyed it and plans to take summer classes at the Seminary on furlough to keep up his studies. Next, our whole family plans to head west to see Grandma and Grandpa Wendland and Aunt Naomi in Zambia!

Today I woke to several leaks above the stove. In an attempt to cook without dirty water dripping into the food on the stove, I popped open an umbrella to finish. God bless, Rebecca

Sent: August 27, 2010
Subject: Zambia
Rob writes: We're back in Blantyre after a great trip to Zambia. We thoroughly enjoyed our time "back home" with Mom and Dad and sister Naomi. We took an amazing trip to see Victoria Falls. The kids were in awe. As we were touring, someone died at the "Boiling Pot," a deep pool carved out by the rushing waters. Thankfully for us, the victim was not one of our children. The safety measures are not extensive. That means you get to experience Victoria Falls up close and personal—which is awesome, since it is one of the seven natural wonders of the world.

My birthday present was whitewater rafting on the Zambezi. Naomi, Rebecca and I hiked down the Batoka Gorge (which is downstream from Victoria Falls) to the rafts on the Zambezi River. The rapids were terrific. In one area we went through a place called "The Washing Machine." It twirled us around and almost bent us in half, but we didn't flip. It was a wonderful experience in Africa!

Two other enjoyable highlights were a sundowner river-cruise on which we saw crocodiles, hippos and a group of elephants drinking and eating at the river's edge. The second highlight was canoeing six miles down the Zambezi. Those highlights were punctuated with games with Grandma, Grandpa and Aunt Naomi, evening meals under the African night sky, and roasting imported marshmallows over a *mopani* wood fire.

We had an uneventful return trip home to Kabula Hill. A neighbor dumped a load of sand too close to our back wall and broke part of it, but there were no other emergencies. Thanks to the Lord for the special trip, time with loved ones and safe journeys! Love, Rob

Family by mighty Victoria Falls

Sent: September 17, 2010
Subject: Mt. Not So Pleasant
Rebecca writes: The pace here has picked up dramatically with three kids now in school!

Last evening was not great for Beautiful Saviour church. A gang of thieves managed to get past the electrified wire, wall, and guard (who was hiding). They tied up both the watch-dog and dog-handler, and they used a crow-bar to force open a door and gain entry to the hallway. They broke the trelli-door frame from the wall, kicked in another door and stole all the sound system equipment from church. They also gained access to the Reading Room and took all the People's Bibles. Just kidding…seeing if you were really reading. They did take the computer, TV and related equipment.

This wasn't a total surprise. There have been many break-ins in the Mt. Pleasant area lately. Recently that neighborhood, which includes the Lawrenz property, has had two town meetings to address the security breaches. The thieves have tools (a crow-bar and knife for sure, but no guns) and seem to make quick work of burglar bars and wooden doors. They are particularly interested in laptops and electronic equipment. The security people say the key is to have layers of security (to alert us and stall them) and to get an alarm ringing to send reinforcements. The police have actually started posting camouflaged guards with guns throughout that area now. We saw three of them on Monday evening. Rob wondered: Were those REALLY police men? And if they were, do their guns even work? And if they do, is there any ammunition? Those are all good questions.

It has been a good wake-up-call to reassess our personal security measures. I'm so glad we added the extra burglar bars to the bedroom windows. I know our coming and going is always in the Lord's care, but a few extra prayers for safety would be appreciated. Evidently there is NO safe area, since Mt. Pleasant was the touted "safe haven" all these years. Once again, we take it to the Lord in prayer and know that He has not only Malawi, but the whole world in His hands! God bless, Rebecca

Take the world, but give me Jesus! Sweetest comfort of my soul.
With the Savior watching o'er me, I can sing, though thunders roll.
Oh, the height and depth of mercy; Oh, the length and breadth of love!
Oh, the fullness of redemption,
Pledge of endless life above! (CW 355:2)

Sent: October 23, 2010
Subject: Ntcheu ladies' man
Rebecca writes: Last week our Ladies' Bible Study focused on the topic of the sixth commandment. A Malawian lady led the Bible Study. She began by showing us this article from the local paper:

Ntcheu Man Marries, Divorces 11 women WEEKEND NATION
Oct 8, 2010
Alfred Nyirenda of Ntcheu is an unshakable believer in the biblical saying

that man should populate and fill all corners of the earth. He has taken it upon himself to be the embodiment of this 'holy calling' by marrying and divorcing women. So far, he has married and dumped 11 of them, has a new wife, 5 girlfriends and 15 children. "The Bible says we should multiply like the sand of the earth. This is what inspired me to have this number of wives and children," says the 42 year-old. He added: "It is not like I use magical charms to entice women to accept my love overtures. Maybe they believe that I am handsome." He also adds that he has fortified his body with charms that stop 'infected women' from crossing his love path. He also gives other men charms to protect them from the vices that come with this practice. He claims, "Because of the power I have over the women, it is within my power to have extramarital affairs, but I don't expect any of my wives to do the same and dump them without delay if they betray me." He described the Malawi government's proposal that a family should have a maximum of 4 children as 'a joke.' He continues, "A man needs to work with dedication and commitment in the family, not having just 10 children. That is laziness. It is a man's duty to have as many children as his body allows."

The lady leading the Bible study shared that her own grandfather had married four wives. When his first wife could only produce one daughter, he decided to marry more wives. The lady's stories of the resulting family dynamic in her grandfather's household were really interesting. She stated that the "neutral ground" was under a nearby mango tree, where the four wives each got their food supplies, such as a cup of salt (not heaping, or the women would fight). Her grandfather would take his single blanket from hut to hut as he visited his wives. In the end, the first wife divorced him since it was terrible living in such ungodly conditions. In his later years the grandfather got very sick with cancer. None of his current wives would help him. He ended up going to his first wife for help, and she helped him until he died.

Such is life in Africa, especially when astray from God's Word. The older I get, the more His rules seem truly for our good instead of a "hindrance" to fun and freedom.

Rob is at the installation of Pastor Mwanancho today. He was a vicar at Khanyepa for the last year (working with Rob) and now is the first national pastor—in decades—to be called in Chiradzulu! This is a major step forward for those parish union congregations. I'm happy they can have consistent spiritual care with their own *abusa* (pastor). Praise the Lord! Rebecca

For many Malawians, Christianity is intertwined with traditional African practices and beliefs. It is not uncommon to find men who consider themselves Christians but have multiple wives or mistresses. The man quoted in the newspaper article found a convenient way to mesh his plural living partners with his "Christian" beliefs.

Sent: October 26, 2010
Subject: By the way…
Rebecca writes: Interesting signs are posted all over Malawi. I recently jotted down several word-for-word. Some are intriguing and give an insight into the culture…you can see for yourselves: **"Double-vision Private Secondary School," "Pu Pu Driving School," "Stop early marriages—let girls finish school," "Difficult to Understand Shopping Center and Tea Room," "J.C. Car Breakers," "Heaven-bound Parlor," "Who God Bless No Man Cure," "Concern Universal Limited," "Fizzle Wholesale"**…and finally, **"Pray Until Something Happens"** shop. Enjoy! Rebecca

Sent: November 26, 2010
Subject: "Witch" ya gonna do?
Rob writes: What would you do if, when you got to church, you found only two people there—one holds the keys to open the building, and the other is accused (secretly, by the key holder) of being the very witch who has scared the rest of the congregation away from ever coming to church again?

That's the question I had to answer when I went down to N'singano the other day with Ev. Master and Rev. Meja. We had been noticing that attendance had been dropping at N'singano over the past few months, but it was a real surprise to find only two people there. After visiting some of the members at their homes in the area, we had the story. The congregational treasurer had been accused of "eating" the offerings and he was removed from his position. His alleged response to the removal was, "Okay, but you will see if anyone ever worships in that church again." That was enough for the rest of the members. They were convinced that this former treasurer would curse the building and anyone who went to worship the Lord there. The fact that he would still come when it was time for worship was even more intimidating to the people. To the members it was as if this man was seeing who would be brave enough to violate his ban, and then they would become objects of his harmful witchcraft. So all the men stayed away. A few women, including the key holder, Fragrance Diamond (her given name), continued to come despite the threats.

I was pretty burned up when I heard this story. My plan was to walk up to this former treasurer and confront him right there on the front steps of the church. There is no place for witchcraft in the church, especially if it causes others to lose their faith. However, my national co-workers responded to my plan with a shocked, "No pastor, you can't do that!" When I asked why not, they replied,

"Where is the proof? That is what the former treasurer will say. He will say, 'Show me the holes around the church that I dug to put medicine and charms inside; show me where I have placed those things in the building.' Unless we have concrete proof, we cannot accuse him without empowering him more. If we can't prove anything, he will remain in the church and the members will see that not even the pastors can do anything against the man now." My colleagues also told me that using witchcraft in this way is illegal in Malawi, so if we would make an accusation like this we would have to also involve the police. Without evidence we would be the ones looking powerless and foolish.

Yet, I just couldn't let it go. Could I do nothing while the rest of the congregation cowered from worship because of what was going on? I reminded my brothers of the responsibility of the watchman and read for them Ezekiel 33:1-6. We are the watchmen for the people around N'singano, so we had to do something…but what?

We revised our service for the day. Our readings were changed to deal with the Lord's anger against witchcraft (Dt. 18:9-12), our new life because of and for Christ (Eph. 5:1-21), and Jesus' harsh response to the hypocritical leaders of his day (Mt. 23:27-39). Rev. Meja crafted a new sermon around those readings that connected the dots to witchcraft.

The national brothers also came up with another plan. The keys of the church building would be given to the former treasurer. In the future if he would refuse to open the building for worship, we would have something concrete to call him out on. If, however, he would open up the building, it would be as if he was negating his own (alleged) magic by inviting people to church.

We invited members who lived nearby to come to worship for the day—it was still on. In the end we had about 30 adults and 20 children for the service. When our service began, faces were long and people were subdued, but after the service was over and our plan for the keys was announced, everyone was laughing and smiling and greeting one another. Blessings, Rob

Rob has returned to N'singano several times since this incident, although his visits have been limited by the ongoing Malawi fuel shortage. The former treasurer ended up giving his keys away, but he is still attending church. This scenario shows the kind of grip that African traditional religion has on Malawi, even in a Christian community. Merely a whiff of possible witchcraft caused an entire church to cower. In this case, the church members were the victims, and their faith-life was threatened.

Like many other situations in Malawi, witchcraft is not a straightforward issue. The national church workers had a built-in cultural awareness of the Pandora's Box that would be opened had they directly accused the elder of witchcraft. It is this "insider's view" of a culture that makes it such a blessing for missionaries to work alongside national called workers.

There are so many opportunities to proclaim the gospel of Jesus here. When His disciples cowered in fear after His death, the first word that the risen Christ spoke to them was, *"Peace."* (John 20:19) Peace! It is the peace foretold on the night of His birth—peace between a holy God and sinful human beings. It is a peace guaranteed by God the Father from eternity, won by God the Son and sealed by God the Spirit as He works through His Word. Thousands in Malawi already rejoice in this joyous, confident peace of Jesus. Thousands more still need to hear.

Sent: December 18, 2010
Subject: Merry Christmas update
Rebecca writes: **"Were the whole realm of nature mine, that were a tribute far too small; Love so amazing, so divine, demands my soul, my life, my all." (CW 125:4)**

Indeed, that *love so amazing*, so divine—which was demonstrated so visibly during Holy Week—was first clearly revealed on Christmas Day! The promise of a Savior has been fulfilled! I mull over these hymn words often. They put things into clear perspective throughout the year. I am merely a steward of His unending gifts—great and small.

This past year has been <u>full</u>. The kids never fail to keep our days full of action with school schedules and various activities. My schedule has been full with church activities and a writing project. Rob has had a full schedule serving a dozen village congregations, attending meetings and with the related travels. Even the rains have begun in full force. Our yard is full of life.

One tree in particular is full of fruit this year—our peach tree. We planted it when we moved here. For the first time it is loaded. This recent fruitfulness "bears" a fitting analogy to Rob's ministry. Several rural Malawian churches were planted over 40 years ago, long before we arrived in 2003. Rob has personally served these village congregations for over seven years now. These churches do not have a pastor; they have always relied on the current missionary to "make the rounds." Now, like the peach tree, they are beginning to bear fruit.

One example of this visible fruit is that a national pastor is currently accompanying Rob to the village churches in the Lower Shire Valley. Traveling to these village churches is not a small commitment, particularly with the difficult driving conditions; but it has been a blessing for Rob to have national insight on how best to serve these congregations in southern Malawi. We pray these Lower Shire churches can call a pastor in the future to minister permanently to their congregational needs.

Another example of visible fruit is that a national pastor was called to serve a parish union of 5 churches in Chiradzulu, the northeast region of Blantyre. Chiradzulu is where our mission started in Malawi in 1963. Rob has served there since 2003. Over the decades, the membership has grown to over 2000 communicants...by the power of the Holy Spirit working through the Means of Grace. Praise God that these believers now have their own shepherd, Pastor Mwanancho.

Transferring five churches to the care of a national pastor has allowed Rob to open two new congregations and one preaching station in the Lower Shire. Thank God for this opportunity to tell more souls of the Good News of Jesus Christ, who descended from His celestial dwelling to rescue us—lost and condemned clay-in-motion. That salvation fills our lives with beautiful meaning, purpose and endless reasons to bloom!

Christmas blessings, Robert and Rebecca Wendland
Hannah (age 10,) Nathanael (8,) Caleb (5,) and Bethany (1)

Seven years of emails have provided a written log of our family's Malawi "journey" thus far. That journey is one that you have now shared—without making airplane ticket reservations, crossing time zones, receiving yellow-fever shots or stepping foot on the continent of Africa. My prayer is that through this book you have a deeper appreciation of what life is like for a Mission Mom serving in Malawi, but also that you have a broader appreciation for each blessing, big or small, that God sends *you* in your part of the world. We can each bloom where we're planted, sustained by the Son-shine of God's grace and nourished by the living water of His Word!

Sharing the gift of eternal life in Christ has been our family's daily mission and privilege in Malawi, Africa. Lord willing, one day in heaven we will rejoice with the souls who have heard our witness, and with countless believers through time and around the world...including you!

To God be the glory; great things he has done!
He so loved the world that he gave us his Son,
Who yielded his life and atonement for sin
And opened the life gate that all may go in.
Praise the Lord! Praise the Lord!
Let the earth hear his voice!
Praise the Lord! Praise the Lord!
Let the people rejoice!
Oh, come to the Father through Jesus the Son
And give him the glory—great things he has done! (CW 399:6)